Strategic Thinking

There are many strategy books available in the marketplace for today's student or business professional; most of them view strategy from the 10,000 foot level, while *Strategic Thinking* looks at this important business topic through a different lens. Written from the perspective of a manager, this book builds on theories of managerial and organizational cognition that have had a powerful influence on many business fields over the last two decades. As other books on business policy and strategy cover a broad range of topics, models, frameworks, and theories, the unique feature of this book is that it covers all this, but also focuses on how managers of business firms understand their business environments, assess and marshal their firms' resources, and strive for advantage in the competitive marketplace. It examines the economic, structural, and managerial explanations for firm performance.

Offering professors and business people who are intrigued by the ideas introduced in Peter Senge's books ways to apply those ideas and principles in the classroom and in the companies in which they work, the book puts managers front and center.

Irene M. Duhaime, Senior Associate Dean and Professor at Georgia State University.

Larry Stimpert, Professor of Economics and Business at Colorado College.

Julie A. Chesley, Assistant Professor of Organization Theory and Applied Behavioral Science at the Graziadio School of Business, Pepperdine University.

Strategic Thinking

Today's Business Imperative

Irene M. Duhaime

Georgia State University

Larry Stimpert

Colorado College

Julie A. Chesley

Pepperdine University

Routledge
Taylor & Francis Group

NEW YORK AND LONDON

Publisher:	John Szilagyi
Development Editor:	Felisa Salvago-Keyes
Editorial Assistant:	Sara Werden
Production Editor:	Sarah Stone
Companion Website Designer:	Marie Mansfield

First published 2012
by Routledge
711 Third Avenue, New York, NY 10017

Simultaneously published in the UK
by Routledge
2 Park Square, Milton Park, Abingdon, Oxon OX14 4RN

Routledge is an imprint of the Taylor & Francis Group, an informa business

© 2012 Taylor & Francis

The right of Irene M. Duhaime, Larry Stimpert, and Julie A. Chesley to be identified as authors of this work has been asserted by them in accordance with sections 77 and 78 of the Copyright, Designs and Patents Act 1988.

Library of Congress Cataloging in Publication Data
Dulhaime, Irene M.
    Strategic thinking : today's business imperative / Irene M. Dulhaime, J.L. "Larry" Stimpert, Julie A. Chelsey.
        p. cm.
    Includes index.
    1. Strategic planning. 2. Decision making. I. Stimpert, J.L. (John Lawrence) II. Chesley, Julie A. III. Title.
    HD30.28.D835 2011
    658.4′012—dc22
    2011009765

ISBN13: 978-0-415-87502-8 (hbk)
ISBN13: 978-0-415-87503-5 (pbk)
ISBN13: 978-0-203-80762-0 (ebk)

Typeset in Times New Roman
by RefineCatch Limited, Bungay, Suffolk

Printed and bound in the United States of America on acid-free paper by Edwards Brothers, Inc.

To Walter, always, for everything—I. M. D.

To my students, past and future—L. S.

To Bruce, Abbey, and Alex for their gracious support and love …
and for keeping me grounded—J. A. C.

Brief Contents

Full Contents

CHAPTER 10

CHAPTER 11

CHAPTER 12

Preface

Probably every business manager and professor would agree with the statement that "[t]he critical resource of the modern ... firm is general management skill."[1] But, most strategic management textbooks view firms as a "faceless abstraction," giving little attention to the managers and executives who make the decisions that are the building blocks of their firms' strategies.[2] As a result, we are left with a paradox: An implicit acknowledgment of the importance of managers and executives, but business and management texts that give little attention to the roles of managers, how managers make decisions, and the knowledge and learning that are so essential to managers as they must guide their firms successfully through dynamic business environments. This book aims to fill this critical gap.

The field of strategic management is multidisciplinary, and has built upon many other disciplines, including marketing, political science, psychology, and, above all, economics. In fact, some of the most influential and well known contributions, such as Michael Porter's *Competitive Strategy*, have their theoretical grounding in microeconomics and industrial organization economics.[3] According to this perspective, firm performance is largely a function of industry structure and how competitive an industry is. This kind of thinking leads to many commonly accepted expectations, for example that firms operating in less competitive industries will enjoy higher performance than firms operating in highly competitive environments.

This book examines these economic and structural explanations for firm performance, but our underlying thesis is that the task of strategic management is not only structural but also *managerial*. This book does not argue that industry structure is unimportant—in fact, two chapters (Chapters 4 and 5) are devoted to developing ways of thinking about and analyzing industry structure. But, we begin with a premise that *managerial* thinking about such issues and *managerial* decision making are fundamentally important to the success of business organizations.

Another reason why many books on strategy tend to have a structural rather than a managerial perspective is because "the human variable" is elusive and difficult to study. As organizational theorist James Thompson has described:

> The human actor is a multidimensional phenomenon subject to the influences of a great many variables. The range of differences in aptitude is great, and the learned behavior patterns ... [are] quite diverse. Neither we nor organizations have the data or the calculus to understand organization members in their full complexity.[4]

More recently, advances in management research, specifically efforts to understand managerial and organizational cognition, have provided us with a vocabulary, key constructs and variables, and methodological tools for understanding how managers and executives process information, make decisions, and learn from the decisions they make. This book incorporates these research advances to place managers and executives front and center in the strategic management process.

At the heart of our emphasis on managerial thinking is the concept of mental models, which Peter Senge has defined as "deeply ingrained assumptions, generalizations, or even pictures or images that influence how we understand the world and how we take action."[5] Managerial thinking—embedded in managers' mental models—influences strategic decision making and the actions firms take. Managers' mental models of the situations they encounter determine whether a particular strategic issue or situation will be noticed, how it will be interpreted and understood, and how they will respond to the situation. The study of managerial thinking thus helps to explain why some managers notice important business issues while other managers do not, why some managers correctly interpret these issues while others do not, and why some managers respond appropriately to these issues while others do not. As a result, the linkages among business environments (including industry structure), managerial thinking, and strategic decision making are keys to understanding performance differences across firms and how competitive advantage is developed.

Features of This Book

In addition to giving managers and managerial thinking prominent roles in the strategic management process, this book also highlights two other themes: the dynamic and ever-changing nature of business environments and the value of organizational knowledge and learning. We focus on the dynamic nature of business environments because change is a fact of life in the business world and much organizational success rests on the ability of managers to anticipate and respond to industry change. Furthermore, it has now become imperative for business organizations to learn and acquire new knowledge, but they must also have structures that effectively move knowledge and information from those who have it to those who need it. At the end of every chapter, we describe how that chapter's material is related to these themes.

Throughout the chapters, we not only introduce concepts and ideas, but we also provide many illustrations of these concepts in order to show how these ideas can be applied to actual business situations and to reinforce understanding and learning. While we provide many contemporary examples, we also include some historic examples because we believe they offer timeless truths that are just as relevant today. Finally, the end of every chapter also includes a "key questions for managers" section in which we ask readers to take the most important ideas presented in the chapter and apply them to actual company situations. Students who have worked in companies can apply these questions to the firms where they have worked, or students might select a company and address these questions in a short research project. Current managers can, of course, apply these questions to their own firms and businesses.

Acknowledgments

A project of this scale and scope is only possible with help, and we are grateful to all who helped us at every step. John Szilagyi approached us with the idea for this book, and we are grateful for his encouragement. We hope that the final project warrants his initial confidence in us. Our editor, Felisa Salvago-Keyes, offered us invaluable feedback on each chapter, while also answering a multitude of questions and providing guidance at every step of the way. Our reviewers provided us with helpful feedback and recommendations that we used to strengthen each chapter and the entire book.

Emily Perkins, a Colorado College student, was invaluable as we progressed through this text. She assisted in initial background research on each chapter, helped compile exhibits, and was always available to read and provide thoughtful and helpful comments on each chapter. Almost every page of this book reflects her efforts and contributions. A generous grant from Colorado College supported Emily's contributions to this project.

Finally, we are especially grateful for the support and encouragement we received from friends, colleagues, and family members.

About the Authors

Irene M. Duhaime has taught at the University of Pittsburgh, the University of Illinois at Urbana-Champaign, the University of Memphis, and Georgia State University where she now serves as Senior Associate Dean and Professor of Strategic Management.

Professor Duhaime received her Ph.D. from the University of Pittsburgh. Her dissertation on corporate divestment won the General Electric Award for Outstanding Research in Strategic Management. Before entering the doctoral program, she was responsible for cash management and short-term investments at New England Mutual Life Insurance Company and was an investment officer at Pittsburgh National Bank.

Her research on diversification, acquisition, divestment, and turnaround has been published in the leading management journals including the *Academy of Management Journal*, the *Academy of Management Review*, and the *Strategic Management Journal*. Her research and teaching interests have spanned the range from large, diversified corporations to small entrepreneurial firms and family businesses.

Professor Duhaime has served in a variety of leadership roles in the Academy of Management (including Book Review Editor of the *Academy of Management Review* and chair of the Business Policy and Strategy Division) and in the Strategic Management Society (including two terms on the Board of Directors). She is a Fellow of the Strategic Management Society. She lives with her husband Walter in Atlanta and enjoys music, reading, discovering new restaurants, and weekend exploration of the South Carolina beach.

Larry Stimpert is Professor of Economics and Business at Colorado College, and he has also taught as a Visiting Professor at the Korea University Business School and the United States Air Force Academy. He received his B.A. from Illinois Wesleyan University and his M.B.A. from the Columbia University Business School. Prior to entering the academic field, he worked in the railroad industry and served in various marketing, forecasting, and economic analysis positions at the Southern Railway Company and the Norfolk Southern Corporation. Later, he worked as manager of marketing and pricing for the Chicago and North Western Transportation Company.

Professor Stimpert received his Ph.D. in Business Administration from the University of Illinois where he was recognized for the quality of his teaching while still a graduate student. Professor Stimpert's research interests focus on top managers and their influence on strategic decision making and firm strategies. He has written on many strategy issues, including managerial responses to environmental change and organizational decline, business definition and organizational identity, the management of corporate strategy and diversification, company strategies following deregulation, and corporate governance. His articles have appeared in the *Academy of Management Journal*, the *Academy of Management Review*, the *Journal of Management*, the *Journal of Management Studies*, and the *Strategic Management Journal*, and he has also authored chapters that have appeared in several edited books. He has also served as Essay Editor for the *Journal of Management Inquiry*. He is a member of the Academy of Management, the Southern Academy of Management, and the Strategic Management Society.

Dr. Julie A. Chesley is an Assistant Professor of Organization Theory and Applied Behavioral Science at the Graziadio School of Business, Pepperdine University. Julie holds a B.S. in Management from the United States Air Force Academy, an M.B.A from the University of Colorado, Leeds School of Business at Boulder, Colorado, and a Ph.D. in Organization Theory and Management from the Leeds School of Business at the University of Colorado. Julie has also taught undergraduate management courses at the United States Air Force Academy and at Colorado College.

Dr. Chesley has over 26 years' experience implementing, teaching and researching organization management. She has led critical strategy implementation and change efforts and has been responsible for several national security space staff functions in her 20-year Air Force career.

Dr. Chesley's teaching, research, training, and consulting focus primarily on organization change, team development, leadership development and strategy implementation. She has numerous publications and presentations including articles in *California Management Review*, *Journal of Leadership and Organizational Studies*, *Journal of Business Research*, and the *Journal of Leadership Studies*, as well as the text, *Applied Project Management for Space Systems*.

Chapter 1

Managerial Decision Making and Strategic Management

Strategic management is the process by which managers formulate and implement strategies to generate high performance and to create sustained competitive advantage. Our focus will be on the decisions made by CEOs, presidents, and general managers, as well as mid- and lower-level managers of firms and business units and how, over time, those decisions become the strategies that influence firm performance. The main objectives of this book are: 1) to develop your understanding of the strategic management process and 2) to understand how and why some firms enjoy sustained high performance and why many other firms do not.

This first chapter introduces the field of strategic management and provides an overview of the book. It begins by describing the tasks of general managers and the dynamic and challenging environments that managers face as they develop and implement strategies. We then define strategy, elaborate on the strategic management process, and describe how managerial thinking—the assumptions, beliefs, and understandings contained in managers' mental models—is the source of, and a key to understanding, strategic decision making and firm performance.

Chapter Objectives

The specific objectives of this chapter are to:

- Describe how the study of strategic management is uniquely different from other fields of management study.
- Describe the tasks of general managers and the dynamic characteristics of the business environments in which managers must formulate and implement strategies.
- Define strategy and the concepts of managerial thinking and mental models, and illustrate how managers' mental models influence decision making.
- Show how specific decisions become the building blocks of strategies that ultimately determine firm performance outcomes.
- Provide a model of strategic management that will serve as an organizing framework for this book.

Strategy's Unique Focus on the Management of Firms and Businesses

This book aims to develop your understanding of how managers formulate and implement strategies that lead to sustained **competitive advantage**—the reason some firms enjoy higher levels of performance than their rivals. Our aim is to go well beyond asking whether a firm does or doesn't enjoy high performance; we seek to provide you with the skills and tools to ask how and why some firms do or don't develop a competitive advantage and enjoy high performance. For many, the terms strategy and strategic management are synonymous with an undergraduate or M.B.A. capstone course. Many business education programs expect that the strategy course will provide students with an overview or "big picture" of how other courses in accounting, finance, organizational behavior, marketing, and operations tie together.

But beyond offering you an integrative experience, the field of strategic management should introduce you to concepts, ideas, and theories that will stimulate your thinking about the important roles of general managers, those who have broad responsibilities for the strategic management of entire firms or of the business units of multibusiness firms.

One of the most distinguishing features of strategic management is its unique focus or level of analysis. As illustrated in Exhibit 1.1, the study of economics focuses on more "macro" level—or outside the company—issues. For example, the field of macroeconomics examines employment, price levels, and the growth of the national and international economies, while the field of microeconomics focuses on industries and the nature of competition in various industry environments.

On the other hand, most business fields examine more "micro"—or inside the firm—levels of analysis. For example, the focus of finance is on firms' investment projects and how those projects will be financed. The aim of marketing is to understand the promotion of individual products or services. Similarly, the focus of organizational behavior is on the motivation and job performance of individuals. In fact, motivating colleagues and co-workers is probably one of the most important day-to-day leadership tasks facing any manager!

But the unique focus of strategic management is on the management of *firms and businesses*. Strategists cannot make decisions about firms and businesses in isolation, but must necessarily

Exhibit 1.1 Strategy's Level of Analysis Is Unique

Field of Study	Level of Analysis
Macroeconomics	The economy
Microeconomics	Industries and markets
Strategy	*Firms and businesses*
Finance	Investment projects
Marketing	Products and services
Organizational behavior	Individuals
Operations management	Manufacturing plants

integrate information from across the broader economy, industry, and market levels of analysis while also considering the important roles played by functional departments and individuals within their own firms and businesses. As a result, the tasks of general managers are not only important and demanding, but they are also highly knowledge-intensive because managers use information and knowledge gleaned from experience and a wide range of other sources to make key—strategic—decisions.

The Tasks of General Managers

The Challenge

General managers—presidents, CEOs, and heads of business units—have responsibility for the overall performance of their firms and businesses. Their tasks are multifaceted and challenging. They must analyze their firm's competitive landscape, position their firm or business within its industry, identify and select the most successful ways of competing in that industry, and secure the necessary resources to implement their strategies. And, much is riding on how well they do their jobs. Shareholders expect and demand a return on their investment. Employees, too, are counting on wise decision making to provide them with a secure livelihood. And, the communities in which companies have offices, production plants, and other facilities also depend on companies to pay taxes and help to provide their citizens with a high quality of life.

The tasks of general managers are made even more complicated because the industry environments in which firms and businesses compete do not remain constant. Thus, strategic management is a highly dynamic process, and the strategies that worked well during one time period are unlikely to remain effective indefinitely. Many changes occur in industry environments, but we will focus on three types of changes that confront all firms and businesses:

Demographic Change

First, customers change. If nothing else, customers get older. But any type of demographic change poses both opportunities and challenges for firms and their managers. For example, if products become identified with an older demographic, it can be difficult to attract younger buyers. The average buyer of Lincoln automobiles is now over 60, and Ford wants and needs its Lincoln line to appeal to a younger demographic or else it risks having the Lincoln brand serve an increasingly smaller group of customers.[1] But if Ford changes its Lincoln car line too much, it may run the risk of alienating its loyal, older buyers before it can successfully transition to a strategy that attracts a new following of younger buyers.

Nearly all developed economies are now aging and growing more diverse, trends that offer opportunities for entrepreneurial businesses to provide new products and services to meet an aging and more diverse population. Health care will remain a high-growth industry in the United States as aging Baby Boomers seek to maintain active lifestyles even as they grow older. And, many companies see the benefits of reaching out to and tailoring products to meet the tastes and preferences of ethnic groups that are often among the fastest growing consumer groups in many developed countries.

Throughout this book, we will offer many other examples of how changing demographics provide both challenges and opportunities. But, the key point we want to underscore here is that managers cannot escape from the challenges associated with changing customer demographics.

Technological Change

It's a given that technologies are rapidly changing all of the time. While we are all aware of the ways technology has enhanced a wide array of consumer products from computers and cell phones to consumer electronics and automobiles, technology affects all industries. Technological change not only alters the array of products and services that can be offered to customers, but it also profoundly affects the way products and services are produced and provided. And, it has also fundamentally changed the nature of work, so that the vast majority of workers now make a living not by physical labor, but by communicating and sharing knowledge.

New Products and Services

Shifting demographics create demands for new products and services, and technological change allows entrepreneurs and entrepreneurial firms to develop new products and services that consumers cannot even imagine they might want or need (but can soon become life's necessities). Companies can either be responsible for developing these new products and services, or they can quickly respond to the firms that do, or they can run the risk of falling behind more nimble and opportunistic competitors.

The problem with all three types of change is that they rarely come in steady, predictable increments. As Henry Mintzberg has noted, an industry may be relatively stable for years or even decades, only to be jolted unexpectedly by dramatic change in one or all three of the dimensions described above.[2] Thus, lulled by complacency and a reliance on a "we've always done it this way" mentality, managers can be caught completely off guard by changes. Sometimes their firms are so profoundly impacted by these changes that they cannot adapt and begin to decline. Some firms never recover.

In such a competitive landscape, firms like Apple Computer, founded by two entrepreneurs working in a garage, can so successfully exploit new technologies to develop products that meet previously unknown consumer needs that the firms they start can become some of the largest companies in the world in a very short period of time. Apple, which so fundamentally changed the computer industry, was later eclipsed by the technological and other industry developments that Apple itself set in motion. In the last decade, however, remarkably innovative and elegantly designed products such as the iPod, iPhone, and iPad, and aggressive marketing and advertising campaigns for those products, have restored Apple to its original place as a technology leader. But whether Apple can continue to maintain market relevance in the years ahead will depend on the ability of its managers to formulate and implement successful new strategies, as no company can thrive or ultimately survive if it grows complacent.[3]

If all of these factors are not enough to make the jobs of general managers challenging, their firms and businesses are also now facing much more government regulation and scrutiny from a less trusting public. Accounting scandals that destroyed billions of dollars of shareholder value and shook investor confidence in many once highly regarded companies, including WorldCom, Qwest, Adelphia, Bristol-Myers Squibb, Arthur Andersen, and, of course, Enron led to the enactment of the Sarbanes-Oxley Act, which requires companies to comply with many new regulatory requirements. The regulations have fundamentally changed the responsibilities of corporate directors and managers,[4] but these changes will have a positive effect if they help to prevent the kinds of accounting and ethical gaffes that came to light in the first years of this century.

The deep recession of 2008–2010 led to an unprecedented intervention of the U.S. and other national governments into private business. Rather than let ailing banks and industrial companies fail, the government either took over or assumed a major equity stake in many of the world's largest companies, including AIG, Bank of America, Citigroup, Chrysler, and General Motors. To keep other struggling banks and failing firms afloat, the government directed that they merge with or be acquired by other, healthier firms.

In whatever form they finally take, other major legislative initiatives, including health care reform and limits on carbon emissions, will have far-reaching consequences for business firms and will almost surely involve much more government involvement and regulation of business activity than has been the case for the last several decades.

Consequences and Implications

All of the factors just outlined highlight the need for managers to anticipate and be responsive to industry change and disequilibrium so that their companies can remain viable and vibrant. Unfortunately, it is becoming clear that many traditional management principles are either not particularly helpful or totally inadequate for meeting these challenges. Competitive forces are relentless, and many once "excellent" or "visionary" companies that were doing everything "right" have had difficulties or have faced periods of decline or even failure.

This tendency for high-performing companies to experience difficulties or even fail is vividly illustrated in Exhibit 1.2, which lists a few of the companies that were identified as "excellent companies" by Peters and Waterman in their classic book, *In Search of Excellence: Lessons from America's Best-Run Companies*, or as "visionary companies" by Collins and Porras in their more recent well known book, *Built to Last: Successful Habits of Visionary Companies*.[5] The companies that appear in italics in Exhibit 1.2 have experienced difficulties, decline, and in some cases, failure, and the exhibit vividly emphasizes that success in an earlier time period rarely guarantees success in a subsequent time period.

At the same time, changes in the competitive marketplace also create great opportunities for new wealth creation, and it is the genius of entrepreneurs, who seek out and create these new opportunities, that contributes to the dynamic nature of our economy. Existing companies that are open to change and able to capitalize on changes in their competitive environments can also reap the rewards that come from competing in dynamic industries where change is the rule.[6]

Exhibit 1.2 Decline of Companies Once Considered "Excellent" or "Visionary"

American Express	IBM	Digital Equipment
Boeing	Johnson & Johnson	Sony
Citigroup	K Mart	Motorola
Data General	Marriott	General Motors
Eastman Kodak	Procter & Gamble	Polaroid
Fannie Mae	Walt Disney	Levi Strauss
Ford	Wang Laboratories	Xerox

Source: Peters & Waterman. 1988. *In Search of Excellence: Lessons from America's Best-Run Companies.* New York: Harper & Row; Collins & Porras. 2002. *Built to Last: Successful Habits of Visionary Companies.* New York: Harper Collins.

Managerial Thinking: A New Perspective on Strategic Management

As just described, the highly volatile and competitive business environments in which firms must compete can make the tasks of managing a firm challenging to say the least! But, these environments also highlight an important point—that strategic management is fundamentally a human process. Managers must understand their firms' environments, and they must make the decisions that effectively position and prepare their firms to compete successfully. Note that the definition of strategic management provided at the beginning of this chapter—the process by which managers formulate and implement strategies aimed at creating sustained competitive advantage—emphasizes the key role of managers in the strategic management process.

While it might seem obvious that a focus on the strategic management of firms and organizations would give managers a central role, much of the management literature focuses on economic and structural explanations for firm performance. According to these economic and structural perspectives, firm performance is largely a function of industry structure and how competitive an industry is. This kind of thinking leads to many commonly accepted expectations, for example, that firms operating in less competitive industries will enjoy higher performance than firms operating in highly competitive environments.

This book will also examine these economic and structural explanations for firm performance, but the underlying premise of this book is that the task of strategic management is not only structural but also *managerial*. This book does not argue that industry structure is unimportant—in fact, two chapters are devoted to developing ways of thinking about and analyzing industry structure. We begin, however, with the premise that managers and managerial decision making are fundamentally important to the success of business organizations. This text, therefore, places managers at the center of strategic management. It builds on theories and recent research studies that seek to understand how managerial thinking—managers' attitudes, beliefs, and understandings—influence strategic decision making.

At the heart of our emphasis on managerial thinking is the concept of ***mental models***, which Peter Senge has defined as "deeply ingrained assumptions, generalizations, or even pictures or images that influence how we understand the world and how we take action."[7] Mental models are simplified understandings or representations of the phenomena we encounter. Mental models tell us what is and is not important to us, what we do and do not like, what we should and should not notice. They include our understandings of how things work and what we expect to happen next. When we encounter new and novel situations, our minds quickly construct new mental models to help us understand these new phenomena.

Managerial thinking—embedded in managers' mental models—influences strategic decision making and the actions firms take. Managers' mental models of the situations they encounter determine whether a particular strategic issue or situation will be noticed, how it will be interpreted and understood, and how they will respond to the situation. The study of managerial thinking thus helps to explain why some managers notice important business issues while other managers do not, why some managers correctly interpret these issues while others do not, and why some managers respond appropriately to these issues while others do not. As a result, the linkages among business environments (including industry structure), managerial thinking, and strategic decision making are keys to understanding performance differences across firms and how competitive advantage is developed.

Exhibit 1.3 illustrates this managerial thinking perspective on strategy and how managers' beliefs influence decision making. Specific decisions become the building blocks of strategies. Strategies, in turn, influence business and firm performance outcomes. These performance outcomes provide important feedback to managers, either reinforcing existing beliefs (most likely when performance outcomes are positive) or suggesting to managers that they need to change their beliefs or understandings about the decisions and strategies that lead to high performance (most likely when performance falls short of managers' aspirations or expectations). The exhibit shows that managerial beliefs not only influence the choice of strategies but also that their success or failure provides managers with feedback that can lead to subsequent changes in their beliefs and understandings. Through this ongoing process, individual managers, and their organizations, learn and develop new understandings over time.

Exhibit 1.3 Relationships among Managers' Beliefs, Decision Making, Strategies, and Performance Outcomes

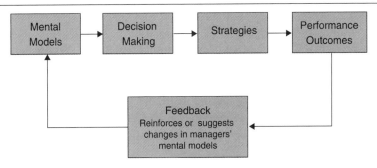

Strategy As a Pattern in a Stream of Decisions

As we've just illustrated, the decisions managers make are critical to the success of their firms, and the overall objective of this text is to understand managerial decision making and how managers' decisions affect the performance of firms and businesses. The decisions managers make are so important because they are the raw material or basis of strategies. In fact, throughout this book, **strategy** will be defined as *"a pattern in a stream of decisions."*[8] In other words, strategies can emerge over time as decisions accumulate to form recognizable patterns of action.

This definition of strategy is quite different from the conventional view of strategy as a "grand plan" that results after careful, comprehensive analyses of competitive environments and organizational capabilities. The problem with the grand plan view of strategy is that it does not reflect how strategies are actually formulated and implemented in most organizations. Typically, strategies do not materialize solely from a corporate headquarters as comprehensive statements of objectives and action plans for achieving those objectives. Although strategies are certainly influenced by and often set in motion by formal **strategic planning** processes, strategies are often shaped or even remade in a piecemeal fashion as managers make decisions in response to a competitor's move, in the face of a pending situation or crisis, or in anticipation of future changes in the business environment.

"Unrealized Strategies" and the "Emergent" Nature of Business Strategies

Two organizational realities exert a great deal of influence on the strategies of business firms. First, many intended plans or strategies do not get implemented; in other words, they become "unrealized strategies."[9] Many factors are responsible for plans becoming "unrealized strategies." Sometimes the plans are simply poorly conceived or inappropriate, and when this fact becomes widely recognized, it's no surprise that these plans are abandoned. One business unit manager has offered this assessment of many corporate plans:

> Let's face it, much "grand" thinking at the top is not. Many otherwise respectable managements permit themselves the delusion that they are providing "vision" when they are merely projecting today's business ahead in time… Genuinely creative thinking about [strategies] that can deliver competitive advantage, say, a decade hence is quite rare at the top.[10]

Other times, problems will arise that prevent implementation—circumstances may change and what was seen as a good idea becomes less attractive, a necessary political coalition required to implement the strategy may not materialize, or key resources that are essential to the implementation of the plan may not be available. And often, the crush of dealing with day-to-day issues and occasional crises prevents managers from implementing even the best-laid plans. One scholar summarized this tendency by stating, "in most … companies the urgent has driven out the important."[11]

Second, it's important to understand and acknowledge that many strategies *emerge* without ever being part of a formal plan.[12] Because of the rapid pace of change that characterizes many business environments, new issues arise frequently and quite unexpectedly (i.e., a competitor will lower prices, a competitor's new marketing strategy negatively impacts a company's sales and threatens its market share, new products with better features are introduced by competitors, new technologies emerge, or totally new competitors enter the market). As managers go about performing their routine, day-to-day activities, they not only have to identify these new issues, but they must also respond quickly to these new issues if their companies are to avoid negative consequences.

In short, managers must make complex decisions quickly and with very little information or very little time to engage in formal planning activities. In the process of making these almost spontaneous decisions, new strategies "emerge" as patterns develop in streams of decision making. Andrew Grove, former chairman and CEO of Intel, described this emergent nature of strategic decision making this way: "People formulate strategy with their fingertips. Day in and day out they respond to things, by virtue of the products they promote, the price concessions they make, the distribution channels they choose."[13]

And, it is not just executives and senior managers who are responsible for "emergent strategies." Because managers at all levels of a business organization must respond to unanticipated events or take action even if no guidance or direction has been previously provided, even mid- and lower-level managers can often be responsible for initiating strategies.

Therefore, Exhibit 1.4 suggests a more accurate depiction of the strategy formulation and implementation process. The "intended strategy" portion of Exhibit 1.4 represents those plans or initiatives that managers *intend* for their firms to pursue. Note also the box labeled "unrealized strategy;" this represents decisions that are not implemented for any of the reasons described earlier. The key point of the illustration is to demonstrate that "realized strategy" is a product, not just of plans or intentions, but also of decisions made in response to emergent issues.

In summary, the strategies that emerge in most firms rarely result solely from a formal planning process. Although the strategies pursued by most companies include many elements from a formal planning process, many aspects of company strategies are conceived "in real time" as managers wrestle with issues that emerge from ongoing day-to-day business activities. The decisions made by managers accumulate and, over time, form patterns that can be recognized as strategies.

Exhibit 1.4 Strategy Formation As a Product of Intended and Emergent Processes

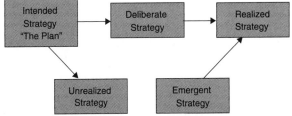

Source: Mintzberg, H. 1978. Patterns in strategy formation. *Management Science*, 24: 945.

Some Case Studies of Intended, Unrealized, Emerging, and Realized Strategies

A couple of examples will illustrate the emergent nature of company strategies. The first is historical, and comes from an article that analyzed Honda's success at entering the U.S. motorcycle market in the 1960s and 1970s.[14] The article first summarized a study prepared by the Boston Consulting Group (BCG). This study attributed Honda's success in the U.S. motorcycle market to a formal strategic planning process that sought to achieve production economies through market share leadership. The article then contrasted the BCG study with accounts by Honda's own managers that described how its successful entry was really a process of learning from trial and error. In the words of one Honda manager:

> In truth, we had no strategy other than the idea of seeing if we could sell something in the United States. It was a new frontier, a new challenge, and it fit the "success against all odds" culture that Mr. Honda had cultivated.[15]

The key idea that the article sought to emphasize was that:

> consultants, academics, and executives express a preference for oversimplifications of reality and cognitively linear explanations of events. To be sure, they have always acknowledged that the "human factor" must be taken into account. But extensive reading of strategy cases at business schools, consultants' reports, [and] strategic planning documents, as well as the coverage of the popular press, reveals a widespread tendency to overlook the process through which organizations experiment, adapt, and learn. We tend to impute coherence and purposive rationality to events when the opposite may be closer to the truth. How an organization deals with miscalculation, mistakes, and serendipitous events *outside its field of vision is often crucial to success over time.*[16]

Another example of the emergent nature of strategy is provided by the strategy formulation activities of two retailers as diverse as Abercrombie and Safeway, the supermarket chain, during the recent severe economic downturn.[17] Prior to the downturn, Abercrombie had pursued a strategy of maintaining high prices as part of a larger effort to position its stores as luxury clothing retailers both in the United States and abroad. Similarly, Safeway had invested more than $8 billion in refurbishing its stores and added many gourmet and prepared food items in an effort to compete for more upscale grocery customers.

Managers at both companies initially responded to the recession by maintaining their firms' high-end strategies and refusing to engage in significant discounting of their merchandise, in order to reinforce the image and perceived quality of their products. As the recession deepened and lengthened, however, both companies were forced to abandon these "intended strategies" of maintaining high prices. As competitors moved quickly to discount their prices to attract customers, both companies saw significant reductions in sales and declines in market share as their shoppers sought better bargains elsewhere. As a result, sales at Abercrombie fell, while sales at another clothing retailer, Aeropostale, which did engage in significant discounting, actually saw its sales increase from 2007 through 2009.

Exhibit 1.5 The Evolution of Strategy at Abercrombie and Safeway

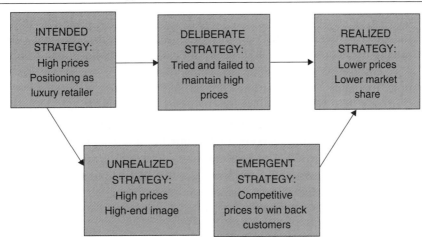

Declining sales eventually forced both Abercrombie and Safeway to abandon their "intended strategies" of maintaining high prices, and at least parts of their high-end strategies became "unrealized strategies." Both retailers have now discounted prices on many items in an effort to win-back customers and to regain lost market share.[18] Neither company moved fast enough, however, to prevent an erosion of market share. As a result, the "realized strategy" for both companies includes lower prices. Exhibit 1.5 illustrates the evolving strategies of Abercrombie and Safeway. It's not that either company had to abandon efforts to differentiate itself from its competitors, but that they had to recalibrate their prices to be more competitive with the lower prices offered by their competitors.

What Makes Strategy "Strategic?"

Now that strategy has been defined and the strategy formulation and implementation processes have been described, let's consider what makes strategic management "strategic." One way to clarify these terms is to distinguish between decisions and actions that are "strategic" and those that are more "tactical." Every day, many times each day, managers must make a variety of decisions. The majority of these decisions will respond to routine issues, while others have the potential to affect the health or direction of the business in a much more fundamental way. These critical, direction-setting decisions are the focus of this book and they are "strategic" for at least three reasons.

Strategic Decisions Are Important

Strategic decisions and strategic management not only shape and define a business organization, but they also have the potential to affect the bottom-line financial health of a business and even the survival of the organization. As a result, strategic management is a fundamentally important activity; how managers respond to important issues can affect the health and prosperity of their firms and businesses in the short run as well as in the long run.

Strategic Decisions Often Involve Significant Reallocations of Resources

Strategic decisions have the potential to change the purpose and direction of a firm and, therefore, lead to major changes in the definition, scale, and scope of the business. Nearly all strategic decisions involve significant allocations or reallocations of organizational resources.

For example, managers will sometimes decide that their firms must target a different set of customers, offer a new line of products or services, or employ new technologies. Cisco, in an effort to maintain the impressive growth it has experienced since its founding, is now expanding beyond the networking markets it has come to dominate, and has announced it will begin to offer a much broader range of products and services. But, the decision to move into 30 new markets, including everything from servers to video cameras, will require Cisco to compete against many established and formidable competitors, including Hewlett-Packard, Dell, and IBM—all companies with which Cisco has long partnered in its traditional network routing businesses.[19] These are strategic decisions for Cisco's managers because they entail a significant expansion of the company's product lines and will result in major changes in Cisco's competitive landscape.

Decisions to acquire businesses, to start new businesses, or to divest existing businesses will also almost always alter the scale or scope of a firm. All these decisions involve major commitments or reallocations of organizational resources and are thus strategic decisions.

Strategic Decisions Usually Involve More Than One Functional Department

Finally, strategic decisions are rarely focused on a "marketing problem" or a "manufacturing problem." Instead, strategic decision making usually cuts across functional departments, involving marketing *and* manufacturing and, possibly, finance, research and development, and engineering. Strategic decision making thus requires the attention of general managers and chief executive officers who must often mediate interdepartmental or interdivisional disagreements and rivalries in order to achieve a consensus or widespread agreement about the overall direction of their firm.

A Model of Strategic Management

Exhibit 1.6 expands on Exhibit 1.3, illustrating a model of strategic management that provides the organizing framework for this book. Like the framework shown in Exhibit 1.3, the model portrayed in Exhibit 1.6 builds on the assumption that managers' mental models—their beliefs and understandings—influence decisions and shape strategies that, in turn, influence performance outcomes and determine whether their firms enjoy a competitive advantage. As in Exhibit 1.3, performance outcomes provide important feedback to managers that will either reinforce existing beliefs or suggest to managers that they need to change their beliefs and understandings. Note in Exhibit 1.6 that all of these decisions occur in the larger environment of industry, customer, technology, societal, and economic forces.

Exhibit 1.6 Managers' Beliefs, Strategic Decisions, and Their Influence on Performance and Competitive Advantage

As suggested in Exhibit 1.6, this book focuses on four important types of mental models and decisions:

1. ***Managers' Beliefs about Industry Environments, and How These Beliefs Influence Decisions about Business Definition and Positioning.*** Industries are the competitive environments in which firms interact with customers, rivals, suppliers, and other stakeholders. Thus, managers must develop beliefs and understandings—mental models—about the nature of competition in their industries. Chapter 4 will describe two widely-used frameworks that are useful for analyzing industry structure, and Chapter 5 will suggest a more dynamic framework that can be helpful for anticipating how industries will evolve over time. These frameworks and tools can be very useful to managers who must develop accurate beliefs and understandings about the environments in which their firms must compete.

   Managers' beliefs and understandings of their industries are important as they seek to define or position their firms and businesses in these ever-changing competitive environments. Chapter 6 takes up the challenges of business definition and positioning. Chapter 6 also emphasizes the need for managers to anticipate how demographic changes and technological innovations will create future arenas of opportunities so that they can proactively position their firms to enjoy "first-mover" and other advantages.

2. ***Beliefs about How to Compete, and How These Beliefs Influence Decisions about Business Strategy.*** Managers' beliefs about how to compete in their firms' industries will influence the decisions that become the basis of their firms' strategies. Of course, business strategies will also be influenced by decisions about business definition. For example, Rolex enjoys a very distinctive yet narrow business definition in the highest

end of the wristwatch market. Because of its distinctive position, Rolex pursues business strategies that are very different from those of Timex, Swatch, or Seiko—all of which compete in much broader segments of the wristwatch market.

Business strategy is the focus of Chapters 7, 8, and 9. Chapter 7 provides a foundation for understanding and analyzing business strategies, and describes several different types of "generic" business strategies or ways firms and businesses can compete in their industries. Chapter 8 builds on this foundation by examining the appropriateness and effectiveness of various business strategies in emerging markets. We will focus on the special challenges of new and rapidly growing businesses. We will also examine the challenges faced by established firms as they seek to compete in new markets created by demographic and technological changes. This chapter will also consider online businesses and the competitive opportunities and challenges introduced by the Internet and other information technologies. Chapter 9 focuses on the challenges of maturing and declining markets. In this chapter, we also focus on how firms in mature markets can maintain a competitive edge by developing innovative products and services.

3. ***Understandings about the Appropriate Scale and Scope of the Business Enterprise, and How These Beliefs Influence Firms' Corporate Strategies.*** A third group of beliefs that are crucial to the success of firms involves managers' beliefs about the appropriate scale (i.e., size) and scope (i.e., breadth and diversity of product offerings) of their firms. Many firms, even many small firms, are diversified, multibusiness firms—that is, they have more than one main business and they compete in different markets or industries. Managers' beliefs about how these businesses are related to each other and how diversification should be managed are also critically important beliefs. These beliefs, in turn, influence decisions about corporate strategy, including decisions about vertical integration, diversification, mergers and acquisitions, and strategic alliances. These topics are considered in Chapter 10.

4. ***Beliefs about How to Organize, and How These Mental Models Influence Decisions about Organizational Structure.*** A fourth group of beliefs that will be explored in this book includes managers' mental models about how their firms should be organized. These mental models influence managers' decisions about the structures they employ in their organizations to implement strategies and to coordinate human resources and information flows. Like effective definitions and business and corporate strategies, effective structures can also be a source of competitive advantage. Chapter 11 describes the various components of organizational structure, assesses the ability of these components to contribute to competitive advantage, and describes a number of companies that have achieved great success by adopting innovative structures.

The book concludes with a look at the challenge of organizational responsiveness. The last chapter of the book addresses the topics introduced at the beginning of this chapter— the rapid pace of industry and environmental change, and how managers can anticipate and respond to these changes so their firms might remain viable and enjoy high levels of performance. Chapter 12 explores reasons why managers fail to respond to changes in their industry environments while also suggesting ways that managers can be more responsive.

We begin, however, with a detailed introduction to the concept of competitive advantage, or why some firms consistently out-perform others. Chapter 2 also describes the factors that are required to build and maintain competitive advantage. The chapter explains how competitive advantage results from asymmetry: high-performing firms either occupy unique positions in their industries, or they develop and possess unique and valuable capabilities that cannot be easily duplicated by their rivals.

Then, in Chapter 3, we provide an in depth look at the work of general managers and the task of building competitive advantage. Before examining the various components of the model illustrated in Exhibit 1.6, Chapter 3 focuses specifically on how managers' beliefs— their mental models—influence strategic decisions and the crafting of strategies that lead to competitive advantage, the reason why some firms consistently enjoy high performance relative to their rivals. The chapter will explore the sources of managerial beliefs while also noting some of the biases and limitations of managerial thinking.

Conclusion: Three Key Themes

This chapter suggests three key themes that will be emphasized throughout this book.

Managers and Managerial Thinking

This text adopts Mintzberg's definition of strategy as "a pattern in a stream of decisions." We also emphasize that managers make the decisions that form the basis of strategies, so to understand company strategies and to understand why some companies outperform others, we must understand the thinking that causes managers to make a particular set of decisions rather than some other set of decisions. The importance of managers will therefore be emphasized throughout the book. We will focus on how managers develop the beliefs and understandings that influence the decisions they make, how managers come to acquire new beliefs and understandings, the inherent problems and weaknesses associated with managerial thinking and decision making, and how those problems can be overcome to produce organizational success.

Change and the Need to Think Dynamically about Strategy

Strategies that are effective today will almost certainly be ineffective in the future because companies compete in dynamic, not static, environments. Consumer demographics, tastes and preferences, the nature of products and services, and the technologies businesses use to provide products and services all change, and so industries will evolve in response to these changes. Sometimes these changes occur rapidly. For example, in some product markets, such as cell phones and personal computers, companies face product life cycles lasting less than one year and sometimes as short as four to six months. Far different from the economic ideal of market equilibrium, it can often seem that these industry environments are in a permanent state of disequilibrium in which demand and supply do not stabilize because technological innovation and changing consumer wants and needs encourage the rapid introduction of new products and services. Management scholars and consultants have coined new terms, including *high-velocity environments* and *hypercompetition,* to describe the dynamics of these rapidly changing competitive environments.[20]

On the other hand, some industries experience little change for decades. As a result, the managers of firms in these industries can grow complacent and be content to pursue the same or very similar strategies for years. When major changes in these industries do occur, these managers can be caught off-guard. They then have to scramble to adapt to dramatically different industry conditions.

Whether changes in business environments occur frequently or more sporadically, they require company managers to anticipate and/or respond quickly both to changing consumer preferences and to the moves of their competitors in order to introduce the right products and services on a timely basis. Adding to the challenge, some, more entrepreneurial, firms will seize the opportunities that are created by these market forces to enter markets and become formidable competitors. Inevitably, some companies emerge as leaders, while others will fail to keep pace with the rapid rate of change in their industries, and some firms will enter periods of decline from which they do not recover.

Thus, the book will emphasize the importance of thinking dynamically about strategic management. All business organizations face the challenge of developing and maintaining competitive advantage while also anticipating or responding to changes in their industry environments. Managers who ignore changes in their industry environments will risk seeing their firms blindsided by new customer wants and needs, new products and services, and new developments in technology. Decline or organizational failure is the price their firms will pay for a lack of diligence.

The Importance of Organizational Knowledge and Learning

We have already emphasized that the tasks of general managers are highly knowledge-intensive in that they must be able to combine knowledge and expertise about their firms and businesses with knowledge of economic and industry forces to position their organizations in the marketplace and formulate effective business strategies. But *all* work today is becoming increasingly knowledge-intensive. Knowledge resides in organizations in the heads of managers and employees, in routines and standard operating procedures, and in the equipment and technologies that are employed.

As the business world becomes increasingly knowledge-intensive, the ability to learn, store, retrieve, and exploit new knowledge and information will become a key source of competitive advantage. Therefore, this book will examine how organizations can capitalize on organizational learning, while also focusing on the factors that can contribute to organizational learning as well as the many barriers that prevent firms from learning.

A Look Ahead

In the chapters to come, we will see that the model of strategic management illustrated in Exhibit 1.6 provides compelling explanations for many contemporary business situations. Take, for example, the dismal performance of two major corporations, General Motors and Kodak. In each case, we can find convincing evidence that the executives failed to keep pace with rapidly changing business environments. As a consequence, both companies' business definitions became dated, and both companies failed to develop the organizational capabilities that would allow them to enjoy a competitive advantage over their rivals.

For both GM and Kodak, the model of business performance illustrated in Exhibit 1.6 suggests that managers, specifically their mental models, failed to anticipate or keep pace with changes in the industry, thus leaving the firms unprepared to maintain or develop a competitive advantage in the new industry environments in which they found themselves. As a consequence, for many years these firms lacked vision, uncertainty prevailed, new strategic initiatives failed to receive sufficient resources, talented employees became dissatisfied and left, and morale problems developed among those employees who stayed. The cost of such failures in managerial thinking is staggering: plants closed, thousands of employees laid off, billions of dollars of restructuring changes, and the loss of shareholder value.

Understanding of the three themes of this book—the central role of managerial thinking, the rapid rate of industry change, and the importance of organizational learning—is critical to organizational success; changes in managerial thinking are fundamental to firm success because managers usually cannot recommend strategic changes without first changing their own mental models. It's not that managers' beliefs are the only thing that must change in order to renew a languishing organization, but a change in those beliefs is often a necessary prerequisite to organizational change and renewal. Unfortunately, GM and Kodak are not isolated examples. Similar patterns are observed almost daily, and this book will point out many examples in which managerial thinking failed to keep pace with changes in the business environment.

On the other hand, we have many exemplary companies that have enjoyed and maintained consistently high levels of performance in spite of significant changes in their industry environments or fierce competition from their rivals. Disney has certainly experienced ups and downs during its history, but the company has long enjoyed an outstanding reputation. And, under the leadership of Bob Iger, Disney has become the largest media company in the world in terms of market value. By focusing on the value of Disney's creative assets and by acquiring Pixar, Iger has improved Disney's performance in its traditional markets, and has also encouraged expansion into Russia, China, and India, including producing films in those countries' local languages.[21]

Coca-Cola has also seen its ups and downs, but few companies have enjoyed as much overall success over such a long period of time. A truly global company, Coca-Cola is sold in nearly every country and its Coca-Cola and Coke brands are among the most familiar in the world. Though the company's competitive environment is characterized by fierce competition from Pepsi and other soft drink companies as well as other beverages including coffee, bottled water, and fruit juices, the company's performance and competitive advantage remain outstanding.

Key Points

This introductory chapter had several objectives. It began by reviewing some of the most important characteristics of today's business environments. The chapter then introduced the field of strategic management. It defined strategy as "a pattern in a stream of decisions,"[22] and described the "emergent" nature of the strategy formulation and implementation processes. The chapter then introduced the model of strategic management that will serve as the organizing framework for this book.

Being able to think strategically, to evaluate business environments, to understand the content, formulation, and implementation of business and corporate strategies, and to appreciate how all employees and departments are an integral part of the larger company mission—these are skills that should be held, not only by general managers, but should be widely distributed among all employees throughout a firm or business. In many "high involvement" companies today, responsibility for decision making has been widely distributed so that employees at all levels must think strategically, and decisions made only from a manager's functional point of view will be inadequate.[23]

Although this book offers many business examples and addresses many contemporary issues, no book can anticipate the issues firms and businesses will confront in the years ahead. As a result, managers, and all employees, need to develop *ways of thinking and learning* that will enhance the contributions they can make to the overall success of their firms and businesses.

Key points emphasized in this chapter include:

- Strategy's focus or level of analysis is unique. Economics focuses on the economy or industries, while most business fields such as finance, marketing, operations management, and organizational behavior tend to focus on more "micro" levels of analysis. Strategy is one of the few fields in business that focuses on the overall management of firms and businesses.
- The tasks of general managers are complex and challenging, and made more difficult because strategic management occurs in dynamic business environments.
- Many management books emphasize the importance of industry structure as a primary influence on firm performance. According to this view, firm performance is a function of operating in attractive industries. In contrast, this book also emphasizes the critical role of managers and strategic thinking in understanding industry environments, defining or positioning businesses in their competitive arenas, developing and maintaining capabilities, and developing organizational structures and other coordinating mechanisms.
- The book is organized around a model of strategic management that emphasizes the importance of the managerial thinking contained in managers' mental models. Mental models are simplified, mental representations of the phenomena we encounter; these models contain our assumptions, beliefs, and understandings about a wide range of phenomena. Specifically, the book examines four types of mental models:
  - Managers' beliefs about industry environments, and how those beliefs influence decisions about business definition and positioning.
  - Managers' beliefs about how businesses should compete, and how those beliefs influence decisions about business strategy.
  - Managers' beliefs about the appropriate scale and scope of their firms, and how those beliefs influence decisions about corporate strategy.

- Managers' beliefs about how to organize, and how those beliefs influence decisions about organizational structure.
- Three key themes that will be emphasized throughout this book include: 1) the importance of managers and managerial thinking, 2) change and the need to think dynamically about strategy, and 3) the value of organizational knowledge and learning.

Key Questions for Managers

At the end of every chapter, we will pose a set of "key questions for managers." This section asks readers to take some of the most important ideas presented in the chapter and apply them to actual company situations. Students who have worked in companies can apply these questions to the firms where they have worked in the past, or students might select a company and address these questions in a short research project. Current managers can, of course, apply these questions to their own firms and businesses.

- What are the key managerial beliefs and understandings that guide strategic decision making in your firm?
- Do you and other managers take a dynamic view of strategy and actively anticipate how your firm's competitive landscape is likely to change?
- What are the sources of change that make your firm's competitive environment dynamic or challenging? Or, if your firm's competitive environment is relatively stable, how might changes in consumer demographics, technologies, or the development of new products and services alter your firm's competitive landscape in the future?
- What are the taken for granted aspects of your firm's industry environment (customer demographics, products and services, technologies) that could change, and how well prepared is your firm to anticipate or respond to these changes?
- What elements of your firm's strategy are/were "intended" or resulted from a strategic planning process? What elements of your firm's strategy have "emerged" and are not a result of the firm's strategic planning process? Does your firm have elements or components of its strategic plans that have become "unrealized?"
- Does your firm value organizational learning and knowledge? Does it have systematic processes in place for capturing and exploiting learning?

Suggestions for Further Reading

Additionally, links to further resources online—such as cases, articles, and videos—can be found on the book's website, www.routledge.com/textbooks/Duhaime.

Collins, J. C., & Porras, J. I. 1994. *Built to Last: Successful Habits of Visionary Companies*. New York: HarperBusiness.

Johansen, R. 2009. *Leaders Make the Future: Ten New Leadership Skills for an Uncertain World*. San Francisco: Berrett-Koehler Publishers.

Martin, R. 2009. *The Design of Business*: *Why Design Thinking Is the Next Competitive Advantage*. Boston: Harvard Business Press.

Mintzberg, H. 1978. Patterns in strategy formation. *Management Science*, 24: 934–948.

Peters, T. J., & Waterman, Jr., R. H. 1982. *In Search of Excellence: Lessons from America's Best-Run Companies.* New York: Harper & Row.

Senge, P. M. 1990. *The Fifth Discipline: The Art and Practice of the Learning Organization.* New York: Doubleday/Currency.

Chapter 2

Competitive Advantage

Chapter 1 described how managers' mental models influence the decisions they make, which, in turn, become their firms' realized strategies. The model of strategic management introduced in Chapter 1, and reprinted here as Exhibit 2.1, suggests that managers must make four major types of strategic decisions. They must:

- *Define or position their firms in their competitive environments based on their understandings of industry structure and dynamics.*
- *Develop a business strategy based on their understandings about how to compete in their firms' industries.*
- *Develop a corporate strategy based on their understandings about the appropriate scale and scope for their firms.*
- *Create an organizational structure based on their understandings about how business firms ought to be organized.*

Before beginning a detailed study of these four key types of strategic decisions, however, this chapter provides an introduction to the concept of competitive advantage. We'll see that, through their decisions, the managers of some firms succeed in creating a competitive advantage by acquiring and developing firm-specific resources and capabilities that are valuable, rare, difficult to imitate, and lack substitutes.

Chapter Objectives

The specific objectives of this chapter are to:

- Provide a definition of competitive advantage, and describe how organizations develop and then maintain competitive advantage.
- Distinguish between strategy content and process and emphasize the importance of organizational processes in developing and maintaining competitive advantage.
- Introduce the concept of the value chain and explain its usefulness as a tool for assessing organizational capabilities.
- Emphasize the importance of socially-complex resources, such as trust, culture, and reputation, in the development and maintenance of competitive advantage.
- Demonstrate that any source of competitive advantage can be rendered obsolete very quickly by changes in firms' competitive environments.

Exhibit 2.1 Managers' Beliefs, Strategic Decisions, and Their Influence on Performance and Competitive Advantage

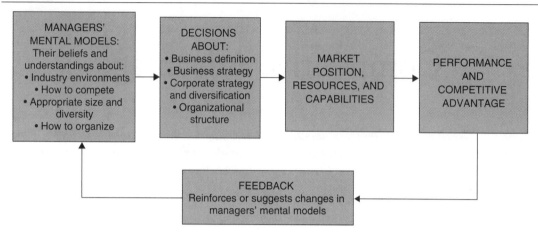

What Is Competitive Advantage?

Competitive advantage is the set of factors or capabilities that allows firms to consistently outperform their rivals. Note that the objective of competitive advantage is to *outperform* rivals, not merely to match the performance of other businesses. Firms with a competitive advantage should enjoy high performance, and, while firms that have a competitive advantage do not necessarily have to be the highest-performing firms in their industries, they should consistently be among the highest performers in their industries and do much better than the average. The book's framework (Exhibit 2.1) suggests that, through their decisions, managers are responsible for making the four types of strategic decisions that lead to the acquisition and development of firm-specific resources and capabilities that can be sources of competitive advantage.

Moreover, another important aim of competitive advantage is for firms to enjoy *sustained* levels of high performance. In other words, a business should not enjoy just one or two or a few good quarters or even years, but it should have a sustainable competitive advantage so that it *consistently* outperforms rival firms and businesses over longer periods of time. Many firms have shown that they have the ability to have a good year or two, but far fewer firms have shown the ability to enjoy *consistently* high levels of performance year after year.

The concept of competitive advantage is closely tied to the concept of economic rent. Economists assume that over the long run, firms in competitive markets will earn average economic profits (profits after all factors of production have been paid) of zero.* Firms that

---

*Note that the key difference between economic profit and the traditional accounting measures of net income is that economic profit would include the cost of equity capital. For example, assume a firm earns an accounting profit of $50 million and has total capital of $200 million and a cost of capital of 15 percent. Its economic profit is $20 million [$50 million – ($200 million * 15 percent)].

earn above-average economic profits over the long run are said to enjoy economic rents. The logic behind economic rents and competitive advantage is essentially the same—firms enjoy economic rents and competitive advantage by possessing and exploiting some set of resources or capabilities that allow them to outperform rivals.

Firm performance is often equated with financial performance, but firm performance can be assessed in many ways and along many different dimensions. Financial performance is certainly one key way in which we assess the performance of business organizations, but firms can also be evaluated by how quickly they are growing and whether they are gaining or losing market share vis-à-vis their competitors. Whether firms are noted for being especially innovative or whether they are known for providing high quality products or services are also dimensions of performance. Because of the important relationship between firm performance and assessments of competitive advantage, an appendix to this chapter provides an overview of the many ways of assessing the performance of firms and businesses.

The main point we want to emphasize is that performance is a multidimensional concept, and it is important to consider a variety of different types of performance measures when evaluating whether a company enjoys a competitive advantage. The best indication that a firm enjoys a competitive advantage would be high performance across many different performance dimensions over a number of years.

Does a company have to outperform every one of its competitors every quarter or every year in order to claim that it has a competitive advantage? There's probably no consensus among business professionals and academic researchers on this point. While outperforming all competitors every year on every conceivable performance dimension would provide a very clear-cut definition of competitive advantage, the fact is that very few, if any, companies would ever be able to claim that they enjoy a competitive advantage if these criteria were the requirement. Even the strongest companies will have a bad year or two or will experience a sustained slump. And, few if any companies have managed to weather the recent severe recession without impacts on their sales or profitability. On the other hand, many companies have succeeded in enjoying strong performance and remaining market leaders for many years or even decades. Thus, we will use less restrictive criteria when evaluating whether a company enjoys a competitive advantage, requiring that a company experience strong performance, beating the performance of most of its competitors, in most years in order to claim that it enjoys a competitive advantage.

Competitive Advantage: The Importance of Firm-Specific Resources and Capabilities

The aim of strategic management is the development of sustainable competitive advantage. Given this book's definition of strategy as "a pattern in a stream of decisions,"[1] our focus is on the patterns of decisions that contribute to the development of competitive advantage and sustained high performance. The model of strategic management illustrated in Exhibit 2.1 shows that strategies do not affect firm performance directly, but that strategies affect performance through the development of firm-specific resources and capabilities that can lead both to competitive advantage and to high performance. This chapter considers how managerial thinking and decision making are associated with the development of firm-specific resources and capabilities, including business definitions and market positions, business and corporate strategies, and structures that lead to sustained competitive advantage.

It is only during the last few decades that the field of strategic management has begun to explicitly acknowledge and appreciate the impact that firm-specific factors and capabilities can have on firm performance.[2] Early studies, including studies of the brewing industry, showed that firms in the *same* industry pursuing the *same* strategies had widely varying levels of performance.[3] Such findings were important because they called into question traditional "structural" explanations for firm performance, which predict that firms in the same industry— especially firms pursuing similar strategies in the same industry—would enjoy roughly comparable performance outcomes.

Later studies examining performance differences among firms in the same industry that are pursuing similar strategies hypothesized that these performance differences must result from differences in organizational capabilities.[4] Those subsequent studies did find significant differences in the resources and capabilities across firms, and they also found a significant relationship between firms' capabilities and their performance outcomes. Thus, the key to sustained high performance lies in firm-specific resources and capabilities and in the managerial thinking that marshals and develops these resources and capabilities.

One way to explore the performance implications of firm-specific resources is through the resource-based view of the firm.[5] This perspective is rooted in the important work of British scholar Edith Penrose, who suggested that firms could be viewed as collections of productive resources.[6] The central thesis of the resource-based perspective is that too little attention has been given to the importance of firm-specific resources and capabilities. Advocates of the resource-based perspective do not suggest that industry or market characteristics are unimportant, but they do argue that competitive advantage will be determined by the resources and capabilities firms bring to their competitive arenas.

Criteria that Determine Whether Resources and Capabilities Can Provide Firms with Competitive Advantage

Although researchers have only begun to explore the implications of the resource-based perspective during the past few decades, there is broad agreement on the central tenets of the theory: that firms will enjoy a sustained competitive advantage only if their capabilities are *valuable* and *rare, lack substitutes*, and are *difficult to imitate.*[7]

According to this logic, resources and capabilities that are not valuable obviously cannot be expected to generate any sort of competitive advantage. Similarly, if valuable resources are not rare, but are widely available to all firms, the best that a firm can hope for is competitive parity with other firms. If resources and capabilities are both valuable and rare, and also difficult for rivals to imitate, then those resources can at least be a temporary source of competitive advantage. Finally, if resources and capabilities are valuable, rare, and difficult to imitate, and if those resources also lack viable substitutes, then those resources and capabilities can be the source of sustained competitive advantage. This reasoning is summarized in Exhibit 2.2.

Exhibit 2.2 Estimating the Return-Generating Potential of Organizational Resources and Capabilities

Description of Resources and Capabilities				
Valuable	Rare	Difficult to Imitate	Lacks Substitutes	**Result**
No	-	-	-	*Competitive disadvantage*
Yes	No	-	-	*Competitive parity*
Yes	Yes	No	-	*Temporary competitive advantage*
Yes	Yes	Yes	No	*Competitive parity*
Yes	Yes	Yes	Yes	*Sustained competitive advantage*

Source: Adapted from Barney, J. B. 1991. Firm resources and sustained competitive advantage. *Journal of Management*, 17: 99–120.

Let's consider just one example to illustrate this important concept. Toward the end of Chapter 1, we described Disney as a company that has managed to remain very successful over many decades. At least one reason for Disney's enduring success is the value of its Disney characters—certainly among the most valuable resources owned or controlled by any firm in the world.

Are Mickey Mouse and the other iconic Disney characters valuable, rare, difficult to imitate, and do other companies lack viable substitutes for these valuable assets? There is no question that they are valuable. While there's no shortage of animated characters in the motion picture and entertainment industries, the Disney characters do seem to occupy a unique and very special place in the very competitive world of family entertainment, in spite of considerable efforts on the parts of other companies to imitate their success. And, although there are certainly many different types of films, media, and entertainment, few if any other companies have succeeded in developing a completely viable substitute for Disney's animated characters, the films in which they appear, and the company's highly successful theme parks that are built around the popularity of its characters and movies.

The Asymmetric Nature of Competitive Advantage

The four criteria that determine whether resources and capabilities provide firms with a sustainable competitive advantage—valuable, rare, difficult to imitate, and without substitutes— imply that an essential characteristic of competitive advantage is *asymmetry*. In other words, uniqueness is an essential characteristic of any resource or capability that is to be the basis of competitive advantage. Thus, conceptually, the test of whether a resource or capability can be a source of competitive advantage rests on two questions:

First, does the resource or capability allow a firm to do something that its rivals cannot do? For example, a patent gives one firm the exclusive right to sell a particular product or service for 20 years. Alternatively, a company might enjoy such an outstanding reputation that it is difficult for other companies to gain a significant share of the market (i.e., Gerber in the

U.S. market for baby foods—interestingly, Gerber has never been able to develop this same reputation or level of market penetration abroad).

In marketing, the concept of "master brands" refers to companies that have so successfully branded their products or services that the brand name becomes synonymous with the entire product or service category. Examples include Coke, FedEx, Kleenex, Rollerblades, and Scotch tape. These companies often enjoy significant advantages over other companies because of the way their brands have come to define the market.

On the other hand, such advantages can be very fleeting, especially when customer preferences change or as new technologies emerge. As mentioned in Chapter 1, Kodak dominated the market for photographic film for decades, but it now faces decline and even oblivion as consumers have largely abandoned film photography for digital photography.

Second, since most companies do face major rivals in their markets, another test for competitive advantage is whether a firm has resources or capabilities that allow it to outperform its rivals. For example, many firms sell cellular telephones, so no one firm has an exclusive lock on or dominates this market. But a firm could still enjoy a competitive advantage in this market if it had resources that allowed it to consistently outperform its rivals. The cellular telephone market also offers a good illustration of just how fleeting competitive advantage can be. Over the years, a number of firms have enjoyed a relative advantage in this market—Motorola, Ericsson, Nokia—but no one firm has been able to maintain a *sustained* advantage over its rivals for very long periods of time. Nokia has been the recent market leader, but Apple, Samsung, and others have emerged as formidable competitors.

Although it is easy to identify a wide variety of tangible and intangible resources and capabilities that could be potential sources of competitive advantage, the resource-based view suggests that any resource will only contribute to the development of competitive advantage if it is associated with "barriers" that prevent its acquisition or replication by competitors.[8] If a valuable resource or capability can be acquired or replicated by competitors, then any competitive advantage enjoyed by the firm will soon disappear.[9]

The Challenge of Defending Against Imitation

One of the most important challenges confronting any firm that seeks to enjoy a sustained competitive advantage is to defend against imitation. This challenge is especially difficult in market economies where the managers of business firms not only have easy access to information, but also have powerful incentives to learn about and acquire potentially valuable resources and capabilities.

Past research on the diffusion of innovations is particularly helpful in understanding the challenge of defending against imitation by rival firms. Studies have shown that ideas and innovations are diffused through the economy in a pattern that resembles a slanted "S-shaped curve" as illustrated in Exhibit 2.3. The curve suggests that for a relatively brief time—from t_0 to t_1—innovations may be proprietary to just one or only a very few firms, but that at some point—t_1 in the exhibit—the diffusion process begins. By t_2 in the exhibit, nearly all firms in the market or the entire economy have adopted the innovation. This pattern of adoption—in

Exhibit 2.3 The Diffusion of Innovations

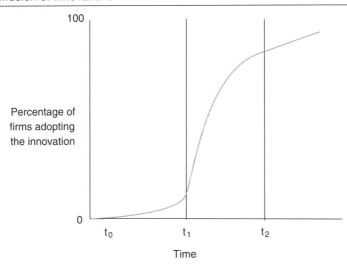

which initially only one firm or very few organizations employ a particular innovation, but very soon afterward nearly all firms have adopted the innovation—is seen across nearly all innovations.

A resource or capability, like the value of an innovation, will contribute to competitive advantage only until the diffusion process begins. At the point t_1, any source of competitive advantage will begin to lose its rareness and, therefore, will no longer guarantee sustained high performance. In fact, the resource-based framework summarized in Exhibit 2.2 suggests that as a resource begins to be diffused through an industry or the entire economy, firms can expect the resource to offer only competitive parity with other firms. As an example, the diffusion of scanning technology in U.S. grocery stores that occurred during the 1970s closely parallels the general pattern portrayed in Exhibit 2.3—some early pioneers in the adoption of scanning technology probably enjoyed a short-lived competitive advantage over rivals by offering faster check-out lines and higher labor productivity, but within a very short time frame these advantages disappeared as nearly all grocery stores adopted the scanning technology.

Retail scanning technology is also an interesting example because there were obvious, early gains in labor productivity that adopting firms could enjoy, which no doubt motivated the rapid diffusion of the technology. At the same time, it remained for Wal-Mart and a few other sophisticated retailers to demonstrate how scanning technology could also lead to even greater productivity and cost-saving advantages through more effective management of inventories, purchasing, and logistics. Though nearly all retailers quickly adopted scanning technology, it took most other retailers much longer to realize these additional productivity and cost savings to be gained from scanning technology, and some lagging retailers have still not effectively exploited these potential gains.

While copying or imitating firms are a threat to a leading or pioneering firm's competitive advantage, it is also important to emphasize that imitation alone will not give copying firms a competitive advantage. As suggested by the framework summarized in Exhibit 2.2, the best that copying firms can expect to achieve will be competitive parity in their industries or markets. And, even parity is unlikely as few firms are standing still and waiting for competitors to catch-up with them.

Only by innovating and developing their own valuable, rare, and difficult-to-imitate resources and capabilities will these firms come to enjoy a competitive advantage. *Imitation can help firms "catch-up," but imitation alone is unlikely to give firms a competitive advantage.*

Ways to Slow Down or Prevent Imitation

Managers can seek to prevent imitation by competitors in a number of ways. They can and often will seek to patent their firm's technologies or other resources. A patent will provide a firm with exclusive rights to a particular technology for 20 years. On the other hand, some managers are reluctant to patent their firm's technologies because they fear that the information contained in the patent might allow rivals to innovate or engineer around the patent, a process quite common in many high-technology industries.

The paradox of patents is that, while their purpose is to protect the ownership interests of those companies that develop new products, services, and technologies, they can actually aid in the diffusion of innovations. Since patents are public documents, any rival can get access to a firm's patent and then exploit this knowledge. Xerox, which pioneered the development of dry copying, protected its processes with hundreds of patents, but it took Canon only a few years to develop its own dry printing process.[10]

Another way to prevent imitation is to own exclusive access to key resources or assets. Inco, for example, long dominated the world nickel market largely by owning a large percentage of all known nickel deposits. Managers might also seek to exploit a resource as fully as possible before the diffusion process begins. For example, managers of a company with a totally new product might seek to lock customers into long-term contractual relationships so that those customers are committed to the company even if other firms develop similar competing products. Or, a firm offering a new product or service based on a new technology might seek to build market share as quickly as possible. Such a strategy would aim not only to build customer loyalty to the firm's product or service, but also to allow the firm to enjoy economies of scale, learning economies, and an absolute cost advantage over potential rivals before they could adopt or exploit the new technology. No doubt the massive advertising and promotion expenditures made by Amazon.com were aimed at developing this kind of customer recognition and buyer loyalty.

In addition, litigation is not typically thought of as a competitive tactic, but it is, in fact, often employed by managers to slow the diffusion process. Intel has frequently and successfully used litigation as a competitive tactic in its efforts to slow competitors that are hoping to catch up with or "leap-frog" over Intel's technological advancements.[11]

Ultimately, the best way to defend against imitation is to remain one step ahead of the competition. Even the most iron-clad patents will fail to insure a competitive advantage for more than a couple of decades. And, often the most formidable competitors are those that emerge from outside the industry offering new products, based on new technologies, designed to meet new or emerging customer needs or preferences (a topic considered in depth in Chapter 5). Thus, constant vigilance, the development of new products and services, and the ability to exploit technological developments are essential to staying out in front of the competition.

How Firms Acquire a Competitive Advantage: The Development of Unique Capabilities

Competitive advantage is most likely to result from the development of unique capabilities that are built up through an ongoing process of resource accumulation.[12] Five factors contribute to this resource accumulation process, making capabilities more difficult to imitate and enhancing the potential of these capabilities to contribute to sustained competitive advantage. These five factors—time, building on past success, the interconnectedness of capabilities, investment, and causal ambiguity—are examined here:

Time

The firm that builds a resource or capability through continuous investments over many years may enjoy a significant advantage over other firms that attempt to replicate this capability through larger investments made over a shorter time period. An analogy is the advantage a student who studies consistently throughout the semester enjoys over other students who attempt to cram an entire semester's worth of study into the week before the final exam.

As suggested by this analogy, time is directly related to the amount of learning that occurs. A firm that uses time to learn and to develop unique capabilities can gain a significant advantage over its competitors. This experience or learning effect is illustrated by the advantages Southwest Airlines enjoys in the airline industry.[13] One of Southwest's biggest advantages is its high levels of asset utilization. Passengers are unloaded, planes are serviced, and passengers are quickly loaded for the next flight. So effective are Southwest's processes and procedures that it routinely turns its planes ten or more times each day, almost twice the level of utilization enjoyed by other airlines. After observing Southwest's success and attributing that success to effective equipment utilization, all of the other major airlines have sought to improve the number of turns they get from their planes.[14]

Southwest's competitors have been unable to match Southwest's success at equipment utilization, however, most likely because they need additional time to learn how to turn their planes faster. Additional time will give them not only more opportunities to learn from experience about how to improve their efficiency, but also time to modify route patterns and flight schedules, rethink maintenance and cleaning procedures, and renegotiate restrictive union contracts that govern the work rules and practices of their flight personnel and ground crews.

Building on Past Success

Most businesses find much truth in the statement, "success breeds success." A history of accomplishments makes it easier to attain future success. Not only are winning firms likely to have more discretionary resources that can be reinvested to expand their businesses, but their reputations for success will also help them attract more assets and resources, helping to guarantee future successes and achievements. This is also the reason why venture capital tends to flow to start-up firms that have executives with proven track records. Similarly, firms enjoying a reputation for success have no trouble recruiting outstanding employees. For example, many marketing students are attracted to Procter & Gamble because of its outstanding reputation as a consumer products company.

Researchers have long recognized the importance of "path dependency"—the idea that decisions made at an earlier point in time will make some current options viable while also foreclosing other options. Although not all decisions are path-dependent, many of the most important decisions made by managers tend to be highly dependent on past decisions and strategies. Firms on more successful paths or trajectories will almost always have a better array of options than will firms whose managers have made less optimal decisions or pursued less successful strategies in the past. As Exhibit 2.4 illustrates, an early bad decision by Firm B will put it on a lower trajectory than Firm A, which makes a good early decision, even if every subsequent decision by Firm B is a good one.

Interconnectedness of Resources and Capabilities

The ability to take advantage of a particular resource or capability may depend on the strength of other capabilities. For example, the extent to which a firm's technological capabilities are a source of competitive advantage may depend on its customer service capability, especially if the firm operates in an environment where customer input and suggestions are an important source of information about future technological requirements.

One industry in which this interconnectedness among capabilities seems to be particularly important is pharmaceuticals. The success enjoyed by many of the leading pharmaceutical firms is due to interconnectedness between their R&D capabilities and their marketing skills. For these high-performing pharmaceutical companies, R&D capabilities provide them with new ethical drug products, but their marketing abilities allow them not only to "sell" these new products to the doctors who will be writing prescriptions for them, but also to gather information and other

Exhibit 2.4 Path Dependency and the Impact of Early Decisions

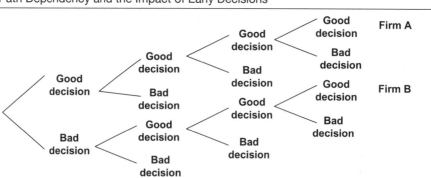

market intelligence that can then be relayed to their R&D departments, further enhancing the R&D process.

Microsoft was sued both by the U.S. government and by European regulators for having an unfair advantage over other companies because of its near-monopoly on the market for personal computer operating systems and its ability to "bundle" its operating systems and software products. Microsoft's Windows operating system for personal computers also typically includes the company's Word software, the company's Excel spreadsheet program, its PowerPoint presentation software, and Microsoft's Internet Explorer. It's little wonder, then, that all of these products have become ubiquitous.

Microsoft was able to overcome the early lead by Netscape and others in the market for Internet browsers by being able to bundle its Internet Explorer with its Windows operating software. This bundling allowed Microsoft to place its browser in nearly all new personal computers. And, as users upgraded to newer versions of Windows, Microsoft was soon able to saturate the market with its Internet Explorer. In the U.S., the court initially found that this ability to bundle its products gives Microsoft an unfair advantage, but this decision was later overturned on appeal. European regulators have been more restrictive of Microsoft's business practices, and their decisions have sought to encourage greater competition in high tech markets.

Investment

Investment is important to the development of unique and valuable capabilities for two reasons. First, the primary way in which firms develop capabilities is through investments that have been made in the past. Furthermore, because any resource or capability tends to deteriorate without sustained investment, resources and capabilities must be replenished if they are to continue to serve as sources of competitive advantage. "R&D know-how depreciates over time because of technological obsolescence, brand awareness erodes because the consumer population is not stationary (existing consumers leave the market, while new consumers enter), [and] consumers forget."[15]

In fact, the value of all resources and capabilities will erode unless sustained by ongoing investment. One example of this resource erosion is in the many brand names that consumer product companies have allowed to lapse over the years. Brylcreem, Aqua Velva, Duncan Hines, and Aunt Jemima are just a few of the once well known brand names that have been allowed to languish as companies failed to maintain them through continued advertising and promotion activities. The auto industry has also seen a number of brand names lose their luster over the last several years. General Motors dropped the Oldsmobile brand several years ago, and it has now also dropped the Pontiac and Saturn brands.

When Hewlett-Packard acquired Compaq, it made the decision to drop the Compaq brand name and consolidate all of the company's personal computer offerings under the HP brand even though the Compaq brand enjoyed a great deal of recognition and respect. In retrospect, this move was probably smart. By focusing its advertising and other marketing expenditures on the HP brand, it probably helped HP strengthen and reinforce the HP brand name, while spreading its resources across two brands might have only served to dilute both brands.

Causal Ambiguity

The preceding four factors, either individually or in combination with other factors, can contribute to the development of competitive advantage. The likelihood of maintaining sustained competitive advantage is greatly enhanced, however, if resources and capabilities are shrouded in "causal ambiguity."[16] In other words, if competitors are unable to determine how or why another firm is enjoying a competitive advantage, their efforts to imitate the high-performing firm's success will be greatly complicated.

What makes resources and capabilities "causally ambiguous?" The first four factors— time, building on past success, interconnectedness, and investment—all play an important role in enhancing casual ambiguity. For example, many managers make the mistake of assuming that if they can simply duplicate the capabilities of an industry leader, then their firms can soon enjoy competitive parity. What they often fail to appreciate is the significant amounts of time, past success, interconnectedness, and investment that have been required to make these capabilities so valuable. Knowing *what* resources and capabilities allow a company to enjoy a competitive advantage can still leave rivals a long way from knowing *how* to exploit those factors or capabilities for their own use.

Going back to the example of Southwest's rapid turnaround times for its planes, other airlines have realized that this is a valuable capability and sought to replicate it at their own firms. Why have they not achieved the rapid turnarounds and high rates of equipment utilization that Southwest enjoys? Because many of the resources and organizational processes associated with Southwest's fast turnarounds are causally ambiguous, and other airlines have not understood that it took Southwest many years to perfect this capability nor have they been able to determine how Southwest has integrated the various resources and organizational capabilities that support its rapid turnarounds.

For example, Southwest's ability to turn its planes quickly is enhanced because the company largely operates a point-to-point route system rather than the hub-and-spoke systems of most other major carriers. Southwest's standard fleet of Boeing 737s also probably plays a role in facilitating its ability to turn its planes quickly. And, as mentioned above, Southwest is not hobbled by the restrictive work rules of the other carriers' union contracts. It is not uncommon for Southwest's pilots to help clean an aircraft or load luggage, activities that would be unheard of at other airlines. Note, however, that what is ambiguous is not any one factor, resource, or capability, but rather how Southwest has combined many factors to improve turnaround times and increase equipment utilization.

Putting the Concepts Together: The Building Blocks of Competitive Advantage

Up to now, little mention has been made in this chapter of managers and the role of managerial decision making in creating and fostering competitive advantage. To tie together the various concepts and ideas that have been introduced in this chapter, with those concepts that have been introduced in the first two chapters, it will be helpful to think about competitive advantage in terms of a conceptual flow chart like the one illustrated in Exhibit 2.5. You might think of this

Exhibit 2.5 A Mental Model of Competitive Advantage

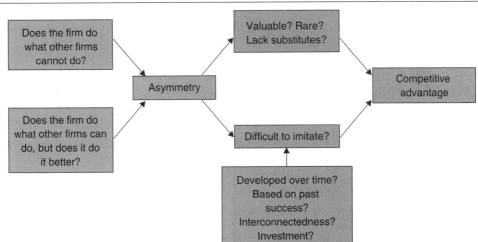

as a "mental model of competitive advantage"—one way of thinking about the resources and capabilities that are associated with competitive advantage.

To assess whether a firm enjoys a competitive advantage, the flow chart begins by asking whether the firm does what other firms cannot do, or whether the firm does what other firms can do, only better. If the answer to either of these questions is yes, then the firm has met the first condition or requirement for enjoying a competitive advantage.

To determine whether the firm will enjoy a sustained competitive advantage from this asymmetry or potential source of competitive advantage, however, other conditions must be met. As already noted, this asymmetry must be valuable, rare, and difficult to imitate, and must lack ready substitutes in order to provide the firm with a sustainable competitive advantage. If all these criteria are met, then the firm can expect to enjoy a sustained competitive advantage over its rivals.

To assess whether a potential source of competitive advantage is difficult to imitate, the flow chart also asks whether that potential source of competitive advantage: 1) was developed over time, 2) is based on past success, 3) incorporates an interconnected set of organizational resources, 4) is sustained by ongoing investment, and 5) is shrouded in causal ambiguity. Again, if these criteria are also met, then a potential source of competitive advantage is likely to be difficult to imitate, thereby increasing its value to firms seeking high performance.

The automobile industry offers a good illustration of how these factors work together to provide firms with a competitive advantage. All of the major manufacturers have the ability to produce automobiles, but some firms consistently outperform other producers in terms of manufacturing efficiency. Though nearly all producers have aggressively imitated these more efficient firms' manufacturing and production processes, they continue to lag behind. As this chapter has already emphasized, imitation alone is unlikely to result in competitive advantage.

Using the Value Chain to Evaluate Organizational Resources and Capabilities

Value chain analysis can be a very helpful tool for evaluating whether an organization's resources and capabilities are likely to contribute to the development of a competitive advantage. The **value chain** is a diagram illustrating the various value-adding processes that occur inside a firm or business. For example, Exhibit 2.6 shows the value chain for a hypothetical manufacturing firm, illustrating the various value-adding processes: engineering and design, component and material procurement, assembly, marketing and sales, and after-sales service.

Analysis of the various links in the value chain can help managers evaluate the extent to which their organizations' processes contribute to competitive advantage. To illustrate, let's use the value chain to compare and contrast Dell with its competitors in the market for personal computers. In the market for personal computers, Dell was a bit of a latecomer, but it went on to enjoy a long period of advantage, consistently enjoying rapid, profitable growth. The last several years have been very challenging for all firms in the personal computer business, Dell included, and it is probably fair to say that Dell has even lost its advantage in the market for personal computers. (We will later examine how Dell stumbled in this market.) Still, it is worth using the value chain to analyze the advantage that Dell once enjoyed in this market.

Two value chains, one for Dell and one representing its industry rivals during the late 1990s, are shown in Exhibit 2.7.[17] As the exhibit shows, neither Dell nor its rivals have focused energy or resources on engineering and design, leaving much of the responsibility for innovation to the industry's key suppliers, Intel and Microsoft. In purchasing, Dell enjoyed a significant advantage over its rivals. Because most of Dell's machines are made to order, it purchases components only as needed; these lower inventory costs saved Dell approximately $86 per machine. Similarly, by not having raw material or finished goods inventory lying around, Dell enjoyed an additional estimated savings of $32 in inventory carrying costs. By selling direct to nearly all of its customers, Dell didn't have to share margin with computer resellers, distributors, or retailers, nor did the company incur a variety of channel-related marketing and

Exhibit 2.6 The Value Chain for a Hypothetical Manufacturing Firm

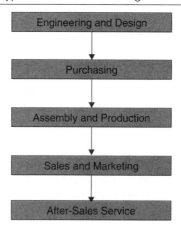

Exhibit 2.7 An Illustration of the Value Chain: Dell and Its Rivals in the Personal Computer Business

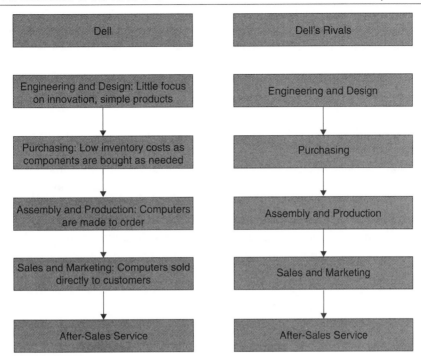

selling costs. Total savings from dealing directly with its customers: another $125. As illustrated in Exhibit 2.7, these cost advantages once allowed Dell to earn, on average, more than twice the margin of its industry rivals.

Value chain analysis is closely tied to benchmarking. **Benchmarking** is the process of comparing and measuring a firm's business activities against the best practice of those processes by any organization in any industry. When a firm decides to undertake a benchmarking effort, it must first begin by analyzing its value chain and breaking down its operations into discrete value-adding activities or processes as we have just done for Dell and its rivals. The next step is to measure those processes and compare and contrast the firm's performance against the best practice of industry leaders or leading firms in any industry.

The type of value chain and benchmarking analysis we've just illustrated for Dell and its rivals in the personal computer market can be performed for any firm in any industry. The process always begins by breaking down firm operations into a sequence of value-adding activities or organizational processes. Once the value-chain is developed, an analysis can allocate company costs to each of the various links in the value chain. Data on industry competitors and other firms employing similar processes can be gathered for comparison purposes.

A company should achieve two objectives from any value chain analysis and benchmarking effort. First, the company should get a set of metrics that compare and contrast its performance of various organizational processes with best practice of those processes, much like we've illustrated in Exhibit 2.7. More important than these numbers, however, a firm engaging in a benchmarking study should gain some tangible ideas about how it can dramatically improve its own performance. These ideas should stimulate organizational learning so that dramatic improvements in overall firm performance can be realized. To managers doing a benchmarking analysis of best practice, some ideas will be quite obvious and can be quickly copied and implemented. Other, more complex ideas will require considerably more "learning by doing" or study in order for the benchmarking firm to match and exceed the level of best practice.

In the example illustrated in Exhibit 2.7, Dell's rivals surely saw that most of Dell's cost advantages were tied to its Dell-Direct approach to marketing and dealing with customers. This approach of building machines to order and dealing directly with customers greatly reduced Dell's inventory and marketing and sales costs. Yet, it was extremely difficult for Dell's rivals to adopt this direct approach to dealing with customers. Their past strategies have committed them to selling through distributors and retailers, and changing these longstanding relationships with their distributors and retailers would invite retaliation. Furthermore, H-P and other PC manufacturers were probably not prepared to handle either the volume or level of customer service that would be required by a shift to Dell's direct strategy.

To summarize, the cost advantages Dell once enjoyed are very much explained by this chapter's competitive advantage framework. Dell didn't offer PC products that are significantly different from the products of its major rivals, however, it did manufacture and sell its PCs in a way that is arguably superior and more profitable than the way other PC manufacturers built and sold their machines.

It is also important to highlight that Dell's recent setbacks in the PC market are also explained by the framework presented in this chapter. The company stumbled badly when it opted to outsource its customer service functions. Customer satisfaction declined dramatically, and Dell's sales suffered badly. The Dell example points to the value of interconnected resources. In the PC market, as is probably the case in most industries, firms must not only offer good products that they manufacture profitably, but most customers also expect a satisfactory degree of customer service. The key organizational processes that support a competitive advantage are often mutually dependent and tightly interconnected.

The Distinction between Content and Process, and the Importance of Core Competencies and Socially Complex Resources

Content and Process as Sources of Competitive Advantage

As suggested by the preceding discussion of the value chain, the distinction between *content* and *process* is particularly germane to this chapter's focus on competitive advantage. **Strategy content** can be thought of as *what* a firm does, while **strategy process** would describe *how* a firm does what it does.

In terms of their ability to provide firms with sustained competitive advantage, organizational processes not only complement but also have distinct advantages over strategy content elements in managers' efforts to develop and sustain competitive advantage. First, because internal organizational processes are much less visible to outsiders, they are less amenable to imitation. Typically, the *content* of firms' strategies is not ambiguous. In fact, the content of firms' strategies, policies, and resource allocation patterns is usually quite apparent in publicly available information. And, competitors do seem to copy or imitate the *content* of their more successful rivals' strategies, but strategy *processes* are less visible and almost always more difficult to imitate.

In short, it is rarely enough simply to spend more than another firm on R&D or advertising. It's not the absolute number of dollars spent on these activities (the "content" of a firm's strategy), but the way those dollars are employed and used (the "process" of a firm's strategy). One article focusing on the value of research and development *processes* in the pharmaceutical industry noted that the success of companies' new product development efforts depends "not on 'research' but with *how* research, or more precisely innovation, is managed."[18]

Core Competencies

Unique and valuable organizational capabilities or processes that give companies a competitive advantage over their rivals have been described as *core competencies*.[19] The academics and consultants, C. K. Prahalad and Gary Hamel, who coined this term, defined **core competence** as "the collective learning in the organization, especially how to coordinate diverse production skills and integrate multiple streams of technologies."[20] This definition implies that core competencies will possess a number of important characteristics:

Interconnected Factors and Resources

Core competencies rarely reside in a single organizational resource, but are based on companies' "collective learning" and the ability "to coordinate diverse production skills and integrate multiple streams of technologies." As mentioned earlier, a pharmaceutical company's success is almost certainly due to the company's strengths in research and development *and* in marketing, as well as its ability to coordinate and integrate the learning that results from these two activities.

Communication

Note that Prahalad and Hamel's definition also emphasizes the importance of communication and collective learning in the development and use of core competencies. Far too often, the important work and learning that goes on in one laboratory, division, or business is not communicated to other parts of firms. As a result, these efforts fail to find their way into other successful products or services. Similarly, companies can be very effective at research and development, but they may not be able to move products and services from the conceptual or design stage to marketable products.

An article on IBM noted that it holds patents covering more than 40,000 inventions, but that the company had been far less successful at moving many of these inventions to the point where marketable products or services result.[21] Prahalad and Hamel reinforce the point that it is not how much companies spend on R&D but rather how R&D dollars are spent and what other organizational processes are in place to allow companies to exploit what is learned through their R&D efforts. They note that "cultivating core competence does *not* mean outspending rivals on research and development," and they document several examples in which highly successful firms have spent considerably less on R&D than their big-spending but less successful rivals.[22]

Getting Smarter over Time

Finally, because core competencies are not based on physical assets but are associated with organizational learning and the ability to coordinate and integrate various processes, they do not deteriorate over time or with use as physical assets do. In fact, the firms that effectively exploit core competencies are likely to get smarter over time. This helps to explain why companies that effectively exploit their core competencies can become such juggernauts in their industries. For example, Honda's engine technology has allowed it to become a dominant player in the worldwide automobile industry, but it has effectively used its engine design and manufacturing competencies to provide engines for everything from motorcycles and boats to lawn mowers and snow blowers.

Socially Complex Resources

The importance of organizational processes has led to a growing interest in human and social capital and other **socially complex resources**. These resources have been defined as factors that enable an organization to conceive, choose, and implement strategies because of the values, beliefs, and interpersonal relationships possessed by individuals or groups in a firm.[23] Some examples include reputation, culture, trust, and friendships among managers in an organization, teamwork among managers and workers, the knowledge of employees, and the learning embedded in organizational processes, routines, and standard operating procedures.

In other words, socially complex resources are the human equivalent of other, more tangible organizational capabilities and processes. Socially complex resources, such as organizational culture or reputation, can be very important potential sources of competitive advantage. The particular value of socially complex resources, and the reason they are described here, lies in the difficulty that competitors will have in attempting to imitate them. For example, a reputation for high-quality products or outstanding service is not only a tremendously valuable competitive asset, but also one that must be developed deliberately over time. It may be difficult for one firm to match or imitate another firm's reputation for excellent customer service unless it is willing to invest considerable resources over a long period of time. As a result, it is no surprise that researchers have concluded that factors such as expertise and reputation are among the most important organizational resources.[24]

Managers seem to have an intuitive feel for both the importance of strategy process and socially complex resources and the inability of strategy content variables to provide their firms with competitive advantage. Researchers have surveyed corporate managers to develop lists of resources that managers see as contributing to their firms' successes. Most of the items that the managers named were either subjective factors like "reputation for quality," "customer service/ product support," and "name recognition," or intangible resources and capabilities, such as "culture" and "know-how."[25]

Jack Welch, former chairman and CEO of General Electric, captured the importance of such socially complex resources when, in an interview, he stated: "our ultimate competitive advantage lies in our ability to learn and rapidly transform that learning into action."[26] Thus, it is worthwhile for firms to invest in socially complex resources. Not only do they have the potential to be important sources of competitive advantage, but they are also likely to be among the most difficult organizational resources and capabilities for competitors to imitate.

Conclusion: The Fleeting Nature of Competitive Advantage

This chapter has described the asymmetric nature of competitive advantage. Firms enjoy competitive advantage either by doing what other organizations cannot do or by doing what other organizations can do but doing it better. Thus, firms can gain a competitive advantage by occupying a unique niche or position in their industries through a particularly effective business definition. Alternatively, firms can enjoy a sustainable competitive advantage by possessing capabilities and resources that are *causally ambiguous* and *difficult to imitate.*

If capabilities are not causally ambiguous and difficult to imitate, then rivals will quickly copy or match them, and this is why many of the resources and capabilities typically associated with high firm performance are not—and cannot be—the sources of sustained competitive advantage: An outstanding manager can be lured away by a more attractive compensation package. A new technology can be "reverse-engineered" and imitated. An organization's internal processes, on the other hand, are characterized by resources and capabilities that are much more difficult to copy.

The factors that make a particular process advantageous may be quite invisible to outsiders. How, for example, can an outsider understand or begin to imitate the knowledge that has been accumulated by years of experience, learning, and trial-and-error by a team of outstanding scientists working in a research lab at a successful pharmaceutical company?

This chapter suggests, therefore, that an organization's internal processes are more likely to be sources of sustained competitive advantage than its strategy content variables. Two firms can spend identical amounts of money on research and development (in other words, aspects of the strategy content of two firms can be identical on that particular dimension), but, in the absence of luck, the firm with the better R&D *process* will enjoy higher performance.

The chapter also reviewed the factors that contribute to the development of unique and valuable capabilities, such as an organization's internal R&D or manufacturing processes. These five factors—time, past success, interconnectedness, investment, and causal ambiguity—will make the capability more difficult to imitate and, therefore, increase the likelihood that the capability can be a source of sustained competitive advantage.

Yet, no source of competitive advantage will guarantee success forever. For example, over the years, Sony has effectively exploited its core competencies in electronics, miniaturization, and manufacturing to offer products that came to dominate their categories. As a result, Sony is a major force in the markets for cameras, VCRs and DVDs, camcorders, video cameras, professional movie cameras, and video games. Sony so dominated the high-end TV market that its models once sold for twice the average selling price of models produced by Sony's competitors.[27] But more recently Sony has fallen behind competitors in key markets. Microsoft and Nintendo have proven to be tenacious competitors in the video game market. And, given Sony's competencies in miniaturization, it's surprising that Sony has failed to become a significant player in either the mp3 or cell phone markets.[28]

And, what about Dell, which has enjoyed such significant cost advantages over its rivals in the PC market? More recently Dell has been eclipsed by Hewlett Packard both in terms of profitability and market share. While many factors explain Dell's decline, a lack of focus on customer service was probably one of the most damaging. Dell is now struggling to improve attention to customers while simultaneously working to improve the distinctiveness of its product line.[29]

In terms of the three key themes that were introduced in the first chapter, this chapter has also had much to say:

Managers and Managerial Thinking

Developing and maintaining a competitive advantage is probably the most significant challenge facing any manager. In Chapters 4 and 5, we focus on ways of understanding industry environments in which firms must compete. Based on their understandings of the competitive landscape in which their firms must compete, managers must then make a wide range of decisions that will directly influence the success of their firms and whether they come to enjoy a competitive advantage. As outlined in Chapter 1 and at the beginning of this chapter, managers must make at least four broad types of decisions, including:

- Decisions that define or position their firms in their competitive environment—the focus of Chapter 6.
- Decisions about appropriate business strategies—the focus of Chapters 7, 8, and 9.
- Decisions about corporate strategy, or about the appropriate scale and scope for their firms—the focus of Chapter 10.
- Decisions about the most effective organizational structures to employ—the focus of Chapter 11.

As we focus on each of these four types of decisions, we will be examining the ways each can be a source of competitive advantage. In the next chapter, we demonstrate how managerial thinking influences specific decisions, and how these decisions can then provide a firm or business with a competitive advantage.

Change and the Need to Think Dynamically about Strategic Management

Any source of competitive advantage can become dated and useless as business conditions change. Furthermore, any source of competitive advantage is likely to be tightly coupled with managerial thinking. In fact, managers' beliefs and the resources and capabilities associated with competitive advantage can mutually reinforce one another so that firms can become quite inflexible and find it difficult to change either managerial thinking or the factors associated with competitive advantage. Thus, managers must be particularly sensitive to changes in customers' needs and wants, the introduction of new product or service offerings, and the development of new technologies, any of which could jeopardize the effectiveness of any particular source of competitive advantage. Managerial thinking must quickly adapt to these changes, or even better, managers should anticipate and be on the cutting edge of changes in their industries.

In addition, this chapter has suggested that a firm's internal processes are a critical resource that can be the source of sustained competitive advantage. It is crucial to remember, however, that a particular internal process can quickly be rendered obsolete due to environmental shifts, such as changes in consumer demographics, regulations, and technologies. Scholars have even noted that organizations can become so good at what they do, that they can be "trapped" by their own competencies, so unable to adapt to changes in their competitive environments that they cease to be viable.[30]

The Importance of Organizational Learning

Managers and their firms and businesses must learn in order to adapt to or anticipate environmental changes. Managerial attention needs to focus not only on the development of competitive advantage in today's environment, but also on how the environment is likely to change and evolve. Managers will succeed in achieving *sustained* competitive advantage for their firm only if they acquire and develop resources that enhance their firm's current position while being mindful of the kinds of resources and capabilities that will be needed in the future. *This kind of creative thinking and foresight is perhaps the most valuable and most difficult to imitate of all organizational capabilities!*

Key Points

- The chapter began by offering a definition for competitive advantage: the set of factors or capabilities that allows firms to consistently outperform their rivals.
- Firms that enjoy a sustained competitive advantage possess factors, capabilities, or competencies that are valuable, rare, difficult to imitate, and lack substitutes.
- As a result, a key characteristic of competitive advantage is asymmetry. Firms enjoy a competitive advantage either by doing what other firms cannot do, or, if they do what other firms can also do, by doing it better.
- Without resource "mobility barriers" to prevent the transfer of resources and skills across firms, capabilities and other sources of competitive advantage tend to be quickly diffused through an industry and the entire economy.
- Five factors that contribute to the development of sustained competitive advantage are time, past success, interconnectedness of resources, investment, and causal ambiguity.

- The value chain can be a very useful tool for analyzing organizational capabilities and processes and for assessing competitive advantage.
- Because they tend to be causally ambiguous and difficult to imitate, a firm's internal processes are more likely than the content of its strategies to be sources of sustained competitive advantage.
- Socially complex resources, such as reputation and culture, can also be important sources of competitive advantage, again because they are so difficult to imitate.
- Because a source of competitive advantage can become dated and useless over time, key management responsibilities are to be mindful of how vulnerable resources and capabilities are to imitation and obsolescence, and to anticipate the kinds of resources and capabilities that will be needed to compete effectively in the future.

Key Questions for Managers

- Does your company enjoy a competitive advantage?
- If yes, is your company's competitive advantage based on 1) doing what other firms cannot do, or 2) doing what other firms do but doing it better?
- What factors make the source or sources of your company's competitive advantage difficult to imitate?
- How has managerial thinking influenced the development and maintenance of competitive advantage (or the lack of a competitive advantage) at your firm?
- Is current managerial thinking about competitive advantage anticipating how changes in the larger competitive environment may require the company to change and adapt in both the short- and long-run?

Suggestions for Further Reading

Additionally, links to further resources online—such as cases, articles, and videos—can be found on the book's website, www.routledge.com/textbooks/Duhaime.

Aaker, D. A. 1989. Managing assets and skills: The key to sustainable competitive advantage. *California Management Review*, 31(2): 91–106.

Barney, J. B. 1986. Organizational culture: Can it be a source of sustained competitive advantage? *Academy of Management Review*, 11: 656–665.

Barney, J. B. 1991. Firm resources and sustained competitive advantage. *Journal of Management,* 17: 99–120.

Barney, J. B. 2001. Is the resource-based "view" a useful perspective for strategic management research? Yes. *Academy of Management Review*, 26: 41–56.

Dierickx, I., & Cook, K. 1989. Asset stock accumulation and sustainability of competitive advantage. *Management Science*, 35: 1504–1511.

Finney, M. I. 2008. *Building High-Performance People and Organizations*, Westport, CT: Greenwood Publishing.

Miller, D., & LeBreton-Miller, I. 2005. *Managing for the Long Run: Lessons in Competitive Advantage from Great Family Businesses*, Boston: Harvard Business School Publishing.

Prahalad. C. K., & Hamel, G. 1990. The core competence of the corporation. *Harvard Business Review*, 68(3): 79–91.

Rapp, W. V. 2002. *Information Technology Strategies*. New York: Oxford University Press.

Spear, S. J. 2009. *Chasing the Rabbit: How Market Leaders Outdistance the Competition and How Great Companies Can Catch Up and Win*, New York: McGraw-Hill.

Wernerfelt, B. 1984. A resource-based view of the firm. *Strategic Management Journal,* 5: 171–180.

Appendix: Ways of Assessing Firm Performance

The term *performance* most commonly refers to financial performance, which can include sales, net income, gross margin, or other absolute accounting or financial measures. Such measures can be helpful in assessing the growth of a particular firm or business over different time periods, but these absolute performance measures are not particularly helpful in comparing or contrasting firms of different size or firms that operate in different industries.

For example, two hypothetical firms might both have a net income of $15 million, but one firm could be very large (say, $1 billion in total sales revenues) while the other firm might be much smaller (say, only $100 million in total sales revenues). Which of the firms is more profitable? If only net income is considered, the answer would be that the two firms are both equally profitable, but this answer is misleading given that one firm is so much larger than the other.

Thus, ratio measures are more useful for comparison purposes because they "standardize" absolute measures, such as net income, by dividing these measures by a common denominator.

Some of the most common ratio measures are return on sales (net income/sales revenues), return on assets (net income/total assets), and return on equity (net income/total shareholders' equity), though many other ratio measures are also commonly used to assess the financial performance of business organizations. The return on sales for the first hypothetical firm mentioned above is only 1.5 percent, while the return on sales for the much smaller second firm is 15 percent. In other words, for every dollar of sales made by the first firm, it earns only 1.5 cents of net income, while the second firm earns ten times as much net income for every dollar of sales. By controlling for firm size, the ratio measure—return on sales—suggests that the second, smaller firm is significantly more profitable than the larger firm.

Financial Statement Analysis

Financial statement analysis can be very useful in analyzing the financial health and prosperity of any business organization. Financial statement analysis can also offer important clues about the strategies firms are pursuing, so it can be an important tool for analyzing the strategies of competitors. In this section, we'll consider three types of ratios to be derived from financial statement analysis. We'll then examine some additional ratios that are of special interest to strategists.

Financial Ratios

Return on assets and return on equity are two of the most commonly used financial ratios; they both examine overall firm financial performance. They are calculated as:

Return on assets = Net income/Average total assets
Return on equity = Net income/Average total shareholders' equity

A number of additional measures are helpful for examining more closely the performance and efficiency of firms' ongoing business operations. These ratios include profit margin, net profit margin, and the asset turnover ratio. They are calculated as:

Profit margin = Gross margin/Net sales
Net profit margin = Net income/Net sales
Asset turnover ratio = Net sales/Average total assets

Note that:

Net profit margin * Asset turnover ratio = Return on assets

This important relationship implies that managers can increase the overall profitability of their firms by 1) increasing the amount of profits earned from their companies' sales, and 2) increasing the volume of sales generated by their companies' assets. Some businesses are high volume—that is, they generate much of their profitability through a very high level of sales. For example, many retail establishments, especially grocery stores, tend to have fairly low net profit margins, but they aim to "make it up in volume" by generating a high level of sales and, therefore, have high asset turnover ratios. The most profitable businesses will usually have both a high profit margin and a high sales volume or turnover ratio.

Liquidity Ratios

Liquidity ratios assess the ability of firms to meet current financial obligations. The two best known measures of liquidity are the current ratio and the quick ratio (sometimes called the acid-test ratio). They are calculated as:

Current ratio = Current assets/Current liabilities
Quick ratio = (Current assets – Inventory – Prepaid expenses)/Current liabilities

The quick ratio is a much more stringent measure of a firm's ability to meet its current financial obligations because it includes only the most liquid current assets in the numerator.

Leverage Ratios

The most common measure of debt and leverage is the debt-to-equity ratio. It shows the extent to which companies' assets are financed by debt rather than equity, and it is calculated as:

Debt-to-equity ratio = Total liabilities/Total shareholders' equity

Another widely used measure of debt, which also measures an organization's solvency or its ability to meet its long-term financial obligations, is the times interest earned ratio. It is calculated as:

Times interest earned = Earnings before interest and taxes/Interest charges

In other words, the times interest earned ratio examines the extent to which a firm's current earnings are sufficient to meet its current interest payments.

Ratios Providing Information about Strategy Content

Some financial ratios are of special interest to strategists. For example, in addition to assessing firm performance, liquidity, and capital structure, financial ratios can offer important clues to understanding organizational strategies. Companies with high ratios of selling, general, and administrative expense to total sales or, more specifically, high levels of advertising and marketing expenditures to total sales, may be trying to build consumer awareness or customer loyalty through advertising and other marketing activities. Companies with high ratios of R&D expenditures to total sales may be working to develop new products or services or working to lower costs by developing more efficient production processes. Similarly, companies with high ratios of capital expenditures to total sales may be planning to increase production capacity.

Economic Value Added and Market Value Added

Closely tied to the concept of economic profits is the measure of economic value added. Many financial analysts argue that economic value added is a better measure of performance than net income because it includes the cost of invested capital. More specifically, economic value added is calculated as:

> Economic value added =
> Operating income – Interest expense – Taxes – Cost of capital

To illustrate the concept of economic value added, consider the example of a company that reports net income of $7,242 million, operating income of $10,888 million, interest expense of $1,599 million, and taxes of $4,097 million. In addition, assume that the company's cost of capital is calculated as $4,874 million, based on its shareholder equity of $32,491 million and an assumed cost of equity of 15 percent. Plugging these numbers into the formula gives an economic value added of $318 million, far less than the company's reported net income of $7,242 million, but a much more accurate portrayal of its economic profit since it includes the company's imputed cost of capital.

Market value added measures the increase in the value of shareholders' investment. It is a company's current market value less the value of shareholders' original investment in the company. Expressed as a formula:

> Market value added = Market value – Book value of capital stock and paid-in-capital

To illustrate, consider an example, in which a company has a market value of $100,425 million and the book value of the company's capital stock and paid-in-capital is $15,425 million. In this example, the company's market value added over and above the value of shareholders' original investment in the company would be approximately $85,000 million.

Strengths and Limitations of Financial Statement Analysis

One major strength of financial statement analysis is the availability of data. Financial data for publicly held companies is widely available through company annual reports, documents filed with the Securities and Exchange Commission, and many popular databases. Many companies' financial statements are available on their websites and through EDGAR, an online service that provides access to records maintained by the Securities and Exchange Commission. Another advantage of financial statement analysis is that it relies on ratio measures so that companies can be readily compared with each other.

At the same time, financial statement analysis has a number of limitations. First, financial ratios and other measures are fairly meaningless in isolation. In other words, to be useful, financial ratios for a particular company must be compared against industry averages, other firms' ratios, or the firm's own past performance. Second, all financial data, no matter how recent, reflect what has happened rather than what will happen. Thus, financial ratios evaluate company performance by looking back rather than by looking ahead. This can be a problem, especially in high-velocity environments in which a firm's performance today says little about its ability to perform effectively tomorrow.

When using financial data to assess performance, users must be aware of the impact of extraordinary items and other accounting adjustments on net income. For example, an otherwise outstanding firm that enjoys a consistent record of excellent financial performance could have a major loss due to a fire at one of its facilities. This extraordinary item may, however, take little away from the company's strengths, and the company may well bounce back to high levels of profitability after one year of losses due to this extraordinary item. At the same time, a firm reporting a series of restructuring charges over a period of several years should raise some skepticism: Why exactly is the firm undergoing so much restructuring? Why can't the company's managers get it on track?

These points highlight the need to "look behind the numbers" when using financial data to assess competitive advantage. The "Management Discussion and Analysis" and "Notes to Accompany the Financial Statements" sections that are included in companies' annual reports are often invaluable—indeed, essential—supplements to the financial statements. These observations also suggest the importance of consulting a wide variety of resources when evaluating companies, including newspaper and magazine reports, interviews with company executives, and even comments by the managers of competing firms. Recent accounting scandals should only further reinforce and emphasize the importance of looking beyond the numbers.

Other Dimensions of Firm and Business Performance

In addition to annual reports, other useful sources of firm performance data include company 10Ks (documents that all publicly traded companies must file annually with the Securities and Exchange Commission), Standard and Poors' *Industry Surveys*, Moody's *Manuals*, and industry and other trade publications. Many libraries have databases that can be very helpful for conducting research on firms. For example, the Hoover's online and Standard and Poors' Research Insight databases contain current and historical accounting and market performance data on thousands of firms.

Performance is, however, a multidimensional concept and, though financial performance measures are probably the most common, many other types of performance measures are also used to assess the performance and health of business firms. For example, stock market performance measures are commonly used, such as one- and five-year market returns, which assess increases in the value of companies' stock prices over a particular time period. Earnings per share (EPS) is a ratio of a firm's net income divided by the total number of its common shares outstanding. Price/earnings (P/E) ratios are calculated by dividing the current market price of a company's common shares by its EPS. The resulting number is referred to as a company's "multiple." Historically, the average P/E ratio for stocks has been around 15, however, some stocks have very high P/E ratios. The P/E ratios of outstanding consumer products companies are often much higher than the historical average, as high as the 30s, 40s, or even higher, reflecting investor confidence that these companies will continue to enjoy high earnings well into the future.

Market share is another important performance measure, especially in industries or markets in which important advantages can be derived from large size (i.e., economies of scale). On the other hand, firms that are deliberately pursuing very focused or niche strategies may find market share an irrelevant performance consideration. BMW, with only about 3 percent of the U.S. automobile market, is obviously a niche player. But the company enjoys tremendous brand equity and its U.S. sales operations are highly profitable.

Many other performance measures are more industry specific. In retailing, for example, sales per square foot of retailing space is a common performance measure. In banking, net interest earned—the interest banks earn on their loans and other activities less the interest banks must pay to their depositors and other providers of funds—is an important measure of bank profitability. More recently, "cycle time" and "time to market"—the time it takes to get new product ideas into production and available for consumer purchase—have become important performance measures, especially in high-tech industries or any markets in which new-product development efforts are critical to success.

Stakeholder analysis has become another important way to evaluate company performance. The stakeholder approach argues that business firms have multiple constituencies, including internal stakeholders (employees and stockholders) and external stakeholders (customers, suppliers, communities). Since all of these constituents contribute resources to firms, they all have a "stake" in how those resources are used. Stakeholder theory also suggests that each stakeholder may apply its own yardstick for measuring firm performance outcomes. Over the years, various approaches to stakeholder analysis have been developed, including the "balanced scorecard," which suggests that high performance is a function of balancing various stakeholder claims and objectives.[31]

While many performance measures are fairly straightforward and objective, other performance measures are more subjective. For example, customer perceptions of quality and business reputation are frequently measured, and the major business magazines publish lists of "Most Admired Companies." But these assessments lack some of the objectivity of measures based on financial and stock market performance data. Just because some measures are more subjective than others does not mean, however, that they are unimportant or less relevant. For example, highly subjective customer perceptions of product or service quality can make or break a company.

Chapter 3

Managers and Strategic Decision Making in Business Firms

Chapter 1 emphasized the key role of managers in the formulation and implementation of strategy. Our definition of strategy as "a pattern in a stream of decisions" emphasizes that managerial decision making is the basis for strategies. And, to a large degree, the quality of a firm's strategies—and ultimately its overall performance—will reflect the quality of its managers' decisions. Chapter 2 then focused on competitive advantage, and specifically examined the requirements for developing and maintaining a competitive advantage. Chapter 2 again highlighted the role of managerial thinking in influencing the decisions that determine whether a firm will develop or maintain a competitive advantage.

Thus, a better understanding of decision making processes and the managerial thinking that guides decision making is essential to understanding how strategies are formulated and implemented. As Chapter 1 noted, many books on strategy will acknowledge the importance of managers, but then ignore the role that they play in decision making and strategy formulation and implementation. This book, in contrast, puts managers "front and center" and takes the view that we can't really understand strategic management processes without understanding the managerial thinking and decision making that guide these processes.

Chapter Objectives

The specific objectives of this chapter are to:

- Illustrate the linkages among managerial thinking, decision making, strategy, and performance.
- Review the sources of managerial thinking, and demonstrate how managerial thinking reflects learning and expertise.
- Identify and illustrate some of the problems associated with managerial thinking.
- Emphasize the practical usefulness of understanding the concepts of mental models and how decisions are made.
- Describe the qualities of effective managers and leaders.

How Managerial Thinking Influences Decision Making, Strategies, and Firm Performance

Every day, managers at all levels are making a multitude of tactical and strategic decisions that shape strategies and determine performance outcomes. Chapter 1 introduced the concept of **mental models**—assumptions, beliefs, and understandings—that guide and influence decision making. One management author defined the concept of mental model as:

> an interconnected set of understandings, formed by frequently implicit views of what one's interests and concerns are, what is important, and what demands action and what does not. It is a cognitive representation of the world and ourselves in it.[1]

Exhibit 3.1 reproduces the model of decision making introduced in Chapter 1. The exhibit illustrates that decisions are not made in a vacuum, but in the context of the larger business, economic, and cultural and social environments in which we live and work. The exhibit also emphasizes that decisions stem from our mental models—our assumptions, beliefs, and understandings.

The aim of this chapter is to help you develop a better understanding of the concept of mental models, and of how mental models guide strategic decision making in business organizations. This section describes different types of mental models and then illustrates in more detail how mental models influence decision making. Subsequent sections examine the sources of mental models as well as the characteristics of decision making processes, including some of the problems associated with managerial thinking. The chapter concludes by emphasizing the practical usefulness of understanding the concept of mental models and by describing the qualities of effective managers and leaders. (In an appendix to this chapter, we also offer some illustrations of a simple mental mapping technique—or a way of making the beliefs and understandings contained in managers' mental models explicit so that they can be examined and analyzed.)

Exhibit 3.1 Relationships among Managers' Mental Models, Decision Making, Strategies, and Performance Outcomes

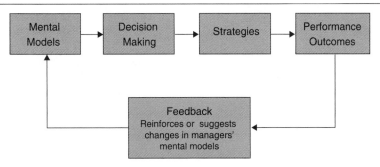

Types of Mental Models

Though mental models are inherently unobservable, individuals can "map" or otherwise make explicit their own thinking or the thinking of other individuals. For example, if you were asked to distinguish between a good professor and a bad professor, you would have no trouble identifying a set of characteristics that would distinguish between the two. Psychologists call this type of thinking *categorical knowledge* because it is the knowledge individuals use to distinguish between and among categories of people, objects, and other phenomena (i.e., "good professor" and "bad professor"). Stock analysts also use categorical knowledge whenever they analyze companies and sort their stocks into "buy," "sell," or "hold" recommendations. One way business executives use categorical knowledge on a daily basis is to distinguish firms that are competitors from those firms that they do not consider competitors.

Another type of mental model describes understandings of *causality*. Individuals have causal beliefs about all kinds of phenomena. For example, the well known proverb, "Early to bed and early to rise makes a person healthy, wealthy, and wise," contains two causal assertions—that if you go to bed early and if you wake up early, you will then enjoy personal health, wealth, and wisdom. As with categorical knowledge, managers of business firms have causal beliefs about a wide array of phenomena. For example, many executives believe that advertising leads to higher sales revenues. Likewise, many executives believe that R&D spending leads to innovative products or more efficient production processes. Exhibit 3.2 illustrates the causal reasoning embedded in these simple causal beliefs.

Managers, like all individuals, also have mental models of elaborate processes. Some simple examples of process models would include understandings of how to change a flat tire. Business examples might include managers' understandings of the processes of developing a new product or about entering a new geographic market.

Like all mental models, categorical knowledge, beliefs and understandings of causality, and understandings of individual or organizational processes can change over time. For example,

Exhibit 3.2 Maps of Some Simple Causal Beliefs

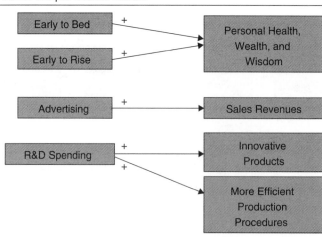

two decades ago, business executives rarely mentioned quality, and few stories about quality appeared in the business press. Today, nearly all top executives have come to realize the importance of quality, and most executives now have a causal belief that quality will have a very significant positive impact on the image of a company's products or services, which, in turn, can lead to higher sales and market share.[2]

Similarly, understandings of processes can become significantly more complex over time as an individual gains additional experience. As managers gain experience at their firms, they develop elaborate understandings of processes, routines, and standard operating procedures. This firm-specific knowledge is highly valuable—and a great example of the socially complex resources described in Chapter 2—and can contribute in important ways to the development and maintenance of competitive advantage.[3]

Mental Models and Decision Making

As noted in Chapter 1, we have mental models about a vast array of phenomena, including people, hobbies, music, how to play a particular sport, politics, religion, and, of course, a host of business phenomena. And our minds are able to construct new mental models very quickly when we encounter new or novel phenomena. Because mental models are cognitive representations—i.e., "models"—of the phenomena we encounter, they may be more or less complete. For example, for some phenomena—a favorite hobby or sport—an individual's mental models might be very complete, including understandings of the key features as well as more peripheral aspects of the hobby. For other less well understood phenomena, mental models might contain only very cursory or superficial understandings. Later, the chapter will show how the accuracy and completeness of mental models can significantly influence the quality of decision making.

The power of mental models is that they allow us to function and make decisions in a complex world in which we are bombarded by stimuli—far more than we could possibly comprehend or process—and only a few of these stimuli receive our attention. Mental models play three key roles in the decision making process. First, they focus our attention and determine what stimuli we do and do not notice. Second, they influence how we interpret the information and stimuli we do notice. And, finally, mental models also determine how we act on our interpretations of the information we process. Here we will provide a brief description of each of these components of the decision making process:

Noticing

A key function of mental models is to filter information and focus attention. As an example, consider how most of us read a newspaper. We could, obviously, read every single news story, either online or by reading a physical newspaper, something that might take several hours or a day or more depending on the newspaper. Most people read through a newspaper fairly quickly, however, by focusing on those news stories that are of greatest interest. Mental models are responsible for this "selective perception" or focusing as we read through a newspaper.

Like all individuals, managers use mental models to filter what would otherwise be an overwhelming amount of information and stimuli they receive from interactions with their environments. The days of most business executives are crammed with meetings, telephone calls, emails, and reports that offer far more data than they can possibly process. Their mental models focus their attention on those stimuli that are deemed most important and relevant, so that they can then focus on those aspects of their environments that they perceive to be most critical. At the same time, other stimuli—including potentially very important stimuli—may well be ignored.

Interpretation

Because mental models contain our attitudes, beliefs, and understandings, they also influence our responses to the stimuli we notice. So, for those stimuli that are noticed—for those newspaper stories we choose to read, for example—our mental models help us to interpret and understand what we have just read. For example, how is a particular piece of business news related to the larger economic environment? What implications will that piece of business news have for stock prices in general or for the stock price of a particular company? Similarly, business executives will zero in on particular stimuli and then process and interpret these data to determine what implications they may have for their firms.

Deciding

Finally, the beliefs and understandings contained in our mental models also guide decision making. After reading and interpreting a newspaper story about a particular company, we might decide to buy or sell that company's stock. Similarly, a business executive might read a marketing report and focus on a part of that report showing poor sales in a particular geographical region. The executive might then interpret this piece of information and conclude that the company needs to spend more on advertising for its products in that region and subsequently make a decision to commit more advertising and promotion dollars to that particular market.

As suggested by the framework illustrated in Exhibit 3.1, this hypothetical decision—to spend more advertising dollars in a particular region—will result in a change in the company's marketing strategy, and most likely then have some impact on company performance. The change in performance will, in turn, provide the executive with feedback. If sales performance in the particular region increases, the executive's mental model—in this case, a causal belief about the relationship between advertising and sales levels—will be reinforced. This executive will probably come to believe even more strongly that advertising is positively linked with sales increases. This learning-by-doing or trial-and-error learning is a very powerful source of personal learning; beliefs acquired through trial-and-error learning can become widely and firmly held in organizations. We will also see that such beliefs can be very difficult to change once acquired.

Exhibit 3.3 illustrates the model of strategic management introduced in Chapter 1. As seen in the exhibit, managers' mental models influence different types of decisions that serve as the basis for company strategies. Managers make an array of both large and small decisions. In this book, we focus on four of the most important types of decisions managers make, all of which will have a profound impact on their firms' market positions and their resources and capabilities. As illustrated in Exhibit 3.3, these include 1) decisions about industry competition

Exhibit 3.3 Managers' Beliefs, Strategic Decisions, and Their Influence on Performance and Competitive Advantage

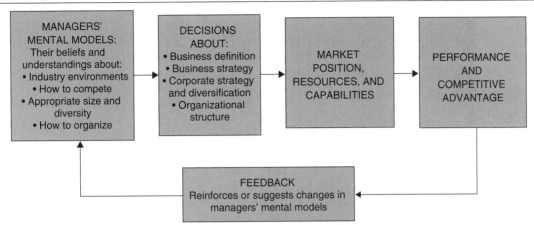

and business definition, 2) decisions about business strategy, 3) decisions about corporate strategy and diversification, and 4) decisions about organizational structure. Many factors will influence firm performance levels and whether firms enjoy a competitive advantage, including the larger economic environment and industry competitors, but to a significant degree we expect that a company's market position and its resources and capabilities will have a major influence on its performance.

As shown in Exhibit 3.3, performance outcomes provide important feedback to managers that will either reinforce existing mental models (most likely when performance outcomes are positive) or suggest to managers that they need to change their beliefs or understandings about the decisions and strategies that lead to high performance.

To illustrate the model, let's consider the case of Southwest Airlines. Compared to the CEOs of other airlines, Southwest's leaders, including its iconoclastic former CEO, Herb Kelleher, and its current CEO, Gary Kelly, hold beliefs—mental models—about the airline industry that differ fundamentally from most other airline executives, including how to compete in the airline industry and how their company ought to be organized. These very different mental models have resulted in unique strategies. For example, Southwest's low-fare strategy has traditionally targeted customers who might have driven rather than flown to their destinations, a fundamentally different type of customer than the customers pursued by most of the major airlines.

In addition, management decisions have also resulted in a very different business strategy. Southwest has relied primarily on a point-to-point route system rather than the expensive hub-and-spoke systems of the other major carriers. Southwest does not serve meals, and uses only Boeing 737 aircraft to minimize maintenance and other aircraft costs.

Perhaps most important to Southwest's success are management's decisions that have led to a novel approach to organizing. Southwest has avoided many of the union work rules that hamstring the efficiency of other air carriers. Other aspects of its novel labor agreements also raise the productivity of Southwest employees far above their counterparts at other airlines, and, as noted in Chapter 2, give Southwest the fastest turnaround times at airports and the highest level of aircraft utilization in the industry. The company also attributes its customer service rankings to its focus on employees.[4] Despite the fact that Southwest is one of the most unionized firms in the industry, it experiences little labor conflict in relation to other commercial airlines. As Jody Hoffer Gittell explains in her book *The Southwest Airlines Way*:

> The respect that Southwest managers demonstrated for employees and their elected representatives reinforced frontline employees' trust for their company and their identification with the company's goals. In addition, the respect demonstrated by top management also helped to foster respectful relationships between the unions themselves. In short, the considerate and friendly relations that Southwest has with unions appear to set the tone for respectful and trusting relationships throughout the company.[5]

The result is that Southwest enjoys one of the best positions in the airline industry. It benefits from the lowest costs in the industry and it is the only major carrier that can consistently be relied upon to generate a profit. Though Southwest recorded losses in 2009 during the worst economic downturn since the Great Depression, the company had previously posted a profit in each of the past 36 years, a record unmatched by any other commercial airline. The company also has remarkable organizational capabilities that other carriers have sought to imitate but cannot seem to duplicate. The success the company has enjoyed almost certainly has reinforced the mental models of its top executives. In fact, it's easy to conclude that Southwest's executives are the only managers in the airline industry who have a winning "formula" or set of managerial beliefs for operating a profitable carrier.[6]

The aim of this example is to illustrate that managers' mental models exert a powerful influence on strategic decision making. Where did Southwest's winning "formula" come from if not from the beliefs and understandings of its top managers? And, even after decisions are made and action is taken, Southwest's managers monitor the outcomes of their decisions. Such monitoring of performance outcomes provides the company's managers with feedback from which they can "learn" about the effectiveness of their decisions.

Another example showing the importance of mental models can be seen in the aircraft manufacturing industry. The current aircraft designs that Boeing and Airbus are pursuing reflect the different mental models that executives from each company have. Boeing executives, believing that most customers want to fly point-to-point with no connecting flights and who have seen their company enjoy great success with smaller planes designed for point-to-point destinations, concluded that the company should focus its efforts on developing the 787 aircraft. The 787 is a mid-sized plane that will be more efficient than Boeing's previous planes in terms of maintenance and fuel costs. On the other hand, Airbus executives, concluding that there is a significant market for very large aircraft connecting large metropolitan areas around the world, has developed the A380, a large, 550-passenger plane. The two planes are very different, stemming from the difference in mental models that led to the pursuit of different aircraft types.

In both examples, we see the powerful linkage between executive beliefs and each company's strategies, but just how powerful is the influence of mental models? We suggest that nothing is a more important influence on the success of business organizations than the mental models of their managers. And, to back up our claim, we offer these opinions from a successful business leader and from management scholars. Here are the thoughts of Thomas Watson, Jr., the legendary former chief executive of IBM, on the importance of mental models:

> [An organization] owes its resiliency … to the power of what we call beliefs and the appeal those beliefs have for its people. In other words the basic philosophy, spirit and drive of an organization have far more to do with its relative achievements than do technological and economic resources, organizational structure, innovation and timing.[7]

And, two Harvard Business School professors who have studied the influence of managers' beliefs on decision making have concluded that managers' mental models provide them with

> a shared commitment to a vision of their organization's distinctive competence, the risks they are willing to take, and the degree of self-sufficiency they desire. As a result, these beliefs are themselves a powerful constraint on the options the executives will consider and the decisions they make.[8]

The Sources of Managerial Beliefs

How are managers' mental models developed and how do managers come to hold certain beliefs and understandings? Here, we'll take a close look at five key sources of mental models:

Experience and Trial-and-Error Learning

First, as noted above, experience is a major source of beliefs. In fact, much of what is contained in our mental models is a product of learning-by-doing or trial-and-error learning. Many children have touched a hot stove and learned that the resulting burn is quite painful. Later on, we acquire interpersonal skills, study habits, hobbies, clothing and recreational preferences, and a multitude of other beliefs and understandings based on trial-and-error learning of what does and doesn't work for us as individuals.

Managers learn all the time from the impact their decisions and strategies seem to have on the performance of their companies. As described above, firm performance provides managers with a good deal of feedback about the accuracy of their mental models and the effectiveness of their decision making. Wal-Mart serves as a great example showing how a company uses trial-and-error to become a more successful company. After missteps in the South Korean and German markets, Wal-Mart executives used the lessons they learned in these failures to successfully enter China, Mexico, and Great Britain. In South Korea and Germany, the company did not sufficiently take into account the importance of foreign culture and its effects on globalization strategy. After learning from its mistakes, though, not only has Wal-Mart increased international sales by more than $20 billion since 2007, but foreign sales now account for almost one quarter of Wal-Mart's total sales.[9]

It's also important to emphasize that managers can learn the wrong lessons from their experiences. The result can be inaccuracies in their mental models or superstitious beliefs. For example, the major U.S. automobile producers had no trouble beating back efforts by foreign producers to gain significant shares of the U.S. market during the 1950s and 1960s. These early successes against foreign producers may have given executives at General Motors, Ford, and Chrysler a sense of invulnerability that left them poorly prepared to deal with the successful arrival of Japanese producers in the 1970s and 1980s. This example also illustrates why it is so important for managers to continually test their assumptions, beliefs, and understandings against developments in their firms' competitive environments.

Education

Education—defined broadly to include formal primary and secondary schooling, undergraduate and graduate education, on-the-job training, and executive education programs—is another important source of managerial beliefs and thinking. Education includes both the delivery of knowledge content and the processes associated with learning. Obviously, both aspects of education are important. A good part of education involves the delivery of knowledge content. Lectures, books, exercises, problems, and tests are all aimed at the mastery of knowledge content. Probably even more important, however, are the processes associated with learning, including critical thinking skills, since they determine our ability to process new information and acquire new beliefs and understandings.

While education can be an important source of mental models, all educational programs face a number of challenges or limitations in their ability to convey management knowledge. First, we know that much that is learned in any educational program must be reinforced through trial-and-error learning. The experience with corporate training is instructive. Companies spend hundreds of millions of dollars each year to train employees, yet studies have shown that much of this training fails to significantly upgrade employee skills. One simple reason for this disappointing outcome is that many training programs simply do not provide employees with meaningful exercises to reinforce the training.

Another challenge for education is the problem of tacit knowledge—or that we know more than we can say. Oftentimes some of the most important information we would like to be able to communicate is knowledge that has been developed over years of experience or is so specialized that it cannot be easily communicated to or shared with others. In such cases, education and training programs are rarely able to facilitate the transfer of tacit knowledge. To make matters even more complicated, much specialized knowledge can be so taken for granted that we don't even realize how important it is. Thus tacit knowledge is truly an important, but sometimes overlooked, component of management ability. Educational and training efforts need to acknowledge the importance of tacit knowledge and place greater effort on making such tacit knowledge more explicit and transferring it to colleagues and co-workers.

Culture and Values

Culture is another important source of our mental models. Culture can be thought of as "the way we do things" in a particular setting. As a result, culture carries with it a number of usually implicit beliefs and understandings, and even a language and vocabulary that gets passed on to newcomers as they are socialized into an organization or any other type of environment. A story told by sociologist Erving Goffman illustrates how culture and socialization influence our thinking.[10] According to the story, a young boy, whose grandfather owned a baseball team, was asked by his teacher, "What is one and one?" The boy responded, "A ball and a strike." This little story vividly demonstrates how cultural or social contexts shape our beliefs and understandings.

Many smaller, family businesses, as well as very large corporations have strong cultures. These cultures exert significant influences on employees' beliefs and understandings of company policies and how the firms should compete. Often, these strong cultures yield significant benefits. For example, often the employees of companies with strong cultures will develop a great deal of loyalty to their company. Customers will benefit if one aspect of the culture is a commitment to outstanding customer service. And, a culture that values creativity and innovation is likely to foster new product development.

At the same time, a strong culture can have some significant risks. A strong culture can so shape our mental models that we can have difficulty understanding the perspectives and beliefs of those from other cultures. For example, managers of many companies have made foolish mistakes when they've sought to do business in other countries because they failed to understand how differently people from other cultures might view their products, services, technologies, and even their marketing and advertising strategies.

A strong culture can also give managers a "we've always done it this way" mentality, so that they are unable to understand how changing industry conditions could render their firm or its strategies obsolete.[11] Because the "we've always done it this way" mentality limits the ability of executives to accept new ideas or to challenge the conventional wisdom, boards of directors sometimes conclude that they have to turn to executives from other firms and even from firms in other industries when searching for new CEOs. The aim is to find executives whose thinking is not so tied to traditional beliefs or conventional ways of doing things. The main point we want to emphasize is that even when companies have strong cultures, the mental models of managers and top executives must remain flexible and open to new ideas. One research study summarized:

> firms must recruit or develop executives who have the ability to remain flexible in their thinking, so that their beliefs do not become ossified but their firms successfully adapt and respond to changes in their competitive landscape.[12]

In summary, while culture can be a powerful, motivating force in a company whose employees share similar beliefs and understandings about the company, its strategies, and performance objectives, a strong culture can also be hostile to new ideas and influences. Furthermore, as recent corporate scandals make plain, companies can have dysfunctional cultures or cultures that ignore the importance of ethical values. For example, Enron was well-known for having a corporate culture that included the view that Enron employees were the "smartest guys in the room." This arrogance, condoned and enhanced by Enron's culture, was partly responsible for the scandal that led to the company's downfall.

Imitation

Imitation also provides raw material for mental models. Many of our attitudes, beliefs, and understandings come from observing and then adopting the attitudes, beliefs, and understandings of others. The trends in fashions, clothing styles, and other patterns of personal expression are spread by people imitating each other. Likewise, such sports as snowboarding and mountain biking became popular through rapid imitation.

Similarly, company managers might observe other companies adopting a particular strategy. If they conclude that this strategy leads to positive performance outcomes, they will probably develop a belief in the efficacy of that strategy. Imitation probably explains the rise of airlines like JetBlue, AirTran, and America West—all seeking to copy Southwest's low-cost strategy (and also its profits!). After *Fast Company* magazine published a flattering story on JetBlue, a reader wrote the following letter to the magazine that emphasizes that company's imitation of Southwest:

> In 90 percent of your article on JetBlue, if you take the name "JetBlue" and replace it with "Southwest Airlines" and take the name "David Neeleman" and replace it with "Herb Kelleher," it could have been an article written 25 years ago on Southwest Airlines and its chairman. Much of Neeleman's modus operandi with his employees and his basic business model isn't so innovative but simply a copy of Southwest. Apparently, he learned a lot during his time there.[13]

As emphasized in Chapter 2, one weakness of imitation is that strategies based on or copied from other firms are necessarily less distinctive than innovative strategies, and they are much less likely to provide firms with a competitive advantage. Executives may see that a particular strategy works very well for another firm and they may develop a belief that the same strategy will work well for their firms. And, the strategy may indeed work well at their firms, but a strategy taken out of its context will usually not be as successful for a number of reasons. First, the original firm has probably been pursuing the strategy for a long period of time and will therefore have had more time to fine-tune and hone the strategy and its implementation. In addition, the original firm will have had additional time and opportunities to fully integrate the strategy into its existing structure, systems, and culture. So while managers at another company can easily copy or imitate other companies' strategies, they will probably find it much more difficult to match the level of success enjoyed by those companies.

Creativity

Researchers consider something creative if it is both *novel* and *appropriate*.[14] In a management context, this would include ideas that are original, different, or innovative and also potentially useful or offering economic value. Creativity and imagination thus provide a basis for new thinking or for the development of totally new mental models containing new beliefs and understandings. Research by Teresa Amabile and others and a book by Rollo May, *The Courage to Create*, suggest some of the characteristics of the creative process.[15] For example, May concluded that creative insights occur suddenly, that they are particularly vivid, and that they usually provide the individual with a sense of certainty about the appropriateness of the insight.

Furthermore, May found that creative insights tend to run counter to the beliefs that individuals have held or maintained in the past. They also tend to follow long periods of hard work on a particular problem or question. Amabile, too, emphasizes the importance of creative working and thinking skills. But creative insights frequently occur during a period of rest during which the unconscious mind has an opportunity to work through the problem or question, thus underscoring the importance of unstructured or "play" time.[16] In any event, this creative encounter represents an "ah-ha" experience in which an individual comes to a new belief or understanding about a particular phenomenon. Perhaps it should come as no surprise, then, that a highly creative firm like Google insists that employees spend time on projects unrelated to their specific work assignments and that the company has designed its office space to encourage "play" and creativity.

Regardless of what triggers creative insights, the ability to see the world in a new way is a gift or talent vitally important to the success of business organizations that must continually renew themselves due to changes in their industries. However, new ideas may require companies to try new things or totally rethink how they do things. The great irony is that change is a fact of life for all business organizations, yet their managers, structures, and cultures are often reluctant to embrace, if not downright hostile to, new ideas.

Not surprisingly, some of the most noteworthy recent examples of creativity in the business world are found in technology. For example, computers had existed for at least three decades— primarily the domain of scientists and engineers—before Apple Computer's founders concluded that computing power should be accessible to the general public. In fact, the genius of Apple's founders, Jobs and Wozniak, was to see that the development of microprocessors could be exploited to place a great deal of computing power into a relatively small box *and* to see that this development could equip a whole new segment of the population with "personal" computers. Their innovation has, of course, changed the computer industry and everyday life in our society in profound ways. As a *Fortune* article explains:

> Apple has demonstrated how to create real, breathtaking growth by dreaming up products so new and ingenious that they have upended one industry after another: consumer electronics, the record industry, the movie industry, video and music production… Apple's philosophy goes like this: Too many companies spread themselves thin, making a profusion of products to defuse risk, so they get mired in the mediocre. Apple's approach is to put every resource it has behind just a few products and make them exceedingly well.[17]

Similarly, Jeff Bezos took the insights he had gained from studying the computer industry and the potential of the Internet to found Amazon.com. Bezos saw that the Internet could give a company the opportunity to offer 24-hour service to customers and that technology could personalize the shopping experience in ways that bricks-and-mortar stores could not match.

John Mackey, the CEO of Whole Foods Market, has done something very similar in the grocery industry. Taking the insights he developed while previously running his own natural foods store, a small store named SaferWay, Mackey has not only helped to carve out a natural foods niche in the grocery industry but has also used creativity and changing consumer demand to put Whole Foods at the forefront of this niche. With $8 billion in sales for the year 2008, the company is the biggest organic and natural food seller in the country. One of Mackey's key beliefs is that a firm can not only serve to make a profit for its shareholders, but it can also serve a greater purpose of providing healthy food to a large community. As Mackey puts it:

> A business that is not profitable is going to fail. At the same time, I've never felt comfortable with people who think the purpose of business is to make a profit. That doesn't make any sense to me. It's like saying that the purpose of life is to eat. Well, you can't live if you don't eat, but you don't live to eat. And neither does business exist primarily to make a profit. It exists to fulfill its purpose, whatever that might be.[18]

Note that these entrepreneurs weren't simply lucky; nor did their creative insights just "spring forth" from unprepared minds. Jobs and Wozniak were electrical engineers, so they fully understood microprocessor technology and its capabilities. Bezos had previously worked on Wall Street, and had a solid grasp on both business finance and the potential of computer and Internet technologies. Mackey had owned his own natural foods store for many years before deciding to expand. Hard work and a deep understanding of an industry or technology are almost always prerequisites for developing insights. Amabile emphasizes that skill in a particular domain is an essential prerequisite for creativity. Similarly, Rollo May emphasizes the importance of what he calls "form" or structure to provide a crucible for the creative experience.

Characteristics of the Decision Making Process and Problems Associated with Managerial Thinking

Now that we have described mental models and how managerial thinking influences decision making in more detail, it's important to step back and focus on some of the key characteristics of the decision making process and also examine some of the problems associated with managerial thinking. The stories reported in *The Wall Street Journal*, *Business Week*, *Fortune*, *Fast Company*, and other business publications may give the impression that managerial decision making is a highly rational process in which managers assess their industry environments, consider their firms' strengths and weaknesses, and then make carefully considered decisions based on thoughtful analysis of all relevant data. In fact, as emphasized in the first chapter, managerial decision making is typically anything but a linear, rational, and well informed process, and many of the most important strategic decisions are made under a number of limitations:

Incompleteness

One key characteristic of mental models is that they are just that—models or representations of the phenomena we encounter. Put another way, our mental models are "constructions" rather than "imprints" or pictures.[19] Thus, mental models can be more or less accurate or complete. A good analogy is a set of instructions for assembling a product that you've just purchased. Some instructions are very detailed, will include a complete parts list with pictures, and provide a step-by-step guide to assembling the product. Some instructions are far less detailed and may even contain inaccuracies. Similarly, for some phenomena we will have very detailed mental models, but for other phenomena, we may have only very vague understandings or beliefs. Obviously, the more complete our mental models, the more likely we are to make sound interpretations of the phenomena we encounter and the more likely we are to make good decisions.

Even the best-informed executives must often make important decisions with less than adequate data, especially when firms are trying to create something new. Amazon's recent creation of the Kindle is a good example. The executives at Amazon had no way of knowing that its e-reader, a completely new device unlike anything else in the gadget world, would be such a hit. Not only does the Kindle have the opportunity to completely revolutionize the publishing industry, but initial sales far exceeded expectations. In fact, Barclays Capital predicts that Kindle sales will account for 20 percent of Amazon's total sales by the year 2012.[20]

Similarly, Verizon CEO Ivan Seidenberg recently took a big bet on investing in the company's new FiOS technology without having a solid prediction of the outcome. Starting in 2007, Verizon began to rip out and replace 100-year-old copper telephone wires across the country with thin strands of fiber-optic glass in order to not only provide customers with a faster connection but to gain an advantage over rival AT&T as well. As Verizon is traditionally seen as a conservative company when it comes to taking risks, the decision to invest $23 billion was huge and raised many eyebrows. These examples illustrate that, even though they may lack accurate or adequate information, managers must still make important strategic decisions, and more often than not, business leaders make some of their boldest decisions based on incomplete data.

A lack of accurate data can also contribute to management mistakes. Early on, AT&T owned the rights to cellular telephone technology but its executives concluded that fewer than one million customers would be using cellular telephones by the year 2000. It therefore sold the rights to cellular telephone technology to other companies. Demand has, of course, significantly exceeded earlier forecasts: Cell phones have now reached almost 90 percent of the United States population, and the industry is still growing worldwide.[21] By the mid–1990s, AT&T realized that it needed to get back into the cellular telephone business and paid $12 billion to acquire McCaw Cellular Communications—a company using the very same technology AT&T once owned! Since then, AT&T and its wholly-owned subsidiary AT&T Wireless have been acquired by SBC Communications and subsidiary Cingular Wireless respectively in order to be able to compete on a large scale with rival Verizon.

It might be tempting to think that the explosive growth of information technology would be accompanied by a corresponding growth in the ability of managers to process information flows, but this does not appear to be the case. Few companies have modified their internal structures to take advantage of the information they gather, and they have been slow to exploit the power of information technology to process the information and data that are available. As a result, managers often face the problem of information overload, so that they are overwhelmed by information and their mental models either cannot notice what is really important in the flood of data or they are unable to interpret the data in order to understand the situations they are facing. In such cases, the availability of data hinders rather than helps managers as they wrestle with important decisions or immediate problems. Here's how one business executive has described this challenge:

> There are limits to the information [managers] can absorb and the operating details they can monitor. Managers can be spread so thin that they overlook areas of true opportunity. The information age has not necessarily been accompanied by an ability to interpret and use the greater fund of information advantageously.[22]

Top Executives Are Often Insulated from and Out of Touch with Reality

Another problem facing key decision makers is that they may not get accurate information so their mental models do not reflect an accurate understanding of the situations they face. In spite of assertions that they don't want to be surrounded by sycophants, many executives do find themselves surrounded by other managers who rarely want the task of telling their superiors that things aren't as good as they seem. As a result, "bad news" tends to travel up through a company's ranks very slowly, leaving many top managers poorly informed about the very problems for which they need the most information.[23] Andy Grove, former chairman and CEO of Intel, is a strong believer in creating environments where people feel comfortable sharing their real thoughts as well as bad news. In his book, *Only the Paranoid Survive*, he stresses that fear is a necessary part of any company because it is what stops firms from being complacent. On the other hand, he also notes that:

> Fear that might keep you from voicing your real thoughts is poison. Almost nothing could be more detrimental to the well-being of the company. If you are a senior manager…under no circumstance should you ever "shoot the messenger" or allow any manager who works for you to do so… From our inception on, we at Intel have worked very hard to break down the walls between those who possess knowledge power and those who possess organizational power. Ideally, each will respect the other for what he or she brings to the party and will not be intimidated by the other's knowledge or position.[24]

Cognitive Biases

Thinking and learning are also impaired by a number of cognitive biases. These biases undermine rational thinking so that decisions are often made more on the basis of hope than evidence. We are likely to trust our "hunches" and "gut feelings" far more than objective evidence would suggest we should. Research also demonstrates that we make decisions based on very little information or in spite of evidence that supports a different decision. Managers often put inordinate and unwarranted faith in optimistic forecasts. And, when we desire a particular outcome, we are likely to exaggerate the possibilities of that outcome. For example, a large percentage of the population buys lottery tickets, and, week after week, many people are convinced that they have at least a reasonably good chance of buying a "winner," even though statistically they have a much better chance of being struck by lightning or even drowning in a bathtub.

Superstition can also be a source of bias and lead to poor decision making. Superstition is really nothing more than a false understanding of cause and effect, and superstitions often result from making incorrect inferences from past experiences. Business managers can also be very superstitious. For example, a company may try a new strategy and it may fail. As a result, the company's managers may conclude that the strategy is unworkable, even though it may have failed because of poor implementation or for a multitude of other reasons that have little to do with the actual merits of the strategy.

Another bias very common in the business world is that most managers will pay a great deal of attention to those stimuli or aspects of the environment that confirm their mental models while ignoring or discounting evidence to the contrary. As a result, managers will often base their decisions on optimistic or unrealistic forecasts even though the available evidence would warrant more modest expectations. This unchecked optimism might explain the fiasco of the merger between Daimler and Chrysler in 1998. Neither Chrysler nor Daimler executives considered carefully the challenges of merging the two companies' corporate cultures and, as a result, the merger failed to successfully integrate the two companies or provide promised synergies.[25] It may also explain why Toyota's managers were so slow in addressing a rash of recent quality problems; their existing beliefs would not allow them to accept the idea that their cars could actually be seriously defective.[26]

Timeliness and the Difficulty Associated with Altering Managerial Beliefs

As already emphasized, business environments will change, so managers' beliefs and understandings are likely to become obsolete. In fact, a major challenge for managers, who must function in rapidly changing environments, is to keep their mental models aligned with the pace of changes in their industries. If this updating of mental models does not occur, then new or novel issues may be interpreted using dated or obsolete understandings. This can lead to incorrect interpretations of issues and poor decision making. Organizational decline and even failure can result. Jack Welch, GE's former chairman and CEO, summarized the dilemma well:

> We've long believed that when the rate of change inside an institution becomes slower than the rate of change outside, the end is in sight. The only question is when.[27]

Unfortunately, the cognitive processes that are required to change attitudes, beliefs, and understandings don't always work very well. As we become more and more familiar with a particular phenomenon, we are likely to develop very strongly held beliefs about it:

> The mind is an inference machine that strives mightily to bring order, simplicity, consistency, and stability to the world it encounters. In other words, where nature is ambiguous, people develop strong beliefs and act upon them.[28]

New information, especially information that should cause us to change our beliefs about a particular situation may or may not be absorbed into our thinking. Researchers have shown that we tend to be "cognitive misers."[29] In other words, once we have "figured-out" a particular phenomenon or situation—i.e., formed a mental model about it—we are reluctant to commit additional cognitive energy to deciding whether we need to change that mental model. As a result, we continue to use and reuse a mental model over and over again, even, in many cases, after we have begun to receive feedback that suggests that the mental model is no longer appropriate given environmental and other types of changes.

The experience of U.S. railroad companies provides an illustration both of how once-accurate beliefs can become increasingly inaccurate as the business environment changes, and also illustrates how reluctant managers can be to change their beliefs. Before the development of a national highway system, the railroads had a virtual monopoly on most freight transportation. An analysis of railroad corporate documents from that era has shown that nearly all railroad executives held a fairly reasonable belief, given their monopoly position, that charging customers higher freight rates would lead to higher financial performance. Yet, this same analysis has also suggested that most railroad executives continued to hold this belief long after a new national highway system had allowed trucks to become a major presence in intercity freight transportation. They simply failed to grasp that ever higher freight rates would only divert more and more freight traffic to the emerging trucking industry.[30]

Likewise, the mental models of managers and executives in the music industry have had to adapt to an ongoing series of changes in the distribution of music—from LP records to tapes to CDs to online distribution. Apple upended the music industry when it opened up its iTunes store—and the changes brought about by the Internet aren't just confined to the music industry. The development of the Internet has executives in many different media industries rethinking their mental models because of the shift in the distribution of content. As Rupert Murdoch, CEO of News Corp., puts it:

> The Internet is almost the ultimate way of giving people choice. Young people use it more. Before, we were pushing media at them. Now the new generation and the generations to follow are going to be pulling out of the universe what media they want.[31]

Because music and other media executives have been slow to embrace understandings about how online distribution is fundamentally changing their industries, they are now scrambling to keep their firms relevant.

Part of the problem is that we often take our beliefs and understandings for granted and rarely take (or find) time for reflection. As a result they remain quite implicit and unexamined. Here's another example that illustrates how unexamined beliefs undermined the competitiveness of U.S. automakers in the 1980s:

> The problems with mental models lie not in whether they are right or wrong—by definition, all models are simplifications. The problems with mental models arise when the models are tacit—when they exist below the level of awareness. The Detroit automakers didn't say, "We have a mental model that all people care about is styling." They said, "All people care about is styling." Because they remained unaware of their mental models, the models remained unexamined. Because they were unexamined, the models remained unchanged.

As the world changed, a gap widened between Detroit's mental models and reality, leading to increasingly counterproductive actions.[32]

These illustrations suggest that beliefs and understandings that have been developed over long periods of time are unlikely to be easily shaken, even when individuals are confronted by widespread disconfirming evidence.[33] The incompleteness of mental models and the challenge of keeping pace with changes in the larger environments in which we live and work are further complicated by a number of social-psychological factors, including *groupthink* and *escalation of commitment.*

Social-Psychological Factors: Groupthink and Escalation of Commitment

Two additional problems or pathologies are also likely to contribute to the tendency for managers' mental models to be inflexible. One is the danger of *groupthink,* in which intragroup pressures enforce a uniformity of thinking on group members.[34] As a result of the groupthink phenomenon, a top management team or other group will explicitly or implicitly limit its consideration of fundamental assumptions, causal factors, and likely outcomes. Furthermore, groups that fall victim to groupthink will often intentionally disregard information that would serve to disconfirm their predetermined opinions or chosen courses of action.

A related phenomenon is *escalation of commitment*, in which managers continue to pursue a particular course of action or strategy even though performance outcomes and other sources of feedback indicate that the strategy is not working or is inappropriate.[35] One good everyday example of the escalation of commitment phenomenon is the tendency to keep on driving even after we know we are lost. Probably the wisest thing to do in such a situation is to stop for directions as soon as we think we are lost, but many of us will instead keep on driving, which usually only increases the number of miles we have to backtrack.

Recall also the hypothetical example, given earlier in the chapter, of the executive who is concerned about company sales levels in a particular region. The executive decides that the appropriate response is to spend more on advertising the company's products in that region. We saw that if sales do increase, the executive's mental model—the belief that advertising is associated with higher sales—will be reinforced. What if, on the other hand, sales in the region do not increase? The executive might then decide to spend even more money on advertising in a particular region. But this could easily result in the company "throwing good money after bad" and not really addressing more fundamental problems with the company's strategy in the region.

It's conceivable that many other factors may explain the declining sales in this region, and ideally, the failure of the advertising strategy to reverse the sales decline would encourage the business executive to question what else might be affecting sales. For example, the executive might conclude that this particular region is a special case that requires more complex strategizing. The executive might seek more data and discover that a competitor has launched a new product in this region or that the company's products lack features that are needed by customers in this region. New decisions might be made—perhaps a new product is developed specifically for this region—and if these new decisions result in sales increases, then new trial-and-error learning will take place.

Unfortunately, when performance doesn't respond as company managers hope, they often find it difficult to shake their beliefs or to engage in this kind of experimentation. Often they respond by trying harder, or "escalating their commitment" to a failing course of action. Psychologists have noted that once individuals commit themselves to a particular course of action, it is very difficult to get them to change their minds, even when they are confronted with considerable evidence that they have made a wrong decision.

This tendency to commit psychologically to a particular course of action explains a variety of management mistakes, including the all-too-common mistake of investing heavily in failing product lines or businesses, and "bidding wars," in which acquiring companies end up paying too much for their acquired businesses. Another example is the troubled merger of AOL and Time Warner, which became almost inevitable as the top leaders of the two companies became psychologically committed to its consummation, even though many other executives inside both organizations could foresee significant problems in uniting these two very different companies.[36]

Research suggests that escalation is often due to individuals or managers attempting to appear consistent rather than waffling in their decision making. Managers will also continue in a particular course of action or strategy in order to justify or reinforce past decisions. What is remarkable about research on the escalation of commitment phenomenon is the degree to which subjects will persist in pursuing a particular strategy in spite of disconfirming or negative feedback. This research suggests that individual and organizational learning is not always a straightforward, rational process.

Summary

While this section has focused on the weaknesses and limitations of mental models and decision making processes, it is important to acknowledge how well these mental processes often work. We are able to function in a world containing an overwhelming amount of information and stimuli because our mental models usually do a heroic job of distinguishing between the important and the trivial. And, we have a keen ability to interpret the stimuli that our brains notice. Almost always, we make informed and wise decisions.

At the same time, this chapter would not be helpful if we didn't also underscore, as we have here, that mental models are prone to a number of limitations and biases. They may fail to alert managers to changes or other important stimuli in the larger environment. And, even when change in the environment is noticed, mental models are not easily changed. Two noted organizational scholars have summarized the problem this way: "Managers operate on mental representations of the world, and those representations are likely to be of historical environments rather than of current ones."[37] Thus, firms face the very real danger that their top managers may be operating on outdated or even inaccurate assumptions, beliefs, and understandings. Moreover, the last few sections have shown that managers' mental models are also subject to biases and social-psychological factors that can interfere with effective decision making.

It's no wonder, then, that many firms wind up in trouble. And, because of the rigidities, biases, and other limitations in managerial thinking, chief executive officers and other top managers of troubled firms must often be replaced before strategies can be altered and a turnaround in company performance occurs. Unfortunately, most boards of directors do not do an effective job of monitoring either the performance of their companies or the performance of their firms' chief executive officers. Dismissal of a CEO is usually a final desperate measure taken by boards only after companies have experienced a severe decline in market standing, a severe downturn in financial performance, or—even worse—the threat of bankruptcy or failure.

Practical Usefulness of Understanding Your Own and Others' Mental Models

This chapter has sought to underscore the importance of managerial thinking in the strategy formulation and implementation processes. But managerial thinking and mental models should not be viewed as abstract management concepts. Instead, the managerial thinking or mental models approach to the study of strategy that is emphasized in this book has a number of practical implications:

First, if you can develop the ability to "map" mental models—in other words, begin to understand the assumptions, beliefs, and understandings that you and others hold—and observe how they influence decision making and the formulation and implementation of strategy, you can better understand firms' strategies and their competitors' likely reactions to those strategies. This understanding can help you: 1) have a better perspective on why the firms where you work pursue the strategies that they do, 2) help you make better decisions and recommendations, and 3) allow you to make better predictions about the future actions of competitors. Success at recommending and making better decisions and predicting competitors' actions should lead to greater influence and higher levels of responsibility.

Second, understanding that our mental models are incomplete, that they are subject to a number of biases, and that our beliefs may be outdated given ongoing changes in our industry environments should lead to companies establishing formal mechanisms for testing our mental models. One way to do this would be to engage in scenario planning exercises in which managers debate the effectiveness of their beliefs in a wide range of possible industry contexts. For example, what if technologies change in revolutionary ways, what if major new competitors emerge, or what if customer wants and needs radically change? Alternatively, companies can create teams that challenge both the key beliefs of, and the strategies pursued by, company managers so that everyone in the organization can acknowledge the strengths as well as the limitations of the company's strategies as well as the beliefs behind those strategies.

Furthermore, an understanding of mental models can improve your interpersonal skills. How many times have you said, "She just doesn't understand my point of view" or "He and I just don't see eye to eye?" Most interpersonal relations problems can be traced to the fact that individuals hold different mental models. In such cases, individuals who are trying to communicate with each other really *don't* understand each other's points of view. Understanding that disagreements and disputes often emerge because different individuals hold very different underlying assumptions, beliefs, and understandings about a particular phenomenon can, however, go a long way toward achieving consensus.

Often, consensus requires making each individual's underlying assumptions or beliefs explicit. Then, the various parties can evaluate the mental models held by the other parties and better appreciate why they hold the particular views they espouse. One advantage of making underlying assumptions and thinking explicit is to allow the various parties to learn from each other. Quite often it is not so much that one individual is "right" and that other individuals are "wrong," but rather that each individual is viewing the issue through a different lens. Such discussions about different underlying assumptions and thinking often lead to comments like, "Oh, I've never thought about it that way"—statements that suggest individuals are beginning to learn from one another.

Finally, an understanding of mental models will help you better appreciate the need for updating your mental models on a timely basis. This chapter has already noted the tendency for mental models to be used over and over again, even when new information suggests that they should be updated, and the chapter has described the risks associated with this reusing of old or dated models. By simply being aware of the inertia associated with your thinking and the risks associated with the use of outdated or inappropriate models, you are much more likely to discipline yourself to pursue a program of continuous learning. Here's how one management scholar has described the importance and also the practical relevance of continuously updating our mental models:

> The manager who realizes he [or she] is following a conceptual map [or mental model] has taken an important first step toward being able to manage ambiguity. Our maps can be priceless guides, but they can also limit our perceptions, sometimes becoming rigid and confining. Understanding a map as a revisable model generally induces a healthy skepticism as to its infallibility, and engenders more flexible thinking. Mapping and remapping is a fundamental process that a manager facing ambiguity and change must master.[38]

Conclusion: The Qualities of Effective Business Leaders

The overall aim of this chapter is to provide you with an understanding of mental models and how mental models influence strategic decision making. The beliefs and understandings contained in managers' mental models determine what they notice, shape how they interpret the events, data, and environmental stimuli that they do notice, and influence the decisions that they make in response to these interpretations. Thus, mental models play a key role in strategic decision making and in the strategy formulation and implementation processes.

The chapter also examined the sources of beliefs and understandings contained in mental models, including trial-and-error learning, education, imitation, culture, and creativity. Powerful as they are in influencing decision making, mental models are also subject to a number of biases and limitations. The chapter reviewed these weaknesses and showed how they can lead to poor decision making and a failure of mental models to keep pace with changes in firms' competitive environments. Finally, the chapter discussed the practical usefulness of understanding the concept of mental models.

To conclude this chapter on general managers, it is worth considering the qualities that are associated with effective business leaders. And one way to think about the qualities of effective leaders is in terms of the three key themes that will be emphasized throughout this book, as the material presented in this chapter certainly reinforces each of these key themes:

Managers and Managerial Thinking

This chapter has emphasized that strategies are not formulated in a "black box," but are the product of managerial thinking—managers making decisions based on their mental models. Clearly, it will be difficult for managers to make effective decisions if they lack some level of basic knowledge about the particular issues they face, their firms, or their industry environments. Thus, it is fair to conclude that *effective leaders are experts.* Managers must develop mental models that allow them to make good decisions, and one of the best ways to avoid making mistakes due to inaccurate thinking, biases, and other weaknesses is to become knowledgeable. Effective decision making and strategic management require competence and expertise.

What does it mean to be an expert? Herbert Simon, the Nobel Prize-winning scholar, insists that an expert is an individual who knows 10,000 pieces of information about a particular phenomenon! Simon also argues that few individuals can develop such a body of knowledge in less than ten years. Malcolm Gladwell, in his book, *Outliers*, stresses the research of neurologist Daniel Levitin, who has similar ideas to Simon. Levitin believes that it takes 10,000 hours of practice to become an expert, and Gladwell shows in his book that social circumstances and contexts determine the ability of a person to become an expert in something.[39]

It's important to recognize, however, that it is not just the quantity of information or knowledge, but rather the quality, content, and timeliness of the knowledge possessed by individuals that will make them effective leaders. And, as people move through the ranks of any business organization, the content of the knowledge employed will have to change considerably. For example, an effective marketing manager and an effective engineer will have to acquire totally new types of knowledge as they rise through the ranks and take on more general management responsibilities. The knowledge will have to be less specific to marketing or engineering and more focused on addressing general management concerns and issues.

Moreover, research suggests that *effective leaders are able to link disparate strands of information and to consider a broad array of scenarios and outcomes.* Effective general managers are able to see many different points of view and consider many different possible outcomes. Moreover, effective managers must strike a balance between thinking broadly and focusing on specific issues, between "seeing the forest for the trees" and "sweating the details," and between thinking about the future and thinking about today.

Change and the Need to Think Dynamically about Strategic Management

Nothing in the business world is more certain than change. Demographic changes, the development of new technologies, and the introduction of new products and services—all are potentially major changes facing business firms and their managers. What makes change even more challenging is that it rarely comes in steady, predictable, or incremental patterns. Firms may enjoy the luxury of operating for years, a decade, or even many decades in the same competitive environment. Then, seemingly overnight, new competitors arrive on the scene, customers begin to want and demand new products and services, and new technologies render existing products and services obsolete. Strategies that used to work are no longer effective.

Some firms cope with such changes very effectively and some firms even seem to thrive on change, but many firms have a great deal of difficulty responding to changes in their competitive environments. Thus, *effective leaders must be able to think dynamically about strategic management and they must be able to anticipate the future.* Management professors and consultants, Hamel and Prahalad, insist that managers must "compete for industry foresight."[40] In other words, managers must anticipate and understand how their firms' competitive environments are likely to evolve so that they can adequately position and prepare their firms for these changes. As noted in Chapter 1, a more appropriate name for the field of strategic management would be *strategic change management.*

The Importance of Organizational Learning

Finally, the text has already emphasized that managers' mental models must remain flexible and open to change if they are to keep pace with changes in business environments. Otherwise, managers risk having their firms pursue strategies that are no longer appropriate given changes in customer preferences, competitors' product and/or service offerings, and the development of new technologies.[41] Therefore, *managers (and their firms and businesses) must be good learners.* The scholar, James March, writes that managers must "exploit the known" while also "exploring the new."[42] According to March, exploiting the known is about gaining and maintaining a competitive advantage in what the firm already does, while exploring the new is learning about the future. If a firm focuses only on getting better at what it already knows how to do, it will be blind-sided by the future. If it focuses only on the future, it will probably never achieve a competitive advantage today. Thus, managers must balance optimally their organizational resources between these two learning activities.

Another way in which top managers can maintain flexibility and open-mindedness, while also avoiding the groupthink phenomenon, is to surround themselves with opinionated colleagues and to encourage them to offer dissenting opinions. Peter Drucker tells this anecdote about Alfred Sloan, GM's legendary chief executive:

> Sloan is reported to have said at a meeting of one of his top committees: "Gentlemen, I take it we are all in complete agreement on the decision here." Everyone around the table nodded assent. "Then," continued Mr. Sloan, "I propose we postpone further discussion of this matter until our next meeting to give ourselves time to develop disagreement and perhaps gain some understanding of what the decision is all about."

Drucker then makes this insightful observation:

> Sloan … always emphasized the need to test opinions against facts and the need to make absolutely sure that one did not start out with the conclusion and then look for the facts that would support it. He knew that the right decision demands adequate disagreement.[43]

Key Points

- The content of managers' mental models will influence the decisions they make and the strategic management of their firms.
- Mental models are developed through trial-and-error learning, through education, as a product of culture and values, by imitation, and through creativity.
- Mental models are incomplete representations of phenomena and are also subject to a variety of biases and social-psychological factors that can result in poor decision making.
- Mental models tend to be used over and over again even as the environment changes, so that they become less and less accurate or appropriate. One key point of this chapter is that, just as business environments are changing all the time, so, too, must mental models change if managers hope to make appropriate and effective decisions.
- An understanding of the mental model concept can offer a number of practical advantages, including the ability to make better strategic recommendations, an improvement in interpersonal relationships, and an acknowledgment of the need to change and update mental models on an ongoing basis.
- The qualities of effective leaders include: being an expert, being able to link disparate strands of information and to consider a broad array of scenarios and outcomes, being able to think dynamically about strategic management and to anticipate the future, and being good learners.

Key Questions for Managers

- What are the mental models (i.e., fundamental beliefs and understandings) that appear to be guiding your firm's strategies?
- What are the sources of these mental models?
- Are there any problems associated with these mental models? For example, what inaccuracies or biases do they include? Have we resisted changing our beliefs, even though changes in the larger competitive environment might be suggesting the need to change beliefs?

Suggestions for Further Reading

Additionally, links to further resources online—such as cases, articles, and videos—can be found on the book's website, www.routledge.com/textbooks/Duhaime.

Ashby, M. D., & Miles, S. A. (Eds.) 2002. *Leaders Talk Leadership*. New York: Oxford University Press.

Charan, R., & Useem, J. 2002. Why companies fail. *Fortune*, May 27: 50–62.

Donaldson, G., & Lorsch, J. W. 1983. *Decision Making at the Top*. New York: Basic Books.

Finkelstein, S. 2003. *Why Smart Executives Fail: And What You Can Learn from Their Mistakes*. New York: Portfolio.

Freedman, M., with Tregoe, B. B. 2003. *The Art and Discipline of Strategic Leadership*. New York: McGraw-Hill.

Gardner, H. 1995. *Leading Minds: An Anatomy of Leadership*. New York: BasicBooks.

Hamel, G., & Prahalad, C. K. 1994. *Competing for the Future*. Boston: Harvard Business School Press.

Hartley, R. F. 2000. *Management Mistakes and Successes* (6th ed.). New York: John Wiley & Sons, Inc.

Senge, P. M. 1990. *The Fifth Discipline: The Art and Practice of Learning Organization.* New York: Doubleday/ Currency.

Wren, D. A., & Greenwood, R. G. 1998. *Management Innovators: The People and Ideas That Have Shaped Modern Business.* New York: Oxford University Press.

Appendix: Mapping Mental Models to Understand Strategic Decision Making

Mental models are unobservable; we have no direct process for obtaining an understanding of another individual's attitudes, beliefs, or understandings. Yet, we can construct "cognitive maps" of mental models by analyzing what we or others do, say, or write that can serve as powerful tools for understanding why we engage in some behaviors and not others. Many business researchers have used a variety of techniques for mapping managers' mental models to understand why their firms pursue some strategies and not others.

Here, we will examine only one simple, yet effective, method for constructing cognitive maps. We use this mapping technique to illustrate the link between managers' mental models and the strategies of their firms. The two examples we offer provide compelling evidence of the powerful influence of managerial thinking on decision making and the formulation of firm strategies.

The cognitive mapping methodology illustrated here involves content analysis of written documents. The written materials used in these examples are the letters to shareholders taken from firms' annual reports. Annual reports are a convenient data source for the analysis of managerial thinking because all publicly held companies provide these reports to their shareholders, so this data source is widely available and updated annually.

Content analysis of annual reports has been criticized because annual reports are believed to be biased and written to frame issues in the best possible light for public relations purposes. Although annual reports are no doubt written in a way that portrays management as favorably as possible, content analysis of annual reports can still be useful because managers cannot (or should not) intentionally mislead shareholders and because the material almost certainly reflects the views of top managers. Furthermore, analysis of annual reports can be supplemented by content analysis of other company documents as well as the texts of speeches and interviews given by the chief executive officer.

The mapping technique we employ involves constructing simple maps by counting executives' use of key words. The goal of this content analysis technique is to identify key factors or issues emphasized in the thinking of top executives. The implicit hypothesis is that the thinking of executives—as revealed in their use (or lack of use) of key words—will be reflected in their firms' strategies. So, for example, if a particular firm's CEO mentions research and development over and over again in his or her letter to shareholders, then we can hypothesize that the firm emphasizes R&D, possibly spends more on R&D, and develops more new products than other competing firms whose managers do not mention research and development as often in their letters to shareholders.

Content analysis using this word count technique has been employed to examine the relationship between thinking and action in a variety of fields, including not just management, but also journalism, political science, and sociology.

Illustration #1: Two Different Leaders; Same Company

After Carleton "Carly" Fiorina was abruptly fired as CEO of Hewlett-Packard, the company selected Mark Hurd as the new CEO. Many articles have examined the differences in the two executives' management philosophies and approaches, but nearly all articles agree that Hurd has focused much more than Fiorina on efficiency and profitability. Using the word count technique to analyze the letters to shareholders written by these two executives, can we find evidence that this difference in strategies is tied to their management beliefs? To explore this question, we obtained the letters to shareholders from Hewlett Packard's annual reports for 2000, a year when Carly Fiorina was CEO, and for 2005, a year when Mark Hurd was CEO. We then counted the number of times each CEO used the following sets of words: 1) product and customer, 2) revenue and growth, 3) technology, research, development, innovation, and 4) cost, efficiency, and profit, and we then adjusted the results to reflect that the two letters were not the same length.

The results reveal different patterns of word use (and thus may reflect very different thinking about the management of Hewlett Packard). As shown in Exhibit 3.4, Fiorina used the words "product" and "customer" almost twice as often—43 times, compared to Hurd, who used these words 28 times. Similarly, Fiorina used the words "revenue" and "growth" almost twice as many times as Hurd; 74 times versus 49 times. Both used the words "technology," "research," "development," and "innovation" about the same number of times; 15 for Fiorina and 12 for Hurd. On the other hand, Hurd used the words "cost," "efficiency," and "profit" nearly three times as often as Fiorina; 28 times versus 10 times.

The results of this very simple application of the word count technique suggest that Fiorina was more focused on expansion and growth than Hurd, who certainly appears to be focused more on costs and efficiency. Perhaps it is no surprise that, given her emphasis on growth, Fiorina pushed Hewlett Packard to acquire Compaq Computer in what was at that time the largest technology acquisition ever. Hurd, on the other hand, has been praised for improving Hewlett Packard's profit margins and overall performance through his emphases on cutting costs and improving efficiency.[44]

Exhibit 3.4 An Illustration of Mapping Mental Models Using the Word Count Technique to Examine the Beliefs of Two CEOs of the Same Company

	Number of times CEOs used a particular set of words in letters to shareholders			
	Product and Customer	Revenue and Growth	Technology, Research, Development, and Innovation	Cost, Efficiency, and Profit
Carly Fiorina	43	74	15	10
Mark Hurd	28	49	12	28

Illustration #2: Two Different Leaders; Two Companies

For most banks, 2006 was a good year. But, by 2007, many banks began to experience major credit losses as customers, especially homeowners, began defaulting on their loans. The ensuing banking crisis soon spread to other sectors of the economy, and we have since experienced one of the worse worldwide recessions since the Great Depression of the 1930s.

Yet not all banks suffered equally dramatic performance downturns. Many banks failed entirely, many banks received large infusions of capital from the U.S. government in order to avoid bankruptcy, many weak banks were forced to be acquired by stronger banks, and a few banks were able to weather the storm with only a modest decline in performance. Could examining the mental models of banking CEOs allow us to have predicted which banks would have suffered the most significant declines due to poor credit management policies?

Using the word count technique, we examined the 2006 letters to shareholders written by the CEOs of two large banks, Citi, the largest U.S. bank, which experienced one of the worst performance downturns in the banking industry, and JP Morgan Chase, also a very large bank, but one that has now emerged from the crisis relatively unscathed.[45] We counted the number of times the CEOs of these banks used the following sets of words: 1) profit, performance, return, and equity, 2) growth, and 3) loans, risk, default, conservative, subprime, and quality, and then, as in the Hewlett Packard illustration above, we adjusted the results to take into account that the two letters were not the same length.

The results of this word count technique are quite striking. As shown in Exhibit 3.5, the CEOs did not differ significantly in their use of the first group of words (i.e., profit, performance, return, and equity), with the Citibank CEO, Charles Prince, using these words about 26 times and the JP Morgan Chase CEO, James Dimon, using these words 36 times.

On the other hand, the Citibank CEO used the word "growth" 44 times compared to the JP Morgan Chase CEO's use of this word only 14 times. Even more striking, the Citibank CEO used the words that all had to do with credit quality (i.e., loans, risk, default, conservative, subprime, and quality) only 11 times compared to the 67 times the JP Morgan Chase CEO used these words. Clearly, the CEO of Citibank placed relatively more emphasis on growth, while the JP Morgan Chase CEO placed relatively more emphasis on credit quality.

While this does not demonstrate or "prove" causality, it certainly suggests that the leadership of Citibank was placing more emphasis on growth than the leadership of JP Morgan Chase, and

Exhibit 3.5 An Illustration of Mapping Mental Models Using the Word Count Technique to Examine the Beliefs of Two Banking Industry CEOs

	Number of times CEOs used a particular set of words in letters to shareholders		
	Profit, Performance, Return, and Equity	*Growth*	*Loans, Risk, Default, Conservative, Subprime, and Quality*
Citi	26	44	11
JP Morgan Chase	36	14	67

that this emphasis on growth could possibly account for Citibank taking on riskier and less credit-worthy loans, while the leadership of JP Morgan Chase may have placed much more emphasis on credit quality so that it incurred a less risky loan portfolio, and, as a consequence, faced fewer foreclosures during the recent severe economic downturn.

These are obviously very simple illustrations of just one technique that has been employed to map mental models. While much more careful and detailed analysis would be required: 1) to fully understand and document the thinking of the four executives highlighted here and 2) to verify or "prove" a linkage between their mental models and thinking about management and their company's strategy. Still, in each case, the striking differences between the executives' patterns of word use and their firms strategies and performance outcomes suggest an important and powerful linkage between thought (i.e., mental models about management) and action (i.e., firm strategies).

Chapter 4

Frameworks for the Analysis of Industry Environments

In terms of the model of strategic management introduced in Chapter 1, Chapter 2 defined the concept of competitive advantage and described the ways in which competitive advantage can be developed and maintained, and Chapter 3 emphasized the importance of general managers in strategic decision making. Chapters 4 and 5 begin our consideration of industry environments, the competitive arenas in which firms and businesses compete.

As illustrated in Exhibit 4.1, managers' beliefs and understandings of their firms' business environments are important because they influence decisions about business definition and positioning and business strategy, topics covered in later chapters. Managers who develop insights about, or novel understandings of, their firms' industries may be able to uniquely define or position their firms or formulate particularly effective business strategies that can lead to the development of competitive advantage. Thus, the overall objectives of this chapter are to introduce you to ways of thinking about the characteristics of industries as well as ways of analyzing the competitiveness of industry environments.

Chapter Objectives

The specific objectives of this chapter are to:

- Develop your understanding of industries, the competitive environments in which firms offer products or services in an effort to compete for resources, customers, sales revenues, and profits.
- Introduce and illustrate SWOT Analysis and the Five Forces Model, two of the most commonly used industry analysis tools.
- Assess the strengths and limitations of SWOT Analysis and the Five Forces Model as tools for analyzing industries.

What Is an Industry?

Industry is a taken-for-granted concept—the term is widely used in the world of business, so it is easy to assume that everyone shares the same understanding of the word's meaning, when that is not true. So, before beginning a discussion of industry analysis, we will clarify the

Exhibit 4.1 Managers' Beliefs, Strategic Decisions, and Their Influence on Performance and Competitive Advantage

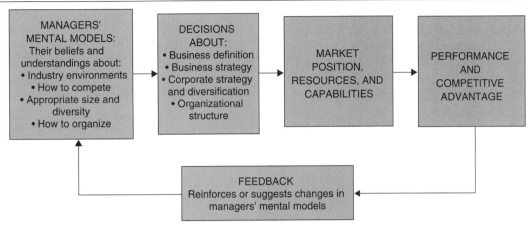

meaning of this important concept. When we write about an industry, we are referring to a group of companies that share similar customers, offer similar products and services, and use similar technologies to provide those products and services.

Given this definition of an industry, it is important to emphasize a couple of points. First, an industry is not an "entity." It is neither a structure, like a building or machine that you can touch or hold, nor is it an organization like a company or a corporation that has a legal charter or definition. Instead, an industry is largely a cognitive and social construction—firms and businesses become a part of an industry because their managers and external parties believe or perceive them to be a part of the industry or to share common characteristics with other firms.

Moreover, this definition of an industry also recognizes the dynamic nature of the environments in which business firms compete. Chapter 5 will emphasize that the boundaries of industries—far from remaining fixed over time—are quite fluid as customer demographics change, as new technologies are created and exploited, as new products and services are developed, and as new firms enter and as other firms exit. Consistent with the book's emphasis on strategic change, it is important to view industries not as static phenomena, but rather as dynamic "competitive spaces" or arenas.

Why Analyze Industry Environments?

When a roomful of executives is asked, "Is it fair to say that your industry is competitive?" a resounding "Yes!" is usually heard. This tends to happen regardless of industry, the size of the executives' firms or businesses, whether the companies are domestic or global enterprises, or even whether they are businesses or not-for-profit organizations. Indeed, all organizations face competition—for resources, customers, sales revenues, and profits. All organizations also face uncertain and turbulent environments. And, given the rapidly changing and competitive nature of today's business and economic landscape, never has it been more important for managers to position their organizations strategically in order to compete successfully in the future.

Successful positioning, or what we call *business definition* (a topic we take up in Chapter 6) requires that managers thoroughly understand the dynamics of their industries, the trends in their firms' external environments, and the basic economics of their firms' markets—in short, managers must know how to analyze their industries. Once they have developed understandings—mental models—of their industry environments, managers must then craft the strategies that will effectively position or define their firms in their industries. They must also formulate and implement strategies aimed at building unique capabilities and competencies that will provide them with competitive advantage (all topics considered in Chapters 7, 8, and 9).

Probably the most noteworthy characteristic of industry environments is the great extent to which they can vary. Some industries are highly competitive and consequently not very profitable on average, while other industries are relatively less competitive and consequently enjoy much higher levels of average profitability. Some industries are mature, with growth coming primarily from replacement purchases or growth in the economy; other industries are only now emerging and beginning to experience rapid growth as large numbers of customers purchase the products or services for the first time.

Rapidly growing markets tend to be less competitive and often attract entry by new or existing firms. Emerging industries will provide managers and their firms with considerable discretion, opportunities to pursue a variety of different strategies, and even room for making mistakes. On the other hand, mature, concentrated industries provide competitors with very little breathing room; one firm's strategies or mistakes can have significant ramifications for the entire industry. For example, one firm's price reductions can set off an industry-wide price war that reduces the margins of all companies in the industry. At the same time, many industries offer examples of firms that can do very well in spite of a hostile industry environment—Southwest Airlines in the airline industry is just one example—again, demonstrating that structural or economic approaches to strategy cannot completely explain variations in firm performance.

How Much Does Industry Matter?[1]

When an industry with a reputation for bad economics meets a manager with a reputation for excellence, it's usually the industry that leaves with its reputation intact.

Warren Buffett

It should come as no surprise that firm performance levels depend a great deal on the attractiveness of the industries in which firms compete. Exhibit 4.2 shows the median return on assets of several different industries, including computer, airline, beverage, and pharmaceutical industries, illustrating the wide variation in average industry performance levels. For example, aside from a few outliers, nearly all companies in the pharmaceutical industry enjoy high performance levels that would be the envy of many firms in lower-performing industries.

Just how important is the influence of industry membership on firm performance? In other words, how advantageous is it to be in a high-performing industry, and will a firm in a low-performing industry be at a serious disadvantage relative to firms in other industries? Research evidence suggests that the influence of industry membership on firm performance is very strong.

Exhibit 4.2 Average Return on Assets in Different Industries

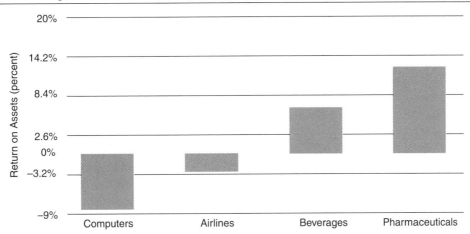

For almost any sample of firms, a regression equation using industry performance data (for example, average industry return on assets) to explain firm performance such as

$$ROA_{firm} = f(ROA_{industry})$$

will yield an r² of about .20. In other words, the variation in just this one variable—average industry performance—will explain a great deal (approximately 20 percent) of the variation in the performance of any single firm in that industry. In fact, no other variable or set of variables will consistently explain so much variation in firm performance.

Some economists seize on such findings to argue that industry is "all that matters,"[2] yet, as discussed in Chapter 1 and reiterated above, such an industry "structuralist" argument is incomplete for several reasons.[3] First, performance can vary widely from year to year. For example, Dell enjoyed an ROA of 14.5 percent in 1999, but had a ROA of –13.4 percent in 2009. Similarly, the entire computer industry enjoyed significantly higher profitability in 1999 than it did in 2009, reflecting many economic and market forces, but also reflecting changing *company* fortunes.

Moreover some industries are much more cyclical than others, meaning that average industry performance levels are heavily impacted by the macroeconomic business cycle. Firms in the motor vehicle and semiconductor industries have enjoyed some very good years when the economy has been strong and demand has been high, while the weaker economic environment of 2008 and 2009 tended to exacerbate competition in both industries and depress profits. The future performance of firms in these industries will depend, of course, on a variety of factors, including intraindustry rivalry, but macroeconomic factors including gas prices, exchange rates, and global demand will continue to play a major role in determining the performance of firms in these industries.

Finally, industry averages also mask considerable variation in firm performance levels *within the same industry*, and some firms will perform well or perform poorly regardless of the average profitability of their industry. For example, Apple's ROA was nearly five times greater than the ROA of the computer industry in 2009. Southwest Airlines is again a good example of a firm that consistently out-performs its competitors in the airline industry. Coca-Cola's ROA in 2009 was more than twice the average of its industry ROA, and the highest performing pharmaceutical company enjoyed a ROA that was nearly three times the industry average ROA.

In fact, looking across all industries, research has found that variations in average *intraindustry* profitability are approximately six times greater than the variations in average *interindustry* profitability.[4] In other words, researchers have found that the difference between the performance of the highest- and lowest-performing firms in any particular industry will be six times greater than the difference between the performance of the highest- and lowest-performing industries! This evidence again underscores the important point that industry is not all that matters when looking for explanations for differences in firm performance.

In spite of these significant *intraindustry* differences in performance, Warren Buffett's comment at the beginning of this section still holds a great deal of truth, and given the choice of doing business in an industry that enjoys a consistently high level of profitability or doing business in an industry that suffers consistently low levels of profitability, most managers would opt to see their firms compete in the former. And all managers must develop beliefs and understandings—mental models—about how their firms should be positioned and how they should compete that reflect the characteristics of their industry environments.

What is needed, then, are models or tools for assessing the *relative* attractiveness of industries. Such models or tools are useful in developing beliefs and understandings of the factors that will tend to make an industry more or less attractive. Once managers come to have beliefs and understandings about their industry environments, these same beliefs and understandings are fundamentally important in guiding the decisions managers must make about business definition and the development of competitive strategies.

This chapter introduces two widely used tools for analyzing industries, SWOT Analysis and the Five Forces Model. Both frameworks are well known by academics and industry practitioners alike, and both frameworks have enjoyed widespread application in the business world. In fact, the managers of almost every business firm, whether large or small, have at one time or another conducted a SWOT Analysis or analyzed their industry using the Five Forces framework.

SWOT Analysis

What It Is and How It Is Used

SWOT Analysis has been used for many years to analyze industry environments. Not only can SWOT Analysis be used to analyze firms' external, environmental opportunities and threats, but it can also be used for analyzing firms' internal strengths and weaknesses (and therefore to assess whether firms are likely to enjoy a competitive advantage, the focus of Chapter 2). Hence, the acronym SWOT, derived from ***Strengths***, ***Weaknesses***, ***Opportunities***, **and *Threats***. SWOT Analysis is performed in two steps. First, managers thoroughly evaluate their *firm's* (internal) strengths and weaknesses and its *environmental* (external) opportunities and threats. In the second step of SWOT Analysis, managers use the evaluation developed in

Exhibit 4.3 The Strengths, Weaknesses, Opportunities, and Threats Matrix

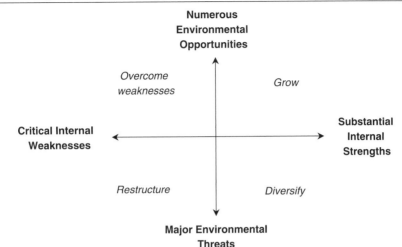

the first step to place the firm into one of the four quadrants of the SWOT grid or matrix as shown in Exhibit 4.3.

For example, if SWOT Analysis revealed that a firm enjoyed many internal strengths and few internal weaknesses, and many environmental opportunities and few environmental threats, the firm would be placed in the upper right quadrant on the SWOT matrix. Likewise, a firm with many internal weaknesses and many environmental threats would be placed in the lower left quadrant of the matrix.

As illustrated in Figure 4.3, SWOT Analysis is also prescriptive, and different broad categories of strategies are associated with each of the four SWOT quadrants. For example, if a firm's managers determine that it has both considerable internal strengths and many external opportunities, then SWOT suggests that the firm should "grow" through merger and acquisition or internal development of new business opportunities. On the other hand, if a firm's managers determine that it has internal weaknesses but external opportunities, then SWOT recommends that the firm "overcome weaknesses" by engaging in joint ventures, vertical integration, or unrelated diversification. Similar sets of recommendations are associated with the other two SWOT quadrants.

Use of SWOT Analysis is very straightforward, and this ease of use is one of its great strengths. In addition, SWOT can provide a very helpful framework for getting managers to think constructively about their firms' external environments and internal strengths and weaknesses. SWOT is particularly helpful as a tool for beginning company or business unit planning discussions. Nearly all managers will have assumptions, beliefs, or understandings—mental models—about their firm's or business unit's strengths, weaknesses, opportunities, or threats, so SWOT Analysis can be a very effective tool for making this thinking explicit and "getting it out on the table." Rarely will managers agree on their assessments of strengths, weaknesses, opportunities, or threats—reflecting the idiosyncratic nature of managers' mental models—so SWOT Analysis can also help managers identify areas of concern and fundamental disagreement.

Often, these differences of opinion can lead to insights or suggest new opportunities while also helping organizations identify sources of concern that can be addressed in planning processes.

Limitations and Drawbacks of SWOT Analysis

Although it is certainly helpful in stimulating thinking and discussion about firms and their external environments, SWOT Analysis also has some significant drawbacks as a tool for industry analysis. Perhaps the most serious limitation of SWOT is its subjectivity. Evaluating the position of a firm along the two SWOT dimensions will be quite subjective, and managers attempting to use SWOT are likely to encounter widespread disagreement among individuals within the same firm about the firm's position along these dimensions.

Like the problem of one individual seeing "lemons" where another sees "lemonade," firms using SWOT Analysis will find managers disagreeing about whether a particular phenomenon in the firm's external environment is an opportunity or a threat. In fact, almost any event will offer a particular firm some opportunities while also posing some threats. A new technology, for example, can offer a firm the opportunity to develop a new product or it can represent a threat if the firm lacks the ability to develop or exploit that new technology. As noted above, however, these differences of opinion can be very helpful in planning discussions, giving companies and business units opportunities to address previously unacknowledged issues and questions.

Assessments of environmental opportunities and threats will also be biased by managers' perceptions of their firms' strengths and weaknesses. Managers of firms with many strengths are more likely to view environmental phenomena as opportunities, while the managers of firms with many internal weaknesses may view these same environmental phenomena as threats. Such interpretations will no doubt influence the strategies of these firms.

If one firm's managers agree that their firm has a major opportunity while its competitors view this same phenomenon as a threat, the managers of the first firm are much more likely to pursue this opportunity while their competitors are more likely to take a defensive approach. For example, based on their organization's R&D strengths, managers might conclude that a rapid technological change offers their firm an important opportunity to develop new products, but the managers of a competing firm might see this same rapid rate of change as a threat. The first firm is much more likely to take an aggressive or proactive posture with respect to that industry change.

Another drawback of SWOT Analysis is that its use is likely to yield few clear-cut recommendations. Very few firms are fortunate enough to have *only* external opportunities and internal strengths and very few firms are so unfortunate to have *only* external threats and internal weaknesses. In fact, almost all firms are going to face some combination of threats and opportunities in their external environments and they are also likely to possess some combination of internal strengths and weaknesses. So instead of providing managers with an obvious or clear-cut set of recommendations, SWOT Analysis is likely to suggest many contradictory strategies.

To summarize, then, SWOT Analysis will almost always encourage good thinking and dialogue about the firm and its industry, and managers using SWOT Analysis will almost always be able to list many strengths, weaknesses, opportunities, and threats. SWOT Analysis also brings together not only the external analysis of a firm's industry environment, but also provides an internal analysis of the firm's internal strengths and weaknesses. As a result, it can be very helpful in assessing a firm's potential for achieving or maintaining a competitive advantage. And, as noted above, management discussions employing SWOT Analysis will often help uncover issues, opportunities, and questions that have not previously been addressed. At the same time, the subjective nature of SWOT Analysis is a major drawback. As a result, managers often employ additional industry analysis tools, and we next consider one of the most common.

The Five Forces Model

Given both the positive and negative aspects of SWOT Analysis, Harvard Business School professor Michael Porter sought to fill this void first with a now-classic *Harvard Business Review* article[5] and then with his best-selling book, *Competitive Strategy*.[6] Porter's work offered a new tool for industry analysis that has enjoyed considerable popularity among business executives and has received a good deal of interest from the academic community as well.

The **Five Forces Model** is based on the structure-conduct-performance framework of industrial organization economics. This framework suggests that the structure of an industry (e.g., the number and relative size of firms in the industry, barriers to entry, etc.) will have an impact on the conduct or competitive behavior of the firms in that industry (e.g., prices charged, rate of innovation, etc.). Industries characterized by a relatively small number of firms and industries that allow incumbent firms to erect entry barriers to keep new firms from entering the market will tend to be less competitive than industries that are populated by more firms. Firms in these more concentrated industries can charge higher prices than they would be able to in more competitive industries.

The second part of the structure-conduct-performance framework suggests that the conduct of firms will influence the average performance of firms in that industry. Logically, if the structure of a particular industry allows firms in that industry to charge higher prices, then those firms will enjoy higher performance than would be the case if the industry were more competitive.

The implicit aim of industrial organization economics has been to understand the structural characteristics that allow industries to deviate from the perfectly competitive "ideal." Porter's model adopted the structure-conduct-performance framework, but Porter's work departed from the traditional industrial organization economics perspective in two significant ways. First, he recognized that if firms could either make their industries less competitive or shield themselves from the competitive forces in their industries, then they could enjoy higher performance. Second, Porter's approach identified and described five specific "forces" that could be used to evaluate the structural characteristics of an industry. For each of the five forces, Porter identified sets of factors that would determine the presence and power of the force in a particular industry environment.

The Five Forces Model is almost always depicted as shown in Exhibit 4.4. Exhibit 4.4 also provides a comprehensive list of factors for evaluating the power or intensity of each of the five forces. The logic behind the model is straightforward: *As the intensity of the forces increases, the industry environment becomes more hostile and overall industry profitability will decline.* In the following sections, the five forces and the sets of factors associated with each of the five forces are examined in more detail.

Exhibit 4.4 The Five Forces Model

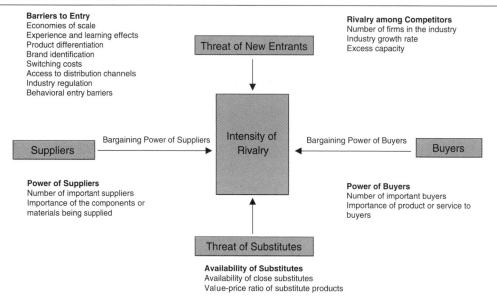

Barriers to Entry
Economies of scale
Experience and learning effects
Product differentiation
Brand identification
Switching costs
Access to distribution channels
Industry regulation
Behavioral entry barriers

Rivalry among Competitors
Number of firms in the industry
Industry growth rate
Excess capacity

Threat of New Entrants

Bargaining Power of Suppliers

Suppliers

Intensity of
Rivalry

Bargaining Power of Buyers

Buyers

Power of Suppliers
Number of important suppliers
Importance of the components or
materials being supplied

Power of Buyers
Number of important buyers
Importance of product or service to
buyers

Threat of Substitutes

Availability of Substitutes
Availability of close substitutes
Value-price ratio of substitute products

The Threat of Entry

If new rivals can enter an industry relatively easily, then the industry will probably be more competitive and it is less likely that the industry will enjoy a high level of average profitability. For example, the lack of entry barriers allowed retailers like Wal-Mart and Target to become major sellers of toys. As a result of their entry and aggressive pricing strategies into this retail segment, longtime toy retailers FAO Schwarz and KB Toys have been forced into bankruptcy. Thus, it is desirable for incumbent firms—those already in an industry or market segment—to erect barriers to prevent other firms from entering. What factors can serve as entry barriers, minimizing the threat of new firms entering an industry? In general, four types of factors can make entry less likely.

The first set of factors can be thought of as cost barriers. For example, if incumbent firms enjoy scale economies, the benefits of experience and learning effects, or privileged access to key raw materials or technologies, then potential entrants will necessarily enter the industry at a serious cost disadvantage. Economies of scale exist when unit costs decline with increases in production as fixed costs are spread over a larger volume of output. Larger firms that can realize economies of scale can enjoy significant cost advantages over smaller rivals. The concept of minimum efficient scale (MES) is closely related to the concept of economies of scale and refers to the level of production that is required in order to produce at the lowest level of average unit cost. Firms operating at MES are operating at a level of output that allows them to enjoy the lowest possible unit costs, as illustrated in Exhibit 4.5.

The concepts of scale economies and MES are important because firms that do not produce at a volume of production to achieve minimum efficient scale necessarily incur a cost penalty relative to competitors with higher levels of output. Similarly, any firm that hopes to enter an

Exhibit 4.5 The Concepts of Scale Economies and Minimum Efficient Scale

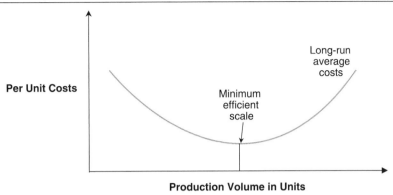

industry must either enter at the level of MES or risk facing a serious cost disadvantage relative to any incumbent firms that are already operating at the MES level. Exhibit 4.6 shows the minimum efficient scale estimated for several key industries, and also shows the cost penalty incurred by firms that operate at only half of the level of minimum efficient scale.

As Exhibit 4.6 suggests, scale economies often offer firms operating at the level of MES a significant cost advantage over other firms or new entrants that are forced to operate at levels

Exhibit 4.6 Minimum Efficient Scale in Several Industries

	Minimum Efficient Scale as Percentage of U.S. Output	Percentage Increases in Unit Cost at Half MES
Flour mills	0.7	3.0
Bread baking	0.3	7.5
Printing paper	4.4	9.0
Sulfuric acid	3.7	1.0
Synthetic fibers	11.1	7.0
Auto tires	3.8	5.0
Bricks	0.3	25.0
Detergents	2.4	2.5
Turbogenerators	23.0	n.a.
Diesel engines	21–30.0	4–28.0
Computers	15.0	8.0
Automobiles	11.0	6.0
Commercial aircraft	10.0	20.0

Source: Scherer, F. M., 1980. *Industrial Market Structure and Economic Performance* (2nd ed.). Chicago: Rand McNally; U.S. Department of Commerce, Washington, D.C.

of output below the MES level. For example, firms manufacturing commercial aircraft must have plants that produce one-tenth of the total market in order to operate at minimum efficient scale. And, plants that are only half that size may have considerably higher costs, as much as 20 percent higher. The same is true for beer producers. Though many successful microbreweries (defined as producing less than 10,000 barrels per year) have found attractive market niches, nearly all the breweries owned by the major beer producers are much, much larger. In fact, to realize scale economies and operate at minimum efficient scale, a brewery needs to be capable of producing at least four million barrels per year.[7] The significant scale economies that exist in these industries probably explain the small number of large firms that dominate these industries.

Due to the shape of the long run average cost curve, scale economies are less of a factor in some other industries, however, so firms can enter these industries at a fairly small scale and not suffer a serious cost disadvantage. Smaller firms and new entrants to an industry can also compete successfully against larger competitors by finding attractive market niches (like the microbreweries) or by developing innovative production and distribution methods that allow them to match their larger competitors' cost advantages. For example, Amazon has almost none of the facilities and inventory costs of bricks-and-mortar bookstores like Barnes and Noble and Borders. Dell also realized significant cost savings by adopting its "Dell Direct" approach to sales and distribution of its PCs and other products.

In later chapters, we will also focus on the problems—"diseconomies"—associated with large size. Firms in many industries encounter additional costs as their size increases. For example, in spite of the wave of consolidation that is sweeping through the banking industry, research evidence suggests that smaller banks (those with total assets between $50 million and $500 million) are more efficient and profitable than medium or large banks (those with total assets greater than $500 million).[8] Similarly, during the recent recession, the big airline companies in the U.S., AMR (parent of American Airlines) and United Airlines, have certainly taken bigger hits than the smaller airlines. American Airlines went from a net profit of $504 million in 2007 to a $2.8 billion loss in 2008, a 510 percent change from the year before.[9] United Airlines lost $5.3 billion in the fiscal year of 2008.[10]

Sheer size can also give a firm a cost advantage, because often these very large firms can afford to put tremendous resources into innovation and leap ahead of competitors. Take Samsung, for example. Often thought of as an older Asian electronics company, many people forget that Samsung has long been the largest maker of computer memory chips and flash memory chips, and in 2008 it became the world's largest TV maker and recently became the second largest cell phone producer. The company's scale allows it to spend more funds on innovation, so that it can launch new products like its line of premium, LCD TVs with ultra-thin screens.[11] This ability to innovate creates barriers for smaller firms trying to compete, especially in the fast changing world of consumer electronics.

Cost advantages that incumbent firms enjoy due to experience or learning are another type of cost barrier. The concept of experience or learning effects suggests that as a firm's cumulative output doubles, unit costs of production will fall by some set percentage because the business is continually learning how to operate more efficiently and effectively. This experience effect, also called the "learning curve" effect, has been documented in a wide range of manufacturing and service activities in many different industries.

The concept of experience effects can be seen in the production of the Boeing 767 aircraft. The forward cabin on the first 767 required 6,000 hours and 47 days to construct. In addition, more than 12,000 production and design changes were made during the course of assembling the first 767. By the time Boeing had assembled the 70th 767, however, far fewer hours were required and only 500 production changes needed to be made.[12]

Cost economies due to scale and learning are not guaranteed and do not occur without management effort. Products and services must be designed to capture economies of scale. Production and distribution must be centralized, and engineering, research and development, and marketing must also be coordinated in order to achieve economies of scale. And, managers must also balance the efficiencies that come with increased centralization and coordination with the loss of motivational and customer service advantages that come with decentralizing many of these activities.

A second set of factors that can minimize entry includes the marketing and distribution advantages enjoyed by incumbents and switching costs. For example, if incumbent firms enjoy brand loyalty, then potential entrants will have to take satisfied customers away from products or services they are presently using and enjoying. Similarly, if incumbents enjoy access to retail distribution channels, such as grocery store shelf space, then potential entrants will have to convince retailers to provide them with shelf space or similar opportunities to distribute their products. Grocers and other retailers understand all too well the important control they have over access to customers, and they often charge companies wanting to introduce new products thousands of dollars in "stocking fees" to place these new products on their shelves.

The credit card market offers some interesting illustrations of ways companies have tried to prevent entry by limiting access to distribution. Until 2001, MasterCard and Visa did not allow member banks to issue American Express, Discover, or any other competing credit cards. As a result, American Express and Discover had a great deal of difficulty getting banks to offer their cards since this would have required banks to drop their MasterCard or Visa franchises. A federal court ruled, however, that these policies and bylaws were a violation of U.S. antitrust laws.[13] In a more recent case, retailers, led by Wal-Mart, challenged MasterCard and Visa policies that required any retailer that accepted their credit cards to accept their debit cards as well. In addition, MasterCard and Visa had informally encouraged customers to sign for their debit card transactions rather than use their PIN numbers, since that required debit card transactions to be completed in the same way as credit card transactions and at much higher fees to the retailers than PIN number transactions, which were processed through different and far lower-cost clearinghouses. In a settlement reached with retailers, MasterCard and Visa have now agreed to reduce their fees on debit card signature transactions.[14]

In addition, if customers of incumbent firms will incur switching costs by buying products or services from another firm, they will be more hesitant to shift their allegiance from an incumbent firm to a new entrant. Although not quite as relevant in recent times, switching from personal computers or laptops using Microsoft's Windows operating system to Apple's Macintosh system is an example of a switching cost. People have to incur the cost of the actual computer or laptop itself as well as the time and effort it takes to learn how to use a Mac. As Apple is making its applications more compatible with other Windows-only applications, people are finding the switch much easier, and this is boosting the market share of Macs. Another example of a switching cost can be seen with cell phone carriers. Usually carrier companies charge a high fee for canceling a contract in hopes of reducing the number of customers who switch companies.

Government restrictions are another set of factors that can minimize entry. In spite of considerable deregulation over the last two decades, many industries still remain heavily regulated and some firms in the communications and media industries must receive regulatory approval before they can offer services to customers. And, it appears likely that new government regulations will be a fact of life for firms in the health care and banking industries.

Deregulation is often viewed as opening industries to more free-market competition and is also often accompanied by a greater threat of new entry. Yet, this is not always the case. For example, the airline industry has now been deregulated for three decades, but many start-up airlines have been unable to reach potential passengers traveling to and from East Coast cities due to an important structural barrier—namely, the lack of access to boarding gates and takeoff and landing slots at eastern airports.[15] Similarly, major U.S. airlines have had difficulty expanding into Asian markets, which are still heavily regulated by governments that have been reluctant to allow entry to U.S. carriers.[16]

Finally, a fourth set of entry barriers, referred to as "behavioral" entry barriers, can be very effective in limiting entry. For example, incumbent firms might maintain low prices in order to discourage entry into what appears to be a low-profit industry. Or, incumbents might signal that they will lower prices considerably if another firm enters the industry. Other types of "signaling" are also common. For example, firms often announce that they are planning to add additional capacity. Such a move may be aimed at discouraging entry by signaling to potential entrants that the industry could develop excess capacity that would push down prices and profits. Or, companies could announce that they are about to unveil the next generation of a product, so that potential entrants would be concerned that they would be entering the industry with an obsolete product. Intel has used many of these behavioral tactics very effectively over the years as it has built its dominance in the market for certain types of microprocessors.[17]

Signaling can often accomplish legally the same goals as collusive behavior that would violate antitrust laws. For example, the managers of one firm in an industry can announce that they intend to lower prices in an attempt to ward off entry by other firms. The managers of other firms can quickly follow the lead of the first firm's managers and also lower their prices. Such signaling behavior is perfectly legal and relatively common. On the other hand, if the managers of these same firms explicitly colluded by meeting in a hotel room or by telephoning one another to discuss pricing policies, then they would be engaging in illegal activities.

The Threat of Substitute Products and Services

The second of the five forces is the threat of substitute products and services. If substitute products or services are readily available, then firms in the industry are likely to suffer lower average profitability. A classic example of a substitute product is the personal computer for the typewriter, or the use of aluminum versus the use of steel in manufacturing automobile engines and other automotive parts. More contemporary examples include teleconferencing for business travel, e-mail instead of letters (i.e., using the post office), and DVRs like TiVo for videocassette recorders at home.

The extent to which products and services are substitutes for each other will depend on the value-price ratios of the two products. Two products or services might offer the same value or satisfy the same need or desire, but the extent to which they will be true substitutes for each other will also depend on the relative prices of the two products or services. For example, when DVD players were first introduced, their price was much higher than it is today. This meant that DVD players were viewed as luxury products that only a few consumers chose to buy. For most of the public, the high price of DVD players meant that the value-price ratio of going to a movie theater or keeping an old VCR was much better than purchasing a DVD player. As prices of DVD players have fallen, however, their value-price ratios have become much more comparable to movie theaters and VCRs, and they are now truly substitute products. The availability and comparable value-price ratios of first VCRs and now DVD players, are surely two of the reasons why movie theater attendance has been growing on average by only 2 to 3 percent over the last decade and has even fallen in some years in spite of a wave of new theater construction.[18]

It is important to distinguish between *substitute* and *competing* products and services. In the Five Forces Model, "substitute products and services" refers to alternative products and services that can fulfill the same function (personal computer for typewriter), not to another competitor's offering of the same product or service. A cereal manufacturer and a fast food company serving breakfast are offering substitute products that compete with each other, but they are offering customers different products. On the other hand, two cereal companies making competing cereal products are "rivals" manufacturing the same product— breakfast cereal.

The Power of Suppliers

The third force in the Five Forces Model is the power of suppliers. If the suppliers to an industry have enough power, they may be able to extract higher prices for critical components, thereby reducing average industry profitability. Though many factors influence the power of suppliers (see Exhibit 4.6), two factors are generally the most critical in determining supplier power. First, if only a few suppliers of a particular component exist relative to the number of buyers, then those suppliers will tend to have greater bargaining power. Second, if the component is a critical one, or if it incorporates proprietary technologies that are only available from one supplier or a very few suppliers, then those suppliers will generally have greater power.

The personal computer market offers some interesting examples of supplier power. The most critical component in any personal computer is the microprocessor. In the early history of personal computers, IBM was so powerful that it was able to demand that suppliers of critical components agree to license their products and technology to other suppliers to guarantee a "second source." For example, IBM had selected Intel to make the microprocessors for its personal computers, but had also required Intel to license its technology to Advanced Micro Devices. With its significant technological capabilities and with the microprocessor so critical to the performance of personal computers, Intel's power grew considerably. By the time it had developed its 486 (pre-Pentium) line of microprocessors, Intel declared that it would no longer license its proprietary technology to other semiconductor manufacturers.

At that point, IBM and other PC manufacturers had become so dependent on Intel's technology and innovation capability that they could do little but go-along with Intel. Certainly no PC manufacturer was in a position to force Intel to share its proprietary technology. Thus, Intel and Microsoft, which enjoyed a similar lock on personal computer operating system software, were in a position to extract a large amount of the profit-generating potential from firms in the PC market.

It is worth emphasizing that the near-monopoly positions Intel and Microsoft have in supplying chips and operating system software for the PC industry allow them to extract a great deal of the profit-making potential from the personal computer industry. For example, in 2009, when the average ROA of computer manufacturing companies was –8.5 percent, Intel and Microsoft enjoyed ROAs of 10.4 percent and 24.3 percent respectively.

On the other hand, many different companies produce other personal computer components, including disk drives, monitors, and keyboards, most of which incorporate less proprietary technologies. In these markets, producers enjoy very little supplier power, and personal computer makers can generally extract liberal price concessions from the producers of these components.

Supplier power also led to tensions between Nike and Foot Locker, the number one retailer of athletic shoes. More powerful than other athletic shoe manufacturers, Nike routinely gave retailers, including Foot Locker, little flexibility in terms of product selection and forced all retailers to accept lower margins. In 2002, in an effort to get Nike to give it more flexibility in merchandize selection and pricing, Foot Locker announced that it was going to reduce its orders of Nike merchandise by 15 to 25 percent, or between $150 and $250 million of its total sales of approximately $1 billion. In response, Nike upped the ante by announcing that it was going to reduce its shipments to Foot Locker by 40 percent or $400 million less than the previous year. Even more punitive, Nike announced that it would no longer ship its most popular styles to Foot Locker. By the end of 2003, Foot Locker was forced to concede on its demands and resolve its feud with Nike, and a strong rebound in the sales of Nike shoes helped to boost Foot Locker sales in 2004.[19]

The Power of Buyers

Just as powerful suppliers can make an industry less attractive, so too can powerful buyers extract price concessions for products or services, also reducing industry profitability. As with the power of suppliers, two factors appear to be most critical in determining the power of buyers. First, if only a few buyers of a product or service exist relative to the number of firms in the industry, then those buyers will have greater bargaining power. Second, if the product or service is not particularly important to buyers or does not incorporate proprietary technologies, then buyers will have greater power. On the other hand, if the product or service is critical to the buyer or if the product or service is based on proprietary technology, then the power of buyers will be reduced.

One very good illustration of the power of buyers is in the automotive components industry. Hundreds, if not thousands, of small automotive components manufacturers exist around the world. Because there are so few buyers (i.e., automobile manufacturers) relative to the many component manufacturers, the buyers exercise a great deal of leverage over the firms in this segment of the automotive industry. The auto producers thus enjoy a great deal of buyer power, routinely dictating product specifications, delivery schedules, and even the prices they will pay to these suppliers.[20]

Best Buy has gained significant clout as several of its major competitors have gone out of business, including CompUSA and Circuit City. As the largest remaining electronics retailer, Best Buy has gained increasing power over electronics manufacturers, including Hewlett-Packard, Sony, and Toshiba. Best Buy aims to use this clout to offer its customers products that they cannot find at other retailers.[21]

Because Wal-Mart is so large, commands so much retail market share, and is the largest buyer for many of its supplier companies, it is in a position to exercise significant buyer power, even dictating the prices it will pay its suppliers. As a result, even large companies like Dial and Procter & Gamble must submit to Wal-Mart's demands for pricing restraint or even price reductions. The overall impact of Wal-Mart's power over suppliers is so extraordinary that many economists give a great deal of credit to the "Wal-Mart effect" for low rates of inflation experienced in the United States during the last decade.[22]

The company is increasing its power over suppliers even more by requesting specific product innovations from numerous companies, including Coca-Cola and PepsiCo. Products like Diet Coke with Splenda, Slice ONE (a diet-soda line from PepsiCo), and super-concentrated laundry detergent would not have been developed if Wal-Mart had not pushed its suppliers to create them with specific requirements.[23] Usually the relationship between supermarket retailers and its suppliers entails product promotion and in-store displays only; thus Wal-Mart is transforming the relationship between supplier and buyer in the supermarket industry.

Rivalry

The last of the five forces is the extent of rivalry among existing firms in an industry. Greater rivalry usually reduces average industry profitability because rivalry will either drive down prices or increase the costs of doing business (as firms seek to add more features to their products and services without raising prices for those features). Many factors will tend to increase rivalry in an industry. Generally, the more firms in an industry, the greater will be the rivalry (e.g., the trucking industry), though highly concentrated industries with only a few major players can also be the scene of considerable rivalry and protracted price cutting (e.g., the steel industry). As the number of firms in a particular industry increases, the industry will come closer to matching the conditions associated with perfect competition (i.e., many firms producing similar products, firms "taking" prices established by market competition, etc.).

Mergers and acquisitions, which necessarily reduce the number of firms in an industry, are often pursued in an effort to reduce rivalry and competition in an industry. For example, several years ago, the Federal Trade Commission argued against the acquisition of Office Depot by Staples, alleging that the acquisition was an effort by the managers of Staples to improve profit margins by reducing competition and rivalry in the market for office supplies. A federal judge agreed, and issued a ruling forbidding the merger.[24]

More recently, the U.S. government did give its approval to a merger between Ticketmaster and Live Nation, the country's biggest concert promoter. Since they compete in different industries, the merger between the two firms will create vertical integration, with Ticketmaster and Live Nation playing a part in virtually every step between musicians and consumers. Some argued that this would give the combined company too much control on the concert business, especially control over ticket prices.[25]

The growth rate of an industry will also affect rivalry, and slower growth or declines in overall industry sales will tend to increase rivalry. Unable to meet their sales growth objectives from growing demand in the market, rivals in slow growth industries must compete to take market share from each other.

Excess capacity in an industry also tends to increase rivalry and usually results in lower prices, lower profit margins, and a less attractive industry. As firms in an industry with excess capacity seek to make full use of their own plant capacity, they collectively tend to create excess supply that in turn drives down price levels. Industries, such as airlines, steel, and telecommunications that are characterized by a high level of fixed costs, seem particularly prone to this sort of behavior. The automobile industry is another example of an industry with excess capacity. Because the U.S. market is very well saturated, the many firms that compete in the market have seen an increase in rivalry. Thus, the recent financial troubles of GM, Chrysler, Ford, and other major car manufacturers are not solely the result of the economic crisis. In fact, quite a few of the problems that the car companies are dealing with, including too many cars sitting idly at the dealerships, seemingly-endless cycle of rebates and price cuts, and increased competition with other firms, are a result of excess capacity.

This section has focused on factors that tend to increase rivalry in an industry, but just as many factors tend to *increase* rivalry, so will several other factors *decrease* the level of rivalry in an industry. For example, in many emerging industries, firms must work together to gain consumer acceptance of new products and services, develop distribution channels, and establish industry standards. Similarly, any type of government regulation tends to decrease rivalry among firms in the regulated industry.

Summary

Nearly all the five forces are present to at least some extent in most industries, but it is the intensity of the various forces that will determine whether they have a significant impact on the profitability of a particular industry. The logic behind the Five Forces Model is straightforward: *As the intensity of the forces increases, the industry environment becomes more hostile and overall industry profitability will decline.* The next section describes how the Five Forces Model can be applied to analyze industry environments.

Application of the Five Forces Model

The best way to illustrate the application and implications of the Five Forces Model is to use it to analyze an actual industry. This will demonstrate how the structural characteristics of an industry influence the average profitability of firms in that industry. To get you started and to help you conduct your own industry analyses using the Five Forces Model, we've provided you with the guidelines summarized in Exhibit 4.7. These guidelines will help you to assess the intensity or strength of each of the five forces in Porter's framework.

To illustrate how you can use the Five Forces Model to analyze industries, we'll use the guidelines and criteria listed in Exhibit 4.7 to analyze the market for personal computers. At first glance, the PC manufacturing industry may seem like a profitable industry to be a part of. Technology has seen a boom in the last few decades, and computers and laptops are now essential to our daily lives. As illustrated in Exhibit 4.8, the Five Forces Model shows us, however, that certain aspects of the industry make it an unattractive one to compete in.

Exhibit 4.7 Guide to Using the Five Forces Model for Industry Analysis

The aim of this guide is to help you develop your skill at using the Five Forces Model to analyze a company's competitive environment. Using the following questions, you can assess the relative power of each of the five forces. Once you have completed this analysis, you will be prepared to answer a number of strategic questions:
1. What are the major competitive advantages of each player in the business (including the focal company)?
2. What are the "rules of the game" in this industry? What are the factors that make the industry attractive or unattractive?
3. What can a company in this industry do to alter the structure of the industry to make it more attractive?

Threat of New Entrants
a. What are the barriers to entry? Are we able to raise them? What factors are tending to lower them?
b. What firms are potential or imminent new entrants? What are their characteristics (size, number, growth, customer base, etc.)?
c. What are the entrants' competitive strategies likely to be? How might the new entrants and their strategies reshape the industry?
d. When will they enter our market?

Power of Suppliers
a. What firms are suppliers, and how large or concentrated are they?
b. How concentrated is our industry (their buyers) relative to them? That is, how many of us buy what percent of the output?
c. Can firms in the industry switch suppliers easily?
d. What percent of their total output is purchased by our industry? How large are the quantities?
e. How important is their product or service to the quality of ours?
f. How much of our cost does their product or service represent?
g. What is the threat of forward integration by each supplier? (Conversely, what is the opportunity for backward integration by one or more of us?)
h. What is their relative bargaining power over us?

Industry Rivalry
a. What firms are the major competitors (today)? What are their basic characteristics (size, growth, product lines, customer base, geographic coverage, etc.)?
b. What are their relative positions in the industry?
c. What is the competitive advantage of each? (What switching costs have they built?)
d. How do they compare? What "weapons" or strategies does each use?
e. What form does competition take—open warfare, polite détente, secrecy, open signaling?
f. How is product differentiation achieved?
g. How competitive is the industry? Are any competitors in the industry? Are any competitors attempting to shape the industry? How?

Power of Buyers
a. What firms are the customers for this industry? How concentrated are they?
b. How fast is demand growing overall and in different segments? What is the potential for finding or creating new markets or niches?
c. What are the switching costs? How high are they?
d. How price sensitive is each customer segment for each of the industry's services?
e. How large is the threat of backward integration (i.e. buyers' self-supplying our products or services)?
f. What is the customer's relative bargaining power?

Threat of Substitutes
a. What are the substitutes or alternatives for our products or service?
b. How big an impact will the substitutes have? (That is, how viable are they as direct replacements for our product or service?)
c. How quickly will they penetrate?
d. Which players in the industry will consider substitutes as an opportunity for diversification?

Exhibit 4.8 Five Forces Analysis of the Personal Computer Market

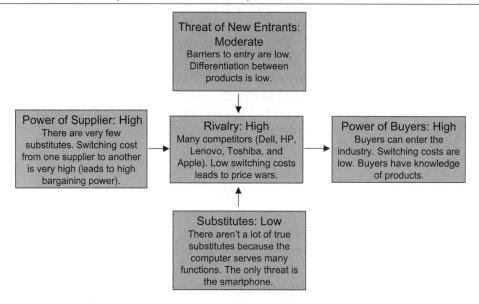

First, the power of buyers is quite high in the PC industry. Buyers, whether individuals and companies purchasing directly from manufacturers or retailers and distributors who then sell to individual buyers, face almost no switching costs if they move from one computer brand to another, especially with Apple recently making its Mac applications more compatible with Microsoft and PC applications. Not only is the switching cost from one computer to another computer low, but buyers have more knowledge about all of the companies in the industry and each company's products because of the widespread availability of product information on the Internet.

The buyers in the PC industry aren't the only ones with power. Suppliers like Microsoft and Intel that provide operating systems and microprocessors respectively—hold enormous power over PC companies. Because there are few suppliers of these components and because the cost to switch from one supplier to another is large, each of these suppliers have high bargaining power over the companies it deals with.

Rivalry in the PC industry also makes the industry an unattractive one to compete in. Since there are many companies that manufacture personal computers—Dell, HP, Lenovo, Toshiba, and Apple, for example—and since the switching cost from one computer to another is so low, this fierce rivalry leads to price wars and decreased profitability.

The PC industry used to enjoy a lack of any true substitutes. The computer serves many functions, and although there are many products to satisfy one or two of these functions, until recently, no other product existed that served all of its functions. The typewriter, calculator, television, radio, music players, and other products fulfill one or two of the functions of a computer, but no product did it all. However, the industry now faces substitute products such as the iPad and smartphones from Apple, RIM, and others that have PC-like capabilities, like e-mail, Internet, ability to read e-books, music storage, built-in keyboards, along with traditional phone use in the case of the smartphone (and probably soon for products like the iPad).[26]

As for the threat of entrants, low barriers of entry make the threat of new entrants into the industry moderate. There aren't many legal or governmental barriers to enter the PC industry, and with the low differentiation of the products between brands (as all computers mainly serve the same functions), the only thing standing in the way of potential new firms gaining significant market share would be a lack of brand recognition. As a result, the threat of new entrants is moderate. Thus, even though the PC industry is continually updating its products to be more useful and technologically sophisticated, an analysis using Porter's Five Forces model shows that from a company's perspective, it is not a particularly attractive industry.

Limitations of the Five Forces Model

By offering a more concrete tool and by suggesting specific criteria or factors for evaluating the strength of each of the five forces, the Five Forces Model is very helpful for conducting industry analysis and for explaining differences in average industry performance levels. Still, the model is not without its limitations. One key limitation is its inability to suggest strategies for managers. Porter concludes that managers have two options if they find their firms in unattractive industries. First, they can simply diversify their firms away from—or exit completely—the unattractive industry. Alternatively, they can attempt to minimize the impact of any of the five forces that are acting to make the industry unattractive.

The problem with the first recommendation is that few totally attractive industries exist. Almost every industry involves at least some unattractive characteristics, and the more attractive industries will generally be the most difficult to enter (because many of them have significant entry barriers). In addition, some firms lack the resources necessary to diversify into other industries. Acquisitions of firms in other industries and the development of totally new products and services usually require a great deal of capital, and many low-performing firms will lack either the necessary capital or access to capital from external sources. Moreover, diversification can be especially risky for firms that have little or no previous experience with diversification (an issue considered more fully in Chapter 10).

Managers can and frequently do pursue the second option, seeking to make their industries more attractive either by 1) reducing the power of the five forces, or 2) shielding or protecting their companies from the power of the five forces. For example, nearly all companies attempt to build brand loyalty through advertising or by offering good customer service. Companies also frequently seek to minimize the power of suppliers through backward integration in which they begin or threaten to manufacture their own components or merchandise.

It is important to emphasize, however, that many activities aimed at reducing competition in an industry are illegal. Firms must not be so eager to reduce competition in their industries that they unwittingly violate antitrust laws. For example, many activities aimed at preventing firms from entering an industry can be construed as restraint of trade. Collusion and price fixing are sometimes temptations for the executives of firms caught in intense rivalry and competitive pricing, but such collusive activities are, of course, also illegal.

Several years ago, an unlikely group provided an excellent illustration of collusion. Admissions and financial aid personnel from 21 elite private colleges and universities in the U.S. would meet regularly to discuss the financial aid packages that they planned to award to admitted students.[27] Was this practice collusive? The meetings offered an opportunity to minimize intercollegiate rivalry for promising college students by agreeing on tuition levels and the terms of the financial aid packages that would be offered to admitted students. And, the colleges' tuition charges suggested collusion; at the time, tuition levels at Harvard, the University of Pennsylvania, Dartmouth, Columbia, Yale, and Princeton differed by less than $150! The colleges and universities finally agreed to stop meeting collectively after the U.S. Justice Department announced that it was planning to launch a full-scale investigation of the schools' admission practices.

The case the Justice Department brought against Microsoft—alleging that Microsoft's bundling of its Windows operating system, software applications, and its Internet Explorer browser products gives the company an unfair advantage over its rivals—was important because of the implications it will have for many high-tech companies.[28] In the past, antitrust laws have been interpreted to discourage the bundling of products, but many of today's high-tech products—especially the programs included in computer software packages—involve some type of bundling. Microsoft has argued that its bundling is similar to an automobile manufacturer that includes air conditioning, radios, and CD players in the cars it sells. A U.S. appeals court has largely accepted this reasoning, but the case remains controversial in Europe and elsewhere.

Synthesis: How Tools for Industry Analysis Relate to the Three Key Themes Emphasized throughout This Book

The Importance of Managers and Managerial Thinking

This book places a special emphasis on the role of managers and managerial thinking in the strategy formulation and implementation processes. The book's model of strategic management suggests that managers' assumptions, beliefs, and understandings about their firms' competitive environments will influence two crucial sets of decisions. First, managers' mental models of the competitive environment will influence decisions about business definition—decisions that position firms and businesses in the competitive space or arena. Decisions that place firms and businesses in more or less competitive segments or decisions that redefine the competitive arena can have a major influence on profitability.

Managerial thinking about a firm's or a business's industry environment will also be an important influence on decisions about how the firm or business should compete. For example, we know from research on retail companies that managers tend to view larger stores and those that are physically closer as more significant competitors, even though more objective data might indicate other stores are actually more direct competitors.[29] Again, the business strategies that evolve from these decisions about how to compete can have a major influence on profitability. In the next chapter, we will emphasize that unique and novel managerial thinking about industry structure or the ability to anticipate industry changes can provide firms and businesses with significant advantages if the managers of rival firms lack such foresight. Thus, mastery of industry analysis and the development of mental models to guide industry analysis are key managerial skills.

Change and the Need to Think Dynamically about Strategic Management

Though SWOT Analysis and the Five Forces Model are both fairly straightforward and relatively easy to understand and use, many users of these industry analysis techniques often fail to appreciate the dynamic nature of the industries they are analyzing. Both frameworks provide their users with "snapshots" of industry environments, but many users then assume that the nature of competition in those industries will remain stable over time. In other words, many users of SWOT Analysis and the Five Forces Model apply these tools to study a particular industry at a point in time, but then fail to recognize how that industry is changing. As two leading management authors have argued:

> Traditional competitor analysis is like a snapshot of a moving car. By itself, the photograph yields little information about the car's speed or direction—whether the driver is out for a quiet Sunday drive or warming up for the Grand Prix.[30]

As will be demonstrated in the next chapter, many—if not most—industry environments are very dynamic, and to use this same analogy, it makes all the difference in the world whether competitors and would-be rivals are "out for a quiet Sunday drive or warming up for the Grand Prix." Developments in customer preferences, technologies, and product and service offerings can revolutionize industries overnight. This point is underscored and amplified by the authors of *Blue Ocean Strategy*, who advocate a new tool for examining and creating market space (more on this in Chapter 5).[31] So, while SWOT Analysis and the Five Forces Model are widely used and can be very helpful in analyzing industries, these tools must be used with a recognition that any observations and conclusions may be quite fleeting as industry conditions change.

The Importance of Organizational Learning

This discussion of industry change implies that managers must insure that they and their companies and businesses are taking little for granted and are continually learning. Complacency is a major problem in many business organizations. One way for firms and businesses to promote learning through industry analysis would be to initiate conversations among top managers about the industry environment using SWOT Analysis and the Five Forces Model. These initial conversations could be especially helpful in developing an understanding of a particular industry and identifying key competitive issues and factors. These same issues could then be further examined using a more dynamic model of industry structure and evolution, such as the one that will be introduced in the next chapter.

In addition, companies and businesses using SWOT Analysis and the Five Forces Model might also ask a wide range of company insiders and outside consultants to play devil's advocate or otherwise challenge the management thinking that emerges from any discussions about industry analysis. Such sessions could promote learning by asking managers to question their basic assumptions, beliefs, and understandings about their industry environment.

Key Points

- Industry environments vary considerably. Some industries are relatively young, emerging industries while others are more mature; some industries are characterized by fierce competition while others are characterized by very little rivalry; and some industries are, on average, more profitable than others in any one year.
- Industry performance is an important influence on firm performance, but high- and low-performing firms are found in all industries. While industry performance is important, it is not all that matters; differences in firm performance within an industry will usually be much greater than the differences in average performance across industries.
- SWOT Analysis can be used to analyze industry environments and organizational capabilities. This tool specifically examines (internal) organizational *Strengths* and *Weaknesses* and (external) environmental *Opportunities* and *Threats*. The major limitation of SWOT Analysis is that it lacks objective dimensions, so any conclusions tend to reflect managers' subjective evaluations of their industry environments.
- The Five Forces Model analyzes five aspects of industry structure—the threat of entry, the threat of substitute products and services, the power of suppliers, the power of buyers, and industry rivalry—in order to assess the relative attractiveness of different industries. The basic reasoning behind the Five Forces Model is straightforward: *As the intensity of forces increases, the industry environment becomes more hostile and average industry performance will suffer.*
- Finally, both SWOT Analysis and the Five Forces Model are *static* frameworks. Users must recognize that most industry environments can be quite dynamic, and that any conclusions based on these models may not be appropriate in the future.

Key Questions for Managers

- What are the major strengths and weaknesses of your firm? What are the key opportunities and threats in your firm's external environment?
- Have you and your colleagues discussed differences of opinion about your company's strengths and weaknesses as well as the environment's opportunities and threats? What accounts for differences in your interpretations of strengths and weaknesses; opportunities and threats?
- Have you analyzed your firm in terms of the five forces in Porter's Five Forces Model? What options are available for minimizing the strength of each of the five forces?
- Have you considered how possible changes in the competitive environment will alter any of the five forces? What forces that are favorable today are likely to become more intense in the future?

Suggestions for Further Reading

Additionally, links to further resources online—such as cases, articles, and videos—can be found on the book's website, www.routledge.com/textbooks/Duhaime.

Adams, W., & Brock, J. 1990. *The Structure of American Industry* (9th ed.). Englewood Cliffs, NJ: Prentice-Hall.

Hamel, G., & Prahalad, C. K. 1989. Strategic intent. *Harvard Business Review,* 67(3): 63–76.

Hamel, G., & Prahalad, C. K. 1994. *Competing For the Future*. Boston: Harvard Business School Press.

McGahan, A. M., & Porter, M. E. 1997. How much does industry matter, really? *Strategic Management Journal,* 18 (special issue): 15–30.

Miniter, R. 2002. *The Myth of Market Share: Why Market Share is the Fool's Gold of Business*. New York: Crown Business.

Porter, M. E. 1980. *Competitive Strategy*. New York: Free Press.

Rumelt, R. P. 1991. How much does industry matter? *Strategic Management Journal,* 12: 167–185.

Schmalensee, R. 1985. Do markets differ much? *American Economic Review,* 75: 341–351.

Chapter 5

A Dynamic Model
of Industry Structuring

This chapter continues our focus on industry environments. Chapter 4 described two frameworks for analyzing industries, SWOT Analysis and the Five Forces Model. The chapter concluded its discussion of these frameworks by observing that both SWOT Analysis and the Five Forces Model can provide "snapshots" of industries at a particular point in time, but managers who rely on these tools can fail to anticipate how industries will change over time or how firms and their rivals will respond to these industry changes.

The objective of this second chapter on industries is to emphasize the dynamic nature of nearly all industry environments and to help you develop ways of thinking—mental models— about how industries evolve, how new firms are likely to enter industries, and how incumbent firms are likely to respond.

Chapter Objectives

The specific aims of this chapter are to:

- Introduce a dynamic model of industry competition and evolution.
- Offer several propositions about the ways industries will evolve based on this dynamic model, focusing specifically on the likely actions of new entrants to an industry and the responses of incumbent firms.
- Illustrate how this dynamic model can be used to analyze industries.
- Emphasize the managerial implications of this dynamic model of industry structuring.

Introduction

Let's begin our more focused look at the dynamic nature of industry environments by considering the firms and industries that are included in Exhibit 5.1. The firms and industries included in the exhibit should help to underscore two important points about industries. First, *industries change*—often evolving in modest or incremental ways but sometimes in surprising and profound ways that can completely change their character. A second key point is that the most profound changes are often produced by industry "outsiders," while incumbent firms—those firms already in the industry—are frequently caught off guard by these new

Exhibit 5.1 Industry Change and Evolution: New Entrants, the Industries They Entered, and the New Markets They Created

New Entrant	Existing Industry	Market Created
Procter & Gamble	Diapers	Disposable diapers
EMI	Medical technology	CT scanners
Apple	Computers	Personal computers
Southwest	Air travel	Low-cost air travel
Staley (Gatorade)	Beverages	Sports drinks
Canon/H-P/others	Photography	Digital photography
Burton	Winter sports	Snowboarding

entrants. Some incumbents do respond effectively, but others never regain the dominance they once enjoyed.

The competitive dynamics of these industries (and many others that are not included in Exhibit 5.1) are inconsistent with structuralist views of industries. The Five Forces Model and the structure-conduct-performance framework from industrial organization economics on which Porter's Five Forces Model is based suggest that firms can erect a variety of entry barriers in order to prevent potential new rivals from entering an industry. Yet, in spite of entry barriers, new firms not only *do* enter industries, but frequently enjoy remarkable success in competing against powerful incumbent firms.[1] It's not that the Five Forces Model or SWOT, which we examined in detail in the last chapter, are ineffective tools for industry analysis, but they may not be particularly helpful in anticipating how industries will evolve over time.

Thus, new frameworks and ways of thinking—mental models—are needed so that managers are not only better prepared to anticipate the forces of industry change, but also understand the need for their firms to recreate themselves so that they can prosper in future competitive environments. As Gary Hamel and C. K. Prahalad emphasize in their book, *Competing for the Future*:

> It is not enough for a company to get smaller and better and faster, as important as these tasks may be; a company must also be capable of fundamentally reconceiving itself, or regenerating its core strategies, and of reinventing its industry. In short, a company must also be capable of getting different.[2]

This chapter offers a model that explains how and why industries evolve. The model suggests that two factors that have already been emphasized in this book will play major roles in the process of industry structuring. First, the chapter emphasizes the changing nature of industry environments, describing the ways that industries can change and evolve over time. Second, building on the concepts and ideas introduced in Chapter 3, we will see that managers often fail to respond effectively or anticipate changes in their industries because of the biases, limitations, and inertia that are inherent in their thinking. When combined, these two factors help to explain why newcomers rather than industry incumbents tend to reshape industries in such fundamental ways and why managers of incumbent firms often have great difficulty in responding to these changes.

The chapter will also suggest how managers can be more responsive to, anticipate, and change their firm's industry. Later chapters elaborate on these suggestions, emphasizing not only how managers can develop competitive advantage, but also how they can maintain competitive advantage in the face of industry change. Note that the title of this chapter uses the word "structuring" rather than "structure." This choice is deliberate, emphasizing that industries are not static but that they are continuously being structured and restructured over time—an ongoing process of industry structuring.

The Nature of Industry Change

In an important book on management, author Derrick Abell suggested that an industry can be thought of as an arena or a competitive space in which rivals compete along various dimensions. Abell defined an industry as a group of firms that serves the same customers, meets similar customer needs, and employs common technologies.[3] If we adopt this conceptualization of an industry, then we can depict an industry as a three-dimensional "competitive space," as illustrated in Exhibit 5.2, delineated by customers (the "who" an industry serves), products and/or services (the "what" an industry offers), and technologies (the "how" those products or services are produced or provided).

Traditional perspectives on industry analysis and the two industry frameworks that we examined in Chapter 4 assume that changes in the dimensions of industries are relatively unimportant, that the size and shape of the competitive space are relatively stable over time, that industries remain in equilibrium, and that the locus of competition remains fixed

Exhibit 5.2 Industry As a Three-Dimensional Competitive Space Consisting of Customers, Products, and Technologies

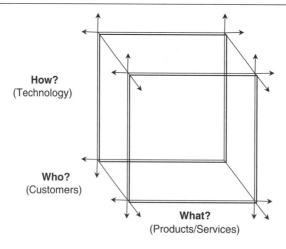

How?
(Technology)

Who?
(Customers)

What?
(Products/Services)

on traditional patterns of interaction among participating firms. But, this is rarely the case. Customer demographics change, new technologies emerge, and new products and services are constantly being developed, so that industry dimensions are, in fact, changing all the time. What complicates this process is that change rarely comes in steady, predictable increments. While firms in high tech industries have come to expect that microprocessor capability will double every 18 months based on Moore's Law, few other industries can count on such a steady or predictable pace of change. Mintzberg makes this point quite compellingly:

> An organization may find itself in a stable environment for years, sometimes for decades, with no need to reassess an appropriate strategy. Then, suddenly, the environment can become so turbulent that even the very best planning techniques are of no use because of the impossibility of predicting the kind of stability that will eventually emerge.[4]

The key point is that almost any industry environment or competitive space can be very fluid, and the arrows on each of the three dimensions of the figure in Exhibit 5.2 underscore the many forces that can be sources of change.

The examples offered in Exhibit 5.1 provide specific illustrations of the many ways in which industries can evolve. Demographic changes and the emergence of new customer wants and needs can create new competitive space, which is then filled as firms develop new products and services to meet these emerging wants and needs. For example, just as increasing numbers of women were beginning to work outside the home, disposable diapers began to appear in the marketplace and proved to be very much the right product at the right time because they offered busy families a great deal more convenience than cloth diapers. As illustrated in Exhibit 5.3, the customers (new parents) who needed diapers didn't change, but their new need for convenience created an opportunity for Procter & Gamble and Kimberly Clark to expand the market for diapers along the product dimension.

Exhibit 5.3 Procter & Gamble and Kimberly Clark Expanded the Competitive Space along the Product Dimension When They Introduced Disposable Diapers

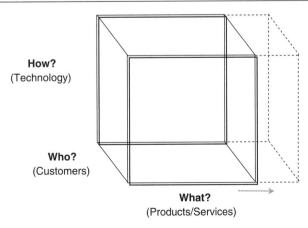

Exhibit 5.4 Southwest Airlines Expanded the Airline Industry along the Customer and Product/Service Dimensions

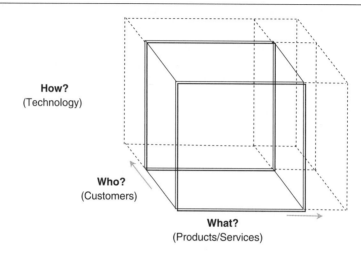

Alternatively, entrepreneurial firms can develop new products and services that create new customers and thereby expand the competitive space along both the product/service and the customer dimensions. For example, Southwest Airlines was conceived on a novel notion of airline travel—that a desire for speed and convenience would attract passengers (who otherwise might drive their cars) to short-haul flights if those flights were priced competitively. As a result, Southwest expanded the competitive space of airline travel by introducing economy, short-haul service that has attracted and continues to attract large numbers of new airline passengers who otherwise would drive their cars to their destinations. Exhibit 5.4 illustrates how Southwest Airlines expanded the airline industry along the customer and product/service dimensions.

What Southwest Airlines did for air travel, Kendall Jackson, Mondavi, Yellowtail, and others did for the wine industry, by introducing quality wines at reasonable prices that brought many new customers into the wine market. Starbucks has grown a global business by developing gourmet coffee and convincing customers that they need to spend $3.00 or more for a cup of coffee. Starbucks and its imitators have created a vast new competitive space; in 1989, only a handful of coffee shops were scattered throughout the United States, while today there are nearly 15,000 coffeehouses in the U.S. alone, not to mention thousands more Starbucks and other coffeehouses worldwide.[5]

The competitive space can also expand as new technologies evolve. Unmanned U.S. aircraft, for example, are turning the defense industry upside down. Relatively inexpensive in comparison, military drones took up $3.5 billion of the U.S. national defense budget in 2010, and the government is relying more and more on small companies that are producing these unmanned aerial vehicles. These small companies, like General Atomics Aeronautical Systems, are gaining an edge over the bigger, well known companies like Boeing that have struggled to produce comparable combat-ready UAV technology. These larger companies haven't given up just yet though—they've turned to partnerships and acquisitions to compete. For example,

Boeing acquired Insitu, while Northrop Grumman partnered with General Atomics to supply drones for a Navy contract.[6]

Similarly, the Internet and the emergence of other high-tech information technologies are allowing many firms to expand their industries' competitive space along the technology dimension. Amazon.com, eBay, Facebook, and Google are just *four* of the many relatively new companies that owe their existence to the commercialization and popularity of the Internet. Amazon.com has exploited Internet technology to become the largest bookstore in the United States by using a different business model. Traditional booksellers, Barnes and Noble and Borders, have been forced to copy Amazon.com and offer their own Internet sites.[7] And, Amazon has not remained content just selling books, but has expanded the scope of its retailing operations to include a very broad spectrum of consumer products. Google, likewise, has exploited Internet technology to become a search engine giant, with most of its profit coming from selling advertising, especially the text ads that pop up next to search results when a person uses the search engine.

Finally, consider the founders of Apple Computer, who had the foresight and entrepreneurial creativity to transform the computer industry along all three industry dimensions. They saw that the emergence of new microprocessor technologies could allow them to package a great deal of computing power in a small box to create a new product—the personal computer—and that they could then sell that product to customers who had not previously thought they needed a computer. So, as illustrated in Exhibit 5.5, Apple and other personal computer manufacturers expanded the computer industry along all three industry dimensions.

Apple also illustrates another important point about industry evolution and change—that great ideas rarely wait for customer needs or wants to become obvious. Few of the customers who purchased PCs knew they needed or wanted them before personal computers first appeared on the market. Apple doesn't even conduct focus groups or market research. Steve Jobs is quoted as saying, "You can't ask people what they want if it's around the next corner."[8] And this mantra has held true in recent years with the iPod and iPhone products, as well as with the new iPad products, resulting in a complete upheaval of one market and industry after another.

Southwest Airlines, Apple, Nike, Trek, Burton, Nucor, Starbucks, and the others share many characteristics. First, many were "outsiders," entering established industries that were already occupied by incumbent players. In most cases, however, the incumbent firms failed to respond quickly (if at all) to the entry of these new competitors. In fact, they often failed to develop competing products or services until the entrants had gained dominant positions in the market. For example, before any of the major makers of condiments offered their own salsa products, salsa had already become the largest-selling condiment product. Heinz started developing its first salsa product only after sales of salsa exceeded sales of ketchup.[9]

To summarize, then, as one or more of the dimensions in an industry changes, "holes" or new areas of opportunity are created. Sometimes these holes will be created independently—by the development of new technologies, or by demographic changes that create new groups of customers with new needs and wants. But, the most entrepreneurial firms often create these new competitive spaces by proactively exploiting new technologies and developing new products and services, and only later creating desire for these products and services

Exhibit 5.5 Apple and the Other Personal Computer Manufacturers Expanded the Computer Industry along All Three Dimensions

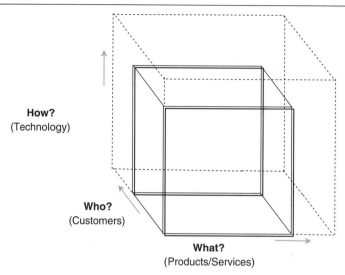

How?
(Technology)

Who?
(Customers)

What?
(Products/Services)

through marketing and advertising efforts. In effect, *they are shaping, rather than being shaped by, their competitive space.*

The Role of Managerial Thinking in Industry Evolution

This last section has described the nature of industry change—that all industries have the potential to change, but that change rarely comes in steady, easy to anticipate increments, and that firms can either react and respond to changes or proactively anticipate and create changes in their industries. We now focus on the limitations and inertia in managerial thinking that leave managers poorly equipped to deal with the dynamic nature of their firms' competitive environments.

Limitations and Inertia in Managerial Thinking

Why exactly do the managers of incumbent firms often fail to anticipate, detect, and respond to changes in their industries or to notice the entry of new rivals? Don't their firms employ sophisticated market research, forecasting, planning, and R&D departments that should alert top managers to important new developments in their industry environments? Evidence suggests that even with all of these resources, managers still often fail to notice and accurately assess important changes in their firms' industries. Several factors help to explain why.

Noticing

First, managers may simply fail to notice changes in their firms' environments. Mintzberg emphasizes that "[t]here is no process in organizations that is more demanding of human cognition than strategy formation. Every strategy-maker faces an impossible overload of information (much of it soft); as a result he can have no optimal process to follow."[10] Nor do strategic issues "present themselves to the decision maker in convenient ways; problems and opportunities in particular must be identified in streams of ambiguous, largely verbal data."[11] Psychology researchers suggest that this problem is compounded because individuals make sense only of what they perceive to be key or important events. Thus, managers will naturally be inclined to focus attention on issues that were important in the past because they have no way of knowing for sure what issues are most likely to be important in the future.

Not only will managers tend to focus most on those issues that have been important in the past, but as noted in Chapter 3, individuals also seek confirmation for their beliefs and will, therefore, pay greater attention to events that support their views—views that were formed by past experiences.[12] Managers, like all individuals, tend to use mental models that are based more on our past experiences.[13] "When faced with a totally new situation, we tend always to attach ourselves to the objects, to the flavor of the most recent past. *We look at the present through a rear-view mirror.*"[14]

Is it any surprise, then, that executives in the recording industry—an industry that has always coped rather well with such evolutionary changes as the shift from LP records to cassettes to CDs—have responded so ineffectively to the emergence of file sharing and other much more revolutionary Internet-based technologies that allow consumers a great deal more discretion in how they obtain music?[15]

The Difficulty of Making Accurate Interpretations

Furthermore, managers often cannot make objective or rational evaluations of the data they collect, so a new rival offering a new and different product or service or employing a new and different technology might easily be ignored or rationalized away by incumbents. Traditional industry analysis tools assume that defining the nature of threats or rivals is not a problem. Yet, considerable evidence suggests that *defining the nature of a competitive threat is a problem* for the managers of incumbent firms. Changes in industry dimensions may not be perceived as important by the managers of incumbent firms, *especially if their firms continue to enjoy satisfactory levels of performance.*

Perhaps the most remarkable feature of organizational behavior is that the managers of complex organizations often develop and implement sophisticated strategies that are based on assumptions or understandings of the environment that may no longer be appropriate.[16] Moreover, many researchers have concluded that these understandings are so strongly held that they can be altered only by a crisis or calamity, such as a loss of profitability or even bankruptcy.

Noticing and Interpretation Are Difficult Because Most Changes Occur and Most New Rivals Enter on the Periphery of the Competitive Space

Traditional perspectives on industry structure suggest that following the entry of a new rival into an established industry, incumbent firms will move quickly to counter the initiatives of the new player. Yet, many factors may prevent the effective retaliation predicted by traditional models. First, as already suggested, managers of incumbent firms may simply fail to "see" the entrant. Given the effects of industry norms and managers' cognitive limitations, a new entrant could easily proceed to carve out a niche and establish a presence without being detected.

Second, even after a new entrant is detected, managers of incumbent firms will have to determine whether the new rival poses a serious threat, and, if so, how they should respond. This task is made more complicated because new entrants are likely to be working in a previously unoccupied area of the industry or competitive space, and they may not look like a competitor. The managers of incumbent firms could easily assume that the niches occupied by new entrants are neither viable nor large enough to be of concern.

Executives at Coke and PepsiCo almost certainly "noticed" an upstart called Red Bull, and they have responded quickly to the emergence of a new portion of the competitive space called "energy drinks," but not before Red Bull was able to establish a dominant place in that market.[17] Canon applied a similar strategy as it emerged as a major player in the photocopier industry. It entered the industry offering only small, "personal" photocopiers and has effectively executed a strategy of operating just beyond the peripheral vision of Xerox until it became an industry leader, offering a full range of photocopier and printer products.[18] Red Bull, Canon, and many other companies demonstrate that while the Five Forces Model emphasizes the importance of establishing "credible deterrence" to prevent other firms from entering the industry, *the more relevant issue is whether incumbent firms identify the "credible threats" posed by new entrants.*

Many food companies are currently struggling with the emergence of customer interest in more healthy, natural foods. But consumer interest in natural foods is not new, and dates back to at least the early 1970s when a number of natural cereal products began appearing on supermarket shelves. Then, as now, the major food companies were caught off-guard by these new products:

> After a rise in consumer interest in "health foods," all-natural cereals together had a market share of about 0.5 percent in early 1972. By early 1973 the naturals' share had climbed to about four percent, and in mid-1974 natural cereals accounted for about ten percent of the market. Testimony and documentary evidence suggest that the shifts in consumer taste that led to this sharp increase in demand *were not well anticipated by most of the established firms*. As a result, a substantial new market segment was up for grabs.[19]

Additional research also suggests that when confronted by a threatening situation, managers seek more information in order to better understand the threat, but the information overload that results can create confusion. In this confusion, the true nature of the threat is obscured, and managers are more likely to shift their focus back to less strategic concerns. The paradox of information gathering is that, instead of developing a better understanding, managers are likely to develop a "threat rigidity" so that they end up *actively ignoring* new rivals.[20]

Furthermore, even if the managers of incumbent firms do perceive the seriousness of the threat, new rivals will still enjoy a number of "first-mover" advantages. Once they recognize the threat posed by new entrants, the managers of incumbent firms will still have to determine how and when to retaliate. Some responses could emerge quickly. For example, incumbent firms could simply lower prices in order to improve the value-price ratio of their products. More elaborate responses, such as developing new products or services that are true substitutes for those offered by the entrant, may require large investments and considerably more time to implement, especially if the incumbent firms are large and bureaucratic.

Even fast responses may come too late, however. Research suggests that "first-movers" enjoy market share, pricing, and other advantages not enjoyed by "second-movers." Most studies conclude that first-mover advantages can continue for many years, so that even if incumbent firms respond quickly and are able to offer products that are close substitutes, a new entrant could still enjoy many advantages for many years.[21]

Industry Norms

Firms in the same industry typically share a common language and similar understandings about how to compete.[22] These shared industry norms result as managers of firms in the same industry move through the same educational programs, develop common professional networks, attend the same professional meetings, and read the same industry trade publications. These activities promote and reinforce conformity to industry norms, and managers of firms in the same industries develop a "common body of knowledge."[23]

On the positive side, these shared norms help in providing industry standards, in encouraging consumer acceptance of products and services, and in facilitating incremental technological developments and improvements. On the other hand, these shared understandings remain relatively stable over time and can easily fail to keep pace with changes in the environment. As a result, the managers of incumbent firms might be vigilant in watching for new products and services, new customer groups, new technologies, and potential rivals, but they are likely to be watching for products and services, customers, technologies, and rivals that are consistent with or similar to current industry norms.

The Likely Outcome—Retreat and Decline of Incumbent Firms

The evidence from many industries suggests that the likely outcome of the combination of the preceding factors is not only that new firms enter established industries, but also that incumbent firms often retreat and enter periods of decline. For example, the newspaper industry is suffering a financial crisis due to declining readership. Gannett, the largest newspaper publisher in the U.S. based on total circulation, is scrambling to cut costs with job lay-offs and eliminating other operating expenses in order to squeeze a profit out of an industry that customers are finding more and more outdated. And Gannett isn't the only company. Customers are turning to the Internet for free news, and even the big newspapers are feeling the effects. *USA Today*, published by Gannett, has seen its industry-leading circulation fall by 400,000 in just one year.[24] If the industry can't find a new business model, newspaper publishers will face a grave future.

Managers of incumbent firms, like Gannett, typically describe their firms' retreats as a "rationalization" or a "downsizing," yet rarely do these strategic retreats result in a strengthened position. New rivals are rarely content to remain in smaller niches when they have opportunities to exploit their newly won customer loyalty, innovative products or services, and technologies to move into additional market segments. Recall that Canon was hardly content to remain a manufacturer of small, personal copiers, but moved on to challenge the full range of Xerox's photocopier products.

Drucker calls the advance of new rivals "entrepreneurial judo":

> Entrepreneurial judo aims first at securing a beachhead, and one which the established leaders either do not defend at all or defend only halfheartedly… Once that beachhead has been secured, that is once the newcomers have an adequate market and an adequate revenue stream, they then move on to the rest of the "beach" and finally to the whole "island."[25]

Even when an incumbent's strategic retreat does provide it with a period of relief, the continuing advances of its rivals will sooner or later make the incumbent's situation untenable. The managers of incumbent firms may actually believe they are moving their companies to more defensible market segments; the paradox of strategic retreat is that competition usually intensifies along two fronts. First, competition increases because industry incumbents retreat to smaller segments of the industry, forcing them to compete more intensively for a smaller piece of the pie. Additional competition comes from the new rival or rivals that are seeking to expand from their "beachhead" into larger parts of the "island" or competitive arena.

Traditional industry analysis tools, such as SWOT and the Five Forces Model, assume that *incumbents and their rivals play the same game, battle on the same turf, and abide by the same rules*. From a strategic point of view, however, new entrants would be much more likely to think and act in new and totally different ways. Rather than invading an already crowded playing field, an entrant might seek to find or even create a new, more promising "game" to play—a game that has become possible due to changing industry dimensions, including new consumer demands and technological developments. In fact, this is what authors Kim and Mauborgne advocate in their book, *Blue Ocean Strategy*. And, because a new rival might choose to develop a totally new game rather than take on established firms in an old game, the rules of the game will also be different.

The managers of incumbent firms may not even see this new game as a threat to their organizations, and the decisions they make may be totally inappropriate given changes in their industry environments. Research has shown that when confronted by new technologies, the managers of incumbent firms do not embrace the new technologies but instead seek to improve their own technologies even as these old technologies are quickly becoming obsolete.[26] For example, the most efficient steam locomotives and the most powerful vacuum tubes were developed *after* the introduction of diesel locomotives and transistors.[27]

Patterns in the Evolution of Industries

The model of industry structuring that we've just developed suggests that industries will evolve in common and fairly predictable ways. In this section, we describe some important characteristics of industry evolution and offer examples from many industries. We begin by examining the "attack" of new entrants and then consider how incumbent firms respond.

The "Attack" of New Entrants

The attack of new entrants tends to have three characteristic patterns:

Entry Occurs on the Periphery or at the "Holes" in the Competitive Space

First, the managers of successful new rivals generally do not attack incumbent firms directly, but instead are more likely to enter an industry at the "holes" that are created by changes in industry dimensions, such as new consumer preferences and the adoption of new product and process technologies. The most dangerous new rivals are unlikely to attack the products or markets of incumbent firms directly. Potential rivals would be foolish to attack incumbent firms' positions when lucrative opportunities exist to create or meet new demands. New rivals are more likely to offer new or different types of products or services or to provide these products or services using new or different technologies.

For example, the successful entry of the Japanese automobile manufacturers into the U.S. market in the early 1970s was possible because their small cars filled a new market demand for fuel-efficient vehicles that had not been well met by any of the domestic U.S. producers. In fact, the Japanese entry to the U.S. automobile market closely follows the dynamic model developed in this chapter. The Japanese manufacturers exploited changes in industry dimensions, namely the demand for more fuel-efficient cars and new "lean" production technologies. Because the U.S. producers held a quite different understanding of their environment, their managers failed to appreciate the seriousness of the threat posed by the Japanese producers.

The Japanese producers further exploited the "blindness" of the Big Three producers by not attacking directly. Instead, the Japanese producers carved out and then dominated the small-car market, selling in what the Big Three producers regarded as an unattractive market segment because of the low margins of small cars. In describing the Japanese strategy, Yutaka Natayama, Nissan's representative in the United States, was quoted as having said, "What we should do is get better and creep up slowly, so we'll be good—and the customer will think we're good—before Detroit even knows about us."[28] Using the three-dimensional model of industries, the Japanese entry to the U.S. automobile industry involved altering or expanding the industry along both the technological and product dimensions. This same pattern—of new entrants moving into "holes" in the competitive space or creating new competitive space rather than attacking incumbent firms directly—is observed in the experience of many industries.

The Most Successful New Entrants Will Take Advantage of Changes in Two or Three Industry Dimensions

The dynamic model also suggests that the managers of successful new entrant firms generally offer new products or services that capitalize on changes in more than one industry dimension. For example, a successful new entrant is likely to introduce a new product that not only responds to a change in consumer preferences but also incorporates a new technological development or a new production process. New rivals have many incentives to capitalize on changes in more than one industry dimension. By moving into a "hole" in the competitive space and by not only filling an unmet customer need but doing so in a novel way, a new entrant may be able to disguise itself even better from incumbent firms. Such a new rival might look sufficiently "different" to the managers of incumbent firms that they will have quite a difficult time recognizing the new entrant as a serious threat.

Again, the Japanese automobile manufacturers provide an example. Not only did they offer a new product—the small, fuel-efficient car—but they also exploited developments in manufacturing technology, specifically lean manufacturing techniques. Wal-Mart stores not only provided customers with a unique product mix, but the company also incorporated technological developments that allowed it to operate with a very low cost structure.

Similarly, Apple not only sought to tap an unserved market for personal computing, but, to do so, the company took advantage of important advances in microprocessor technology. In fact, Apple offers a classic example of exploiting changes along more than one industry dimension. As previously illustrated in Exhibit 5.5, Apple's development of the personal computer involved the exploitation of a new technology (microprocessors) to develop a new product (the personal computer) that was then marketed to a totally new segment of computer users (individuals and households).

Entrepreneurial Judo

The model also suggests that the managers of successful new entrant firms seek to establish strong niches from which they then expand into ever larger areas in the competitive space. New entrants are rarely content to occupy niche positions in their industries. Although their initial presence may be modest, new entrants will have many incentives to move beyond their initial market segments. Consumers may develop a loyalty to the new entrant, and this loyalty can be exploited by offering a broader range of products or services.

Similarly, the possibility of enjoying economies of scale from a broader application of the technology will also encourage a new entrant to expand beyond an initial niche position. Nugget Market, a supermarket chain in California, illustrates this concept well. By developing a strong, loyal customer base, the firm has been able to expand its number of stores and at the same time adopt a "unique food experience," complete with a large collection of organic foods, wine-tasting events, inviting décor, extensive array of house wares, and most importantly, competitive prices.[29]

Over the years, the Japanese automobile manufacturers gradually expanded their car lines, introducing products that now fill the complete spectrum of the automobile market, from small, fuel-efficient cars to sports cars, pickups, sport-utility vehicles, minivans, and luxury cars. In a very short time, Wal-Mart grew from a small, regional company to surpass Sears, Kmart, and many other companies to become the nation's largest retailer.

Asleep at the Switch: Patterns in the Responses of Incumbent Firms' Managers

The preceding section focused on the characteristics of new firms entering established industries. This section focuses on three patterns that are common in the response of incumbent firms' managers to the entry of new rivals.

The Difficulty of Matching the Products, Services, or Technological Capabilities of New Entrants

First, as noted in the introduction, managers of incumbent firms are rarely able to match new entrants' products, services, or technological capabilities. Why? In Chapter 3, we emphasized that managers' mental models are often locked in understandings of their competitive environments that do not allow them to recognize either changing industry dimensions or the presence of new rivals. In fact, managers may often fail to appreciate the challenges posed by new entrants until long after decline has already crippled their firms.

The result of this lack of awareness is that incumbent firms are rarely able to match the developments of new rivals. In those situations in which managers of incumbent firms are aware of the important developments in their industries, their companies will probably lack the necessary understandings (i.e., mental models), expertise, and technologies to respond effectively to the new entrants' initiatives. And, even in those cases in which incumbent firms can match a new rival's initiatives, the new rival may have already accrued significant first-mover advantages.

Retreat

The second interesting pattern associated with incumbent response is that, instead of trying to match the capabilities of their new rivals, the managers of incumbent firms are likely to respond 1) by withdrawing to supposedly "safer" areas in the competitive space, 2) by diversifying, or 3) by improving current offerings of products and services. When confronted by a new entrant, incumbent firms might respond by vigorously challenging the new entrant's products or services or by acquiring, developing, or even improving on the new entrant's technology. The model offered in this chapter suggests, however, that such a vigorous response is unlikely. Asleep at the switch, the managers of incumbent firms are more likely to let considerable time pass before noticing the threat of a new entrant, and, then, they are likely to let even more time pass before taking action. By this time, the new entrant may have already secured a comfortable niche, may be enjoying a number of first-mover advantages, and may already be on its way toward challenging incumbent firms' positions of dominance. As a result, a counterattack by incumbent firms, if launched, will typically come too late to be effective.

At this point, incumbent firms will consider a number of other responses. For example, the managers of incumbent firms will often complain about unfair competition. This was certainly the case among managers of the automotive and steel industries who asked for quotas on imported automobiles and steel. Diversification into unrelated businesses is another strategy many industry executives have adopted in order to "escape" from markets that are becoming less attractive.

At the same time, managers are reluctant to abandon long-standing markets and to write-off what had been productive investments.[30] A good deal of research evidence suggests that managers caught in such a situation may seek to "fight it out" by retreating to what they believe to be a more defensible niche. In fact, managers of incumbent firms often pursue improvements in existing products or services even though these products or services may have already been rendered obsolete by the products, services, or technologies introduced by a new entrant.[31] Whatever the initial response, the result is that incumbents tend to be more reactive than proactive. Incumbent managers are much more likely to retreat to what they believe will be more defensible positions than to launch effective counterattacks.

Retreat Rarely Offers Long-term Benefits

Finally, it is important to emphasize that the managers of incumbent firms rarely enjoy any sort of long-run benefit from a strategic withdrawal from market segments invaded by new entrants. As already described, this retreat to supposedly more defensible positions is a paradox. Instead of finding a safe harbor, managers of incumbent firms are likely to find that competition has actually escalated. Competition among incumbent firms is likely to intensify as they begin serving a smaller segment of the industry. These incumbent firms will have excess capacity, and they will be fighting even more vigorously for shares of a smaller pie. Furthermore, competition from successful new entrants is likely to intensify as they proceed to move beyond their initial niche positions into additional areas in the competitive arena. Often, successful new entrants totally restructure the industries they enter.

Using the Dynamic Model for Industry Analysis

Now that we have introduced a dynamic model of industry structuring and offered some specific propositions about the ways in which industries evolve, we want to describe how this dynamic model can be used to conduct analyses of specific industries. Although the dynamic model suggests that any industry can be analyzed along three dimensions—customers (the "who" dimension), products and services (the "what" dimension), and technologies (the "how" dimension)—use of the model requires that the analyst identify the relevant labels for the three dimensions.

For example, in analyzing the food industry, labeling groups based on chronological age might be relevant and provide useful labels for the customer (or "who") dimension. Babies have needs that are quite distinct from the wants of younger children. Similarly, working parents with school-age children have needs and wants different from those of older consumers.

On the other hand, customer groups based on chronological age might not be particularly useful for analyzing the customer dimension of the automobile industry. For example, the automobile industry cannot really target buyers younger than 16 years old in most states. Furthermore, car-buying habits are much more likely to be influenced by such factors as disposable income and driving habits than by chronological age. Thus, for analyzing the customer dimension of the automobile industry, a far more useful set of labels might be "first-time," "repeat," "basic transportation," "luxury," and "performance" buyers.

The major automobile companies develop much more detailed customer segmentation information through their market research efforts, but even this simple segmentation will be very helpful in understanding changes in the industry. For example, all of the major automobile producers spend a great deal of resources on developing entry-level vehicles because these cars are aimed at attracting first-time car buyers. First-time car buyers are so important to automobile companies because many car buyers tend to buy the same brand of automobile again if they have a positive experience.

As mentioned earlier, authors of *Blue Ocean Strategy* offer additional ways to examine customer needs and patterns in an attempt to identify untapped markets. They suggest asking four questions to start analyzing dynamic industries:

- Which of the factors that the industry takes for granted should be eliminated?
- Which factors should be reduced well below the industry's standard?
- Which factors should be raised well above the industry's standard?
- Which factors should be created that the industry has never offered?

Exhibit 5.6 An Analysis of the Products and Services Dimension of the Computer Industry

Comcast, Verizon, AT&T, AOL	Linux, Microsoft, Orade	Intel, AMD, Cisco	Nokia, RIM, Samsung, Apple	Dell, HP, Apple, Lenovo	Dell, HP Sun	Andersen, EDS, IBM, Unisys
←						→
Internet service providers	Software	High tech components	PDAs, Smart phones	Personal computers	Servers	Consulting services

Similar types of analyses are required to develop labels for all three dimensions. The "what," or products and services, dimension poses some challenges. On the one hand, because any firm could hypothetically manufacture just about any product or provide any service, analysts might be tempted to define the products and services dimension too broadly. On the other hand, the products and services dimension must be broader than current conceptualizations of the industry or a single firm's own line of products or services so that the analysis can consider how the industry is likely to evolve. For example, Exhibit 5.6 offers one possible analysis of the products and services dimension of the computer industry.

Note that the analysis illustrated in Exhibit 5.6 includes not only personal computers, but also cell phones, PDAs and other hand-held devices, Internet service providers, software writers, high-technology components (such as microprocessors), other hardware components, workstations, minicomputers and mainframes, and information technology consultation services. By including such a broad range of products and services and by also labeling the various firms that produce and provide these products and services, the user can quickly get a feel for or an understanding of how the industry has evolved and which portions of the product dimension are more "crowded" than others. By doing some further research and attaching revenue and net income figures to the various products and services, the analyst can also get a feel for the relative size of these various product and service markets. Such an analysis would reveal, for example, that software, microprocessors, and consultation services generate the vast majority of the total net income generated by the computer industry.

In analyzing any of the three dimensions, it is important to keep in mind the objectives of the analysis—to understand how the industry has changed and is likely to change, to identify areas of opportunity, and to rethink the structure of the industry. Thus, the choice of labels must help managers understand not only the nature of competition in the industry at the present time, but also how the various dimensions will be changing and how these changes will affect competition and the structure of the industry in the future.

Industry Restructuring and the Key Themes of This Book: Some Specific Implications for Management Practice

The model introduced in this chapter suggests that industries are "structuring" over time, the result of an ongoing process that is tied to the cognitive understandings of managers. This model suggests that two factors: 1) changing industry dimensions, and 2) the limitations, biases, and inertia inherent in managerial thinking are helpful in explaining patterns in the evolution of most industries.

The model suggests that entrepreneurial activity plays a key role in the process of ongoing industry structuring because entrepreneurs see opportunities to satisfy consumers' new wants and needs, exploit new technological developments, and offer new products and services. Entrepreneurs are also helped by the managers of incumbent firms who, because of their cognitive limitations and inertia, fail to see and exploit these same opportunities.

How is the dynamic model of industry structuring introduced in this chapter related to the three key themes emphasized throughout this book, and what are its implications for management practice? Before we suggest answers to these questions, consider how one noted researcher has described the strategy formulation process:

> In general terms, strategy formation in most organizations can be thought of as revolving around the interplay of three basic forces: a) an environment that changes continuously but irregularly, with frequent discontinuities and wide swings in its rate of change, b) an organizational operating system, or bureaucracy, that above all seeks to stabilize its actions, despite the characteristics of the environment it serves, and c) a leadership whose role is to mediate between these two forces, to maintain the stability of the organization's operating system while at the same time insuring its adaptation to environmental change.[32]

Note the similarities between the characterization of the strategy formulation process and the three key themes of this text. Both highlight the importance of managers and leaders. Both emphasize that industry environments are constantly changing, often in ways that are quite unexpected. And, both highlight the importance of organizational learning in helping firms adapt to changing environments. We focus our recommendations for management practice around each of these three key themes:

Managers and Managerial Thinking

Our model of strategic management suggests that managers must not only understand the current relevant dimensions of their firms' industry environments, but they must also think about how these dimensions will change over time. They must also think creatively and imaginatively about where their firms should be in the evolving competitive environments. How, for example, can their firms be on the cutting edge, creating "new" competitive space by developing consumer interest in new products or services or by developing new technological capabilities? This kind of managerial thinking, insight, and creativity may be the most valuable resource organizations can possess, and it is certainly a key source of competitive advantage.

Many of the examples offered in this chapter suggest that managers tend to do too little monitoring of their industry environments. The answer is not, however, for managers simply to do more monitoring. As we've already suggested, monitoring is likely to be focused by past experience and industry norms. As a result, managers are likely to miss potentially important developments, and they are likely to search for potential new entrants that look like their own firms. In addition to monitoring, *managers must more actively anticipate the future by exploring the unoccupied and newly emerging areas of opportunities both within and outside their industries.*

The chapter also suggests that *it is important to think like an industry outsider*. Innovations and strategic alternatives will not necessarily emerge from a better understanding of the industry's current context. Successful innovation requires that managers think like outsiders so that they can better see the opportunities that changes in industry dimensions will offer. This may mean that research and development staff members should be separated from the company bureaucracy. It might also mean paying more attention to the contrarian voices or iconoclasts within the organization who may offer radically different perspectives. New employees from outside the industry can also offer insightful ideas and suggestions. As Gary Hamel suggests, the managers of even the most successful industry incumbents must think like heretics and struggle against industry orthodoxy.[33]

Change and the Need to Think Dynamically about Strategic Management

A key assumption of the model of industry structuring presented in this chapter is that industry environments are evolving over time as customer demographics change, as new products and services are introduced, and as new technologies emerge. Thus, an important insight is that *managers must continuously reposition their firms over time in order to keep pace with changes in their firms' competitive environments*. Entrepreneurial managers can anticipate changes in industry dimensions and literally create whole new markets. This is, of course, the genius of the founders of Apple Computer: They had the ability to see how changes in microprocessor technology would allow a great deal of computing power to be placed in a very small box, making possible a totally new product, the personal computer, that would appeal and be marketed to a totally new group of unsophisticated computer users.

This means that more companies must adopt the strategies of companies like 3M and Rubbermaid. Both of these companies have explicit goals that a certain percentage of annual sales must come from products that did not exist in previous years.[34] Rubbermaid has described its emphasis on new products as one of its fundamental strengths: "Our goal is to have 30 percent of sales each year come from products which were not in the line five years earlier."[35] Some companies have gone even further. News articles about Sony have noted that the company schedules dates for the introduction of extensions to a new product and the date a replacement for a new product will be introduced *before the new product itself is introduced into the marketplace.*

Nor are the impacts of this entrepreneurial activity limited to intraindustry changes. Entrepreneurial activity in one industry can have profound effects on other industries; in some cases, changes can cause two or more industries to collide with each other, and totally new industries can emerge as a consequence. Chapter 1 described how traditional boundaries around industries are falling and new industries are emerging due to technological and other changes. For example, regulatory changes that initiated competition among banks, savings and loans, insurance companies, and investment banks have resulted in the emergence of a new financial services industry. Similarly, personal computers and the Internet have created a new means of distributing media content, and firms in industries as diverse as publishing, motion picture production, cable and network television, and computer software are now pursuing a variety of strategies in order to exploit these technological changes. These strategies and competitive interactions will result in a very different competitive landscape and possibly the emergence of totally new industries.[36]

The Importance of Organizational Learning

The dynamic model of industry structuring introduced in this chapter also highlights the importance of organizational learning, and it also suggests that *a higher level of learning—or major innovation—is likely to be more valuable and important than mere imitation or copying other firms*. When the dimensions of industry environments are changing continuously, imitation should be less useful than innovation. In fact, as suggested in Chapter 2, competitive advantage is much more likely to result from innovation than from mere imitation. Firms that do copy other firms' innovations must focus more attention on adding knowledge and value to those innovations.

The chapter also highlights the need to *beware of success*. It appears as though success in an earlier period is often responsible for decline in a subsequent period. In fact, although prosperity is the goal of the managers of every business enterprise, it appears that advantage is associated with some degree of adversity or struggle. Success often leads to contentment and a self-satisfied sort of complacency among managers. Managers of these firms stop paying attention to changes in their industries, they do less monitoring of the competitive landscape, they tend to discount the activities of their competitors, they tend to assume that new technological developments will have no significant impact on their businesses. In short, these companies stop *learning*. Certainly an important challenge for managers of all firms is to unlock and stimulate the kinds of individual and organizational learning that will be associated with organizational renewal and vitality.

Conclusion

The dynamic nature of industries is what makes business enterprise so interesting. Every day holds the promise of new developments and the opportunity to exploit changes in the competitive environment to create new products or services. Nothing can be assumed to remain stable or fixed for very long, as entrepreneurs rush to take advantage of changes in industry dimensions. Not only do these entrepreneurial efforts lead to the development of new products and services, but this activity is also a source of society's well-being. A company like Apple, founded in a garage, becomes a *Fortune* 500 company within a decade, and along the way creates thousands of jobs, develops many new supporting industries, and generates millions of dollars of sales and profits.

Key Points

The fundamental assumption of this chapter is that industries are continuously structured and restructured over time:

- The model we have introduced suggests that an industry can be thought of as a competitive arena or a "space" defined by firms sharing similarities along three dimensions—customers (the "who" dimension), products and services (the "what" dimension), and technologies (the "how" dimension).

- This model assumes that these three dimensions are continuously changing as customers develop new needs and wants, as new products and services are developed, and as new technologies emerge.
- These changes in industry dimensions create "holes" or opportunities in industry environments, and these holes invite invasion by entrepreneurial firms.
- At the same time, industry norms and cognitive limitations prevent the managers of incumbent firms from recognizing these same opportunities. They also prevent the managers of incumbent firms from recognizing the threat posed by entrepreneurial firms.

The chapter offered three observations about the entry of new rivals into an industry:

- Successful new rivals generally do not attack incumbent firms directly, but instead are more likely to enter an industry at the "holes" that are created by changes in consumer preferences and the adoption of new product and process technologies.
- Successful new entrants generally offer new products or services that capitalize on changes in more than one industry dimension. For example, a successful new entrant is likely to introduce a new product that not only responds to a change in consumer preferences but also incorporates a new technological development or a new production process.
- The model also suggests that successful new entrants seek to establish strong niches from which they then expand into ever larger areas in the competitive space.

The chapter also offered three observations about the response of incumbent firms to those new entrants:

- Incumbent firms are rarely able to match new entrants' products, services, or technological capabilities.
- Incumbent firms confronted by new rivals are more likely to respond by withdrawing to supposedly "safer" areas in the competitive space, by diversifying, or by improving current offerings of products and services.
- Incumbent firms rarely enjoy any sort of long-run benefit from a strategic withdrawal from market segments invaded by new entrants.

Key Questions for Managers

- Do the managers of your firm have a dynamic view of industry structuring?
- In what ways or along what dimensions is your firm's industry changing?
- How might norms within your industry prevent managers of your firm (and your firm's competitors) from anticipating or responding effectively to changes in the industry environment?
- What holes or "white spaces" exist in your industry that might invite entry by new rivals?

Suggestions for **Further Reading**

Additionally, links to further resources online—such as cases, articles, and videos—can be found on the book's website, www.routledge.com/textbooks/Duhaime.

Abell, D. F. 1980. *Defining the Business: Starting Point of Strategic Planning.* Englewood Cliffs, NJ: Prentice-Hall.

Afuah, A. 2003. *Innovation Management: Strategies, Implementation, and Profits.* New York: Oxford University Press.

Brown, S., & Eisenhrdt, K. M. 1998. *Competing on the Edge: Strategy as Structured Chaos.* Boston: Harvard Business School Press.

Christensen, C. M. 2000. *The Inovator's Dilemma.* New York: HarperBusiness.

Cooper, A. C., & Schendel, D. 1976. Strategic responses to technological threats. *Business Horizons*, 19(1): 61–69.

D'Aveni, R. 1994. *Hypercompetition.* New York: Free Press.

Drucker, P. F. 1985. *Innovation and Entrepreneurship.* New York: Harper & Row.

Hamel, G., & Prahalad, C. K. 1994. *Competing for the Future.* Boston: Harvard Business School Press.

Harris, L. M. (Ed.) 2003. *After Fifty: How the Baby Boom will Redefine the Mature Market.* Ithaca, NY: Paramount Market Publishing.

Kiesler, S., & Sproull, L. 1982. Managerial response to changing environments: Perspectives on problem sensing from social cognition. *Administrative Science Quarterly* 27: 548–570.

Kim, W. C., & Mauborgne, R. 2005. *Blue Ocean Strategy: How to Create Uncontested Market Space and Make the Competition Irrelevant.* Boston: Harvard Business School Press.

Mathews, R., & Wacker, W. 2002. *The Deviant's Advantage: How Fringe Ideas Create Mass Markets.* New York: Crown Business.

Tushman, M. L., & Anderson, P. 2004. *Managing Strategic Innovation and Change: A Collection of Readings* (2nd ed.). New York: Oxford University Press.

Urban, G. L., Carter, T., Gaskin, S., & Mucha, Z. 1986. Market share rewards to pioneering brands: An empirical analysis and strategic implications. *Management Science* 32: 645–659.

Yates, B. 1983. *The Decline and Fall of the American Automobile Industry.* New York: Empire Books.

Chapter 6

Business Definition and Positioning

This chapter focuses on managers' decisions about business definition and positioning—decisions that are among the most important that they make. As illustrated in Exhibit 6.1, this chapter describes how managers' mental models about their firms' industry environments influence their decisions about business definition and positioning.

Chapter Objectives

The specific objectives of this chapter on business definition are to:

- Emphasize the connection between managers' understandings of their competitive environment and their decisions about business definition and positioning.
- Define the concepts of business definition and positioning, and emphasize the importance of these strategic activities.
- Describe the ways in which business definition can be a source of, or contribute to, the development of sustained competitive advantage.
- Illustrate some effective business definitions.
- Since firms and businesses operate in changing industry environments, the chapter will also emphasize the importance of *redefinition*, and illustrate the challenges associated with redefinition.

What Are Business Definition and Positioning?

The text has defined strategy as "a pattern in a stream of decisions," and one of the most important sets of decisions managers make involves defining and positioning their firms and businesses. **Definition** is the way a firm or a business describes itself to employees, customers, and other constituencies while also distinguishing it from other business organizations that may or may not be competitors. Thus, definition conveys what is most important about that company while also distinguishing the company from its competitors. In short, definition provides an organization with an *identity* that describes what is "central, distinctive, and enduring" about it.[1]

In Chapter 2, we described the differences between *strategy content*, or *what* a firm does, and *strategy process*, or *how* a firm does what it does. Business definition is both strategy content *and* strategy process. Business definition is strategy content in that, building on the model of industry dynamics developed in Chapter 5, it describes *which customers the firm or business*

Exhibit 6.1 Managers' Beliefs, Strategic Decisions, and Their Influence on Performance and Competitive Advantage

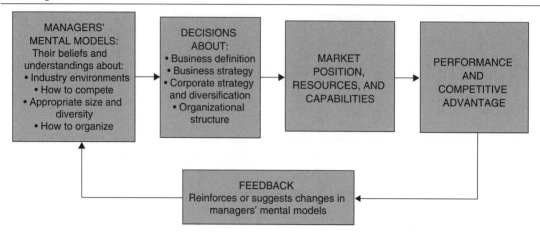

will serve, what products or services the firm or business will offer, and what technologies the firm or business will employ. But business definition is also a strategy process—*the process by which firms and businesses select positions in their industry environments.*[2]

The content and process of business definition are illustrated in Exhibit 6.2. The exhibit depicts an industry as a locus of customers, products and services, and technologies—the three-dimensional competitive space introduced in Chapter 5. The left side of the exhibit illustrates definition as the darker cube representing a particular firm or business choosing to serve certain customers, offering certain products or services, and employing certain technologies within the larger competitive arena. Obviously, managers of the firm or business could choose to occupy a larger or smaller part of the industry's competitive space.

Exhibit 6.2 Business Definition within the Larger Competitive Space of a Market or an Industry

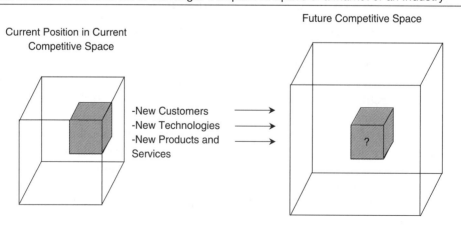

While we tend to think "bigger is better" and size can offer many advantages, this chapter and the next chapter will show that firms can also be very successful by focusing on relatively small market niches. The competitive space in which firms compete may have one or many "sweet spots," just as it may have market segments that aren't viable. And, as we emphasized in Chapter 5, industry environments are also likely to have "white space" or unexplored areas—areas that offer opportunities for entrepreneurs and enterprising incumbent firms.

The exhibit also illustrates the major challenge associated with business definition—that successful definition requires an ongoing process of *redefinition*. Notice in Exhibit 6.2 that, over time, the arrows imply that the dimensions of the industry change due to shifts in customer demographics and preferences, the development of new products and services, and the emergence of new technologies. As a result, managers must redefine their firms and businesses in order to keep pace with these industry changes. Alternatively, managers can be proactive—pushing their firms to develop new products, services, and technologies and identifying new customer wants and needs—so that their firms are instrumental in reshaping industry boundaries.[3] Apple Computer is a good example of a firm that has proactively and fundamentally reshaped not just the computer industry in the early 1980s, but has also more recently had a huge impact on the personal electronics, telecommunication, music, and, most recently, the publishing industries.

On the other hand, the consequences of failing to respond to or to anticipate changes in the competitive space can be severe. Levi's is a good example of a company that once held a leading position in the competitive space for casual apparel. Yet in the early 2000s, Levi's managers missed key changes and trends in the U.S. market and its clothes lost much of their appeal to makers of designer jeans. As a result, Levi's managers have had to struggle to re-energize the Levi's brand in the volatile and highly competitive U.S. market for casual clothing.

Business definition occurs at both the firm *and* business level. If a firm is a "single business firm," that is, if it engages in only a single business activity, then it will probably have a simple, straightforward business definition. On the other hand, diversified or multibusiness firms, which have business segments engaged in many different industries, will need to have unique business definitions for each of their different businesses. And, in addition to developing unique definitions for each business, diversified firms will also need to develop some sort of overall definition for the firm—what Porter has called a "corporate theme"—that describes the firm and suggests how (or whether) its various businesses are related to one another.[4] We will focus more attention on the subject of business definition in diversified firms when we examine corporate strategy and diversification in Chapter 10, but the key point we want to emphasize here is that as firms become larger and more diversified, the task of business definition becomes more complex and challenging.

This chapter focuses on both the content *and* the process aspects of business definition. We focus first on the *content* of business definitions, and how an effective business definition can be a source, or contribute to the development, of competitive advantage. We then describe the creative *process* by which business definitions are developed. Because firms and businesses operate in dynamic markets and industry environments, *business redefinition* is also a very important process, and so the chapter will also focus on the challenges of business redefinition.

Business Definition and Competitive Advantage

Both practicing managers and academic researchers have shown great interest in concepts of "mission," "purpose," "strategic intent," "vision," and "identity," all of which emphasize the importance of organizational "self-knowledge"—that the organization's definition and what distinguishes it from other organizations is somehow critical to its effectiveness.[5] The underlying premise is that business definition can be an important source, or at least contribute to the development, of competitive advantage—the reason some firms enjoy higher performance than their rivals. This is not only because business definition determines how the organization sees itself and how others relate to the organization but also because it influences a wide range of other strategic decisions.

Here, we describe four ways in which business definition contributes to the development of competitive advantage. As noted in Chapter 2, the key consideration in evaluating any source of competitive advantage is always the ease of imitation: Any source of competitive advantage that can be easily duplicated by rivals is unlikely to offer sustained levels of high performance.

Business Definition "Positions" a Firm or a Business in Its Competitive Space or Industry Environment

Business definition is the major way in which companies describe themselves to customers, employees, suppliers, and investors. It is also the primary way customers, employees, and other constituencies develop an image of companies. Exhibit 6.2 showed that, based on their understandings and beliefs (mental models) about the competitive environment, they then define their firm along three dimensions—customers, products and services, and technologies. For each of these three dimensions, business definition allows managers to describe or identify their companies while also helping customers, employees, and other constituencies develop an image of their companies and how they differ from other business organizations.

Business definition is therefore closely related to the concepts of positioning, branding, and differentiation—concepts that will be more fully considered in Chapter 7. The most successful business definitions will not only communicate to customers and other stakeholders how a particular business is positioned in the marketplace but it will also create an emotional bond with the business's stakeholders.

Harley-Davidson enjoys a competitive advantage in the motorcycle industry largely because of its successful definition and positioning. Harley's distinctiveness and the image it has developed have engendered tremendous loyalty among Harley riders. Joanne Bischmann, Harley's vice president of marketing has noted: "I am still awed by the lengths our customers will go to show their commitment. Recently, I saw a man who had tattooed a portrait of our four founding fathers and our 100th anniversary logo on his back."[6]

Within almost any industry, one will find a number of different "strategic groups"—groups of firms pursuing similar strategies. For example, in the brewing industry, Anheuser Busch InBer and MolsonCoors pursue a national strategy in the United States. Microbreweries pursue a very different strategy, with most serving only a local or small regional market. The objective of business definition is to somehow distinguish the firm from its competitors even though it might be pursuing a strategy that is very similar to the strategy being pursued by other companies that are in the same strategic group.

The J. M. Smucker Company provides an excellent example of a company that has developed a very effective business definition, and consistently enjoys high performance. While several other firms produce jams and jellies, the J. M. Smucker Company has successfully defined itself as a manufacturer of the highest-quality jams, jellies, and other fruit products, using the finest inputs. The company's high-quality products have, in turn, attracted a loyal group of discerning customers who will pay a premium to use Smucker's fine products. Customers have so strongly accepted this definition that Smucker's products consistently receive more supermarket shelf space and sell for higher prices than their competitors' comparable products.

Like Smucker, Gerber has succeeded in establishing a definition as the highest quality producer of baby food products. Beech-Nut, Heinz, Gerber and other companies participate in the U.S. baby food market, yet Gerber dominates, commanding nearly 70 percent of the U.S. baby food market. Parents prefer Gerber's products so much that most supermarkets will carry only two of the three leading baby food makers' products—Gerber and either Beech-Nut or Heinz. And, as with Smucker's jams and jellies, Gerber's products always command a large share of the shelf space devoted to baby food and tend to sell for a few more cents per jar than competitors' comparable products.

It is not that Smucker and Gerber do what other companies cannot do—in fact, both companies have well established competitors. Rather, they have so carefully and effectively invested resources into crafting their definitions that they have come to be seen as closely aligned with their product markets. In fact, so closely are they identified with their product markets that consumers often do not consider other brands, even though choosing Gerber's baby food products or Smucker's jams means paying more per jar. Exhibit 6.3 illustrates the pricing advantages Smucker and Gerber enjoy from their business definitions.

Exhibit 6.3 How Effective Definitions Provide Two Companies with Pricing Advantages

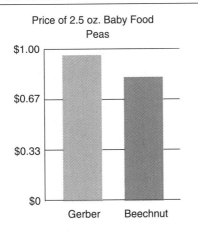

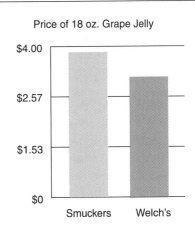

Business Definition Helps to Focus Management Attention on the Firm's Key Objectives, Its Most Significant Strategic Issues, and Its Most Important Rivals

There is an old saying that "the main thing is that the main thing must remain the main thing." Business definition can help to focus management attention on *the main thing*. Not only does business definition allow organizations to describe themselves to internal and external constituencies, but it also helps to focus management attention on key objectives, competitors, and other issues in the competitive landscape. In a classic business article, Ram Charan, management consultant and former Harvard professor, has argued that before managers can effectively address other questions of strategy or competitive tactics, they need to address key business definition questions, including:[7]

- Where are we now? Where are we taking the business?
- How are we going to position our business vis-à-vis the competition and the marketplace?

These are simple questions, yet they have profound implications for the success of any business organization. Business definition, by placing a firm or business in a particular portion of the industry or competitive arena vis-à-vis its competitors, helps managers focus their attention on a set of key strategic objectives and on the competitors, opportunities, and threats that are most relevant. It's not that managers can ignore more peripheral issues and competitors, or developments affecting the industry, but business definition allows managers to focus more of their attention on the most important objectives, the most direct competitors, and the most relevant issues.

Business Definition Influences Other Strategic Decisions

A third way in which business definition will contribute to competitive advantage is by making other strategic decisions more obvious and by helping managers to make decisions that are more consistent with their firm's definition and strategies. Once the business has been defined, managers will be able to quickly identify many other strategic issues that must be addressed. In other words, managers' mental models about their firm's definition will influence their thinking, beliefs, and understandings about a wide array of other issues, including business strategy and the resources and capabilities that will be required. Together, these mental models and the decisions that follow from them should share a consistency or logic that reinforces the business definition.

Consider, for example, the luxury watch maker, Rolex. Given the company's definition as the producer of the finest luxury watches, many other decisions necessarily fall into place. The company continually innovates to maintain the luxury image of its timepieces. Pricing is also carefully aimed at reinforcing the brand's luxury image. (The company could almost certainly increase its sales by lowering its prices—at least initially—but lower prices would also jeopardize the company's image as the preeminent luxury watch manufacturer.) The company distributes its products through only the finest jewelry and watch retailers around the world, and the company's advertisements appear only in those venues that are likely to enhance its image and reputation. It also carefully selects a limited number of cultural and sporting events to sponsor, including opera productions, horse races, tennis matches, and yacht races, again, with an eye toward those events that will enhance its image and puts its name before current and potential customers who are most likely to be able to afford the company's products.

Business Definition Provides Meaning and Can Be Very Motivational

Finally, a fourth way that business definition can contribute to competitive advantage is that an effective definition has the ability to motivate managers and other employees. Many business articles and books, including the best-selling book, *Built to Last*, by Collins and Porras, have emphasized the motivational aspects of such concepts as business definition, organizational identity, strategic intent, and vision. Firms that have strong business definitions provide managers and employees with a sense of meaning, purpose, and excitement that can arouse commitment and even passion. Hamel and Prahalad state, "we believe that any strategic intent must contain pathos and passion. Too many mission statements fail entirely to impart any sense of *mission*."[8]

Research also suggests that effective business definitions can be much more tangible and motivational than financial objectives. Goals such as "increasing earnings per share" or "increasing shareholder value" are *not* examples of business definitions, and Collins and Porras offer this criticism of such goals:

> "Maximize shareholder wealth" does not inspire people at all levels of an organization, and it provides precious little guidance. "Maximize shareholder wealth" is the standard "off-the-shelf" purpose for those organizations that have not yet identified their true core purpose. It is a substitute ideology, and a weak substitute at that. Listen to people in great organizations talk about their achievements and you'll hear very little about earnings per share. ... HP people talk with pride about the technical contributions their products have made to the marketplace. Nordstrom people talk about heroic customer service and remarkable individual performance by star sales people.[9]

A Case Study of Business Definition and the Characteristics of Effective Business Definitions

This chapter has already highlighted a number of examples of businesses and companies that have very successfully defined themselves in their industries, including Rolex, Harley Davidson, Smucker, and Gerber. To further demonstrate how business definition can contribute to competitive advantage, let's consider a classic case study that will help to illustrate the influence of business definition on firm performance. We will also use this case study to identify the characteristics of effective business definitions.

General Motors in 1921

The problem General Motors faced in the early 1920s was that the company had seven different car lines that had been acquired by William Durant, GM's founder, but the separate car lines lacked clear identities and vigorously competed with and took sales from each other. For example, Chevrolet, Oakland (later Pontiac), and Oldsmobile models all had similar specifications and sold at similar price points. As summarized by Alfred Sloan, who succeeded Durant as the head of GM, this confusion had occurred because "we did not know what we were trying to do except to sell cars which, in a sense, took volume from each other."

To make sense of this chaos, Sloan argued that General Motors, like any other business, needed a definition, within what he called a "concept of the automobile business:"

> After the two great expansions of 1908 to 1910 and 1918 to 1920—perhaps one should say because of them—General Motors was in need not only of a concept of management but equally of a concept of the automobile business. Every enterprise needs a concept of its industry. There is a logical way of doing business in accordance with the facts and circumstances of an industry, if you can figure it out. If there are different concepts among the enterprises involved, these concepts are likely to express competitive forces in their most vigorous and decisive form.[10]

Here, Sloan is making several points that have been emphasized thus far in this book. First, he notes the importance of definition (e.g., "General Motors was in need not only of a concept of management but equally of a concept of the automobile business"). Second, he reinforces the fact that effective definitions are based on managers' understandings or mental models of their firms' industries (e.g., "Every enterprise needs a concept of its industry. There is a logical way of doing business in accordance with the facts and circumstances of an industry, if you can figure it out"). Finally, Sloan emphasizes that, by positioning firms in their industries, definitions determine how companies will compete for customers and sales (e.g., "If there are different concepts among the enterprises involved, these concepts are likely to express competitive forces in their most vigorous and decisive form").

The definition or "concept" that Sloan imposed on the chaos of General Motors was the view that each of the different GM car lines should serve different but overlapping price points. Exhibit 6.4 illustrates GM's car lines and the actual price ranges assigned to each line in 1921.

Fundamental to Sloan's concept was the idea that the lowest-priced car line, Chevrolet, would offer automobiles that would not compete directly with Ford's Model T (which at the time sold for $355 and enjoyed a market share of about 60 percent), but would be "so near the Ford price that demand would be drawn from the Ford grade and lifted to the slightly higher

Exhibit 6.4 GM's Car Lines and the Price Ranges Assigned to Each Line in 1921

Chevrolet	$450–$600
Oakland (later Pontiac)	$600–$900
Buick (four-cylinder)	$900–$1,200
Buick (six-cylinder)	$1,200–$1,700
Oldsmobile	$1,700–$2,500
Cadillac	$2,500–$3,500

price."[11] Similarly, each of the other GM lines, Oakland, Buick, Oldsmobile, and Cadillac, respectively, would offer more features and slightly higher quality for which consumers might be willing to pay a premium. Implicit also in Sloan's concept was that GM's customers would trade-up as they moved through their own life stages. Chevrolet would be GM's entry level vehicle, and as customers advanced in their careers and had more disposable income, they could trade-up to GM's more expensive car lines. Over time, GM's definition came to be summarized as "a car for every purse and purpose."[12]

So successful was Sloan's "concept" or business definition that General Motors quickly overtook Ford as the leader in overall market share, and this scheme of differentiated product lines selling at different price points also became a central component of GM's business definition. In addition to helping the struggling General Motors describe itself to customers, investors, and other external constituencies, Sloan's concept had several internal benefits that influenced strategic decision making at the company for many decades, helping GM's managers focus on a more finite set of competitive priorities, motivating managers to develop unique designs and styles, and improving manufacturing efficiency.

Sloan's concept of the car industry and his definition of GM's positioning within the industry was effective for more than 50 years. And, so successful was Sloan's definition that as GM began to experience loss of market share and declines in performance in the 1970s and 1980s, many observers concluded that the company's troubles were the result of its failure to remain true to Sloan's definition. Indeed, by that time, many of GM's car lines shared common styling and the prices of cars offered by the various divisions had begun to overlap considerably.

Characteristics of Effective Business Definitions

This short case study suggests three key characteristics of effective business definitions:

Distinctive

The best business definitions give companies distinct identities and place them in a unique position in the competitive space. In fact, if business definition is to be a source of, or contribute to, sustained competitive advantage, then business definitions must not only be unique, but they must be difficult for other firms to imitate. Note in the General Motors example, Sloan did not seek to imitate Ford's standardized, mass-production definition of the automobile, but rather sought to have GM pursue its own very different definition—one that allowed the company to dominate the industry for a half century and, in the process, revolutionized the automobile industry by emphasizing car design and styling.

Timely and Appropriate given the Industry Environment

Second, a definition must be timely and appropriate given the industry. Sloan's insight, that it would be "suicidal" to go after Ford directly, and that GM needed to position its various automotive brands in varying steps or segments above Ford's Model T, was both at the time and in retrospect nothing short of brilliant, and laid a foundation for General Motors to dominate the automobile industry for half a century.

Clear and Readily Understandable

Not all business definitions can be unique and difficult to imitate, and, given the rapid rate of change in most industry environments, some business definitions will be less timely than others. Yet, all business definitions should be clear and readily understandable. Smucker's and Gerber have so well positioned themselves in their respective marketplaces that their names convey to customers their distinctiveness and quality.

Note, too, how simply the phrase "a car for every purse and purpose" captured the definition that Sloan adopted for GM's automobile business. The ability to distill a company's definition into a single phrase helps to insure that it will be widely understood not only by customers, but also by those inside a company so that employees know the company's definition and support and buy into that definition. As we have already emphasized, wordy mission statements can never provide this same degree of clarity and sense of mission or purpose.[13]

Summary

Thus far, we have defined the concept of business definition, described four ways that business definition can contribute to, or be a source of, competitive advantage. We then provided a short case study of business definition that allowed us to identify three key characteristics of effective business definitions. We now focus on the key aspects of the business definition *process*.

Characteristics of the Business Definition Process

In this section, we focus on the key characteristics of the process by which business definitions are developed:

Business Definition Is Fundamentally a Creative Process

First, business definition is fundamentally a creative process that can vitally influence the success of firms and businesses.[14] Many people think of business as a "science," much like engineering, because many business problems are addressed by applying frameworks, formulas, or models to a particular situation. For example, to address many finance questions, we apply discounted cash flow techniques to calculate the present or future value of a stream of cash flows. Similarly, many marketing questions are addressed by applying statistical techniques to analyze market research data. As a result, it can be easy to think that many if not most business decisions can be guided by more or less "scientific" principles or tools. And, business people can grow frustrated sometimes by the very subjective and challenging nature of leadership, motivation, and many other organizational behavior and human resource management issues that defy easy application of objective criteria or "formulas."

While business school curricula tend to offer students very little exposure to the subject of creativity, many business activities require creative thinking, and entrepreneurship is very much a creative endeavor. While researchers are making good progress at understanding creativity and creative processes, much of this new knowledge and understanding has yet to find its way into business courses and teaching materials or into the popular business press.

As a result, many business managers are poorly prepared for the creativity challenges associated with definition and positioning. Like the work of artists, the process of business definition brings something new into being—deciding that a business will provide a particular product or service, that it will serve a particular group of customers, or that it will make use of a particular technology. And, given the dynamic, evolving industry environments in which business activity takes place, creativity becomes even more important. The psychologist, Rollo May, made these observations about the importance of creativity:

> Every profession can and does require creativity. In our day, technology and engineering, diplomacy, business, and certainly teaching, all of these professions and scores of others are in the midst of radical change and require courageous persons to appreciate and direct this change. *The need for creativity is in direct proportion to the degree of change the profession is undergoing.*[15]

Yet, May was also aware of the forces in our society that work against creativity; most specifically, May was concerned about a lack of will or passion:

> The fact that talent is plentiful but passion is lacking is a fundamental problem of creativity in many fields today, and our ways of evading the hard work of creativity have played directly into this trend. We worship technique and talent, so that we can evade the anxiety and struggle associated with creativity.[16]

Teresa Amabile and her colleagues have done considerable research on creativity, and their findings have important implications for creativity in business organizations. For example, the natural tendency of businesses is to evaluate and critically assess new ideas, and this critical approach can work to retard individual creativity. Amabile also emphasizes the importance of working environments that limit stress, encourage playfulness, and provide employees with time for experimentation. Employees should also feel that they have a good deal of autonomy and freedom to pursue their interests and ideas. Finally, research has suggested that various personality traits are associated with creativity. Specifically, individuals with a preference for independence and complexity are likely to be more creative.[17]

It's not surprising, then, that Google, a firm known for the creativity and originality of its employees, has sought to create a work environment that is consistent with these qualities. And, these newer, high-tech companies are not the only firms adopting this kind of work environment; many established firms have also worked to develop cultures that foster creativity. Without the creative impulse as well as the entrepreneurial passion or will to transform ideas into reality, our business landscape would be far less vibrant and our society would have far less economic growth and a lower standard of living than we presently enjoy. As a result, it is worth valuing and enhancing those aspects of work environments and of society that encourage and foster creativity and inspiration.

The Business Definition Process Requires Knowledge and Understanding of the Competitive Space and Its Opportunities

A second characteristic of the business definition process is that effective business definitions rarely emerge without an extensive knowledge of the business and competitive landscape. In other words, *effective* business definitions are rarely the result of luck or whims, but are instead the outcome of expertise and hard work. May argued that creativity results from "encounter" or "engagement" with a particular issue or problem.[18] Furthermore, even though we tend to think of the *status quo* or "conventional wisdom" as the opposite of creativity, May argued that an understanding of the structure of the problem or situation—what he called "form"—will actually increase the quality of the creative effort. May reasoned that an understanding of the problem or situation provides a context so that creative thinkers can know the full range of both the possibilities and the limitations associated with that particular problem or situation.

The experiences of many important entrepreneurs confirm this characteristic of the creative process. John Deere's steel plow and Goodyear's development of vulcanized rubber followed years of experimentation and trial-and-error learning. Apple founders Steve Wozniak and Steven Jobs did not stumble onto the idea of personal computers, but, as electrical engineers, they were fully knowledgeable of the potential for microprocessors to place a great deal of computing power in a very small box. Jeff Bezos had extensive knowledge of the power of Internet technologies, and he used this knowledge to develop keen insights about how Internet technologies could make amazon.com an e-commerce powerhouse.

Business Definition Is Not the Same as Writing a Mission Statement

These characteristics suggest another important feature of the business definition process: An effective business definition will not only answer, usually in a brief sentence or two, the Who (i.e., what customers to serve?), What (i.e., what products and services to offer?), and How (what technologies or distribution channels will be employed?) questions, but also will be much more creative, unique, and meaningful than almost any corporate mission statement. Nearly all mission statements are long on lofty ideals and objectives, but they usually lack anything distinctive that would distinguish the organization from its competitors. In their book, *Competing for the Future*, Gary Hamel and C. K. Prahalad share this observation about the lack of distinctiveness that characterizes most company mission statements:

> Recently one of us made a presentation to the top 15 officers of a large multinational company. We showed them their company's mission statement. No one demurred; yes, that looked like their mission statement. Only what was there on the screen was actually the mission statement of their major competitor!
>
> … if we took the mission statements of 100 large industrial companies, mixed them up tonight while everyone was asleep, and reassigned them at random, would anyone wake up tomorrow morning and cry, "My gosh, where has our mission statement gone?"[19]

Definition Implies Doing Some Things but Not Doing Others

People think focus means saying yes to the thing you've got to focus on. But that's not what it means at all. It means saying no to the 100 other good ideas that are there. You have to pick carefully. I'm actually as proud of many things we haven't done as the things we have done.

Steve Jobs[20]

As this Steve Jobs quotation captures so well, another characteristic of a successful business definition process is that it will require that firms choose to engage in some activities and necessarily not engage in others. The word *decide*, like the word *scissors*, comes from the Latin *caedere*, which means "to cut," and it is important to remember that a decision to engage in one activity almost always means that it will not engage in some other activities; they will be "cut" or eliminated as options.[21] In developing and focusing on a particular business definition, a firm is deciding that it will serve certain customers but *not* others, provide certain products and services but *not* others, and employ certain technologies but *not* others.

One reason many firms underachieve is because they fail to focus. They fail to commit to a particular business definition and therefore dissipate their resources and capabilities by trying to do too much. No firm has the ability to be "all things to all people," but the managers of too many firms fail to realize how important it is to focus their firms' capabilities, resources, and energies.

Sometimes, business definitions result from not deciding. In other words, business definition can be the product of proactive decision making, but business definition can also result from a passive acceptance of or being "boxed in" by market forces. Again, Alfred Sloan, GM's legendary chairman, reflecting on his company's position in the 1920s, captured this tension between efforts to proactively create a business definition and falling victim to the forces of the marketplace:

We did not know what we were trying to do except to sell cars... Some kind of rational policy was called for. That is, it was necessary to know what one was trying to do, apart from ... *what might be imposed upon [us] by the consumer, the competition, and a combination of technological and economic conditions.*[22]

The italicized portion of this quotation emphasizes the point made earlier—that without a proactive approach to definition and redefinition, managers can let their firms fall victim to market and competitive forces that can severely limit their flexibility and competitive options. For example, Motorola once held a leading position in the cellular telephone market, but it allowed an array of competitors, including Ericsson, Nokia, and Samsung to gain technological and marketing advantages that allowed these companies to occupy the most favorable positions in this industry. And, then, these firms also failed to anticipate how companies like Research in Motion, Apple, and other "smart phone" manufacturers would also change the competitive landscape and carve out new, profitable segments of this market.

As these examples illustrate, when managers fail to proactively define or redefine their firms, new competitors, market forces, and changes in the dynamics of the industries can have a profound impact on the effectiveness and value of firms' business definitions. This last point underscores the importance of one final characteristic of the business definition process:

Effective Business Definitions Are Fleeting and All Businesses Must Redefine Themselves over Time

A final characteristic of business definition (and therefore of the business definition process) that must be noted here is the fleeting nature of an effective business definition. Drucker also emphasized this point quite eloquently when he wrote, "what exists is getting old" and that "any leadership position is transitory and likely to be short-lived."[23] Thus, business definition is an ongoing process.

Though business definitions are typically built over time and with considerable investment, they can quickly become dated or irrelevant either by changes in the larger competitive environment or by the actions of managers. For example, the development of transistor and semiconductor technologies doomed firms that had defined their businesses as vacuum tube manufacturers, disposable diapers created an entirely new market in which cloth diaper manufacturers were unable to compete, and the emergence of digital photography has completely changed the markets for cameras and photography.[24]

For decades, every segment of the publishing industry has experienced competition from alternative media. Television and other media brought an end to *The Saturday Evening Post*, in the 1960s, and later years saw the end of other general interest magazines such as *Life* and *Look*. Today, newsstand sales of most magazines are falling rapidly and sales of magazine advertising are also in a freefall.[25]

Newspapers have also been hard-hit by competition from alternative media. It was once common for all major cities to have at least two, and often many more daily newspapers—with at least one major newspaper publishing a morning edition while another newspaper would publish an afternoon edition to update readers on the happenings of the day. Television news doomed many of these afternoon newspapers, and the advent of cable television news stations and widespread access to the Internet have had a devastating impact on the entire newspaper industry.

What is perhaps most interesting about the decline of the old media companies is that their managers have had ample warnings to alert them to the changes in their industries, but few if any of the major newspaper chains—or hardly any of the media companies for that matter—have successfully adapted to the new competitive environment. Many newspapers have experimented with digital strategies, but few of these have gained significant traction. None of these strategies have offered newspapers a fast-growing or profitable new line of business.[26]

On the other hand, consider the case of Ziebart, which has successfully redefined its business in response to changing market forces. Founded in 1962, Ziebart became a highly successful automotive rust-proofing company, and Ziebart's rust-proofing business could do nothing but thrive at a time that rust and road salt could eat through the body of a car within just a few years. But the market for automotive rust-proofing became almost superfluous in the 1980s as the quality of automobile paints and the car companies' own rust-proofing efforts improved and warranties were extended.

Recognizing that these trends could almost certainly drive the company out of business, Ziebart's managers decided that the company needed to diversify into additional automotive services including window tinting, sunroof installation, auto detailing, and security services.[27] Ziebart has also seized on the growing popularity of pick-up trucks to begin selling and installing bed liners. It's important to emphasize that if Ziebart's managers had not taken a proactive approach to business redefinition, the firm could easily have been overwhelmed by trends in its industry environment and found its primary business irrelevant.

Not only must managers be cognizant of the need to redefine their firms over time in order to maintain alignment with the larger competitive environment, but managers must also invest resources in their firms' definitions in order to build and maintain their strength. It is not enough to have a good concept or idea for a business definition; managers must invest continuously in order to establish their firms' definitions and then maintain the strength of those definitions in the marketplace. Chapter 2 emphasized that all assets—including an effective definition—will erode over time without a program of ongoing investment.

The Challenges of Continuous Redefinition

As we have emphasized all along, industry environments can be incredibly dynamic, and the ongoing evolution of those environments requires that companies' definitions anticipate and respond to changes. An outstanding business definition at one point in time is not sufficient.

While firms must redefine themselves in order to respond to changes in their industry environments, redefinition can also be proactive, undertaken by managers to re-position their firms to a more attractive part of the competitive space. For example, Hyundai, at the time it entered the U.S. automobile market, was positioned as a low-cost alternative. But, through very effective advertising and promotion strategies, the company has had good success in repositioning itself as a more distinctive brand.

To explore the need for continuous redefinition and to also highlight the challenges associated with the redefinition process, this section includes three short case studies of companies that either have struggled or are currently struggling with the redefinition process.

Business Redefinition Case Study #1: Intel's Exit from the Memory Chip Business

Intel had pioneered the development and manufacture of memory chips, and by the early 1970s, Intel had a commanding 90 percent share of the market for memory chips. Intel managers held a mental model of the company's business definition that "Intel meant memory." So, even as Intel was becoming a very competitive and profitable microprocessor manufacturer and low-cost competitors were flooding the market for memory chips causing Intel's share of the memory market to fall to about 5 percent by the 1980s, Intel's executives still held on to the concept of Intel as a "memory company."

How did Intel make its break from the memory business to focus and become a dominant player in the microprocessor market? The widely told story is that Intel's top executives, Gordon Moore and Andrew Grove, visualized what would happen if the board replaced them with outside executives. Grove and Moore quickly concluded that outsiders would exit the memory business. Grove proposed that he and Moore walk out the door—figuratively speaking—return, and do themselves what outsiders would do if brought in by the board. Grove and Moore did exactly that and exited memory to focus on Intel's microprocessors.[28]

While Intel's break with its roots in the memory business was difficult because of the emotional ties the company's top managers had for the business, the decision to focus on the microprocessor market and *not* to participate in the memory business opened the door for the extraordinary success Intel has enjoyed over the last three decades and the dominance it continues to hold, especially in the market for PC microprocessors. While one door was figuratively shut, its closure allowed Intel to commit its organizational resources more fully to a business in which the company had an opportunity to enjoy a sustainable competitive advantage.

Business Redefinition Case Study #2: Eastman Kodak Company and the Rapidly Changing Photography Market

Kodak provides a vivid illustration of a company that has been frantically trying to redefine itself. Kodak is the victim of technological change—change that has required the company to discard its longstanding definition as a leading manufacturer of photographic film. Kodak dominated the photography industry ever since its founder, George Eastman, developed silver halide film in the 1880s. Digital photography has, however, quickly overtaken film photography, forcing Kodak to adapt.

For many years, two factors limited digital photography. First, digital photography offered less clarity than film photography because digital photographs did not contain the same amount of "photographic information" as a typical 35 mm negative.[29] Second, the price of digital cameras—once costing anywhere from several hundred to several thousand dollars each—put them beyond the means of most consumers.

Digital competitors moved rapidly to overcome these obstacles, however. For example, new models of digital cameras are priced very affordably.[30] Most of Kodak's digital competitors are not only offering reasonably priced digital cameras, but firms also offer reasonably priced computer printers that are capable of producing high-quality, color photograph-like prints. This wave of innovation has quickly enticed consumers, and, as illustrated in Exhibit 6.5, in 2003 the sales of digital cameras exceeded the sales of traditional cameras in the amateur photography market for the first time. Since that time, the market for traditional cameras diminished rapidly and, today, is virtually non-existent.

Kodak's efforts to redefine itself in an increasingly digital world highlight two key points about the redefinition process. First, it may take years before consumers accept a new technology, but, as the market for digital photography demonstrates, once consumers come to accept a new technology, their switch away from the old technology can be exceedingly rapid. Kodak's managers were almost certainly hoping that consumers' switch to digital photography would be gradual and occur over a very long time, thus giving them more time to redefine Kodak as a digital photography company. Unfortunately for Kodak, the switch proceeded very rapidly.

Exhibit 6.5 U.S. Camera Sales in the Amateur Market (millions of units)

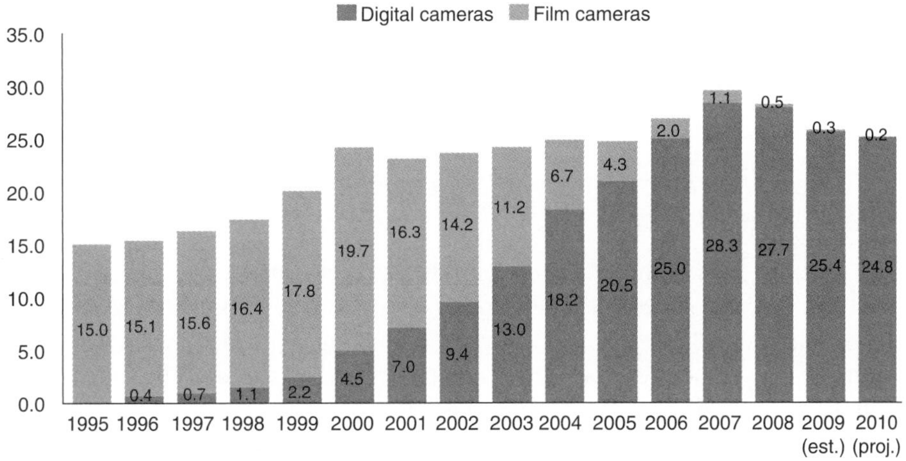

Legend: ■ Digital cameras   ▨ Film cameras

Notes: Excludes single-use cameras and camera phones
Source: PMA Marketing Research

The second point that the Kodak case highlights is how organizational inertia and the resources and competencies developed in an early time frame can slow the redefinition process. Since the early 1990s, Kodak has been working to recast and redefine itself as a digital company. Early on, the company shed businesses that were not central to its core imaging business, including its giant Eastman Chemical Division, and its Sterling Drug unit (best known as the maker of Bayer aspirin).

Yet, the company stubbornly held on to a future in which film photography would play a major part. For example, an early digital product, the Photo CD, introduced in 1992, sought to merge film with digital technologies by allowing users to take traditional film photographs and transfer them to compact disks. Photographs could then be viewed on special photo-disk players. Sales of the Photo CD product were disappointing, largely because consumers refused to pay the high prices for the photo disks (approximately $20 for a 24-exposure film disk) and photo-disk players, which cost between $400 and $800.

The company also sought new, outside management and hired George Fisher, who was the CEO of Motorola, to be its new CEO in 1995. Fisher, in turn, recruited executives from other high-tech companies to help him engineer a turnaround at the insular Kodak, which has had a history of always promoting managers from within the company's ranks. Fisher also consolidated research and development of digital products in a single division, but these and other initiatives have failed to transform the company.[31]

For Kodak, the stakes are quite high. The company's sales peaked at $14 billion in 1999 and have fallen ever since to just half that level in 2009. Moreover, Kodak still earns nearly one-third of its revenues and nearly all of its net income and cash flows from its film products. And, even as Kodak executives have tried for nearly two decades to redefine their company, it remains very much a film company. A reporter has observed that digital technologies are "as out of place in Kodak's silver halide research labs as the first word processors would have been in a typewriter factory."[32]

Thus, Kodak is at a critical juncture, and the steps Kodak's managers take to redefine the company in the next few years will offer an exciting "real time" continuation of this short case study. Depending on their efforts, Kodak "will emerge as either a smart example or a cautionary tale of what happens when a company stops fighting new technologies, and embraces them instead."[33]

Business Redefinition Case Study #3: Gallo Recasts Itself in the Varietal Wine Market

The Kodak example raises the question of whether companies can successfully redefine themselves. Certainly the process of redefinition is fraught with significant challenges, many of which will be reviewed in the next section, but before looking at the factors that make redefinition so challenging, it may be helpful to review a company that has successfully redefined itself and repositioned its products in a competitive market.

For much of its life, the E. & J. Gallo Winery successfully defined itself as a producer of low-cost table wine, typically selling wine for less than $5 to $6 per bottle. Over the last decade, however, Gallo has sought to enter the higher-priced varietal wine segment in which wine sells at various price points ranging from $6 to $16 per bottle. To the dismay of Gallo's managers, the company enjoyed little success in redefining itself as a producer of varietal wines. In spite of critical acclaim for some of its wines and major advertising campaigns aimed at improving the image of the company's products, consumers seem reluctant to pay more than $5 to $6 per bottle for Gallo wines. Apparently, the image that customers have held of Gallo as the producer of low-cost table wines has simply prevented the company from breaking the price threshold that separates the low-cost table wine and varietal wine categories.

For many years, consultants and industry observers suggested that Gallo could enter the higher-priced varietal wine market, but that it would have to use a different name in order to overcome the image consumers have of Gallo as the maker of low-cost table wines.[34] Such a tactic has been employed successfully by many other wine makers; for example, Glen Ellen, a varietal wine maker whose wines generally sell in the range of $5 to $7 per bottle, offers a higher-priced line of wines carrying the Benziger name. Gallo's managers long resisted the suggestion that it offer a wine under any other name, but in the mid-1990s, the company did introduce the Turning Leaf line of wines at a much higher price point. Noticeably absent from bottles of Turning Leaf wines is the Gallo name.

This Gallo example suggests just how important business definition can be. Although Gallo has never enjoyed much success at breaking into the varietal wine segment because of its low-cost table wine image, its Turning Leaf chardonnay rose from obscurity to become the second best-selling chardonnay in less than one year! Gallo's success with its Turning Leaf brand even prompted a lawsuit from Kendall-Jackson, maker of the number-one selling chardonnay. In its lawsuit, Kendall-Jackson argued that Gallo copied its "colored leaf" logo and the "gradual, tapered neck" of its bottles.[35] Kendall-Jackson may well have been concerned about trademark infringement, but it is probably just as likely that Kendall-Jackson was hoping that the publicity surrounding the lawsuit would make wine drinkers aware of Gallo's parentage of Turning Leaf wines.[36]

The Challenges Associated with Redefinition

These three short case studies (and many other business examples) suggest a number of observations about the process of redefinition. First, these case studies underscore a point made at the outset of this chapter: Business definition and redefinition are creative and ongoing processes. Business definition and redefinition are almost always strategic decisions, and rarely, if ever, are they "typical business decisions" in the sense that they are based on financial or quantitative criteria and data.

For example, if Kodak had used present value or rate of return criteria to evaluate whether it should move more aggressively toward a digital future, it would surely reject such an option. It is highly unlikely that investments in digital products and technologies would show higher rates of return than additional investments in Kodak's silver halide film business. Kodak's—and many other companies'—use of these traditional capital budgeting techniques helps to explain in part why companies move so haltingly toward redefining themselves. The message here is that decisions about business definition and redefinition almost certainly have to be made using different criteria and decision processes.

In fact, the capital budgeting practices of most companies are probably inimical to redefinition process. Hamel and Prahalad share this observation about how corporate finance executives are likely to respond to the need for companies to make strategic investments in new products, services, and technologies:

> Find a senior finance person in your company. Tell him or her you need funding for a major "strategic" investment. How do finance executives decode the word *strategic* when it comes in front of the word *investment*? We've asked them this question and almost invariably the answer comes back— "The project is going to lose money!"
>
> In other words, you might just as well say "Las Vegas" as "strategic investment" to most prudent finance officers.[37]

Thus, executives of firms requiring redefinition must be aware that their own capital budgeting processes are likely to work against the commitment of the very resources that will be required to make successful redefinition possible.

At the same time, decisions about business definition and redefinition cannot be made blindly, but instead must be based on a solid understanding (i.e., mental model) of their competitive environment and how it is changing or likely to change. The understandings (i.e., mental models) that Intel's top managers held about the memory market, convinced them they were unlikely to ever be anything more than an "also ran," and also provided them with the insight to focus on and then go on to dominate a market in which Intel could enjoy a competitive advantage. (In Chapter 7, we describe how Intel's now famous "Intel Inside" campaign for its microprocessor technology also contributed to the company's distinctiveness and built enormous brand equity around the Intel name.)

Kodak is probably able to make the decision to move toward a more digital future *because* it has already invested sizable sums in researching and developing digital technologies. In fact, one of the bitter ironies in Kodak's situation is that Kodak has invented many digital technologies and holds more than 1,000 digital technology patents.[38] In fact, licensing agreements allowing companies like Samsung and LG to use Kodak-developed technology are expected to contribute from ten to 15 percent of Kodak's total profits over the next few years, and Kodak has recently sued other companies, including Apple and Research In Motion, alleging that they have violated Kodak patents on a variety of digital technologies that they are using in their products.[39]

These case studies and many other business examples of redefinition also illustrate that redefinition almost always involves some sort of conflict. Employees, customers, and other stakeholders who have an established view of the company will necessarily be forced to change that view as the company changes its focus to different customers, or different products or services, or different technologies (or sometimes all three). It can require tremendous skill to get customers to accept these changes. Sometimes, however, even the best strategies can fail. Gallo ultimately was only able to move into the varietal wine market by offering products with a new name.

Cisco is moving aggressively to expand its definition by moving into new markets and seeking to grow market share in those new markets. As a result, Cisco is now competing with companies like Hewlett-Packard and IBM that were and, in many cases, continue to be, its customers.[40] Again, such a redefinition process requires outstanding execution if it is to avoid completely alienating former strategic business partners.

Many of our examples also highlight another key point about the redefinition process: *Sooner is probably better than later.* As noted earlier, the shift from film to digital photography occurred very rapidly once consumers began to accept digital technologies. Intel's decision to focus on microprocessor technology was very much the right decision at the right time—to exit one highly competitive market and focus on another just as the market for personal computers emerged and began to grow rapidly.

Finally, all of our examples illustrate that business definition and redefinition require a "leap" as well as considerable investment. Hamel and Prahalad have coined the phrase "strategic intent" to describe the significance of these redefinition efforts.[41] Hamel and Prahalad define **strategic intent** as an ideal "destiny" or competitive position that firms hope to achieve over the next several years or even decades of effort and investment. It's probably fair to argue that the success Kodak and the old media companies will enjoy over the next decade will depend both on the effectiveness of the definitions and market positions they stake out for themselves, as well as on the level of investment they are willing to make to redefine themselves.

When General Motors spent billions of dollars to acquire EDS and Hughes in the 1980s (and the company subsequently divested both businesses), it chose not to invest those same dollars in its automotive business. That additional investment could have helped to maintain GM's position in the all-important family sedan and luxury car markets. Similarly, though Kodak developed and now holds the patents on many digital technologies, it chose against commercializing those technologies. Had Kodak chosen to develop products based on its R&D investments in digital technologies, the photography market might look quite different today, with Kodak in the vanguard rather than a big question mark.

Even as we emphasize the importance of timely redefinition, these examples emphasize that redefinition is rarely easy. Many firms have encountered a variety of problems and met considerable resistance as they have sought to change or alter their definitions. The

Gallo-Turning Leaf example illustrates that firms can develop such strong definitions that the loyalty of customers, employees, and other constituencies to those definitions can limit the ability of firms to redefine themselves with anything short of Herculean efforts, or, as in the Gallo case, a willingness to offer its products under a new brand name.

The evidence suggests an important and challenging management paradox: The companies that have the greatest difficulty in changing their definitions are those that have been most effective in forging distinctive definitions in the past. In fact, it is probably safe to argue that *the degree of difficulty associated with business redefinition will be directly related to the level of recognition and distinctiveness that a firm's definition has enjoyed in the past.*

Conclusion: Business Definition and the Book's Three Key Themes

This chapter on business definition and positioning is closely tied to each of the three key themes emphasized throughout this book:

The Importance of Managers and Managerial Thinking

One rather obvious conclusion that emerges from this chapter is that top managers should place a great deal of emphasis on business definition and redefinition. Business definition is the creative task of selecting a mission or vision for the firm, and it includes fundamental decisions about customers to be served, products and services to be offered, and technologies to be employed. As suggested by many of the examples and short case studies offered in this chapter, once managers have made fundamental business definition decisions, other important strategic questions are likely to become more apparent and straightforward.

It is also important to emphasize that business definition is *not* strategic planning, nor is business definition the same thing as writing a company mission statement. Good definitions provide firms with a *vision* or a *strategic intent* rather than a *plan*. Unlike formal planning processes that develop strategies based on analyses of companies' existing competitive environments, the processes of business definition and redefinition should allow firms to shape proactively their own destinies and create totally new competitive environments, transcending the barriers posed by existing industry structures. In other words, through business definition, firms play offense rather than defense.

Furthermore, as managers work to develop their firms' visions or missions and seek to develop unique business definitions, they can then focus their attention on a smaller portion of the competitive environment. While this narrowing of a company's range of vision does pose some increased danger of being "blindsided," it greatly reduces what is perhaps the biggest obstacle confronting most firms: the analysis of too many different business opportunities. Managers who are more certain about their firms' definitions will have less trouble deciding which opportunities are worth pursuing and which would be unrelated to the vision of their firms. It's worth remembering the quote we shared earlier from Steve Jobs about the importance of focus, and that deciding what not to do is just as important as deciding what to do.

Related to this last point, another important advantage of effective definition and timely redefinition is that it should shorten considerably not only the time required to formulate strategy but also the time required to implement strategy. A widely held vision or understanding—a mental model—of a firm's purpose should facilitate decision making by providing managers at all levels of a firm with a blueprint that provides direction for the future of their businesses and firms. Research has revealed that it is not uncommon in most large business firms for 80 percent of middle-level managers to be uncertain about their firms' strategies.[42] Such a situation will greatly complicate the strategy implementation process.

Change and the Need to Think Dynamically about Strategic Management

This chapter has also emphasized that continuous redefinition is essential if firms are to stay relevant and avoid decline. While firms face many "operational" challenges that require management time and energy *to improve what they already do*, changes in the larger competitive environment will create "strategic" challenges that require firms and their managers *to learn how to do entirely new things*. The challenge, as we have emphasized here and in earlier chapters, is that environmental change does not occur in steady, easy to anticipate, installments, but quite erratically. Industry conditions can remain quite stable, so that the same business definition might work well for years or decades. Recall that Sloan's definition for GM's automobile business was effective for 50 years. Kodak and its pioneering film technology dominated photography for a century! Yet, as these case studies illustrate, industry environments can change radically in a short period of time, leaving the industry leaders struggling for relevance and survival.

The Importance of Organizational Learning

Because industry environments are always changing, managers and their firms must emphasize the acquisition of new competencies, skills, knowledge, and resources so that they are prepared to embrace change quickly when it comes. The point made above is worth emphasizing again— if Kodak had followed through and developed commercial photography products based on its digital research and development activities, the photography industry might look quite differently today—starring Kodak as an innovative digital technology consumer products company.

These examples suggest that business definition requires learning on multiple levels. One type of learning involves understanding the industry and the markets a company wishes to serve, and ongoing learning to understand how that industry is or might be changing. Companies must also learn how best to meet the needs and wants of its target customers. This involves taking insights about the market and translating those insights into specific products and services. Learning is also needed to align all aspects of the company with its definition, including hiring the right people and developing appropriate strategies, pricing policies, and marketing campaigns.

___

Key Points

- Business definition is a fundamental, perhaps the most fundamental, business decision that managers must make. Decisions about business definition are based on managers' understandings of (i.e., their mental models) of their industry environments.

- Business definition can contribute to, or be a source of, competitive advantage in four ways:
  - An effective business definition can uniquely position a firm in its industry.
  - An effective business definition can help to focus management attention on a firm's key objectives, its most significant strategic issues, and its most important rivals.
  - An effective business definition does not answer other strategic questions, but it does make those questions more obvious and should improve strategic decision making and the implementation of strategies.
  - An effective business definition provides managers and employees with a sense of meaning and purpose that can be very motivational.
- Effective business definitions share the following characteristics:
  - They are distinctive and set companies apart from competitors.
  - They are timely and appropriate given the industry environments in which companies are competing.
  - They are clear and readily understandable by customers as well as employees, suppliers, and other constituencies.
- The business definition *process*:
  - Is fundamentally a creative process.
  - Requires knowledge and understanding of the competitive space and its opportunities.
  - Is not the same as writing a mission statement.
  - Implies doing some things but not others.
  - Requires that firms are defined and then continuously redefined so that they keep pace with changes in their competitive environments.
- Yet, redefinition poses many challenges. Firms must frequently make significant investments in new markets and technologies without clear evidence that those investments will pay off. Furthermore, redefinition often requires companies to radically alter the perceptions and beliefs (i.e., mental models) of their customers and employees.

Key Questions for Managers

- What is the definition of your business or firm?
- Is your firm's definition distinctive and does it set our business apart from its competitors? Is it timely and appropriate given competitive conditions in the industry? Is it clear and easily understood by customers, employees, suppliers, and other stakeholders?
- Is your firm's business definition a source of competitive advantage, or does it contribute to competitive advantage in some way? If not, how could your company's business definition be more effective?
- Does your business definition reflect a current understanding (i.e., mental model) of the firm's industry. Is it forward-looking, incorporating a vision about where the industry will be headed in the future?
- What trends in your firm's industry threaten or could potentially undermine the effectiveness of your firm's definition? How are customer demographics or customer

needs and wants changing? What technological developments are occurring? What new products and services in our industry or in other industries could render our products and services obsolete?

- What existing or emerging "white spaces" in your firm's competitive environment should you be exploring?

Suggestions for Further Reading

Additionally, links to further resources online—such as cases, articles, and videos—can be found on the book's website, www.routledge.com/textbooks/Duhaime.

Abell, D. F. 1980. *Defining the Business: Starting Point of Strategic Planning.* Englewood Cliffs, NJ: Prentice-Hall.

Amabile, T. M. 1983. *The Social Psychology of Creativity.* New York: Springer-Verlag.

Charan, R. 1982. How to strengthen your strategy review process. *Journal of Business Strategy*, 2(3): 50–60.

Collins, J. C., & Porras, J. I. 1994. *Built to Last: Successful Habits of Visionary Companies.* New York: HarperBusiness.

Dowling, G. 2001. *Creating Corporate Reputations: Identity, Image, and Performance.* New York: Oxford University Press.

Drucker, P. F. 1994. The theory of the business. *Harvard Business Review*, 72(5): 95–104.

Duggan W. 2007. *Strategic Intuition: The Creative Spark in Human Achievement.* New York: Columbia University Press.

Hamel, G., & Prahalad, C. K. 1989. Strategic intent. *Harvard Business Review,* 67(3): 63–76.

Hatch, M. J., & Schultz, M. 2004. *Organizational Identity: A Reader.* New York: Oxford University Press.

Ries, A. 1996. *Focus: The Future of your Company Depends on it.* New York: HarperCollins Publishers.

Ries, A., & Trout, J. 1981. *Posititioning: The Battle for your Mind.* New York: McGraw-Hill.

Rivkin, S., & Sutherland, F. 2004. *The Making of a Name: The Inside Story of the Brands we Buy.* New York: Oxford University Press.

Sloan, Jr., A. P. 1963. *My Years with General Motors.* New York: Doubleday/Currency.

Sull, D. N. 2003. *Revival of the Fittest: Why Good Companies go Bad and how Great Managers Remake Them.* Boston: Harvard Business School Press.

Chapter 7

Business Strategy and Competitive Advantage

Chapter 7 is the first of three chapters on business strategy. This chapter introduces the concept of "generic" business strategies, describing the objectives, characteristics, and limitations of the various generic strategies. Chapters 8 and 9 continue the study of business strategy, with Chapter 8 examining the formulation and implementation of business strategies in emerging, mature, and online business contexts. Chapter 9 also considers the unique challenges associated with developing a competitive advantage in manufacturing and service industries.

Chapter Objectives

The specific objectives of Chapter 7 are to:

- Introduce the concept of generic business strategies and describe the generic business strategies of cost leadership, differentiation, and focus.
- Describe the organizational resources and capabilities associated with these generic business strategies.
- Suggest how managers can identify opportunities for reducing costs and differentiating their businesses.
- Identify and discuss a number of the implications of generic business strategies.
- Identify and discuss the special challenges of commodity markets (e.g., the tendency to compete on price alone) and the factors that limit the effectiveness of differentiation strategies (e.g., private-label competition, discounting, and commodification, the tendency for differentiated products to lose their distinctiveness).

Background

This chapter and the two that follow focus on business strategy. As suggested by the text's model of strategic management (reprinted in Exhibit 7.1), the overall aim of these two chapters is to consider how managers' beliefs about how to compete influence the formulation and implementation of business strategies with the aims of achieving high performance and developing and sustaining competitive advantage. While the previous chapter

Exhibit 7.1 Managers' Beliefs, Strategic Decisions, and Their Influence on Performance and Competitive Advantage

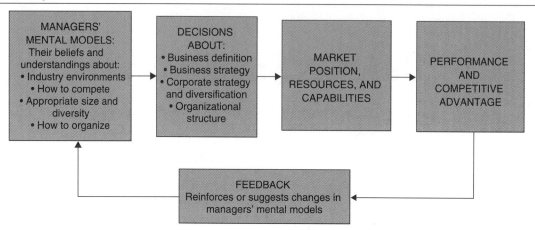

emphasized the importance of business definition, or the task of positioning firms and businesses in their competitive arenas, these three chapters examine how firms should compete in their industries.

Though the text and the model explicitly distinguish between the concepts of business definition and business strategy, it should be fairly obvious that managerial thinking and decisions about business definition and business strategy are very much interrelated and tightly coupled in that they are mutually dependent and can become mutually reinforcing. For example, the managers of companies like Saks Fifth Avenue and Neiman Marcus, which have defined their firms as exclusive, high-end department stores, necessarily pursue different business strategies than Wal-Mart, which dominates the discount segment of the retailing industry and has built its competitive strategy around offering customers low prices yet high value. No doubt the definitions these companies have adopted have influenced their choice of business strategies. In addition, over time, the various strategies that companies pursue further enhance or reinforce their business definitions.

Researchers have sought to develop typologies of business strategies, based on the assumption that there are observable patterns or regularities in the way firms compete. There's no "one single right way" to think about the types of business strategies. One early typology suggested that firms tend to pursue one of four different types of business strategies.[1] According to this typology, firms could be *prospectors*, pursuing entrepreneurial exploration of their competitive environments with the aim of developing new product and market opportunities. Firms could also be *defenders*, seeking stability by maintaining current market positions and defending against encroachment by other firms. The characteristics of a third group of firms, *analyzers*, place them somewhere between prospectors and defenders, balancing the opportunity-seeking nature of prospectors against the risk aversion of defenders. Thus, like prospectors, analyzers seek to exploit new market opportunities, but they will also tend to draw most of their revenue from a stable portfolio of products. Finally, the typology defined a fourth group of firms as ***reactors***. While the strategies of prospectors, defenders, and analyzers are all to some extent proactive, the strategies pursued by this fourth group of firms would be characterized by inconsistencies and a reactionary response to environmental change. Thus, the reactor strategy is not considered a viable one, and firms pursuing such a strategy would either have to adopt one of the other three types of strategy or face eventual decline.

The publication of Michael Porter's widely read book, *Competitive Strategy*, introduced a new categorization of business strategies that quickly gained widespread popularity among both academics and practicing managers.[2] Porter's generic strategies are not necessarily superior to the typology of business strategies just described or to any other typology of business strategies, but, in this chapter, we will examine Porter's generic business strategies of ***cost leadership***, ***differentiation***, and ***focus***, because Porter's writing has had an important impact on the business world, and, as with his Five Forces Model for industry analysis, nearly all managers are familiar with Porter's generic strategies.

In addition to explaining Porter's strategies, the chapter examines some of the "real-world" problems associated with successfully implementing cost leadership and differentiation strategies. We'll highlight some of the specific challenges associated with implementing cost leadership strategies in commodity markets or industries. This discussion will suggest the many benefits companies can enjoy if they can successfully differentiate their products or services. At the same time, the chapter will point to some of the difficulties and challenges of implementing effective differentiation strategies.

Generic Business Strategies

To begin, it is important to emphasize that the underlying goal of any business strategy is to change the shape of the demand curve for a company's products or services. As illustrated in Exhibit 7.2, effective business strategies should make the top portion of a product or service's demand curve more inelastic—in other words, companies' products and services should be

Exhibit 7.2 The Underlying Aim of Business Strategies Is to Change the Shape of the Demand Curve

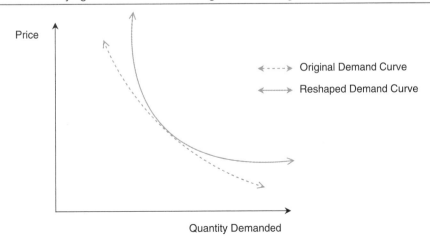

Exhibit 7.3 A Matrix Describing Porter's Three Generic Strategies

Strategic Advantage

		Uniqueness	Low Cost
Target Market	Broad	Differentiation	Cost Leadership
	Narrow	Focus Differentiation	Focus Cost Leadership

so differentiated, attractive, and almost irresistible to buyers that higher prices should lead to relatively small declines in the quantity demanded. Similarly, effective business strategies should make the lower portion of the demand curve more elastic, or in other words, the value consumers perceive in lower prices should translate into relatively larger increases in the quantity demanded. Thus, one of the ways to evaluate the effectiveness of the business strategy a firm adopts is to assess how effectively the firm is succeeding in reshaping its demand curve—this, in fact, is one key way to assess whether a firm's business strategy is providing it with a competitive advantage.

Having established this important conceptual point, let's continue by reviewing the three generic strategies described by Michael Porter in his book, *Competitive Strategy*. Porter's three generic strategies emerge from a two-by-two matrix defined along one axis by market breadth and along the other axis by the source of strategic advantage. Porter argued that any particular company's market breadth can be either broad, aimed at serving an entire industry or a very broad segment of an industry, or narrow, focusing on a particular industry niche. Similarly, Porter suggested that companies can seek to gain a strategic advantage in one of two ways—either by achieving lower costs (and therefore prices) than their competitors or by offering products and services that are perceived as unique in some way. Porter's matrix and its resulting generic strategies are illustrated in Exhibit 7.3. The matrix offers a very useful way of thinking—in other words, a mental model—about business strategy.

Cost Leadership

As seen in the matrix illustrated in Exhibit 7.3, the generic business strategy of cost leadership is aimed at a broad market segment and is based on the strategic advantage of low cost. The idea behind the generic strategy of cost leadership is straightforward: Firms with costs that are lower than those of their competitors are likely to enjoy a competitive advantage in the marketplace because they can offer their customers lower prices and thereby gain increases in sales and market share. They can enjoy a sustained competitive advantage if they can maintain this cost advantage over their competitors over long periods of time. Furthermore, by serving a broad market segment, firms pursuing the generic strategy of cost leadership will be able to exploit economies of scale and experience or learning effects (both discussed in Chapter 4) by maximizing sales volume.

Achieving a low cost position affords a firm greater pricing flexibility than its competitors are likely to have, and this pricing flexibility can be a valuable tool for sustaining competitive advantage. It is important to note that the terms *cost* and *price* are not being used interchangeably here—the strategy the firm is pursuing is *cost* leadership, and having achieved a low *cost* position, the *price* the firm charges its customers is a choice. In a fiercely competitive industry context, a low cost position firm might choose to price below competitors in order to maintain market share, or gain share from other competitors, but in a less competitive industry context a low cost position firm might choose to price at competitors' levels and enjoy the higher level of profitability resulting from its low cost position.

A few points about the strategy of cost leadership are worth emphasizing. First, a strategy of cost leadership is probably most likely to be effective in those industries or markets in which the material or physical characteristics or reputation of a particular product or service are less important than its price. For example, the business strategy of cost leadership is particularly well suited for firms competing in commodity markets or the markets for basic items in which one company's products are more or less indistinguishable from other companies' products. (But, as we will demonstrate soon, with enough creativity, imagination, and work, even the most basic items can be successfully differentiated.)

On the other hand, a strategy of cost leadership is likely to be less effective for firms competing in markets in which products or services are readily differentiated along tangible or intangible characteristics. For example, it's possible that a strategy of cost leadership might be less effective in the market for legal services because most individuals seeking legal assistance would be more interested in the reputation and past success of a particular law firm and be somewhat less concerned about its fees. Or, they might even be skeptical about the quality of the services provided by a law firm that emphasizes low fees.

Second, a successful "cost leader" develops a competitive advantage not by selling products and services that are perceived as "cheap" or inferior or of poor quality, but by offering products and services of adequate quality or levels of quality that are comparable to industry standards, at lower prices than most industry competitors. Especially in the past decade, quality has become a *sine qua non* for companies in all industries, so it is unlikely that any company can survive for very long by offering products or services of poor quality. No matter how low their fares, discount airlines such as JetBlue, Alaska, and Southwest would probably not survive for very long if they offered customers consistently inferior levels of service or were perceived as being unsafe.

At one point, a survey of airline quality gave these carriers the highest service quality ratings of all of the major airlines,[3] but on Valentine's Day in 2007, storms forced thousands of JetBlue passengers to sit on a JetBlue aircraft for many hours. The unfortunate publicity had a very damaging impact on JetBlue's business and even led the company's board to oust the founder, David Neeleman, as CEO.[4] This example underscores the point that even very low costs will not prevent customers from abandoning a company if they perceive that they would be purchasing an inferior product or service.

Furthermore, a successful cost leader need not always offer the lowest prices in the industry. As our discussion of differentiation will emphasize, customer perceptions are often just as important, if not more important, than reality. Thus, what is important to the success of a cost leadership strategy is that the prices of a particular company's products or services are *perceived* by customers to be lower than the prices of other firms in the industry. For example, Wal-Mart, Target, and others compete vigorously with each other in the discount segment of the retailing industry. What is important or significant to the success of Wal-Mart's strategy of cost leadership is not whether its prices are lower than Target's or other stores' prices for every item in its stores, but that customers *perceive* that Wal-Mart's stores offer lower prices than other stores.

Still, given how widely available price data are in our economy, firms are unlikely to enjoy a cost leadership position for long if their prices consistently exceed those of their competitors. As a result, the prices of successful cost leaders must routinely match or beat the prices of other industry competitors.

To achieve an overall low cost position in their industries, firms often seek to have large market shares. Recall again that the goal of cost leadership is to make the lower end of the demand curve more elastic so that relatively small declines in price lead to relatively greater increases in quantity demanded. Thus, cost leadership strategies are often tightly linked with efforts to increase market share. The greater sales volume that is associated with larger market shares allows these firms to exploit economies of scale as well as experience or learning effects (discussed in Chapter 4), helping these firms to lower their per unit manufacturing or production costs. In addition to exploiting economies of scale and learning effects, successful cost leadership strategies are often characterized by:

- Capital-intensive manufacturing or production processes that reduce labor costs.
- Process (rather than product) engineering skills that are aimed at lowering manufacturing and production costs.
- Products that are designed to be manufactured easily and products that are designed to share many common components.

These characteristics help firms minimize production costs and exploit economies of scale. In addition, many successful cost leaders have developed:

- sophisticated materials procurement and inventory management systems, and
- low-cost distribution systems

that can offer significant cost savings.[5] For example, Wal-Mart's state-of-the-art inventory and distribution management systems are almost certainly important factors that contribute to the company's significant cost advantage in the retailing industry. Finally, a management or company culture that emphasizes:

- close supervision of labor,
- tight cost control, and
- incentives based on cost and quantitative targets

can be particularly helpful to firms pursuing cost leadership strategies.

Exhibit 7.4 Using the Value Chain for a Hypothetical Manufacturing Firm to Assess Its Ability to Pursue a Strategy of Cost Leadership

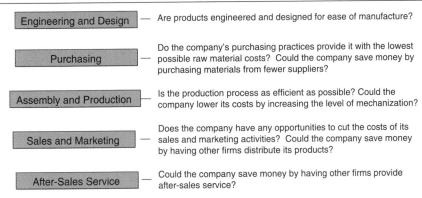

Engineering and Design	— Are products engineered and designed for ease of manufacture?
Purchasing	— Do the company's purchasing practices provide it with the lowest possible raw material costs? Could the company save money by purchasing materials from fewer suppliers?
Assembly and Production	— Is the production process as efficient as possible? Could the company lower its costs by increasing the level of mechanization?
Sales and Marketing	— Does the company have any opportunities to cut the costs of its sales and marketing activities? Could the company save money by having other firms distribute its products?
After-Sales Service	— Could the company save money by having other firms provide after-sales service?

The value chain concept can be a very useful tool for managers who are pursuing a cost leadership strategy. Exhibit 7.4 illustrates the value chain for a hypothetical manufacturing firm first introduced in Chapter 2. Recall that the value chain depicts the various value-adding processes inside a business organization. Analysis of the links in a company's value chain can be particularly helpful in assessing the ability of the organization to pursue a successful cost leadership strategy.

For example, analysis of the value chain depicted in Exhibit 7.4 would lead managers to raise a number of questions: Are the company's products engineered and designed for ease of manufacture? Do the company's purchasing practices provide it with the lowest possible raw material costs? Could the company save money by purchasing materials from fewer suppliers? Is the production process as efficient as possible? Could the company lower its costs by increasing the level of mechanization? Does the company have any opportunities to cut the costs of its sales and marketing activities? Could the company save money by having other firms distribute its products, allowing the company to focus on engineering and manufacturing?

Differentiation

As seen in Exhibit 7.3, firms pursue differentiation strategies when they aim to serve a broad segment of their market by offering products or services that are perceived as unique. This suggests that the strategy of differentiation is likely to work best in those markets with products and services that lend themselves well to differentiation. Many well known firms in the fashion, automobile, and a wide array of consumer goods and personal services industries seek to exploit the advantages of differentiation. The experience of firms in many industries suggests, however, that nearly all products and services—even many commodity products and services, such as colas, hair care, and microprocessors—can be effectively differentiated.

Perhaps no company has been as effective as Morton (a subsidiary of Rohm and Haas, which is a wholly owned subsidiary of the Dow Chemical Company) at differentiating a product—in Morton's case, salt—which is one of the most basic of all commodities. The distinctive blue label showing the company's "When it rains it pours" slogan and the picture of a girl with an umbrella spilling salt is one of the business world's best-known brand icons.[6] Morton's differentiation strategy has helped the company dominate the various markets for its salt products, enjoying higher prices than its competitors for commodity products that are virtually indistinguishable from those offered by its rivals. A trip to the grocery store will show that Morton salt products usually command a 33 percent price premium over identical store-brand products.

Intel offers another remarkable example of a firm that has been able to differentiate a commodity product.[7] Intel's well known "Intel Inside" advertising campaign, on which it has spent more than $1 billion, has been a great success. Developed in 1991 as a way to distinguish its microprocessors from those of Advanced Micro Devices and other semiconductor manufacturers, the "Intel Inside" advertising campaign not only improved the company's name recognition, but also helped to give Intel's microprocessors a premium, higher-quality image in the minds of personal computer buyers. Many PC customers have little idea what features and specifications they might want or need, but they are certain they want a machine with "Intel Inside." These examples illustrate a key point: with enough creativity, imagination, and investment, just about any product or service can be successfully differentiated.

As with the strategy of cost leadership, a few points about the generic business strategy of differentiation must be emphasized. First, it is the *perception* of differences and not the actual material or physical characteristics of competing products or services that is critical to the success of a business strategy of differentiation. True, a strategy of differentiation can be and often is based on very real differences in product or service quality—for example, the shopping experience at Nordstrom truly does have a very different look and feel than shopping at most other retailers—but it is important to emphasize that it is customer perception of the experience that is crucial to successful differentiation. As management professor, C. K. Prahalad, has noted, "experience is the brand," so that the interactions between the customer and a company's products or services and the emotional bonds that are formed between customers and products and services must be intensely managed by companies that aim to be successful differentiators.[8]

Cola is essentially a commodity product, yet the billions of dollars spent each year by Coca-Cola, PepsiCo, and other cola manufacturers on advertising are aimed at convincing consumers that there are significant differences among the various brands of colas. A *Wall Street Journal* article honoring Roberto Goizueta, Coca-Cola's legendary former chief executive, included this quote on the importance of product differentiation:

> If the three keys to selling real estate are location, location, location, then the three keys of selling consumer products are differentiation, differentiation, differentiation.
>
> In recent years, we can honestly say that every marketing victory we have won has been the result of our total commitment to making our brands clearly distinctive from every other item on the grocery shelf... The most notable action has been our ongoing expansion of the famous trademarked contour bottle throughout the entire world-wide packaging line for Coca-Cola, arguably the single most effective differentiation effort the soft-drink industry has seen in many years.[9]

The automobile industry also illustrates the important relationship between differentiation and customer perceptions. For several years, U.S. automobile manufacturers have worked very hard to improve the quality of their cars, and data now indicate that cars sold by the U.S. companies have quality ratings that are roughly comparable to those of cars produced by Japanese and other automobile companies. Still, many customers believe that the quality of U.S.-built cars lags behind that of Japanese cars, and it is this perception that counts in the marketplace. Several years will probably be required before consumer perceptions of quality catch up with or match reality in the U.S. automobile industry, though the problems facing Toyota and the massive recalls the company has had to make may simultaneously boost the quality image of competitors' vehicles, while also doing long-lasting harm to the Toyota brand.[10]

Indeed customer perceptions can long outlive reality. For many years, Maytag, now a unit of Whirlpool Corporation, differentiated its appliances based on reliability and quality. For example, Maytag offered a long-running advertising campaign that featured the "lonely" Maytag repairman, who had nothing to do because Maytag appliances were so reliable. And, at one time, Maytag appliances did enjoy higher reliability and quality ratings than its competitors. Yet, even as Maytag's competitors have matched the reliability ratings of Maytag appliances, customers continue to perceive Maytag as offering greater quality. As a result, Maytag continues to enjoy a significant pricing premium for most of its appliances over those offered by its competitors.

Moreover, because they are often built as much (or more) on customer perceptions as they are on actual or tangible differences in the material or physical characteristics of products and services, successful strategies of differentiation can be "fragile" or short-lived, especially in industries or markets where fads or fashion swings occur frequently. In many markets, the introduction of new products or services can also wreak havoc on companies' differentiation strategies, especially if those new products or services possess real or perceived features that are quickly accepted or come to be demanded by consumers.

All of these differentiating factors take on added importance because many differentiated products are luxury items rather than products consumers actually need. Jewelry; second, third, fourth, and even fifth household television sets; aromatherapy products; vases, urns, china, crystal, and silver are just a few of the many luxuries that highly depend on a strategy of differentiation to convince customers that they should be purchased.[11] As a result, companies that sell these discretionary items must have highly sophisticated market research, advertising, and promotion capabilities to provide customers with the appropriate justification to make these luxury purchases.

Porter underscores many of these points, suggesting that because a successful strategy of differentiation depends on real or perceived uniqueness, firms pursuing differentiation strategies must develop

- strong marketing capabilities, and
- a reputation for quality or uniqueness.[12]

In addition, product (as opposed to process) innovation is important for firms pursuing differentiation strategies because they must develop totally new products or extensions of existing products that will be viewed as unique. Thus, firms pursuing differentiation strategies must also seek to enhance their

- creativity and research capabilities,

Exhibit 7.5 Using the Value Chain for a Hypothetical Manufacturing Firm to Assess Its Ability to Pursue a Strategy of Differentiation

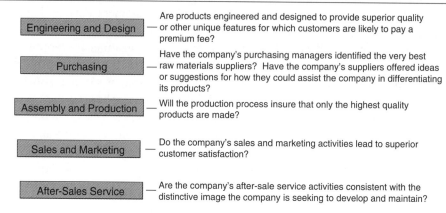

Engineering and Design	Are products engineered and designed to provide superior quality or other unique features for which customers are likely to pay a premium fee?
Purchasing	Have the company's purchasing managers identified the very best raw materials suppliers? Have the company's suppliers offered ideas or suggestions for how they could assist the company in differentiating its products?
Assembly and Production	Will the production process insure that only the highest quality products are made?
Sales and Marketing	Do the company's sales and marketing activities lead to superior customer satisfaction?
After-Sales Service	Are the company's after-sale service activities consistent with the distinctive image the company is seeking to develop and maintain?

- coordination among R&D, marketing, and manufacturing, and
- ability to attract highly skilled labor, scientists, or creative people.

As with the strategy of cost leadership, analysis of the various links in a company's value chain can also be helpful in assessing the ability of the organization to pursue a successful differentiation strategy. Analysis of the links in the value chain of the hypothetical manufacturing firm depicted in Exhibit 7.5 would suggest a number of opportunities to differentiate the company's products: Are products engineered and designed to provide superior quality or other unique features for which customers are likely to pay a premium price? Many aspects of product design may be totally superficial and have nothing to do with the performance of a product, yet design is one of the most powerful and effective ways for companies to differentiate their products. Recent thinking about the importance of design has evolved from focusing on solely the aesthetic aspects of design to a much broader focus on how design influences the way consumers interact with products, services, and companies.[13] Have the company's purchasing managers identified the very best raw materials suppliers? Have the company's suppliers offered ideas or suggestions for how they could assist the company in differentiating its products? Will the production process ensure that only the highest-quality products are made? Do the company's sales and marketing activities lead to superior customer satisfaction?

Focus

As suggested by Exhibit 7.3, when strategies of differentiation or cost leadership are not aimed at broad market segments, but instead are targeted at a narrow industry niche or market segment, they are called focus strategies. Firms pursuing focus strategies seek the same strategic advantage—overall lower cost or perceived uniqueness—as firms pursuing cost leadership or differentiation strategies, but they target or "focus" that strategic advantage on a particular market segment or niche. Thus, there are really two possible focus strategies—a *focus differentiation* strategy of offering products or services that are perceived as unique to a narrow market niche, as well as a *focus cost leadership* strategy of offering low-cost products or services to a narrow market niche.

The automobile business of Rolls-Royce represents one of the best examples of a focus differentiation strategy. Rolls-Royce is obviously not seeking to sell its automobiles to a broad segment of the market; in fact, Rolls-Royce is not even seeking to sell its cars to buyers in the luxury segment of the market. Instead, the company focuses only on those buyers in what might be characterized as the ultra-luxury segment of the market—those consumers who are willing to pay $200,000, $400,000, or even more for an automobile. The "low-end" Rolls-Royce Ghost model sells for $245,000 to $300,000![14]

Similarly, Bang & Olufsen, a Danish firm producing luxury home electronics items, pursues a highly differentiated focus strategy, offering such specialty items as high-end television sets and audio products. A Bang and Olufsen television set might retail for as much as $40,000 and the company has recently introduced a 103-inch flat panel television that retails for more than $100,000.[15]

On the other hand, so-called "dollar stores"—Dollar General, Family Dollar, and Dollar Tree—are good examples of focus cost leadership. Like Wal-Mart, these firms are pursuing cost leadership strategies, but their range of products is much more limited, focusing primarily on products that can be sold for as little as $1 or less. You might guess that such a market would be fairly limited, and, indeed, it will never be a broad market segment, but, for several years now, dollar stores have represented one of the fastest growing segments in the U.S. retailing industry, indicating that even very narrow market segments can sometimes be quite viable.[16]

While companies pursuing a focus strategy are usually segmenting the market based on products (Red Bull focusing on energy drinks within the huge and very broad beverage market, for example), firms pursuing a focus strategy can also segment the market based on customers, demographics, or regions. For example, Dairy Queen has focused almost exclusively on opening stores in smaller towns and cities. Applebee's has grown to be one of the largest restaurant chains in the United States by also focusing on smaller communities.[17]

Though serving only about three percent of all U.S. air passengers, Alaska Air has thrived. The regional air carrier is not only profitable, but it has one of the strongest balance sheets in the highly competitive airline industry. According to Bill Ayer, the company's CEO, "You need to get to a certain size, but beyond that, it's neutral to negative to be bigger." Being small has allowed Alaska to be nimble and to implement many creative ideas quickly. And, the company's size also allows it to avoid much of the complexity that increases the costs of the larger air carriers.[18]

So many firms enjoy high performance by pursuing focus strategies that it's clear that market share is not a prerequisite to high performance. In fact, a research study involving more than 3,000 companies found that firms with the largest market shares rarely enjoy the highest rates of return.[19] Yet focus or low market share strategies can also have their pitfalls and require significant management effort and talent. Recall that a focus strategy applies a cost leadership or differentiation strategy to a very targeted or narrow market niche. As a result, managers of firms pursuing focus strategies must develop the capabilities and resources necessary to be a successful cost leader or a successful differentiator.

A focus strategy requires managers to be particularly attentive to defining the company's target market. Changes in customer demographics, competing products, and new technologies could quickly wipe out narrow target markets. For example, New York City once had a number of African-American community newspapers. Though their circulation numbers were never large relative to other New York newspapers, these newspapers played an important civic and cultural role in their respective communities. As reading habits changed and fewer and fewer households subscribed to newspapers, all newspapers suffered declines in circulation, but many of these very focused newspapers were forced to cease publication.

Furthermore, because managers of firms that are pursuing focus strategies are seeking to serve narrow niches, business definition becomes especially crucial. Managers and employees of companies that are pursuing focus strategies must know and understand exactly what niches they are seeking to serve. And the market size of the niche can be very important. Too narrow a niche will leave a company with too few customers, and sales revenues will be too low to maintain viability. On the other hand, a company that seeks to serve too wide a niche may confuse its customers.

Consider the dilemma faced by companies selling high-priced designer jeans, often selling for $200 or more per pair. These companies could probably serve a larger group of customers and even increase their sales revenues by lowering their prices. Yet, by lowering their prices, they could alienate their current customers if they interpreted the lower prices and larger market as diminishing the exclusivity of the product.

One company that has successfully pursued a focus strategy for many years is Rolex. The company aims to serve only the highest end of the luxury wristwatch market. Its prices reflect this exclusivity, and, to reinforce this image among its customers and potential customers, the company advertises in publications and magazines that cater to its upscale clientele.

On the other hand, niche markets can sometimes grow and become large industries in their own right, and managers must be prepared to take advantage of these opportunities. For example, in its early years, Federal Express served a niche market for a relatively small number of all postal and freight customers—those who had to have their letters and packages delivered overnight. As Federal Express developed this market niche, however, the number of customers who "absolutely, positively" had to have their packages delivered overnight grew substantially, and the overnight mail business has now become an industry in its own right with a very large base of customers and many competitors.

Stuck in the Middle

Porter also argued that some firms do not pursue a viable business strategy, and he labels these firms *stuck in the middle*. According to Porter, firms become stuck in the middle for one of two reasons. First, they might fail to pursue successfully any of the generic business strategies. For example, a firm might pursue a strategy of differentiation, but, failing to become a successful differentiator, the firm becomes "stuck": It has failed to differentiate itself from its competitors, but, by trying to pursue a strategy of differentiation, the firm has also failed to develop the capabilities or resources that would make it a successful cost leader.

Second, Porter suggested that a firm attempting to pursue more than one generic strategy will most likely become stuck in the middle. He argued:

> Successfully executing each generic strategy involves different resources, strengths, organizational arrangements, and managerial style… Rarely is a firm suited for all three.
>
> The firm stuck in the middle must make a fundamental strategic decision. Either it must take the steps necessary to achieve cost leadership or at least cost parity, which usually involve aggressive investments to modernize and perhaps the necessity to buy market share, or it must orient itself to a particular target (focus) or achieve some uniqueness (differentiation). The latter two options may well involve shrinking in market share and even in absolute sales.[20]

Porter's assertion that firms simultaneously pursuing more than one generic strategy will wind up stuck in the middle is challenged later in this chapter as we identify several firms that successfully pursue both cost leadership and differentiation strategies.

Generic Business Strategies: Some Illustrations

The end of this section identifies some specific firms in various industries and describes their strategies in terms of Porter's typology, but first, consider Exhibit 7.6, which provides hypothetical illustrations of successful cost leadership and differentiation strategies. Exhibit 7.6 shows three sets of bar graphs, depicting per unit sales prices, costs of goods sold, and gross margins for the products or services of three hypothetical firms—an "average industry competitor," a "successful cost leader," and a "successful differentiator." Notice that although

Exhibit 7.6 A Hypothetical Illustration of Successful Cost Leadership and Differentiation Strategies

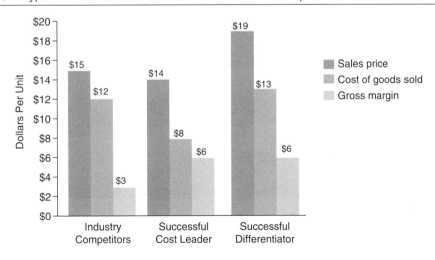

the successful cost leader's product or service is priced just below the industry average, its unit costs are much lower than those of the average industry competitors. Because of this significant per unit cost advantage, the successful cost leader enjoys margins that are much higher than those of the average industry competitors.

The successful differentiator, on the other hand, offers a product or service that is perceived as unique. The successful differentiator, therefore, is able to charge prices that are significantly higher than the industry average. The higher prices the successful differentiator enjoys come at a cost, however: Differentiation requires additional costs either for tangible features, such as more expensive raw materials, or to pay for research and development of unique physical characteristics or for advertising to inform or persuade consumers that the product warrants its higher price. Notice in Exhibit 7.6 that the differentiator's costs are higher than the industry average. Still, the successful differentiator's higher prices provide it with a very satisfactory margin compared to that of competitors.

Exhibit 7.7 goes a step further by applying the same analysis illustrated in Exhibit 7.6 to three firms in the discount retailing industry—Wal-Mart, Target, and Sears Holdings, the parent company of Kmart and Sears. As you can see from Exhibit 7.7, Wal-Mart offers a prototypical example of a successful cost leader. The company's zeal for low costs is reflected in its low level of selling, general, and administrative (SGA) expenses compared to total sales revenues. In 2008, SGA expenses represented only 18.6 percent of Wal-Mart's total sales revenues.

On the other hand, Target Stores provides a very good illustration of a successful differentiator. Though very much a discount retailer, Target seeks to provide customers with unique discount retail shopping experiences. Its motto, "expect more, pay less" captures its goal of seeking to offer shoppers a differentiated experience (i.e., "expect more"), even though they are shopping at a discount retailer (i.e., "pay less"). Target's differentiation or uniqueness, as Porter suggested, comes at a cost, which is reflected, at least in part, in Target's higher selling, general, and administrative expenses that are required to pay for the products, services, and amenities that differentiate the Target shopping experience.[21] Target's SGA expenses represent

Exhibit 7.7 Wal-Mart, Target, and Sears Holdings as Examples of Porter's Generic Strategies and Stuck in the Middle

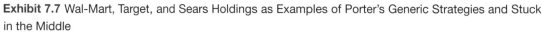

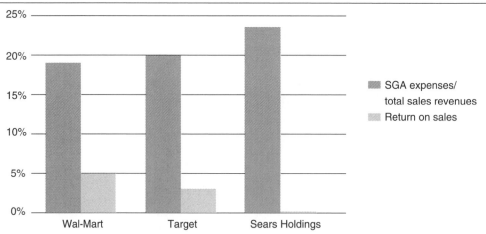

Exhibit 7.8 The Generic Business Strategies of Companies in Various Industries and Markets

Industry	Cost Leadership	Differentiation	Focus
Airline	Southwest	American	Kiwi
Automobile	Kia	General Motors	Rolls-Royce
Retailing	Wal-Mart	Target	Starbucks
Wristwatch	Timex	Seiko	Rolex

19.9 percent of the company's sales revenues. Still, the company's ability to charge higher prices due to the unique shopping experience Target offers its customers allows the company to earn a satisfactory return on sales. Target's 3.4 percent return on sales is less than Wal-Mart's 5.3 percent return on sales, but is still relatively high among retailers.

Sears Holdings, by contrast, offers a classic illustration of a company stuck in the middle. As illustrated in Exhibit 7.7, its SGA expenses as a percentage of total revenues of 23.6 percent are higher than either the segment's cost leader, Wal-Mart, or the differentiator, Target. Yet, Sears Holdings is certainly not a successful differentiator or a cost leader—its return on sales in 2008 was only one-tenth of one percent.

How did this happen to such a successful company? Sears dominated retailing for many decades, and along the way developed many distinctive and highly regarded brand names, including Craftsman tools, Die-Hard batteries, and Kenmore appliances. Kmart was the original big-box discount store. But, as the retailing landscape changed radically, both of these companies failed to maintain effective competitive strategies. In the 1970s and 1980s, Sears was squeezed both by the emergence of specialty retailers at the high end that competed for its apparel and appliance business and by the rise of discount retailers, Kmart, Wal-Mart, and Target that competed vigorously with Sears on the low end. Sears failed to develop an effective response to the rise of these new competitors. Similarly, though Kmart pioneered in developing the discount retail segment, it was overtaken by Wal-Mart and Target. To compound these companies' troubles, the emergence of big-box retailers like Best Buy, Home Depot, and Lowe's, as well as the very focused dollar stores have made significant inroads in both companies' key business lines.[22]

By the 1990s, both Sears and Kmart had lost distinctiveness in their respective markets, and they are perceived as neither distinctive, having merchandise worth paying higher prices, nor as offering the lowest prices for their merchandise. Both companies are unfortunate, but very good, examples of the concept of being stuck in the middle. Now they are combined as Sears Holdings, but it's questionable whether two weak and ineffective competitors can become a viable retailing holding company.

To further illustrate the concept of generic strategies, we've included in Exhibit 7.8 some specific companies classified according to the generic strategy each is pursuing.

The Efficiency and Effectiveness of Generic Strategies

Now that the concept of generic business strategies has been explained and illustrations of successful cost leadership and differentiation strategies have been provided, the next few sections take up additional important issues. This section considers the efficiency and effectiveness of generic strategies, emphasizing two important points:

First, at least in traditional business contexts, none of Porter's generic strategies is, by definition, optimal or better than the other two; the appropriate generic strategy for any particular firm will depend on its managers' beliefs and their decisions, the firm's industry context, its business definition, and its capabilities. Second, cost leadership and differentiation (and focus) strategies can be both *efficient* and *effective*.

The first point is fairly straightforward. Porter has made no claim that any one of his generic strategies is better than the others. The second point may seem somewhat counterintuitive. Because we tend to equate the concepts of efficiency and effectiveness with low costs, it is easy to see how a strategy of cost leadership can be described as "efficient" or "effective"; it is less obvious to see how a strategy of differentiation can be called either "efficient" or "effective" because successful differentiators will almost certainly have higher costs than successful cost leaders.

Efficiency and effectiveness mean more than "low costs," however. A more accurate definition of *efficiency* is "the ratio of outputs to inputs." Similarly, a more complete definition of *effectiveness* is "firm performance relative to average industry performance." Using these definitions, it is possible for both cost leadership and differentiation strategies to be efficient and effective. Cost leadership increases profit margins by lowering costs, while differentiation increases profit margins by allowing firms to charge higher prices for products that are perceived as unique. In either case, the generic strategy can be efficient if it increases the ratio of outputs (i.e., sales price) to inputs (i.e., per unit costs). Note, for example, in the hypothetical examples illustrated in Exhibit 7.7, that both the successful cost leader and the successful differentiator enjoy comparable profit margins that are much higher than the average industry competitor's profit margin, thus both are effective.

Successful cost leadership strategies and successful differentiation strategies are also *efficient* because the resulting ratio of outputs (i.e., margin) to inputs (i.e., cost of goods sold and selling, general, and administrative expenses) is greater than that enjoyed by the average industry competitor. Moreover, successful cost leadership and differentiation strategies are more *effective* because they allow firms to enjoy higher performance relative to the average industry competitor. The breakfast cereal industry illustrates this point. Kellogg, General Mills, and the other name-brand cereal makers are pursuing differentiation strategies. Because of advertising and promotion, their costs are almost certainly higher than those of store-brand cereals. Yet their differentiation strategies can still be *efficient* if they enjoy higher ratios of margin to cost of goods sold than their store-brand competitors. Their strategies can also be *effective* if they enjoy higher levels of performance than their store-brand competitors.

Unattractive Characteristics of Commodity Markets, the Challenge of Price Competition, and Commodification

Firms can be successful and enjoy high levels of profitability in commodity markets, but these markets tend to be less attractive and more challenging than markets that provide greater opportunities for differentiation. Although many firms do well in spite of selling commodity products or services, participation in commodity markets can be particularly challenging for a number of reasons. First, and most important, competition in commodity markets is almost always vigorous, and is primarily focused on price because commodity products or services have few other distinguishing features. Thus, in order to enjoy competitive advantage in commodity markets, firms must 1) become successful cost leaders, or 2) find some way, as Coca-Cola and PepsiCo have done with their colas, as Morton has done with its salt products, or as Intel has done with microprocessors, to differentiate what are essentially commodity products.

Furthermore, the profitability levels of firms in commodity markets tend to be heavily impacted by business cycles. In many commodity markets, firms will have invested heavily in fixed plant and equipment. In these industries, firms are always seeking to spread fixed costs over as large a volume of production as possible in order to reduce overall per unit costs. As a result, firms will attempt to maintain high levels of production even during recessionary periods. The oversupply that typically results almost always depresses price levels in an industry.

Finally, with few features other than price to distinguish among competitors, customers rarely develop a strong loyalty to a particular firm or its products and services and will frequently switch to a different supplier based on only very small differences in price. This lack of customer loyalty can invite entry by additional competitors—remember from Chapter 4 that customer loyalty was identified as an important barrier to entry—and new entrants can further intensify competition, increase supply, and depress prices in the industry.

For all these reasons, commodity markets tend to be less attractive than markets in which firms have more opportunities to differentiate themselves. Unfortunately, over the past several years, firms in several industries have seen their markets become more commodity-like. This commodification has affected a diverse set of industries, including the markets for air travel, personal computers, and toys, and has required firms in these markets to alter their business strategies accordingly.

The Dangers of Price Competition

As just noted, competition in commodity markets often centers on price because the products offered by competitors in these markets tend to be similar, with few distinguishing characteristics. It's not uncommon for price competition to deteriorate into all-out price wars in which firms slash prices to a point where no firms—even those firms with the lowest costs—break even. Many industries have been the scene of past price wars. Wal-Mart and Amazon.com have entered a price war over the sale of best-selling books. On Thursday, October 15, 2009, Wal-Mart announced a price of $10 each for bestselling hardcover books sold through Walmart.com. That same day, Amazon.com announced that it would match Wal-Mart's price. Later on the same day, Wal-Mart announced a new price of $9, with Amazon.com matching this new price on the next morning. But, by Friday afternoon, Wal-Mart announced a further cut in its price to $8.99 in order to be able to claim that it was offering its customers the lowest online prices.[23]

Where will this lead? In light of the intense price competition between Wal-Mart and Amazon.com, it's worth remembering that price competition almost certainly was the undoing of many Internet retailers. A *Harvard Business Review* article noted that:

It was precisely this kind of competition—destructive competition, to use Michael Porter's term—that did in many Internet retailers, whether they were selling pet supplies, drugs, or toys. Too many fledgling companies rushed to market with identical business models and no strategies to differentiate themselves in terms of which customers and markets to service, what products and services to offer, and what kinds of value to create.[24]

Though the business world and the study of management offer very few clear-cut rules or axioms, one almost certain rule is that *price wars are never a good idea!* The important lesson to learn from these examples of vicious price competition is that a price war can hurt all competitors. Consumers would appear to be the big winners in any price war. They relish the low prices, and, at least in the short run, price wars do offer consumers significant savings. Yet, over the long run, price wars are not good for consumers, either. Lower prices will lead companies to reduce spending on R&D and innovations that would improve product features or service. And, if price wars drive some firms out of business, consumers will have fewer choices and they may face higher prices due to less competition.

Though structural factors, such as excess capacity, are often blamed for price wars, there is also a managerial component that is at least as important as any structural phenomena in explaining vigorous price competition. In fact, structural and managerial phenomena are often tied together in mutually reinforcing ways. For example, high levels of fixed investment, underutilized capacity levels, and undifferentiated products or services are all important structural explanations for price competition, but so, too, are such managerial phenomena as the tendency for actions to escalate as discussed in Chapter 3.[25]

Avoiding Price Competition and Price Wars

So, if the axiom is to avoid getting involved in price wars, what *should* managers do if they are confronted by an aggressive competitor that seems all too eager to initiate a price war? This is a difficult question with no easy or clear-cut answers. Matching the competitor's prices could almost certainly result in just the sort of escalation phenomenon that could lead to an all-out price war in which all participating companies could sustain serious losses. On the other hand, if managers fail to match the lower prices of an aggressive competitor, then their firm will surely lose sales and market share.

Perhaps the best advice is for managers to be proactive. Rather than allowing industry conditions to deteriorate to a point where a price war becomes inevitable, managers are well advised to take steps to avert such a calamity. As in many other situations, the best defense is often a good offense. First, managers can work with key customers to negotiate long-term contracts. Such contracts may require managers to offer some price concessions initially, but they would help to maintain price levels during periods of weak demand. Second, managers can signal to their firm's competitors that they are well prepared or positioned to weather a protracted price war as a way of discouraging competitors from lowering their prices. For example, managers could announce that they were working to substantially lower (or had succeeded in lowering) their firm's break-even point.

An even more effective, though more difficult, strategy is for managers to work to differentiate their firm's products or services so that customers will come to perceive them as unique. For example, Gillette and Schick could become complacent and allow consumers to come to the conclusion that one razor is as good as any other. Instead, both businesses have emphasized continuous product development and innovation.[26] To date, these companies' vigorous product development efforts have succeeded in preventing the commodification of wet shave razors.

Such differentiation is, of course, much more difficult to do if the firm participates in commodity markets. As many examples throughout this chapter have demonstrated, however, even commodity-like products can be successfully differentiated. Offering higher quality, greater sensitivity to customers' needs, and more convenient shipping and delivery services, as well as providing such services as warehousing, finishing, or component assembly that are valued by customers, are all additional ways to differentiate even commodity-like products. Though differentiation can be one of the most effective strategies for managers who find their firms in commodity markets, the next section will describe some of the factors that limit the effectiveness of even the best differentiation strategies.

The Limits of Differentiation

Given the discussion in the preceding two sections about the unattractive characteristics of commodity markets and the vigorous price competition that is often present in such industries, differentiation would appear to be an attractive strategic alternative. The success of the generic strategy of differentiation depends, however, on customers valuing the product or service characteristics on which managers have based their differentiation strategies. In addition, differentiation strategies can be thwarted by three factors: private label and store brand competition, discounting, and commodification. We turn now to consider all of these threats to a strategy of differentiation.

Customers Must Value the Product or Service Characteristics on Which Managers Have Based Their Differentiation Strategies

A company can come to dominate a market by differentiating its product or service in a particular way, but if customer tastes change, then the differentiating characteristics or features that have given the firm its dominant position in the market can become irrelevant. This point may seem fairly obvious, but, as suggested in Chapter 3, company managers can become so caught up in their own worlds that they can lose sight of what customers value. Managers must either anticipate or respond quickly to such a trend or else their differentiation strategies will become ineffective or even irrelevant.

This danger of emphasizing product characteristics that consumers do not value explains how Motorola lost its dominance in the market for cell phones to other companies. Motorola, which has long been obsessed with product quality, naturally emphasized quality in its early cell phone advertising, claiming that its phones were so well built that they would last 1,000 years. Many customers—most of whom will live far less than 1,000 years—were less impressed by

Motorola's claim and more attracted to the unique designs and innovative features offered by other companies, including Nokia and Samsung, and now a host of other entrants, including Research in Motion, Apple's iPhone, and Google.[27]

Private-Label and Store-Brand Competition

Another significant threat to the strategy of differentiation is the proliferation of private-label and store-brand products. Private-label and store-brand competition is a threat because it has the potential to change consumers' perceptions of the value-price ratio of name-brand products. Differentiation implies that consumers will pay higher prices for products and services, and that additional value will be derived from such purchases. If consumers purchase lower priced private-label products and find that they enjoy the same level of value as they do from higher priced name-brand products, then they will seriously question future purchases of name brand products and services.

Some product categories have seen considerable private-label competition. For example, store brands of butter now account for nearly half of all sales of this product, and store brands of ketchup now exceed 26 percent of this product. Private labels have won over 20 percent of the market for peanut butter, putting considerable pressure on the Jif and Peter Pan name brands of peanut butter. Overall, private label sales now account for over 17 percent of all grocery sales.[28]

On the other hand, some companies seem to be remarkably immune to the threat of private-label products, and some product categories have seen almost no private-label competition. Exhibit 7.9 shows nine companies that have been market share leaders in their product categories since 1923, and Exhibit 7.10 shows six product categories that have had almost no private-label invasion.

During the last several years, private-label manufacturers have made two advances that threaten the ability of consumer products companies to maintain the perception of uniqueness that their products have enjoyed, thereby undermining their strategies of differentiation. First, the quality of many private label and store brand products has improved while their prices

Exhibit 7.9 Companies That Have Maintained Market Share Leadership Since the 1920s

Category	Leading Brand in 1923	Current Rank
Chewing gum	Wrigley's	No. 1
Canned fruit	Del Monte	No. 1
Crackers	Nabisco	No. 1
Razors	Gillette	No. 1
Soft drinks	Coca-Cola	No. 1
Soap	Ivory	No. 1
Soup	Campbell	No. 1
Toothpaste	Colgate	No. 2

Source: Lander, M. 1991. What's in a name? Less and less. *Business Week*, July 8: 66–67.

Exhibit 7.10 Product Categories That Have Been Immune to Private-label Invasion

Category	Private-label Share
Baby food	0.0%
Beer	0.1%
Shaving cream	0.6%
Bar soap	0.8%
Deodorant	1.3%
Toothpaste	2.0%

Source: Shapiro, E. 1993. Price lure of many private-label products fails to hook many buyers of baby food, beer. *The Wall Street Journal,* May 13: B1, B8.

continue to be much lower than those of name-brand products. As consumers try private label and store brand products and find comparable quality at far lower prices, their perception of the value-price relationship will change, and they may become reluctant to pay premium prices for name-brand products. As a result, the private-label invasion has the potential to seriously erode the loyalty that consumers have traditionally placed in name-brand products.

Many name-brand companies actually manufacture or produce private-label products on the same assembly lines. While this may often make sense from a manufacturing cost standpoint—keeping production lines operating helps to lower the per unit fixed costs and can help companies achieve lower overall costs and higher margins—it rarely makes sense from a marketing or strategic standpoint. Should consumers suspect that private-label products are actually made by name-brand companies, it will surely hurt the ability of the name-brand companies to hold onto those customers and to maintain market share of their name-brand products.

The name-brand cereal companies have seen their strategy of differentiation threatened by many of the factors described here. Kellogg's and General Mills still dominate the ready-to-eat breakfast cereal industry, but they have seen their market shares eroded considerably over the last two decades—first, by sluggish demand as consumers appear to be choosing bagels, fast food, and other more convenient options over cereal for breakfast. Furthermore, not only do Kellogg's and General Mills compete with each other and with other name-brand cereal manufacturers, but the market for ready-to-eat breakfast cereals is also the scene of vigorous competition from private-label and store-brand cereals. Sales of private-label and store-brand cereals, which often sell for $1 or more per box less than the name-brand cereals, grew from approximately $150 million in 1988 to approximately $550 million in 1995—an increase of more than 40 percent annually.[29] The name brand cereal manufacturers fought back by offering new cereal products and by holding the line on price increases, so that sales of store-brand and private-label cereals had only grown to $620 million by 2005.

Discounting

Some companies and whole industries have diminished their ability to maintain their differentiation strategies by engaging in discounting. Discounting weakens the effectiveness of differentiation strategies by giving consumers the idea that they do not necessarily need to pay more for products or services that should be perceived as unique and therefore worth higher prices. Many of the major department stores have lost their distinctiveness and appeal by relying so heavily on sales to attract customers. Many traditional department store customers have now become hesitant to pay full price for any department store items, preferring to wait for the next sale, which, in most cases, will be less than a week away!

Nowhere are the problems of discounting more obvious than among the leading domestic automobile manufacturers. By enticing customers to purchase vehicles by offering hefty rebates, often $3,000 or even more per vehicle, the auto companies have effectively cheapened their vehicles so that many customers are willing to purchase a domestic vehicle only if offered a substantial rebate.[30]

Sergio Marchionne, CEO of Fiat, which acquired an ownership stake in Chrysler in 2009, has moved rapidly to wean that auto maker from a reliance on rebates. According to press reports, Marchionne has demanded improvements in margins, vehicle quality, and pricing policies. A *Wall Street Journal* article quoted Marchionne stating, "Unprofitable volume is not volume I want. ... We have a very good track record for how to destroy an industry—run the [plants] just for the hell of volume, and you're finished."[31]

The recent major recession, however, has forced many consumer products companies to rethink their pricing strategies. For example, Procter & Gamble has long resisted lower prices, believing that consumers equate higher prices with better quality. But with many consumers economizing during the recession by switching to store-brand or private-label brands, P&G was forced to relent on its pricing strategy and to offer lower prices, and in some cases lower-priced versions of some of its leading branded products. For example, during the summer and fall of 2009, P&G began testing a lower-cost Tide Basic version of its classic Tide laundry detergent. But this came only after more than a third of all consumers had experimented with lower-cost laundry detergents.[32]

Commodification

Finally, several factors can lead to a gradual loss of distinctiveness, or commodification. In some cases, famous consumer product brands have suffered from a benign neglect in which companies have failed to invest in maintaining the brand image of these products. Recall in Chapter 2 where investment was described as a key factor associated with the development and maintenance of competitive advantage, it appears that at least some of the problems the major consumer products companies have had with their name-brand products have resulted from their own inaction. Ajax, Brylcreem, Aqua Velva, Lifebuoy, Duncan Hines, Aunt Jemima, Mrs. Paul's frozen seafood, and Log Cabin syrup are all examples of once-famous name-brands that have lost their cachet as well as market share largely because companies failed to sustain adequate levels of advertising and marketing.[33]

In other cases, companies have "crowded out" their own products by introducing new products. For example, Coke's introduction of Diet Coke marginalized the role of its Tab diet cola product. Similarly, Procter & Gamble tried in vain to maintain the market position of its Camay soap, but a good deal of Camay's troubles were due to growing competition from Procter & Gamble's own successful introduction of a similar competing product, Oil of Olay bar soap.[34]

In other cases, companies have simply failed to focus on those qualities that can most effectively differentiate their products from competitors. For example, many automobile companies have probably not emphasized the importance of exciting design. An executive in Chrysler's Dodge division has been quoted as saying, "We were starting to look at the product as a commodity, which is disgusting."[35]

More than a decade ago, Procter & Gamble began to recognize that its own marketing and product proliferation efforts have been a source of confusion for consumers. A *Wall Street Journal* article on the company noted that customers' buying habits have changed significantly in recent years:

> Today's average consumer, more often than not a woman, takes just 21 minutes to do her shopping—from the moment she slams her car door in a supermarket parking lot to the moment she climbs back in with her purchases. In that time, she buys an average of 18 items, out of 30,000 to 40,000 choices. She takes less time to browse; it is down 25 percent from five years ago. She isn't even bothering to check prices. She wants the same product, at the same price, in the same row, week after week.[36]

The article also noted that in spite of these changes in consumer buying habits, Procter & Gamble was routinely "making 55 price changes a day across 110 brands, offering 440 promotions a year, [and] tinkering with package size, color and contents" with the result that the company offered as many as 35 varieties of its Bounce fabric softener just in its North American markets.[37] In response, P&G has taken a number of steps, including drastically reducing the number of variations on each product, and the number of product promotions it conducts, and the company is also working more closely with retailers to improve the promotion and in-store displays of its products.[38] P&G's new approach will probably have several positive benefits. First, greater consistency in pricing and product promotion will help P&G reinforce customers' perceptions of its brands. In addition, by reducing the number of variations of its products, P&G can realize significant cost economies in manufacturing, distribution, and advertising.

Now, many retailers are coming to a similar conclusion—that too much variety can actually hurt sales by making shopping a challenge. "By 2008, nearly 47,000 distinct products filled a typical food retailer's shelves, up more than 50 percent from 1996, according to survey data from the Food Marketing Institute." Many of those retailers are now paring back product offerings in order to simplify the shopping experience.[39]

Negative Brand Equity

Taken to the extreme, customer perceptions of major brand names can become so unfavorable that they acquire negative brand equity, in which customers are *less* rather than more likely to purchase a product or service that carries a particular brand name. Many GM brands, Sears, and Levi's are examples of brands and companies that have struggled with this problem of negative brand equity. So serious was the negative brand equity associated with the Oldsmobile brand that several years ago, General Motors decided to discontinue the brand rather than continue to expend resources to revive it. And, as the company entered bankruptcy during one of the worst economic downturns since the Great Depression, General Motors had also concluded that its Pontiac brand had lost so much equity that the Pontiac brand was also discontinued along with Saturn.

Do Some Companies Enjoy Dual Advantage, or the Ability to Pursue Both Differentiation and Cost Leadership Strategies Successfully?

Porter argued that, because of the resources, capabilities, and skills required, managers will find it very difficult for their companies to successfully pursue more than one generic strategy simultaneously, and he argued that companies pursuing more than one generic strategy are likely to find themselves stuck in the middle. For example, a recent *Wall Street Journal* story highlighted some of the difficulties Wal-Mart has faced in growing its George brand of upscale clothing items. Part of the difficulties faced by the George line are almost certainly because customers are not expecting Wal-Mart to carry fashionable and differentiated clothing. Furthermore, Wal-Mart probably lacks (at least for now) the expertise in merchandising these more fashionable items in its stores. This example demonstrates some of the difficulties a successful cost leader can face in attempting to master the skills of differentiation.[40]

Still, it is worth noting that more than a few high-performing companies seem to be both successful cost leaders *and* successful differentiators, enjoying the benefits of what has come to be known as **dual advantage**. To compete effectively in many industries, firms must have strength along one of these dimensions with at least parity with their competitors along the other dimension.

Consider, for example, Anheuser Busch InBev. The company owns the most modern breweries in the industry and enjoys significant manufacturing, distribution, and marketing cost advantages over its rivals. At the same time, Anheuser Busch InBev has always been very successful at differentiating its beers through highly effective marketing and advertising campaigns. As noted earlier in the chapter, Morton, the famous salt producer, has pursued a very successful differentiation strategy even though salt is one of the most basic of all commodity products. Over the years, however, Morton's managers have also won a reputation as successful cost cutters, and they have had aggressive goals for improving profit margins by further reducing the company's operating costs.[41] The fashion chain, Forever 21, is another example of a firm that is, so far, excelling at both cost leadership and differentiation.[42] Thus, Morton and Forever 21 are also examples of companies that enjoy dual advantage by being both effective differentiators and cost leaders.

The success of a number of global companies also seems to be built on their simultaneous pursuit of both cost leadership and differentiation strategies. Canon's success in the market for photocopiers was built largely on differentiating its products from those of Xerox while also pursuing economies of scale and other cost efficiencies.[43] For many years, Toyota has been one of the lowest-cost producers of automobiles in the world, and Toyota's labor costs per vehicle are roughly half of GM's and about two-thirds of Ford's.[44] Not only does Toyota enjoy significantly lower costs than most of its rivals, but Toyota's innovative automobile designs have also redefined several key segments of the automobile market over the last two decades, especially in the high-volume family sedan segment, where its Camry model has been a best-seller, and in the luxury car segment, where its Lexus models are now viewed as the prototypical luxury model.

Porter is right to be concerned that the simultaneous pursuit of both cost leadership and differentiation strategies will require large commitments of organizational resources (as well as managerial talent). And, it is worth considering whether the quality problems experienced by Toyota aren't a result of the difficulties associated with Toyota's attempts to pursue both differentiation and cost leadership.[45]

The nature of competition in many industries today dictates that firms must frequently compete along both cost and differentiation dimensions. Some recent research studies have also found that the managers of most firms emphasize capabilities associated with more than one generic strategy, further indicating that the strategies do not have to be mutually exclusive.

Similarly, Professors Kim and Mauborgne, authors of the best selling book, *Blue Ocean Strategy*, advocate pursuing a value innovation strategy whereby the focus of competition is changed from beating the competition to making the competition irrelevant by creating a leap in value for consumers and opening up new uncontested market space.[46] Finding what they call a "*blue ocean*," this area of untapped market space, requires an examination of buyer value elements to break the trade-off between differentiation and low cost. They suggest that by examining an industry for value factors that should be eliminated, reduced, raised or created, a company can get a new look—or mental model—of the industry.

Other researchers advocate using design thinking to create advances in both innovation and efficiency, allowing an organization to simultaneously pursue differentiation and cost strategies. Professor Roger Martin, author of *The Design of Business*, suggests:

A person or organization instilled with that discipline [design] is constantly seeking a fruitful balance between reliability and validity, between art and science, between intuition and analytics, and between exploration and exploitation. The design-thinking organization applies the designer's most crucial tool to the problems of business.[47]

As Porter suggested, this is not easy. This approach to design requires a shift in organization structure (Chapter 11), leadership and mindset to achieve desired results.

Finally, a growing body of evidence suggests that many management efforts contribute to both lower costs and greater differentiation. For example, quality improvements enhance customers' perceptions of the value of products and services and can be an excellent way to differentiate a company's products and services. Yet many quality improvement efforts also contribute to lower costs by improving manufacturing processes, reducing scrap and waste, and lowering inspection costs. This is also true of much thinking around "green strategies"—that what is good for the environment may also cost less to produce over the long run.

Developments in many industries are suggesting new competitive dimensions that go beyond cost and differentiation. In some high-velocity manufacturing industries, for example, it can be very important to bring new products to market quickly. Firms in these industries must emphasize design and engineering so that new products move quickly from the concept or idea stage to production. Costs and differentiation may be important in these industries, but fast response or "fast cycle time" may be even more important to firm success.

Conclusion: Generic Strategies and the Book's Three Key Themes

The Importance of Managers and Managerial Thinking

Of course, managers play a critical role in formulating and implementing business strategies that contribute to the development of competitive advantage. One possible way, but certainly not the only way, to think about the role of managers and managerial thinking in developing competitive advantage is depicted in Exhibit 7.11. As illustrated in this exhibit, a company's top managers might begin by defining the business in a particular way. As indicated at the beginning of this chapter, the choice of business definition should suggest an appropriate business strategy, such as cost leadership or differentiation.

The choice of business strategy would be followed by a resource accumulation *process* that would focus on the acquisition of key resources and the development of the capabilities needed to execute the business strategy in a singularly or uniquely effective way. Time, success, interconnectedness, and continued investment would be expected, over time, to provide firms with resources and capabilities that are rare, valuable, nonsubstitutable, and inimitable—unique resources and capabilities that can be sources of competitive advantage. As noted earlier in this chapter, many of these decisions are very much interrelated or "tightly coupled" so that the process is not likely to be as rational or as neat as suggested in Exhibit 7.11. For example, a particularly strong resource or capability might influence managers to define their firm in such a way as to take advantage of that capability.

Two points seem particularly significant: First, as emphasized in Chapter 2 and as this description suggests, it is *not* the choice of generic strategy that leads to competitive advantage, but the resource accumulation *process* that gives rise to unique and valuable capabilities and

Exhibit 7.11 A Mental Model of the Role of Business Strategy and Other Factors in Creating and Maintaining Competitive Advantage

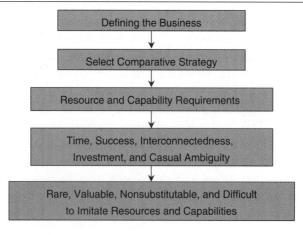

resources that are sources of competitive advantage. The choice of a generic strategy will not, in itself, create a profitable business model. Michael O'Leary, the iconoclastic CEO of Ryanair, an airline known for its fervent commitment to cost-cutting, is almost religious in his commitment to searching for new ways to cut the costs, and therefore the price, of air travel, even considering such seemingly crazy moves as removing airline seats to create space for standing passages who might pay only a fraction of the price paid by passengers with seats. But it is this kind of creative, ongoing, and very hard work that is responsible for developing and sustaining the profitable business models that result in successful cost leadership business strategies.[48]

Second, whether these resource accumulation processes occur in the order illustrated in Exhibit 7.11 or in some other fashion, it is important to recognize that the processes are not random or haphazard, but that they are guided by managers' beliefs and understandings. In fact, the role of "architect" that managers play in guiding their firms through the decisions illustrated in Exhibit 7.11 is crucial or fundamental to the success of business organizations. In the next chapter, we see how these processes play out in a variety of different industry contexts.

Change and the Need to Think Dynamically about Strategic Management

At many points throughout this chapter, we have emphasized that changes in the competitive landscape can undermine the success of business strategies. Changes in customer needs, tastes, and preferences, the development of new technologies, and the introduction of new products and services can render any very successful business strategy ineffective or obsolete. Thus, aggressive efforts to maintain the effectiveness of current business strategies, active monitoring of the competitive landscape, an aggressive and proactive approach to new product and service development, and thinking like an outsider about the industry—all of these management efforts are essential to the ongoing success of firms' business strategies in dynamic competitive environments.

The Importance of Organizational Learning

One question that is certainly appropriate at this point goes back to the discussion of competitive advantage found in Chapter 2: If competitive advantage is based on asymmetry, then how can "generic strategies," such as cost leadership, differentiation, or focus, be sources of competitive advantage? In other words, how can "generic" strategies, which any firm can pursue, possibly give rise to the asymmetry that is the essential characteristic of competitive advantage?

This is a challenging question for the field of strategy. The answer, as we suggested in Chapter 2, is that the ability of any of these strategies to provide a firm with a competitive advantage typically comes not from the *content* of the strategy but from the way the firm chooses to formulate and implement the strategy and the unique capabilities the firm develops. It is not enough for managers to decide that their firm should adopt a strategy of cost leadership because many firms—even many firms in the same industry—will be pursuing a strategy of cost leadership. For a firm to achieve a competitive advantage by pursuing a cost leadership strategy, it will have to pursue that strategy in a distinctive way and develop unique capabilities. In a very real sense, the firms that engage in the most organizational learning will be the firms that will develop capabilities and organizational processes that will be associated with competitive advantage. Thus, the decision to select a particular strategy is only a preliminary step. The array of associated decisions and the associated organizational learning that must follow this first decision about strategy content will prove to be much more influential in determining whether that strategy leads to a competitive advantage.

Key Points

- *Cost leadership*, *differentiation*, and *focus* represent three alternative generic business strategies.
- Each of the generic strategies has its own set of required organizational resources and capabilities.
- Commodity markets, in which products or services of competing companies are perceived to have few differences, have a number of unattractive characteristics—most significant, perhaps, is that firms tend to compete on the basis of price. As a result, managers will often seek to differentiate their firms' products and services.
- Successful differentiation strategies require that consumers value the product or service characteristics on which managers have based their firms' differentiation strategies, and that firms can maintain the perception of uniqueness that is vital to the success of any differentiation strategy. Three additional factors pose a serious threat to the ability of firms to differentiate their products and services, including:
  - Competition from private-label and store-brand products
  - Discounting, which tends to erode customers' perception of product or service uniqueness and value
  - Commodification, or the tendency for once-differentiated products to become more commodity-like over time
- At the same time, a differentiation strategy can also be undermined when customer perceptions of brands become so unfavorable that they acquire negative brand equity— when customers are less rather than more likely to purchase a product or service that carries a particular brand name.
- Though difficult, it appears that some firms enjoy dual advantage, or the ability to be both successful cost leaders and differentiators.
- Competitive advantage is best derived by developing and possessing unique and difficult-to-imitate resources and capabilities.

Key Questions for Managers

- What is your company's business strategy? Is it compatible with its business definition or are there conflicts between the way your firm wants to position its products and services and the generic strategy it is pursuing?
- Does your firm have the necessary capabilities, resources, and skills to execute its business strategy effectively?

- Is your firm or business stuck in the middle? Or, does the business run the risk of becoming stuck in the middle? If so, is this because it is failing to pursue either a successful cost leadership strategy or a successful differentiation strategy, or is it trying to do both but lacks the resources to be successful at both?
- What factors harm your company's efforts to differentiate its products and services? Has it inadvertently undermined its efforts to differentiate its products and services by discounting prices?
- What is your firm or business doing to minimize the possibility of excessive price competition in its market or industry? Has your firm or business exhausted all of the possibilities for creatively differentiating your products and services?
- What factors make your firm's efforts at cost leadership and differentiation difficult for competitors to imitate?

Suggestions for Further Reading

Additionally, links to further resources online—such as cases, articles, and videos—can be found on the book's website, www.routledge.com/textbooks/Duhaime.

Aaker, D., & Joachimsthaler, E. 2009. *Brand Leadership: Building Assets in an Information Economy*. New York: The Free Press.

Beckwith, H. 1997. *Selling the Invisible: A Field Guide to Modern Marketing*. New York: Warner Books.

Brown, T. 2009. *Change by Design*. New York: HarperBusiness.

Danziger, P. N. 2002. *Why People Buy Things They Don't Need*. Ithaca, NY: Paramount Market Publishing.

Esslinger, H. 2009. *A Fine Line: How Design Strategies Are Shaping the Future of Business*. San Francisco: Jossey-Bass.

Fitzell, P. 2003. *Private Label Marketing in the 21ˢᵗ Century: Store Brands, Exclusive Brands on the Cutting Edge*. New York: Global Books.

Forgang, W. 2004. *Strategy-Specific Decision Making: A Guide for Executing Competitive Strategy*. Armonk, NY: M. E. Sharpe.

Magee, D. 2007. *How Toyota Became #1: Leadership Lessons from the World's Greatest Car Company*. New York: Penguin Group.

Martin, R. 2009. *The Design of Business: Why Design Thinking Is the Next Competitive Advantage*. Boston: Harvard Business School Publishing.

Miles, R. E. & Snow, C. C. 1978. *Organizational Strategy, Structure, and Process*. New York: McGraw-Hill.

Porter, M. E. 1980. *Competitive Strategy*. New York: Free Press.

Spear, S. J. 2009. *Chasing the Rabbit: How Market Leaders Outdistance the Competition and How Great Companies Can Catch Up and Win*. New York: McGraw-Hill.

Verganti, R. 2009. *Design-Driven Innovation: Changing the Rules of Competition by Radically Innovating What Things Mean*. Boston: Harvard Business School Publishing.

Chapter 8

Business Strategy and Competitive Advantage in Emerging Industries and for Online Businesses

The previous chapter introduced the concept of business strategy by focusing on and describing Porter's typology of generic business strategies—cost leadership, differentiation, and focus.[1] The chapter focused on how managers' beliefs (i.e., their mental models) about how to compete would influence not only their choice of business strategy, but also the process of accumulating the firm-specific resources and capabilities that would allow them to come to enjoy a competitive advantage. Chapter 7 also suggested some of the unattractive characteristics of commodity markets and the dangers of price competition while also highlighting the advantages as well as the limitations of differentiation.

This chapter and the one that follows continue this focus on business strategies introduced in Chapter 7 by considering the special challenges facing firms in different industry contexts. The overall objective of Chapters 8 and 9 is to develop your thinking—your mental models— about business strategy and competitive advantage in different industry contexts. Because of the many differences across industry environments, developing and maintaining a competitive advantage is much more challenging than merely selecting an appropriate generic strategy. In fact, managers must consider many more competitive dimensions than product or service cost, uniqueness, and market breadth—the dimensions that are the basis of generic strategies. The aim of this chapter is to explore many of these other factors that managers must consider in formulating and implementing business strategies.

Life cycle models suggest that products and services pass through successive periods of emergence, rapid growth, maturity, and eventual decline as illustrated in Exhibit 8.1. Life cycle models have been extended beyond products and services to describe the emergence, growth, maturity, and eventual decline of companies and industries as well. This chapter focuses specifically on the challenges of competing in emerging and high-tech industries, while the challenges of competing in mature industry environments will be considered in Chapter 9.

Although the growth and decline phases are also important, the emerging and mature phases present very difficult challenges that often prove critical to the long-run success of firms. During the growth phase, market demand is growing rapidly, so any one firm's growth does not necessarily come at the expense of other firms in the industry. Furthermore, the growth phase can be very forgiving: Strategic mistakes made during the growth phase can usually be

Exhibit 8.1 The Industry Life Cycle

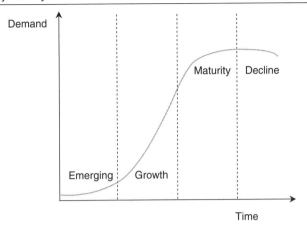

overcome because industry demand is growing so quickly; mistakes made during the emerging and mature phases of the industry life cycle, however, can have much more significant negative consequences. (Chapter 12 deals with the problem of decline, or, more specifically, how managers can avoid seeing their firms enter periods of decline.)

Later on, this chapter also considers online competition and business strategies. We examine the applicability of Porter's generic strategies of cost leadership, differentiation, and focus in these markets and also examine the effectiveness of "pure play" versus "clicks-and-bricks" or hybrid online strategies.

Chapter Objectives

The specific objectives of this chapter are to:

- Describe the characteristics of emerging industry environments.
- Highlight the challenges they pose for firms seeking to develop a competitive advantage in those industries.
- Describe the advantages and disadvantages associated with first- and second-mover strategies.
- Identify some of the factors that are essential to success in emerging industry environments.
- Describe the challenges online businesses encounter in seeking to formulate strategies and develop a competitive advantage.

Competition in Emerging Industries and the Value of First-Mover and Second-Mover Strategies

As emphasized in Chapter 5, industry environments are constantly in flux. Some industry environments have proven particularly dynamic over the last decade as new customer preferences

Exhibit 8.2 Managers' Beliefs About How Their Firms Should Compete in Different Industry Contexts

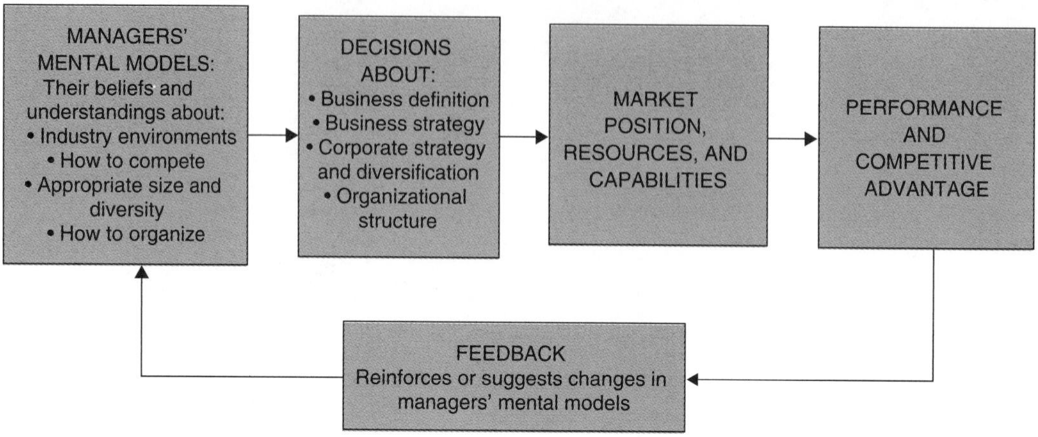

have emerged, new products and services have been developed, and new technologies have been exploited. As suggested by the book's model of strategic management (reprinted in Exhibit 8.2), the managers of firms operating in these dynamic industry contexts will develop mental models about their industry environments as well as mental models about how they should compete. These beliefs and understandings will influence how they position their firms in these emerging competitive environments and will also influence managers' decisions about whether their firm should be a first-mover, that is, whether their firm should be the first to seize and exploit new market opportunities, or whether their firm should wait until another, pioneering firm has entered the market before it enters the market as a follower.

Advantages and Disadvantages of First- and Second-Mover Strategies in Emerging Markets

In many cases, managers do not have the ability to decide whether their firm will be a first- or second-mover in an emerging market. Because successful entry into, and the development of, new markets requires foresight and skill while also entailing a certain degree of luck, firms cannot always be first-movers. And, there are advantages as well as disadvantages associated with both first-mover and second-mover strategies. For example, it is not always advantageous to be a first-mover. And, even when it might be advantageous, a first-mover strategy will not necessarily guarantee a competitive advantage. The next few paragraphs examine the advantages and disadvantages of first- and second-mover strategies, suggesting some of the factors managers must consider in making important decisions about entering emerging industry environments.

Empirical research suggests that first-movers often enjoy a number of advantages that persist over time.[2] Perhaps the most important advantage is a positive reputation effect. A firm that successfully pursues a first-mover strategy can come to be so closely associated with the new product or service in the minds of customers that subsequent entrants will have a difficult time overcoming that loyalty. If a first-mover fills a new portion of a market's competitive space and if that first-mover can achieve a high level of customer satisfaction, then subsequent entrants will have a difficult time displacing the first-mover from its status as market leader because that company will have already acquired some degree, perhaps even a high degree, of name recognition and customer loyalty. So, in many respects, first-mover strategies have many of the same qualities and objectives as the generic strategy of differentiation.

First-movers can also come to be recognized as particularly innovative firms, which can positively influence customers' perceptions of the other products or services these firms offer. Finally, by aggressively entering an emerging market segment before other firms, first-movers have an opportunity to move down the experience or learning curve so that they have the potential to enjoy a significant absolute cost advantage over any firms that enter the segment later.

On the other hand, first-movers sometimes stumble badly, and their strategies can fail to win customer acceptance. Sometimes, in the rush to bring new products or services to market quickly, first-movers will offer products or services that are poorly designed or even defective. First-movers might also launch new products or services with inadequate marketing or promotional efforts. Or, sometimes first-movers are so overwhelmed by customer acceptance of a product or service that they are simply not prepared to meet customer demand. As a result, orders go unfilled and customers can become dissatisfied by being forced to wait. These errors provide opportunities for second-movers, allowing them to learn from and then exploit first-movers' mistakes.

Furthermore, when second-movers can quickly imitate the products or services of first-movers, it is often in their best interest to let first-movers pay for research and development, initial marketing and advertising to introduce the product or service, and the costs associated with opening distribution channels. Second-movers can then "piggyback" on the efforts of first-movers, while avoiding many of the costs that the first-movers have incurred.

So, both first-mover and second-mover strategies have advantages and disadvantages and, as we will see, neither strategy always guarantees success.[3] The risks for firms considering either first- or second-mover strategies are heightened by two factors that characterize the dynamic emerging industry contexts in which these decisions must often be made: 1) the ambiguity of emerging markets, and 2) often short product life cycles.

The Ambiguity of Emerging Markets

First, the managers of firms in these dynamic industry contexts face a great deal of ambiguity and uncertainty about the attractiveness of emerging market opportunities. For example, uncertainty exists with respect to all of the following:

Demand

Will consumers accept a new product or service? Will the new product or service be a fad, selling very well for a short time with demand then falling off sharply? Or, will the new product or service appeal to broad market segments and become widely demanded? How fast will demand grow? Will the product be an overnight sensation, or will it take years for demand to grow and become significant? A product like the mp3 player could very well have been a short-lived sensation, but the iPod, introduced by Apple, has enjoyed tremendous sales, in part because of

Apple's effective marketing, pricing, and the many new models and product extensions that have been introduced.

Industry Infrastructure

Most emerging industry environments lack an infrastructure of established markets, buyers, suppliers, distribution channels, and a common language and set of norms. As a result, the preconditions and requirements for industry success are often unknown by the players in these emerging industries. Furthermore, managers of firms participating in these emerging industries must cooperate and even collaborate to develop the needed infrastructure.

High technology markets offer a number of illustrations of the challenges that firms face in moving into emerging markets in which the infrastructure is largely undefined. While PC users often express frustration over Microsoft's near-monopoly on computer operating system software, the Windows operating system provided a standardized operating system platform that removed much of the ambiguity (and perhaps some of the innovation) that might exist if consumers had to choose from multiple operating systems. As a result, many companies were able to develop applications for the Windows operating system and be assured that millions of users could be potential customers. Something similar is going on now as entrepreneurs and firms rush to develop applications for Apple's popular iPhone and iPad.

Industry Standards

Additional ambiguity exists until an emerging industry settles on a uniform set of product or service standards. Will the firm's product or service set the standards or will a competing product with different standards come to be preferred by consumers? In the latter case, how quickly can other firms adopt the new industry standard? What costs will be incurred by switching to the new industry standard?

Even as DVD players overtook VCR technology, firms began working on developing the next generation of technology to succeed DVDs. Companies as wide-ranging as Sony, Dell, H-P Matsushita, Philips, Samsung, and Thomson aligned behind "Blu-Ray" technology, so named because blue lasers read disks. When Wal-Mart and other large retailers opted for the Blu-Ray technology, firms that were developing a competing HD DVD technology, including Toshiba and NEC, were forced to adapt their strategies.[4]

The Nature of Competition

Perhaps most uncertain of all is the nature of the competitive environment. What other firms will choose to compete in an emerging market? Will those firms seek to dominate the market or will they be willing to accept more modest shares of the emerging market? What strengths and weaknesses will these competitors bring? And, perhaps most important, can a pioneering firm hold on to its lead even after significant competitors enter the market?

Even though many major companies now offer their own mp3 players, Apple's iPod products still represent a large share of this highly competitive market. On the other hand, EMI developed and introduced the CT scanner. But it entered a marketplace that was dominated by other medical technology firms, and its sales of CT scanners were quickly eclipsed by General Electric, which had long been a major player in X-ray machines and other medical technology devices.

The Length of Product Life Cycles in Emerging Markets Can Vary Considerably

In addition to market ambiguity, another troubling characteristic of many emerging business opportunities is that the length of product life cycles can vary considerably. Some products can have very long product life cycles, sometimes spanning decades. But many emerging market opportunities are characterized by much shorter life cycles. For example, sales of a motion picture in the U.S. typically peak just six weeks after a film is released, underscoring the importance of international release, video sales and rentals, and download sales for immediate or later viewing in order to enhance movie industry revenues. In the market for CT scanners, less than two years elapsed between the first sale and market saturation; EMI sold its first CT scanner in 1974 and by 1976, the industry had the capacity to manufacture 900 units even though only 500 units were sold that year.[5]

The product life cycles of many high tech products can be very short. The life cycles of new personal computer and cell phone models can be as short as four to six months from the date of a model's introduction until demand starts to decline! Cisco has adopted an aggressive acquisition strategy, in part, because the company claims that, in the high tech markets in which it competes, it must acquire new technologies very rapidly—more rapidly than it could develop these technologies internally—or otherwise risk missing-out on the sales from these fast-evolving technologies.

As a result, firms that choose to compete in emerging markets—regardless of whether they choose to pursue first- or second-mover strategies—not only face the challenge of introducing their new product or service offerings, but because product life cycles can be so short, they must also quickly establish competitive advantage.

Successful First- and Second-Movers: The Importance of Three Factors

If neither first- or second-mover strategies guarantee success in emerging markets, what factors, then, do determine success? To explore further this question of what distinguishes successful first- and second-movers from those firms that are less successful, we list several successful and unsuccessful first- and second-movers in Exhibit 8.3. For example, the exhibit identifies several successful first- and second-movers such as Chrysler, a successful first-mover in the market for minivans, and Apple, a very successful second-mover in the market for mp3 players. The exhibit also identifies some less successful first- and second-movers, including EMI, a first-mover in the market for CT scanners.

What would be helpful is to have some understanding—a mental model—about the factors that distinguish the winners from the losers in Exhibit 8.3. Such a mental model would then aid managers in making appropriate strategic decisions as their firms compete in emerging market contexts. Research by David Teece, a professor at the University of California, suggests that three factors are significant influences on whether first- and second-mover strategies are successful.[6]

Exhibit 8.3 Successful and Unsuccessful First- and Second-Movers in Various Industries

	First-Mover	Follower
Win	• Chrysler (minivan) • Searle (NutraSweet) • Du Pont (Teflon)	• IBM (personal computer) • Matsushita (VHS video recorders) • Seiko (quartz watch)
Lose	• RC Cola (diet cola) • Bowmar (calculator) • DeHavilland (Comet)	• Kodak (instant photography) • Northrop (F20) • DEC (personal computer)

Source: Adapted from Teece, D. J. 1978. Profiting from technological innovation: Implications for integrating, collaboration, licensing, and public policy. In D. J. Teece (Ed.), *The Competitive Challenge: Strategies for Industrial Innovation and Renewal*. Cambridge, MA: Ballinger: 185–221.

Dominant Design

It appears that much of the success of either first- or second-movers depends on their developing what becomes the dominant design for the new product or service. Arguably, Chrysler was saved from bankruptcy by its introduction of the minivan in 1982. Today, 30 years after the introduction of its first minivans, Chrysler continues to enjoy a market share lead in this market segment in spite of competition from nearly every other automobile manufacturer in the world. Much of the company's success with its minivan product can be traced to the fact that, in spite of considerable imitation, no other manufacturer has got it right the way Chrysler did in its original design and its more recent model updates.[7]

When developing its minivan models, Chrysler executives made the decision that the vehicle should be built on a car chassis. This gave the Chrysler minivan models a low profile and a car-like feel and drivability. Other automobile manufacturers that quickly introduced their own minivan models after Chrysler chose instead to place their minivans on truck chassis. But consumers by and large rejected this design option and showed a clear preference for Chrysler's low-profile design. Apple was a second-mover in the market for mp3 players, but with the introduction of the iPod, which featured significantly longer battery life, the capacity to hold many more songs than other mp3 players, and, above all, a sleek and elegant design, Apple was quickly able to seize the dominant design positioning.

It's probably worth underscoring that technically superior designs do not necessarily become dominant designs. The QWERTY typewriter (and now personal computer) keyboard is often cited as an example of a product that became the dominant design in spite of being technically inferior to other keyboard layouts. Sony's first-mover video recording product employing BETA VCR technology, though widely regarded as technologically superior, failed to become the dominant design as the market converged instead on VHS technology. And, as noted above, history has repeated itself as teams of competitors have more recently battled for the rights to claim the dominant design in the next generation of DVD technology.

Inimitability

If an innovative product or service is easy for competitors to imitate quickly, then it matters little whether a firm is a first- or second-mover. RC Cola has long been one of the most innovative soft-drink manufacturers. It was, for example, the first company to offer soft drinks in cans, and its Diet-Rite cola was the first diet cola to be introduced. Yet none of these innovations has provided the company with any long-term competitive advantage because of the ease with which RC's competitors could imitate them.

Even innovations that are patented are subject to imitation. Many companies have successfully innovated or engineered around patents. Canon's successful entry into the market for photocopiers came after its researchers had developed a "new process" that worked-around and avoided infringing on Xerox's many hundreds of patents.[8]

Still, companies must be careful when attempting to innovate around another company's patents. After Polaroid's success at creating instant photography, Kodak sought to be a successful second-mover in the fast-growing market for instant photography products. After Kodak entered the market with its own instant photography products, Polaroid successfully sued Kodak, charging patent infringement. In its judgment against Kodak, the court awarded Polaroid over $900 million in damages.

The Polaroid-Kodak case shows that litigation can be used by firms to defend against the imitation or infringement of patents, but that it can also be a competitive weapon and is often used by firms to delay or even derail completely their competitors.

Interconnectedness

A final factor that can distinguish between successful and less successful first- and second-movers is whether they possess complementary interconnected resource capabilities. Similar to the logic presented in Chapter 2, if the successful introduction of a new product or service requires an interconnected set of resources or capabilities, then both first- and second-movers will face greater costs to bring new products or services to market. Potential second-movers may find it both time-consuming and expensive to duplicate the success of a first-mover if that success is based on an interconnected set of resources and capabilities. Similarly, first-movers will have a difficult time maintaining their lead if second-movers have a better endowment of the interconnected resources.

EMI's inability to enjoy any sort of long-term advantage from its development of the CT scanner—a technology so important that the EMI research team that developed the scanner won the Nobel Prize in medicine in 1977—was probably due to its lack of interconnected resources and capabilities.[9] For example, EMI had no previous medical technology sales experience and it had no U.S. sales force, even though the United States was likely to be the largest market for the CT scanner technology. On the other hand, EMI's major competitor in the market for CT scanners, General Electric, had long been a major player in X-ray and other advanced medical technologies. And, General Electric had an established sales and marketing organization to support its advanced medical technology products.

IBM, though a second-mover in the market for personal computers, initially enjoyed great success in this business because of its reputation for product quality and service. In many respects, IBM's reputation allowed it to do what Apple and other PC manufacturers could not do—namely, to persuade businesses to buy personal computers in large quantities. It's also worth emphasizing that the success that most of the major pharmaceutical companies enjoy is due to the interconnectedness of their R&D and their marketing capabilities. Without their marketing capabilities, pharmaceutical firms would not know what new drug ideas to pursue nor would they have a mechanism for making doctors aware of their new products.

Pulling All of These Concepts Together: A Case Study of a Highly Successful First-Mover: NutraSweet

As with any other strategy, the test of whether a first- or second-mover is successful in an emerging market comes down to whether the company is able to create a market position or a set of resources and capabilities that are rare, valuable, and difficult to imitate. If a company can obtain the dominant design positioning or definition in a competitive space, if it has a set of complementary interconnected resources, and if its position and resources are difficult to imitate, then it is likely to be successful, regardless of whether it is a first- or second-mover.

To illustrate, let's pull these concepts together and examine a short case study of a highly successful first-mover, Searle, and the artificial sweetener it developed, NutraSweet. A new market for alternative artificial sweeteners emerged when health concerns were raised about cyclamates, an earlier artificial sweetener, so Searle's development of aspartame proved to be very much the "right product at the right time."

After developing aspartame, Searle patented the new product, but several years passed before Searle won approval from the Food and Drug Administration to market its new product. At that point, Searle's managers sought, and successfully won, the right to extend the life of aspartame patents so that the company would continue to have exclusive rights to market aspartame for several additional years after winning FDA approval for sale of the product.

Searle's patents on aspartame expired in 1992, but the company has maintained its dominance in the artificial sweetener market, suggesting that the company's success is based on more than patent protection. In fact, much of Searle's success with aspartame can be attributed to steps the company's managers took to make its success difficult to imitate, and to the interconnected set of capabilities the company developed to support its product. For example, early on, Searle entered into an agreement with a Japanese company, Ajinomoto, the low-cost maker of a key aspartame ingredient, phenylalanine. In this pact, Ajinomoto agreed to supply phenylalanine exclusively to Searle; furthermore, Ajinomoto agreed to provide Searle with the technology to manufacture phenylalanine so that Searle could also become a low-cost producer of this key ingredient. Searle also pursued an aggressive plant construction program here in the United States aimed at insuring more than adequate capacity and thereby discouraging other companies from building their own manufacturing facilities for producing artificial sweeteners.

In addition, Searle developed the NutraSweet and Equal brand names for aspartame in the United States and the Canderel brand name in Europe. The company also developed the distinctive NutraSweet logo that it required all buyers of NutraSweet to place on their packaging.[10] Such marketing efforts were aimed at bolstering the NutraSweet and Equal brands and developing a following for the products among consumers.

These steps not only gave the company a significant cost advantage over any would-be rivals, but they also led to the development of an interconnected set of manufacturing and marketing capabilities that have strengthened the company's position in the artificial sweetener market.

Today, a number of rival products compete in the artificial sweetener market, including Sweet 'N Low (saccharin) and Splenda (sucralose), which is manufactured by Johnson & Johnson's McNeil Nutritionals division. Most recently, a new "all natural" sweetener, Truvia, has emerged. Yet, due to the ways in which NutraSweet has managed the various phases of the product life cycle, no significant competition in the aspartame market has emerged. Nor has NutraSweet, now owned by J. W. Childs Associates, an investment firm, rested on its laurels. The company maintained an aggressive research effort, and NutraSweet has even developed a new artificial sweetener, neotame, that is approximately 13,000 times sweeter than sugar.[11] This product received FDA approval in 2002.

Online Competition

We turn now to examine online competition. Online business activity continues to grow and many analysts expect that Internet sales will soon account for at least 20 percent of all retail sales at some point in the near future.[12] While only about 10 percent of all shopping is currently done online, many online companies, including eBay and Amazon.com, have become some of the top retailers in the United States.[13] While the Internet has already transformed markets for travel and books, many other industries are now being similarly rocked, including jewelry, real estate, hotels, software, and telecommunications.[14]

In this section, we explore how online competition is different. We also examine the viability and expected profitability of online businesses pursuing the generic strategies of cost leadership, differentiation, and focus. Finally, we examine the relative advantages of "pure play" online retailers versus those firms pursuing clicks-and-bricks strategies.

How Is Online Business Different?

One important question is how does online competition differ from prior business contexts? Managers and scholars alike are struggling to understand how economic and business rules have changed and are likely to change in the years ahead. We know, for example, that the Internet allows firms to overcome physical boundaries and distance and it also allows them to serve larger audiences more efficiently. At the same time, and perhaps more importantly, Web technologies allow companies to target specific consumer groups, which may be difficult to do in traditional markets because of the high cost of obtaining information about particular customer segments.

Furthermore, traditional marketing methods usually emphasize only one-way communication from marketers to consumers, while the Internet is a highly interactive medium.[15] Since information flows both ways between retailers and customers, online businesses can use the information gathered through customer interactions to develop more effective marketing methods, to refine their product mix, and to offer better customer support.[16] As a result, the Internet allows firms to go beyond market segmentation to market fragmentation, dividing their markets into ever-smaller groups of customers—even tailoring their offerings to individual consumers as Amazon.com does with its customer recommendations, a process known as collaborative filtering.[17]

Second, the Internet provides firms with more detailed and higher quality information on customer transactions. Information technologies making use of point of sale data have enabled firms to improve inventory management and customer analysis, but this information tends to be rather crude since it usually includes only merchandise descriptions and quantities sold. On the other hand, vast amounts of rich data can be collected, analyzed, and accessed through the Web by marketers and consumers. This gives online businesses potentially very important advantages in being able to target their product or service offerings to specific customers. For example, Amazon.com uses collaborative filtering software to offer its users customized page views based on past searching habits. The software also permits Amazon to engage in anticipatory marketing by suggesting titles that may appeal to its customers. And, consumers gain by obtaining more market knowledge, allowing for easy comparisons across product offerings and retailers.[18]

The Internet also offers significant opportunities for reducing operating costs, particularly for service firms. Studies provide examples of improved transaction efficiency for service industries such as travel and financial services. For example, the average cost of a banking transaction at a local branch is $1.07. Use of an ATM machine reduces this cost to $.27, but performing this same transaction over the Internet costs a mere $.01. The customer support required for a typical reservation made through a travel agent costs $10.00, but this same transaction made over the Internet costs only $2.00.[19]

What Has Not Changed?

All successful firms must have viable and profitable business models. Many online businesses must incur considerable costs and make sizeable investments to provide value to their customers. For example, Amazon.com made large investments in its distribution facilities. Other companies have found that virtual activities do not eliminate the need for physical activities, but often amplify their importance, and the introduction of Internet applications in one activity often places greater demands on physical activities elsewhere in the value chain. For example, direct ordering makes warehousing and shipping more important. Many firms have reaped significant cost savings by employing Internet technologies, but the Internet does not guarantee that firms will experience lower costs. While Internet job-posting services have greatly reduced the cost of reaching potential job applicants, they have also flooded employers with electronic resumes. By making it easier for job seekers to distribute resumes, the Internet forces employers to sort through many more unsuitable candidates. The added back-end costs, often for physical activities, can end up outweighing up-front savings.[20]

Many products and services sold by online retailers are the same as those offered by traditional storefront or catalog retailers. The primary attraction of online shopping is that customers enjoy rich information and convenience. At the same time, consumers can be overwhelmed by information overload, and they may actually perceive an increase in their search costs. Furthermore, consumers often view online shopping as being riskier than traditional shopping channels. Orders are contracted before consumers receive or physically evaluate merchandise, and the delivery process may also generate risks if consumers do not receive their orders in the time frame and condition expected. Consumers also risk privacy loss.[21] To summarize, the Internet provides an efficient means to purchase products and services, but catalog retailers with toll-free numbers and automated fulfillment centers have been around for decades offering a convenient, consumer-friendly interface and speedy delivery. The Internet only changes the customer interface.[22]

Generic Strategies and Online Competition

Cost leadership is widely practiced today among online businesses that sell standardized products and services. Indeed, among first-time online shoppers, price may well be the most important factor influencing their buying decisions. This may be partially attributable to the ease of scanning and comparing prices on the Internet.[23]

But a strategy of cost leadership also has significant downsides. Because it's very easy for customers to make comparisons and those customers usually face very low switching costs, online businesses pursuing a strategy of cost leadership could easily become locked in a vicious cycle of price-cutting. Because the Internet is an open system, companies have more difficulty maintaining proprietary offerings, thus intensifying the rivalry among competitors. Internet technologies tend to reduce variable costs while increasing the significance of their fixed costs, and this can encourage companies to engage in destructive price competition. In addition, online businesses pursuing cost leadership will turn to outside vendors that offer the same products and services to other firms, so that purchased inputs become more homogeneous, further eroding company distinctiveness and increasing price competition.[24] Since the Internet also mitigates the need for an established sales force or access to existing marketing and distribution channels, barriers to entry are further reduced. Given all of these drawbacks, a generic strategy of cost leadership has many disadvantages for online businesses.[25]

Therefore, differentiation, based either on customizable products and services, a customized online experience, convenience, or some combination of all of these factors, is likely to be a more viable strategy. Firms like Amazon.com that reduce customer search costs, engender trust, and offer products, services, and online experiences tailored to end-users' needs are likely to elicit initial and repeat purchases.

As we noted in the previous chapter, cost leadership and differentiation or their equivalents are viewed as equally effective strategies in most business contexts. For online businesses, this may not be the case. For obvious reasons, price competition has probably intensified in nearly all online business environments, and firms with commodity-like products and services will face great pressure to keep their prices as low as possible. Therefore, the preferred strategy choice for online businesses would be differentiation, and some of the most successful online firms are those that have sought to differentiate their products and services.

Furthermore, as discussed above, Internet technologies potentially give all online retailers the ability to target both broad and narrow customer segments. Firms that pursue narrowly focused strategies are unlikely to be as successful as firms pursuing either cost leadership or differentiation strategies because those firms can take advantage of the scalability of Internet technologies to reach simultaneously both broad and narrow customer segments. So, unlike the traditional business context, online businesses pursuing strategies of focus cost leadership or focus differentiation will be less viable than firms that take advantage of the full scalability of Internet technologies.

The Advantages of Integrated or Dual Advantage Strategies

You'll recall from Chapter 7 that Porter has argued that cost leadership and differentiation are fundamentally contradictory strategies, requiring such different sets of resources that any firm attempting to combine them would wind up "stuck in the middle" and fail to enjoy superior performance.[26] At the same time, we argued toward the end of Chapter 7 that some of the very best companies pursue dual advantage strategies that combine or integrate elements of both cost leadership and differentiation. We believe this may be the case with the most successful online businesses as well.

Several online companies have successfully employed a combination of cost leadership and differentiation.[27] For example, Amazon.com's skills at branding, innovation, and channel management have successfully differentiated it from its competitors, but the company routinely offers low list prices on much of its merchandise. As a result, it is difficult to classify Amazon. com into either strategy type; Amazon.com does emphasize low prices and offers many discounts, but it has also been very innovative. Amazon.com's website was designed around a straightforward process that makes the consumer shopping experience convenient and helpful. Amazon's patented 1-Click service greatly simplified online purchases by allowing customers to use previously entered data to make purchases quickly and efficiently. Prompt delivery is also a hallmark of the Amazon.com shopping experience.

Not to minimize the very real challenges of pursuing a successful combination of generic strategies, but a dual advantage strategy combining elements of cost leadership and differentiation is not only possible but it is probably the most successful strategy for online businesses to pursue. As discussed in the previous section, the strategy of cost leadership suffers from many inherent disadvantages. It is thus likely to offer lower performance than a dual advantage strategy that combines the best features of cost leadership and differentiation. We also expect that a dual advantage strategy will have higher performance than a pure differentiation strategy, because a strategy of pure differentiation does not take advantage of the Internet's potential for lowering costs.

Pure Plays, Clicks-and-Bricks, and Firm Performance

Two broad types of online businesses exist: pure online firms (pure plays) and firms with both online and offline businesses (clicks-and-bricks). When online businesses first began emerging, many observers believed pure plays would be in a stronger competitive position. It was thought that pure plays would be more flexible and better able to leverage their first mover advantages, and that they would not be hindered by conflicts between online and traditional marketing channels. They would also enjoy greater flexibility in pricing. Dell, for example, gained significant advantages by pursuing an online strategy. In fact, traditional bricks and mortar firms, which added an online component as second movers, did struggle at first.

Now, however, many clicks-and-bricks firms have become market leaders.[28] Such an outcome now seems obvious. Since clicks-and-bricks firms are already familiar to customers and have credible brands, other things being equal, customers should prefer clicks-and-bricks Internet sites. Brand recognition, reputation, and credibility of clicks-and-bricks firms are important advantages that pure plays often lack. Furthermore, clicks-and-bricks firms can offer product returns and other customer services through their physical storefronts.[29]

Office Depot has employed the Web to improve its catalog services. Without Office Depot printing more catalogs, the company's customers can access updated and accurate information through the Web and complete transactions online. Walgreen's, which has established an online site for ordering prescriptions, has found that its extensive network of stores remains a potent advantage, even as much prescription ordering shifts to the Internet. Fully 90 percent of the company's customers who place orders over the Web prefer to pick up their prescriptions at a nearby Walgreen's store rather than have them shipped to their homes, probably to save shipping costs.

Tight integration between a company's website and its physical store locations not only increases customer value, but it can also reduce costs. It is more efficient to take and process orders via the Web, but it is also more efficient to make bulk deliveries to a local stocking location than to ship individual customer orders from a central warehouse. An article in *The Wall Street Journal* noted that many clicks-and-bricks firms are encouraging customers to pick up merchandise ordered online at their physical store locations. Not only does customer pick up save what are often substantial shipping charges (especially on large or heavy items), but companies also find that customer pick up leads to more impulse purchases. The article cited an executive at REI who estimated that "online shoppers who pick up their items in stores spend an additional $90 before they walk out the door."[30]

Pure plays should, as a rule, have lower costs due to the absence of physical store locations or warehousing facilities, but at least one study has found that pure play firms were not realizing significant real estate-related cost savings over their clicks-and-bricks competitors, perhaps because they must frequently incur substantial costs to develop elaborate supply chain networks.[31] Furthermore, many customers who use the Internet as a source of product and service information still prefer to make their purchases through traditional channels.[32] If this customer segment remains large, then clicks-and-bricks firms will enjoy further advantages over pure plays.

Pure plays face a number of other drawbacks. First, their customers cannot physically examine, touch, and test products, and they often get little or no help in using or repairing them. In addition, knowledge transfer is restricted to codified knowledge, sacrificing the spontaneity and judgment that can result from interactions with skilled sales personnel. It's always possible that advances in Web technology will allow pure plays to offer highly personalized customer service—Amazon.com with its personalized customer recommendations offers an example of what is currently possible—but the lack of human contact with customers eliminates a powerful tool for responding to questions, providing advice, and motivating purchases. Finally, the lack of a physical storefront, fixtures, and amenities limits the ability of pure play firms to reinforce a brand image.[33]

At the same time, unless clicks-and-bricks firms tightly integrate their on- and offline operations, they will see few synergies from having both an online and a physical presence.[34] For example, Gap's online customers will find an almost seamless integration between the company's website and the product offerings at its physical stores.[35] All in all, at this stage of evolution, it appears that clicks-and-bricks firms can enjoy a number of advantages over pure plays, but to realize these advantages, they must effectively integrate their online and physical operations. Pure plays face all of the difficulties of establishing online operations (e.g., intense rivalry, pressure to lower prices, and the difficulty of establishing brand name recognition), without any of the opportunities to leverage their online operations with offline assets that clicks-and-bricks firms enjoy.

Conclusion: The Importance of Managerial Thinking, Environmental Change, and Organizational Learning in Developing Effective Business Strategies

While Chapter 7 introduced the concept of business strategy and described the generic strategies of cost leadership, differentiation, and focus, this chapter has emphasized some of the complexities associated with the formulation and implementation of business strategies in different industry contexts, including emerging and high tech environments. It's not that generic strategies are inappropriate in any of these industry contexts, but the development of competitive advantage requires managers to do more than select an appropriate generic strategy. Although the choice of generic strategy can be helpful in developing the unique, valuable, and difficult-to-imitate resources and capabilities that are essential to the development of competitive advantage, every firm must pursue specific strategies that are tailored to its industry or market. As in past chapters, much of the material in this chapter is directly related to the three main themes of this book:

The Importance of Managers and Managerial Thinking

Managers must make key decisions about the appropriate business strategy for their firm or business to pursue, and they must also make decisions about the resources and capabilities that will be needed to implement these strategies and develop and maintain a competitive advantage. Managers make these important decisions about business strategy based on their beliefs and understandings (i.e., mental models) about their industry environment and how they should compete in this context.

While Chapter 7 introduced and described the generic strategies of cost leadership, differentiation, and focus, the purpose of this chapter and the next is to illustrate how the nature of various industry environments complicates this decision making. While every industry environment will pose its own unique challenges, in this chapter we focused specifically on emerging industry environments and online business contexts. In this chapter, we offered a number of frameworks and examples for analyzing and thinking about the challenges of competing in these environments, but the key point we want to emphasize is that managers must develop a great deal of specialized knowledge and expertise—i.e., mental models—to guide their decision making. As we have noted in the last chapter and in this chapter, business strategy involves much more than simply selecting from one of Porter's three generic strategies.

Managers' mental models must contain good understandings of their competitive environments. These understandings allow them to guide their firms through an effective business definition process. Based on their firm's business definition, managers must then select the most appropriate way to compete. The choice of business strategy must therefore reflect a good understanding of the competitive environment, the definition managers have chosen for their firm, and the resources that will be required to implement the business strategy. Above all, they must strive for a consistency or "logic" among all of these elements. In other words, a firm's business definition, its business strategy, and the resources and capabilities that support the business strategy should all complement and mutually reinforce each other. This chapter and the next only hint at the complexity of these tasks, but they aim to underscore the need for sophisticated mental models to guide all of these processes.

The Need to Anticipate and Respond Quickly to Changes in Industries and Markets

Changing industry dimensions—the emergence of new customer wants and needs, the development of new products, and new technological innovation—create significant opportunities both for entrepreneurs and for established firms. As noted at the beginning of this chapter, the product life cycle concept has been applied to industries, suggesting that industries and markets move through a predictable cycle of emergence, rapid growth, maturity, and eventual decline.

The text has emphasized that many entrepreneurs have ideas that can radically alter their firms' industries or create totally new industries. As markets emerge and rapid growth begins, however, many entrepreneurial firms lack the managerial talent and skill to maintain a competitive advantage. Most entrepreneurs are very knowledgeable about their products or services, but they often lack the managerial know-how to deal with the challenges of emerging industry environments. As a consequence, many start-up firms go through "growing pains" and many even go out of business because their owners do not acquire the necessary managerial know-how or turn their firms over to professional managers.

The Importance of Organizational Learning

Competing in emerging markets and competing online are activities that benefit from knowledge and learning. While many entrepreneurs have succeeded at introducing new products or services into emerging markets and many Internet entrepreneurs have been successful with their first online business, they have no doubt learned much from the experience and not only improved their business as time went on, but they have almost surely also known more when they introduced their second product or service into an emerging market or started their second online business.

All business contexts offer tremendous opportunities for learning. The online context is especially interesting because the highly interactive Web medium provides rich two-way information flows so that customers can not only learn a great deal about the products and services they are interested in purchasing, but companies have heretofore unparalleled opportunities to learn about their customers. Growing interest in social networking and how information gleaned from social networking websites and other media is already beginning to transform the way products and services are marketed. As with all information, the challenge is to manage flows of information so that companies can take full advantage of these information flows. In Chapter 11, we focus specifically on how companies can organize themselves not only to take advantage of these information flows but also create the best possible opportunities for organizational learning to occur.

Key Points

- Managers of firms operating in emerging industries face a number of challenges, including a great deal of ambiguity and uncertainty, as well as industry and product life cycles that can be very short.
- Neither first- nor second-mover strategies are necessarily optimal for firms operating in emerging industries—both have advantages and disadvantages, and firms pursuing both first- and second-mover strategies have been successful and unsuccessful in developing sustainable competitive advantage.
- Producing products and services that become the dominant design in an industry, producing products and services or developing processes and capabilities that are difficult for competitors to imitate, and possessing important and valuable interconnected assets are all ways to improve competitiveness in emerging industry environments, and contribute to success regardless of whether a firm pursues a first- or second-mover strategy.
- The Internet has fundamentally changed the nature of competition in many industries and will continue to have profound impacts on firms and industries in the years ahead. We offer three tentative observations or conclusions about competition in this new era:
  - All other factors equal, we believe online businesses pursuing differentiation strategies should outperform either cost leadership or focus strategies.
  - We believe online businesses pursuing dual advantage strategies that combine elements of cost leadership and differentiation and the infinite scalability of the Internet should outperform online businesses pursuing any one of the generic strategies by itself.
  - We also believe that clicks-and-bricks firms that closely integrate their online and storefront operations and activities should outperform their pure play counterparts.

Key Questions for Managers

- How should the various stages of the industry life cycle influence the development of your company's business strategy?
- Has your firm adapted aspects of its business strategy to meet the challenges posed by the various stages of the industry life cycle? For example, in emerging markets have you and other managers asked whether your firm is likely to be introducing (or responding to) the dominant design in the marketplace? How imitable are various aspects of your company's product or service offerings? Does your firm have the necessary complementary resources to be highly successful with your product or service?

- Have you and other managers carefully considered the ways online business activity is evolving and how your firm can take best advantage of these emerging opportunities and technologies?
- Have you and other managers considered the feasibility of pursuing dual advantage online strategies that combine the best elements of cost leadership and differentiation?
- Have you and other managers considered how the infinite scalability of the Internet might allow your firm to reach both a very wide audience while also tailoring your firm's product and service offerings to specific customers?
- Have you and other managers evaluated the benefits for your business of "pure play" and "bricks and clicks" approaches?

Suggestions for Further Reading

Additionally, links to further resources online—such as cases, articles, and videos—can be found on the book's website, www.routledge.com/textbooks/Duhaime.

Castells, M. 2001. *The Internet Galaxy: Reflections on the Internet, Business, and Society.* New York: Oxford University Press.

Porter, M. E. 2001. Strategy and the Internet. *Harvard Business Review*, 79(2): 62–78.

Rapp, W. V. 2002. *Information Technology Strategies: How Leading Firms Use It to Gain an Advantage.* New York: Oxford University Press.

Schnaars, S. P. 1986. When entering growth markets, are pioneers better than poachers? *Business Horizons,* 29(2): 27–36.

Shiffman, D. 2008. *The Age of Engage: Reinventing Marketing for Today's Connected, Collaborative, and Hyperinteractive Culture.* Ladera Ranch, CA: Hunt Street Press.

Teece, D. J. (Ed.) 1987. *The Competitive Challenge: Strategies for Industrial Innovation and Renewal.* Cambridge, MA: Ballinger.

Teece, D. J. 2001. *Managing Intellectual Capital: Organizational, Strategic, and Policy Dimensions.* New York: Oxford University Press.

Tuomi, I. 2003. *Networks of Innovation: Change and Meaning in the Age of the Internet.* New York: Oxford University Press.

Urban, G. L., Carter, T., Gaskin, S., & Mucha, Z. 1986. Market share rewards to pioneering brands: An empirical analysis and strategic implications. *Management Science,* 32: 645–659.

Chapter 9

The Challenges of Mature Industry Environments and Competition in Manufacturing and Service Sectors

Chapter 8 examined the factors that make emerging industry environments and online competition so challenging. Just as challenging for managers, if not more so, are mature industry environments, the focus of this chapter. As the rate of market growth slows, one company's growth will almost certainly have to come at the expense of other players in the industry. Thus, battles for market share can become quite intense.[1]

This chapter focuses on the challenges of competing in mature industry environments and also examines the special characteristics of the manufacturing and service sectors. The chapter first describes some of the unattractive characteristics of mature industry environments. It then focuses on some of the ways firms can prosper in these more mature business contexts. We also examine the different challenges of competing in manufacturing and service contexts. Throughout the chapter, our focus will be on developing ways of thinking—i.e., mental models—of these special industry contexts.

Chapter Objectives

The specific objectives of this chapter include:

- Examine the challenges associated with achieving and maintaining competitive advantage in mature industry contexts.
- Describe some specific ways to improve competitiveness in mature industries.
- Compare and contrast the characteristics of manufacturing and service businesses.
- Describe the challenges of achieving and maintaining competitive advantage in both manufacturing and service industries.

Competition in Mature Industry Environments

Unattractive Characteristics of Mature Industry Environments

All phases of an industry life cycle present their own challenges, but managers of firms operating in mature industry contexts face especially formidable challenges. Here we focus

Exhibit 9.1 The Tendency for Capacity Expansion to Grow Faster Than Demand in Mature Industry Environments

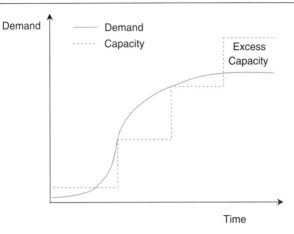

on issues that managers of firms in mature industries must consider as they formulate business strategies:

Stagnant Demand and Excess Capacity

In most mature markets, growth in demand will have either slowed or become stagnant, but because firms in the industry have become used to increasing demand, they are likely to be adding capacity in anticipation of continued growth. And, because capacity tends to be added in "lumpy" increments, there is a tendency for capacity expansion to grow faster than demand as an industry begins to mature. This tendency is illustrated by the figure in Exhibit 9.1 in which demand is depicted as a solid line while capacity is shown as a dotted line.

The strategic challenge this poses for managers is that if capacity exceeds demand over fairly long periods, it tends to invite price competition. If each firm in the industry maintains high levels of output in order to make full use of plant capacity, then the excess supply that results must inevitably put downward pressure on prices as the market seeks to clear the surplus. As suggested in Chapters 4 and 7, excess capacity is a major reason for downward pressure on prices in many industries. Thus, mature industry markets require managers to continually rebalance capacity in light of changes in demand.[2]

Exit Barriers

Exit barriers complicate the problem of excess capacity. Exit barriers are often associated with idiosyncratic or specialized assets that have no "second-best use"—examples of such assets include jet aircraft, steel mills, refineries, and automobile production plants. Managers are reluctant to take these idiosyncratic assets out of production because they have no alternative uses and their firms would most likely incur sizable restructuring charges or write-offs. As a result, exit barriers hinder what might otherwise be a more orderly closing of plants and capacity or a shakeout of weak competitors that would alleviate the excess capacity problem.

A Lack of Innovation

As the growth in demand for products or services slows, managers may stop investing in product or process innovations. Because of stagnant growth, proposals that might improve products or services and lead to higher demand often fail to meet rate of return and other investment hurdles. As a consequence, the rate of innovation in a mature industry will often begin to lag. The ensuing lack of innovation has several unfortunate consequences.

First, a lack of innovation will further customers' perceptions that the industry offers nothing new that would warrant a replacement purchase, further reducing demand. For example, the rapid rate of innovation in many digital technology markets is almost certainly the reason that sales of products in nearly all of these markets have remained robust. Innovation has occurred along many different dimensions. Product development efforts have focused on enhancing the capability and speed of existing products such as personal computers. Other product development efforts have resulted in the introduction of a wide range of totally new products from mp3 players to electronic books. If the pace of innovation in these digital technology markets slowed, demand would almost certainly fall as consumers would find fewer reasons for buying new products or upgrades to existing products.

Second, as firms in an industry engage in less innovation, their products and services may come to appear more and more like commodities. Without discernible differences across products or services, firms will be pressured by consumers to compete on the basis of price, which usually lowers profit margins and can even escalate into all-out price wars.

Pressure from New Entrants

Furthermore, by failing to innovate, incumbent firms in a mature industry actually invite entry because more entrepreneurial managers will see opportunities to appeal to customers by offering new products or services or by employing new technologies. If new entrants do invade, they will further intensify competition in what has already become an unattractive industry. The steel industry offers a good example of how minimills saw an opportunity to employ an alternative technology—the electric arc furnace—in order to enter the steel industry profitably. Their entry put enormous competitive pressures on the established integrated steel companies at a time when they were already suffering from excess capacity and low profitability.

Thus, high-performing firms face the challenge of maintaining their competitive advantage as their industry environments become increasingly unattractive. Alternatively, firms that have never enjoyed a competitive advantage in an industry might see opportunities for developing one as the industry shifts to a more mature context.

Ways to Improve the Attractiveness of and Achieve Competitive Advantage in Mature Industry Environments

This section considers a number of methods or tools that managers have employed in order to thrive in more mature industry environments. We first describe and evaluate the effectiveness of benchmarking. We will then examine how firms have gained competitive advantage by totally rethinking their value chains. Finally, we will describe the importance of aggressive product and process innovation.

Benchmarking and its Usefulness in Developing and Maintaining Competitive Advantage

A technique for developing competitive advantage that many firms have adopted over the last several years is benchmarking. **Benchmarking** can be defined as comparing and measuring a firm's business processes against the best practice of those processes by any organization in any industry. Larry Bossidy, former chairman and CEO of Honeywell, describes the benchmarking process this way:

> Executing well means always taking a realistic view of your company and comparing it with other companies. You're always keeping an eye on what's happening in companies around the world, and you're measuring your own progress, not internally, but externally. You don't just ask, "Have I made progress from last year to this year?" You ask, "How am I doing vis-à-vis other companies? Have I made a lot more progress?" That's the realistic way to look at your situation.[3]

As suggested by Exhibit 9.2, the objective of benchmarking is to foster organizational learning to achieve improvements in firm performance. Note that the illustration in Exhibit 9.2 assumes that ongoing organizational learning and improvement will be taking place. The objective of benchmarking is to accelerate that organizational learning and improvement so that performance "breakthroughs" can be achieved.

When a firm decides to undertake a benchmarking effort, it must first break down its own operations into discrete value-adding activities or processes. One way this can be done is by examining the firm's "value chain." Chapter 2 introduced the value chain concept and the concept's usefulness was also illustrated in Chapter 7. Exhibit 9.3 illustrates the value chain for a hypothetical manufacturing firm, showing the various value-adding processes from design and engineering, to component and materials procurement, and manufacturing, to marketing and sales, and after-sales service.

Exhibit 9.2 Benchmarking, Organizational Learning, and Firm Performance over Time

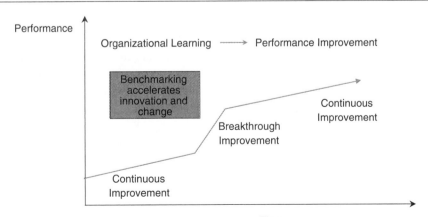

Source: Pappacena, E. *Benchmarking for Success* (presentation).

Exhibit 9.3 The Value Chain for a Hypothetical Manufacturing Firm

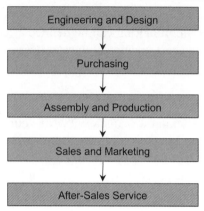

After identifying discrete value-adding activities or processes, the next step in benchmarking is to measure those processes and compare the firm's performance against the best practice of any firm in the world. Best practice of a particular process might be done by a competitor in the firm's own industry. For example, Ford Motor Company has long benchmarked hundreds of its own internal processes against Toyota's performance of those same processes.

One central idea of benchmarking, however, is that firms should not limit their search for best practice to their own industries. Some of the most famous examples of best practice benchmarking involve situations in which firms look at very different industries. For example, to better improve its customer service processes, Xerox benchmarked itself against L.L. Bean, a firm that is widely regarded as one of the very best customer service providers in the world.

A company should achieve two objectives from any benchmarking effort. First, the company should get a set of metrics that contrast its performance of a particular process with best practice. Exhibit 9.4 shows the outcome of a "typical company's" comparison of its procurement activities against best practice.

More important than the numbers or metrics that emerge from a benchmarking exercise, a firm engaging in a benchmarking study should gain some tangible ideas about how it can dramatically improve its own performance. These ideas, in turn, should stimulate a good deal more organizational learning so that dramatic improvements in overall firm performance are realized. During a benchmarking analysis of best practice, some ideas will be quite obvious and can be quickly copied or imitated. Other, more complex ideas will require considerably more "learning by doing" or study in order for the benchmarking firm to match and exceed the level of best practice.

The results of a successful benchmarking effort can be impressive. Exhibit 9.5 illustrates the improvements General Electric was able to achieve in its dishwasher business after a benchmarking study. Note the dramatic improvements in rejection rates, inventory turns, and labor productivity that are documented in the exhibit.

After the emphasis Chapter 2 gave to the asymmetric nature of competitive advantage, a good question is how can benchmarking—with its emphasis on comparing firms' processes and

Exhibit 9.4 A Benchmarking Study Comparing a Firm's Procurement Activities with Best Practice

	Typical Company	World-Class Company
Cost Factors		
Suppliers per purchasing agent	34	5
Agents per $100 million of purchases	5.4	2.2
Purchasing Costs as a percentage of purchases made	3.3%	0.8%
Time Factors		
Supplier evaluations (weeks)	3	0.4
Supplier lead times (weeks)	150	8
Time spent placing an order (weeks)	3.3%	0.8%
Quality of Deliveries		
Late	33%	2%
Rejected	1.5%	0.00001%
Materials shortage (number of instances per year)	400	4

Source: Port, O. 1992. Quality. *Business Week*, November 30: 66–72.

capabilities with best practice—result in competitive advantage? If the essence of benchmarking is the emulation of best practice, then it seems reasonable that benchmarking will be unable to provide firms with the asymmetry that is essential to achieving competitive advantage. According to the logic introduced in Chapter 2, wouldn't it seem that benchmarking, at best, could only result in competitive parity?

The answer to this question is that the aim of benchmarking is not merely to copy or imitate successful firms, but rather to motivate organizational learning and improvements so that firms engaging in benchmarking studies develop their own unique competencies. Furthermore,

Exhibit 9.5 Results of Benchmarking in General Electric's Dishwasher Business

Metric	1980–1981 (actual)	1983 (actual)	1984 (actual)
Service call rate (index)	100	70	55
Unit cost reduction (index)	100	90	88
Number of times handled (tub/door)	27/27	1/3	1/3
Inventory turns	13	17	28
Reject rates (mechanical/electrical test)	10%	3%	2.5%
Productivity (labor/unit index)	100	133	142
Other: number of parts reduced by 70 percent, products 20 pounds lighter, worker attitude improvements			

Source: Adapted from Hayes, R. H., & Wheelwright, S. C. 1984. *Restoring our Competitive Edge: Competing through Manufacturing*. New York: Wiley.

as emphasized in Chapter 2, effective organizational processes will prove very difficult for other firms to imitate. Instead, managers can use benchmarking to spur their own thinking and creativity so that their firms develop their own unique and effective processes. As Steven Walleck, a consultant for McKinsey & Company, has argued:

> Managerial innovation will be required to adapt the important characteristics of successful approaches in ways that best fit a company's own situation. The purpose of benchmarking is to expose managers to new ways of doing things in order to spark creativity, not to create efficient copycats.[4]

In fact, it is safe to say that *the greater the differences or disparity between the focal firm and the firm being benchmarked, then the greater the need for learning and innovation on the part of the benchmarking firm.*

And, it is also important to emphasize that the value of exposing managers to new ways of doing things is to stimulate new beliefs and understandings about the management of their firms—in short, that they develop new mental models that guide decision making and the formulation and implementation of strategies. Oftentimes, the key to successful benchmarking is to get managers to understand the value of changing their mental models—their fundamental beliefs and understandings about how to compete in their markets.

Rethinking the Value Chain

Another way managers can lead their firms to competitive advantage when operating in mature industry environments is to rethink their firms' value chains. Notice the terminology we employ here—rethinking the value chain. The terminology reflects that such a process involves a change in managers' mental models about the ways various value-adding activities contribute value to the firm. Very much related to benchmarking, rethinking the value chain involves careful analysis of each of the various links in firms' value chains. The analysis includes reconsidering which of the various links add or could potentially add value and which of the links are unlikely to contribute to the development of competitive advantage.

How can a company like Nike come to dominate so completely the athletic shoe industry when it owns no shoe manufacturing facilities? The answer is that the managers of many companies, including Nike, have rethought their industries' value chains. In the case of Nike, the company's managers realized that with the widespread availability of low-cost shoe and apparel manufacturing facilities in the Far East, it did not need to have its own production facilities and that manufacturing actually contributes very little to the value of the company's shoe and apparel products.

Furthermore, the company's managers realized that the best way to add value was to develop and exploit new-product development, marketing, and promotion capabilities that would allow Nike to differentiate its products from those of its rivals. Thus, it is fair to say that Nike is really more of a marketing and product development company than an athletic shoe and apparel company. Nike's marketing and promotion capabilities have helped the company to push aggressively into just about every sporting activity.

Like Nike's managers, the managers of many other companies have also come to realize that by rethinking their value chains they can find and exploit new ways to increase profitability. Nowhere are these new tactics more visible than in the way the Internet is changing the retailing industry. Firms like Amazon.com and Shoebuy.com have emerged as major retailers by rethinking the value chain. Rather than operating through traditional retail outlets and building inventories of merchandise to sell to customers, both of these companies first take customers' orders (and their cash) and then fulfill the order by working through wholesalers and distributors. These firms have realized that many consumers will gladly give up some product features or typical services—including the ability to touch, feel, or try-on the product—if they receive some other type of value-added benefits such as additional convenience or product selection as a result.[5]

Travel is another industry that has been revolutionized as major players in the industry have used the Internet and other information technologies to reshape the value chain. The major airline carriers have long employed sophisticated computerized reservation systems to help them with yield management (i.e., filling as many plane seats as possible at the highest possible fares). Companies like Expedia.com and other online travel services have taken much business away from traditional bricks-and-mortar travel agencies. Now, the major airline carriers are also encouraging their customers to book their flights via company websites.[6] And at airports, customers are now using automated kiosks to check themselves and their luggage in for their flights as well as to select seats.

Companies can even find significant value in improving existing components of their value chains. After acquiring Maytag and a number of other appliance brands, Whirlpool found that its warehousing and distribution activities were resulting in inefficiencies and long delays in filling customer orders. By rationalizing and investing heavily in its distribution network, the company has realized significant efficiencies and reductions in inventory, saving it more than $300 million annually. LG has similarly been able to reduce its overall costs by more than $1 billion by re-engineering its supply chain network.[7]

Product and Process Innovation

Innovation is clearly a major source of firm, market, and industry renewal, and considerable research has demonstrated the link between innovation and firm performance.[8] Innovation can occur along two fronts, both of which will change the value-price relationship associated with a given product or service. Product innovations provide new or improved features or attributes that deliver more value. Process innovations typically allow firms to make or deliver better products or services or to make or deliver those products or services at a lower cost and price.

Product innovations have a remarkable record of revitalizing mature markets. For example, consider the impact the mountain bike has had on the bicycle industry. The developer of the mountain bike supposedly tried to sell the idea to Schwinn, whose managers rejected the offer, believing that riders would object to the bike's fat tires. Of course, all that remains of the shortsighted Schwinn company today is its name, which was acquired by another bike manufacturer; the company has gone out of business and been liquidated.

Similarly, an aggressive strategy of product innovation worked well in the automobile industry for many decades. The major producers would routinely alter their cars by adding features (e.g., power steering, power brakes, air conditioning, the automatic transmission) or by making superficial changes in car body design (tail fins, a little more or a little less chrome, changes in the arrangement of the headlights).

Only after the successful invasion of the U.S. market by Japanese manufacturers in the 1970s and 1980s did the U.S. manufacturers begin to emphasize the importance of manufacturing *process* innovations that would improve quality. The results have had been far-ranging and impressive (though manufacturing efficiency at most automobile plants still lags behind the levels achieved by the leading Japanese manufacturers). All automobile companies have also rethought and streamlined the way they develop new car and truck models, with the aim being to shorten both the time and the amount of money required to bring new models to market.[9]

Another example of the impact of process innovation is the adoption of just-in-time production processes by nearly all U.S. manufacturing companies over the last two decades. The impact of this leaner approach to manufacturing on the overall efficiency of the U.S. economy has been profound. In 1983, the ratio of inventory to gross domestic product of the United States was 24 percent; by 2002, this ratio had fallen to just over 10 percent. Deregulation of the transportation sector has also resulted in considerable cost savings in moving goods from manufacturers to final consumers. In the early 1980s, nearly 20 percent of the gross domestic product was accounted for by expenditures on logistics and transportation. By 2002, logistics and transportation costs represented just 8 percent of GDP.

Modular Design

Another important process innovation tool is modular design. The idea behind modular design is to build a number of different product models or variations, all based on a common product "platform." Use of modular design has a number of benefits for companies, including: 1) the ability to offer more product variety, 2) lower product development costs, 3) bring new products to market faster, and 4) keep pace with technological innovations. In short, many companies have realized that modular design offers a relatively less expensive way to offer their customers "mass customization," or a variety of product offerings while also realizing significant economies of scale in procurement and manufacturing.

One company that has benefited from modular design is General Electric. Several years ago, the company considered closing its dishwashing manufacturing operations due to low market share and poor profitability. Given one last opportunity to turn the situation around, the managers of GE's dishwasher business took several dramatic steps, and the results of some of these have already been demonstrated in Exhibit 9.5.

In addition to automating many of the plant's operations and increasing manufacturing efficiency, GE's dishwasher business also adopted modular design. As illustrated in Exhibit 9.6, all of GE's dishwashers incorporate many common "modules," such as the same enclosure, the same interior, and the same motor and wiring harness. Any differences in GE's dishwasher models, such as different wash cycles and other options, are incorporated in the door panel. Thus, the company enjoys the benefits of offering several different models, all based on a common platform. Such an approach to manufacturing allows companies to produce a number of different products or models while also enjoying considerable economies of scale in the production and assembly of common components.

Exhibit 9.6 GE Dishwashers: Several Models, All Based on a Common Platform

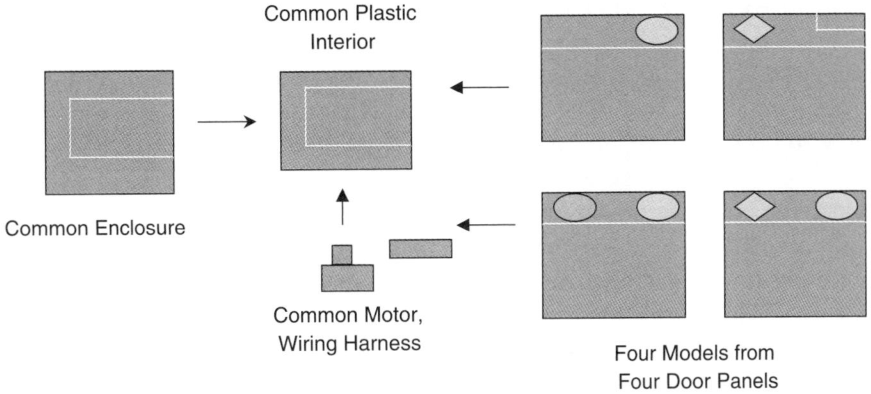

Source: Sanchez, R., & Sudharshan, D. 1993. Real-time market research. *Market Intelligence and Planning*, 11(7): 29–38.

Similarly, the Toyota Camry and Lexus sedans share a common platform, again allowing Toyota to offer two differentiated products targeted at very different market segments while saving inventory, production, and distribution costs. Still, as Chapter 7 pointed out, one of the risks to a strategy of differentiation is that customers can come to perceive that the differences between models based on the same platform are insignificant and then become unwilling to pay for the supposed differences between the two models. As a result, firms that use modular design to offer multiple models of products and services that are based on common platforms must understand how customers respond to these products and the extent to which they perceive the differences in the models as real and worth paying higher prices for models with added features or services.[10]

A Case Study of Product and Process Innovation: Gillette Razors

Throughout this section describing various ways managers of firms in mature industries can seek to gain advantage, we have been offering examples of specific companies. Here, we offer a more detailed case study of how Gillette has used product and process innovation to maintain leadership in the mature, but dynamic wet shave market.

When Bic, the French maker of ballpoint pens, introduced the disposable razor in 1974, Gillette's managers concluded that disposables might win a mere 10 percent of the wet-shave market, but by the late 1980s, 60 percent of all the razors sold were disposables. Though Gillette was able to maintain a market share lead over other razor manufacturers by introducing its own disposable razors, the lower profit margins of disposables were hurting Gillette's overall profitability. The challenge for Gillette was to regain a competitive advantage by developing a razor that would win back customers yet be very difficult for competitors to imitate. The result was the Sensor razor.

The Sensor was a twin-blade razor that offered a very close shave because each of the twin blades is mounted on springs that allow the blades to follow the contours of the shaver's skin. The Sensor was a runaway hit for Gillette, allowing the company to earn high profits and increase its stock price dramatically.

An innovation effort that borders on obsession supported Gillette's development of the Sensor and the many other razors that have followed the Sensor:

Nowhere is the obsession more evident than at the South Boston manufacturing and research plant. Here, some 200 volunteers from various departments come to work unshaven each day. They troop to the second floor and enter small booths with a sink and mirror, where they take instructions from technicians on the other side of a small window: try this blade or that shaving cream or this aftershave, then answer questionnaires. Besides men's faces, the research includes the legs of women volunteers…

For a close look at the mechanics of shaving, Gillette uses a boroscope—a video camera attached to a blade cartridge using fiber optics. Magnifying the film hundreds of times, researchers can precisely determine how twin blades catch the whiskers, pull them out of the follicles and cut them. Sometimes they collect debris after test shaves and measure the angle of the cut whiskers; the flatter the angle, the less force it took to cut the hair.

"We test the blade edge, the blade guard, the angle of the blades, the balance of the razor, the length, the heft, the width," explains Donald Chaulk, vice president of the shaving technology laboratory. "What happens to the chemistry of the skin? What happens to the follicle? We own the face. We know more about shaving than anybody. I don't think obsession is too strong a word." He pauses. "I've got to be careful. I don't want to sound crazy."[11]

But it is precisely this obsession that has helped Gillette to maintain its dominant position in the shaving industry, and it is this same research effort that was behind Gillette's introduction of the Mach3, the first three-blade razor and a runaway hit product that has so-far garnered sales of more than $2 billion annually.[12] In fact, Gillette spent over $750 million developing the Mach3, and the razor's technology is covered by 35 different patents.[13] When the industry's number two, Schick, introduced a four-blade razor, the Quattro, in 2003, Gillette quickly introduced the Mach3Turbo razor featuring "M3Power." The razor incorporates a tiny motor run by an AAA-size battery that causes the razor to vibrate as it moves across the skin for a closer shave.

The Mach3 was followed in 2006 by the introduction of the Fusion, a five-blade razor, and in 2010 by the Fusion Proglide, which features five blades, battery-powered vibration, and an even closer and more comfortable shave.[14] Within a week of Gillette announcing that it will introduce the Fusion Proglide, Schick announced that it will counter Gillette's new product by introducing its own new Schick Hydro, a razor that will include "hydrating reservoir" containing aloe that will moisten the skin.[15]

While Gillette's managers are clearly committed to product innovation efforts, they appear to be equally keen to pursue process innovations, as illustrated in the company's manufacturing processes. To manufacture the Sensor, for example, Gillette had no trouble finding equipment that would attach the tiny springs to each of the Sensor's twin blades. The problem was, the equipment wouldn't operate fast enough to allow Gillette to make a sufficient number of Sensor cartridges profitably. Nevertheless, Gillette acquired the equipment, and the company's engineers then went to work to determine how the speed of the production process could be increased.

Competition in Manufacturing and Service Industries

In Chapters 8 and 9 we have been considering the challenges of formulating and implementing business strategies in different industry contexts, and we have considered the issues faced by competitors in emerging and high tech industry contexts versus those in mature industry contexts. In this section we will conclude our examination of how the pursuit of competitive advantage differs across industry contexts by comparing and contrasting the characteristics of manufacturing versus service firms and describing some of the competitive challenges that are unique to firms in each of these two sectors.

Productivity Improvement in Manufacturing

After several years, in the late 1970s and early 1980s, during which many observers concluded that manufacturing was "dead," the United States and other industrialized nations enjoyed a revolution in manufacturing productivity, and many manufacturing companies enjoyed a renaissance. Richard Schonberger, a consultant to many manufacturers, has pointed out that many American companies grew complacent during the 1960s and early 1970s.[16] Schonberger uses a simple metric, inventory turnover, to illustrate not only the decline in U.S. manufacturing competitiveness (as illustrated in Exhibit 9.7) but also how, after about the mid-1970s, many of these companies began to improve the efficiency of their operations.

What factors have been responsible for the dramatic improvement in manufacturing sector profitability, and why have so many manufacturing companies been successful at establishing a competitive advantage? Here we highlight five factors (and describe the managerial thinking behind each of these factors) that have spurred many firms to improve their manufacturing operations:

Increased Competition

Increased competition from both foreign and domestic rivals alerted many firms to the need for improving the efficiency and productivity of their manufacturing operations. The impact of

Exhibit 9.7 The Decline in Manufacturing Efficiency: Inventory Turnover Ratios of Selected U.S. Manufacturing Companies

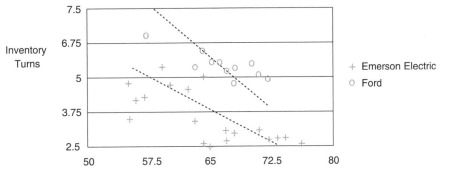

Source: Adapted from Schonberger, R. J. 1996. *World Class Manufacturing: The Next Decade*. New York: Free Press.

competition from Japanese automobile producers on the U.S. automobile industry is perhaps the most obvious example, but the impact on the chemical, electronics, and consumer products industries also illustrates how growing competitive pressures have forced manufacturers to rethink their operations and to engage in the kinds of organizational learning that significantly improved productivity and performance. Technology has also played a role in increasing the level of competition present in many industries. As more entrepreneurial firms have used technology to improve product offerings or generate manufacturing process improvements, more established firms have come under increasing pressure to maintain market share and increase profit margins.

Productivity Improvement

In response to mounting competitive pressures, manufacturing firms have pursued a broad range of efforts to improve the efficiency of their operations. The results of these efforts have provided many firms with significant gains in productivity.

Benchmarking and Value Chain Analysis

Benchmarking was discussed earlier and is mentioned again here only because of its importance in contributing to improvements in manufacturing efficiency and productivity. Nearly all manufacturing operations have conducted some sort of benchmarking or value chain analysis exercises over the last several years, and these studies have proved helpful in identifying those activities or operations that add or contribute value and those that don't.

Reengineering and Outsourcing

Many firms have gone beyond benchmarking studies and value chain analyses and have sought to "reengineer" activities throughout their firms not only to improve efficiency but also to fundamentally rethink all aspects of their business operations and value chains.[17] Reengineering studies at thousands of companies have led to reductions in the number of management layers, staffing cuts, the reorganization of work activities, and the merger or consolidation of various departments.

Even more significant, reengineering also encouraged firms to begin outsourcing more and more activities. Outsourcing is based on the fundamental economic principle of comparative advantage—that there will be certain firms and even nations that enjoy an advantage over others in the production of certain products and services. Though the outsourcing of components has long been a common practice among manufacturing firms, the reengineering movement proved to be a major catalyst for firms to begin outsourcing many more activities that were either not critical to the success of their operations or unlikely to be sources of competitive advantage. Firms found that they could outsource everything from janitorial and secretarial services to data processing, payroll administration, and even, in the case of railroads, train dispatching.[18]

Over the last few years, companies have turned to the international arena for a variety of activities that have not previously been outsourced.[19] Many firms are now turning to companies in India, Taiwan, and China for software development and even the development of new consumer and industrial products. General Electric has opened a research and development center in India. Many companies have taken advantage of telecommunications advances to open service call centers in other countries where labor costs are far cheaper.

Yet, these trends have also caused many managers to question the zeal with which they have pursued reengineering activities. The major concern among managers is that although reengineering efforts can be effective at cutting costs, they do little to increase revenue or market penetration.[20] In other words, reengineering is a defensive strategy that offers managers little guidance about how to grow their businesses. As a result, companies are continuing to pursue reengineering efforts, but they are also giving greater emphasis to strategies aimed at growth in sales revenues.

Quality

Over the past two decades, the importance of quality has become axiomatic among nearly all firms. Although quality improvement had formerly been viewed as a zero-sum game (i.e., improvements in quality would increase costs and come at the expense of lower profit margins), the last several years have shown that improvements in quality that are accompanied by improvements in manufacturing processes can actually result in higher productivity and higher profit margins.

The Growing Service Sector, the Nature of Service Work, and the Problem of Service Productivity

The growth of the service sector is probably one of the most taken-for-granted features of the economic landscape, but it's important to underscore that service sector employment has been growing much more rapidly than employment in the other sectors, a trend that will continue and most likely accelerate.

Firms in service industries have many of the same objectives as manufacturing companies. Both types of firms must attract and keep customers, offer quality products or services, and develop the capabilities that will allow them to compete effectively in their industry environments. At the same time, service industries have several unique characteristics that pose special challenges, and the need for managers to think differently about their business strategies:

Services Cannot Be Inventoried

First, unlike most manufacturing firms, service firms cannot maintain an inventory of services. In other words, most service firms cannot manufacture or make their services "ahead of time" and hold them in inventory for resale at a later date or time. Instead, services—including everything from a haircut to travel on an airplane—are typically provided in "real time" while the customer waits. If a manufacturing company produces a defective product, it may be detected during the manufacturing process and either reworked or scrapped before reaching—and disappointing—a customer. In nearly all service businesses, however, a faulty or substandard level of service will be immediately apparent to the customer.

Although this distinction between manufacturing and service businesses may seem obvious, it is vitally important to the success of service firms. Managers of service firms must attempt to ensure that every encounter with a customer meets a high level or standard of quality.

Many Service Encounters Are Highly Personal

Second, while the relationship between the manufacturers of most products and the customers buying those products tends to be impersonal and somewhat separated due to distribution and retailing channels, the relationship between most service providers and their customers tends to be more personal and based much more on perceptions and other less objective or tangible factors. The personal nature of the relationship between customers and service providers in most service industries suggests that these firms have considerable opportunities to differentiate themselves, and many businesses work very hard to be perceived as offering excellent service.

Consider, for example, the market for something as seemingly mundane as hair care. While some consumers view haircuts and other hair care services as commodity-like services and will seek out low-cost providers, a large percentage of consumers will develop personal and loyal relationships with their hair care professional.

Indeed, such loyal relationships between customers and service providers are a hallmark of many service industries, including the markets for doctors, lawyers, other professionals, and retailing businesses of all types. Often, these relationships are based not only on the quality of the services these professionals provide but also on less objective factors. The personal and less objective nature of the relationship most service providers have with their customers has a number of drawbacks, however. Because of the personal nature of most service businesses, a great deal of organizational knowledge or expertise resides not in the management of the firm but with the actual service provider.

Consider again the example of hair care: Customers are likely to be more loyal to their particular barber or stylist than they are to the hair care establishment because of the personal relationship they have established. If their barber or stylist decides to leave one firm and move to another, customers are likely to follow the barber or stylist to the new salon. As a result, most service firms should emphasize human resource policies and programs that help them retain the best employees.

Automating or Improving the Efficiency of Services Can Be Challenging

Third, because of the personal and "real-time" nature of most service industries, many service firms cannot use the same techniques as manufacturing firms to improve productivity. Many service firms find that employee lay-offs have an adverse effect on service levels and customer satisfaction. For example, when the Carlson Travel Network decided to improve productivity by laying off travel agents, customer service suffered severely—the company's remaining travel agents could adequately handle customers' requests for travel arrangements, but Carlson lost the relationship-specific knowledge of the laid-off agents, who would know that when a particular customer called to request an airline ticket to Los Angeles, that customer would also expect the travel agent to reserve a particular type of rental car and a room at a preferred hotel. As a consequence, the travel agency suffered considerable embarrassment and ill will when customers would arrive at their destinations without rental car and hotel reservations.[21]

Furthermore, many services cannot be automated in the same ways as manufacturing work and it's doubtful that a wide array of services including hair care, legal assistance, and medical care can ever be highly automated. On the other hand, many types of service firms are actively experimenting with ways to automate their activities or otherwise improve their productivity. The banking industry has made great strides in automating many of its services through the installation of automatic teller machines and telephone and online banking systems. Over the last few years, the airline industry has installed thousands of automated check-in kiosks, and now nearly all airline passengers check themselves in for their flights.[22]

Ironically, automation in the service sector does not always result in job cuts. In 1985, the banking industry in the U.S. had 60,000 ATMs and 485,000 bank tellers; now the industry has 360,000 ATMs and 600,000 bank tellers! These numbers reflect the big increase in the number of bank branches and also the expanded array of services offered by banks.

Improving the Productivity of Service Work

Given the dominant role of services in so many countries' economies, firms will be focusing a great deal of effort on improving service sector productivity. As just described, many service firms are automating a wide range of activities, and we should fully expect that firms in many service industries will experiment with ways that many other activities can be automated. In addition to automation, firms in the service sector have pursued many other methods or techniques for increasing productivity, including bundling or cross-selling services, increasing or improving the rate of organizational learning, and restructuring their work practices:

Bundling or Cross Selling

Cross selling involves exposing customers to a broader array of a company's service offerings. Banking offers an excellent example of bundling or cross selling. Many routine banking transactions can now be processed by ATMs or online, but when customers need specialized services or additional assistance, they may seek help from personnel in their bank branch. During this personal interaction with a customer, the bank employee will have an opportunity to ask the customer whether he or she could use any of the bank's other services including loans, credit cards, IRA, or investment services.

Such bundling or cross selling requires a rethinking the role of front line employees—rather than viewing them as mere "transaction processors," bank tellers and other branch personnel become sales representatives. Cross-selling will also usually require that employees have additional training so that they are knowledgeable about their firms' service offerings and how they might identify those customers who would be most likely to make use of the firms' other services. The Web, too, offers companies many opportunities to be sure that customers are aware of the full range of services they offer.

Using Organizational Knowledge and Learning

Managers of service firms are also achieving productivity gains through the more effective use of organizational knowledge and learning. Retailing offers an excellent example of how service firms are realizing significant productivity gains by better using information and organizational knowledge. For example, bar coding and information technology have allowed retailing firms to monitor their customers' buying habits, identify popular items and detect fashion trends, and realize significant improvements in the management of their inventories.

In the years ahead, we are likely to see service firms develop even more aggressive ways to put this information to work. Through its collaborative filtering algorithms, Amazon.com already offers customers purchase recommendations, and it's easy to see how many other retailers might be able to offer their customers personalized advertisements or purchase recommendations. Grocery store chains are now using data on customers' buying habits gleaned from loyalty card programs and computerized cash registers to provide customers with coupons and other incentives based on their buying patterns.

The insurance and financial services giant, USAA, which routinely ranks at the top of *Business Week*'s of customer service providers, emphasizes a high degree of employee training and specialized and focused technologies—all based on the company's heroic efforts to understand and learn about its customers and their needs—in order to offer outstanding customer service.[23]

Employing New Organizational Structures

Managers of many service firms have also reorganized their firms' structures to eliminate inefficiencies and bottlenecks. In many cases, service firms have given "frontline" employees more authority to satisfy customers. Rather than having unhappy customers wait for a manager to show up to rectify unsatisfactory situations, many companies now give employees the authority they need to satisfy these customers. Many service companies are finding that many of the same techniques employed by manufacturing firms can be applied (sometimes in modified ways) to their own activities and customer services.

Many hospitals are using flow models, root-cause, and value stream mapping techniques to smooth the flows of patients and staff, identify the causes of errors and mistakes, and distinguish between those services that do and do not add value to patients. All of these activities, combined with the adoption of the Japanese model of kaizen or continuous improvement, offer hospitals and other health care providers—one of the largest and least productive sectors of our service economy—ways to improve their efficiency.[24]

In the end, the most important force for improving service sector productivity is management and the effectiveness of the strategies they formulate and implement. Some service firms, operating in the same industry with the same technologies using people with the same skill levels, can nevertheless achieve remarkably different levels of productivity from their workers than their competitors. Exhibit 9.8 illustrates one example, comparing the productivity of various companies in the insurance industry. Sustained management attention, the appropriate application automation technology, and the strategies that have been describe above offer significant opportunities for productivity improvement in the service sector.[25]

Chains, Franchising, and Competitive Advantage in Service Industries

Another topic that deserves some discussion in this chapter is the growth of franchising and retailing chains in many service industries. Perhaps the growth of chains and franchising is best illustrated by some statistics from the restaurant industry. Today, the United States is home to more than more than 50,000 McDonald's, Burger King, Wendy's Taco Bell, and Subway restaurants, as well as to thousands more upscale family dining franchises.[26] Independent

Exhibit 9.8 Differences in Productivity Across Three Insurance Companies

	General Expenses + Premiums (in cents per dollar)		
Year	*Connecticut Mutual*	*Phoenix Mutual*	*Northwestern Mutual*
1988	20.9	16.7	6.8
1989	19.8	15.7	6.9
1990	20.2	14.9	7.4
1991	20.9	15.6	6.3

Source: Adapted from Van Biema, M., & Greenwald, B. 1997. Managing our way to higher service sector productivity. *Harvard Business Review*, 75(4): 95–97.

restaurants once dominated the restaurant industry, but chains now generate more than half of all sales in the industry. Nor is the impact of chains limited to the restaurant industry.[27] A drive through any city or a walk through any shopping center will reveal the extent to which retailing chains and franchises have become a dominant feature of the economic landscape.

Much writing has examined the growing presence of retailing chain stores and franchising in developed economies. While the extent of this trend varies by country, it is at a very high level in the United States. Much of the literature takes a very critical view of chains and franchising. Chains and franchising are blamed for the "homogenization" of our cities. This homogenization is so pervasive today in the United States that an individual walking through a shopping mall in suburban Maryland would see almost all the same stores that another individual walking through a shopping mall in suburban Atlanta, Chicago, Denver, Miami, or Los Angeles would see. Critics also associate the proliferation of retailing chains and franchising with the destruction of communities and especially of downtown areas, arguing that the growth of shopping malls on the periphery of cities has required nearly everyone to own a car in order to enjoy "first-class citizenship" in the modern city.[28]

Other articles and books have also argued that chain stores and franchising are responsible for the loss of many small, unique, and locally owned businesses, and that the strategies of chains—and Wal-Mart in particular—have driven many smaller, independent, and locally owned retailers out of business. Some communities have reacted by adopting zoning laws that seek to prevent retailers—specifically Wal-Mart—from entering their borders.[29]

Although much of the literature takes a very dim view of the growth of chain stores and franchising, a few more positive observations are also warranted. First, the chain store and franchising phenomena are likely to be an important part of the economic landscape for many years to come. Most retail chains have ambitious expansion plans, and nearly any retailing concept can be franchised. As a result, it's likely that the role of chain stores and franchising will grow rather than diminish.

Second, it is also important to recognize that chain stores and franchising have a number of important economic and strategic advantages over other forms of business. For example, chains and franchise organizations typically enjoy economies of scale in purchasing, distribution, and marketing and advertising that give them an important edge over smaller, independently-owned businesses.[30]

These economic and strategic advantages will also contribute to the growing dominance of chains and franchises in many retail markets. As noted above, chain restaurants already account for over half of the industry's sales, and the chains' share of restaurant sales is growing approximately one percent annually.[31]

Furthermore, chains and franchise organizations are almost ideally designed to promote organizational learning. Both chains and franchise organizations can develop and perfect a particular concept and then expand by opening other establishments based on this concept or by selling franchises to independent entrepreneurs. Unlike most entrepreneurial activity, however, the chain or franchise is pursuing a concept that has already proven itself at another location. In addition, over time, the chain develops a tremendous amount of information and learning about customer preferences, marketing, sourcing, and logistics. With effective structures (the topic to be addressed in Chapter 11), this organizational learning and knowledge can be widely shared across all chain or franchise outlets. And, as the chain or franchise continues to expand, its knowledge base continues to grow.

These points are not intended as either an endorsement or a critique of chains and franchises, only to emphasize that 1) chains and franchises are already a major force in retailing, 2) they are likely to expand their influence in the years ahead, and 3) they have many economic and organizational learning advantages over small, independent, and locally owned business organizations.

Conclusion and the Book's Three Key Themes

The Importance of Managerial Thinking

This chapter has stressed the need for continuous innovation to keep firms in mature industry environments competitive. We have also emphasized that the remarkable renaissance among U.S. manufacturing companies is almost certainly due to the application of new knowledge and organizational learning that have been translated into strategies that have dramatically improved productivity. Furthermore, improvements in service sector productivity will most likely occur because managers and their firms have developed new insights and knowledge that suggest new strategies.

Many innovations and productivity improvements come about by rethinking a firm's value chain. It's important to emphasize that rethinking the value chain really involves a rethinking of managers' mental models, assumptions, and beliefs about the business. Thus, an openness to new ideas and mental flexibility are the keys to innovation and continued competitiveness.

Change and the Need to Think Dynamically about Strategy

We showed that many successful established firms operating in mature industry environments stop innovating and, as a consequence, their sales begin to stagnate. Instead of pursuing innovations that might invigorate their firms, managers remain content with existing products and services. This is a naïve and short-sighted approach to business strategy. The case study of Gillette and the many other examples we have cited in this chapter demonstrate the value of ongoing innovation, new product development, and continued investment in keeping firms vibrant, even though they may be operating in mature industry environments.

The Value of Organizational Learning

As change impacts every aspect of business activity, companies must encourage learning. We have distinguished between both low-level and high-level learning, and emphasized the importance of each. Companies must encourage both types of learning in order to facilitate adaptation as necessary, but also to encourage proactive rethinking of the business so they can stay ahead of their competitors.

Key Points

- Managers of firms operating in mature industry environments face a number of difficult challenges, including stagnant demand and excess capacity, exit barriers, a lack of innovation that makes products and services less attractive to customers and competition from new entrants.
- Managers of firms in mature industry environments can take steps to develop and maintain competitive advantage, including benchmarking, rethinking the value chain, and product and process innovation.
- The manufacturing sector of the economy has enjoyed remarkable improvements in efficiency and productivity. The much larger service sector has not shared in these efficiency gains.
- Managers of firms in service industries face many challenges that are quite different from those faced by the managers of firms operating in manufacturing industries.
- Close management attention, appropriate use of technology, and the development of efficiency-enhancing organizational routines and standard operating procedures can lead to major improvements in service sector efficiency and productivity.
- One of the most important reasons why chains and franchises have enjoyed great success is their ability to accumulate, store, and apply organizational learning to enhance efficiency and productivity.

Key Questions for Managers

- If your firm has begun to move from the growth phase to the mature phase of the business life cycle, have you and other managers noticed and correctly interpreted this change in market conditions? Has your firm adapted or curbed expansion plans in response to this slow-down in demand?
- At the same time, if your firm has entered the mature phase of the life cycle, do you and other company managers believe that they must still invest in product and process innovation so that your company's products or services do not become stale in the minds of customers?

- Have you and other company managers carefully considered the special ways manufacturing and service businesses differ and have you incorporated the best ideas from any manufacturing and service companies regardless of their specific industry?

Suggestions for Further Reading

Additionally, links to further resources online—such as cases, articles, and videos—can be found on the book's website, www.routledge.com/textbooks/Duhaime.

Cortada, J. W. 2003. *The Digital Hand: How Computers Changed the Work of American Manufacturing, Transportation, and Retail Industries.* New York: Oxford University Press.

Hammer, M., & Champy, J. 1994. *Reengineering the Corporation: A Manifesto for Business Revolution.* New York: HarperBusiness.

Lacity, M. C., & Rottman, J. W. 2008. *Offshore Outsourcing of IT Work: Client and Supplier Perspectives.* New York: Palgrave Macmillan.

Sanchez, R. (Ed.) 2004. *Modularity, Strategic Flexibility and Knowledge Management.* New York: Oxford University Press.

Shiffman, D. 2008. *The Age of Engage: Reinventing Marketing for Today's Connected, Collaborative, and Hyperinteractive Culture.* Ladera Ranch, CA: Hunt Street Press.

Teece, D. J. (Ed.) 1987. *The Competitive Challenge: Strategies for Industrial Innovation and Renewal.* Cambridge, MA: Ballinger.

Teece, D. J. 2001. *Managing Intellectual Capital: Organizational, Strategic, and Policy Dimensions.* New York: Oxford University Press.

Van Biema, M., & Greenwald, B. 1997. Managing our way to higher service-sector productivity. *Harvard Business Review,* 75(4): 87–95.

Chapter 10

Corporate Strategy and Diversification

We now turn to corporate strategy and diversification. In terms of our model of strategic management, illustrated in Exhibit 10.1, decisions about corporate strategy and diversification are influenced by managers' beliefs about the appropriate scale and scope of the business enterprise. Or, to put it differently, managers' beliefs about the appropriate size and diversity of the firm and its businesses will be a key influence on the firm's corporate strategy and the extent of its diversification. We will also show that successful corporate strategy and diversification require managers to develop beliefs about how their firms' businesses are related to each other as well as how diversification and corporate strategy should be managed.

Corporate strategy and diversification are, however, multifaceted topics, and our exploration of these topics will build on many of the issues that have been discussed in previous chapters. We will see, for example, that successful corporate strategy requires the effective management of business definition or positioning at both the business and corporate levels, the development of unique organizational capabilities for the management of diversification, and the use of complex organizational structures (a subject we explore more fully in the next chapter). Above all, this chapter will emphasize the importance of managerial thinking, knowledge, and learning in guiding these management activities. The chapter will emphasize that managerial and organizational learning are essential to the successful management of diversification and the effective formulation and implementation of corporate strategies.[1]

Chapter Objectives

The specific objectives of this chapter are to:

- Define corporate strategy and diversification, describe some of the key reasons firms diversify, identify and describe different types of diversification and corporate strategies, and assess the advantages and disadvantages associated with each.
- Define the concept of synergy and emphasize that the goal of corporate strategy and diversification is synergy across a firm's portfolio of businesses.
- Identify sources of synergy in diversified firms and explain why synergies are so difficult to achieve.

Exhibit 10.1 Managers' Beliefs, Strategic Decisions, and Their Influence on Performance and Competitive Advantage

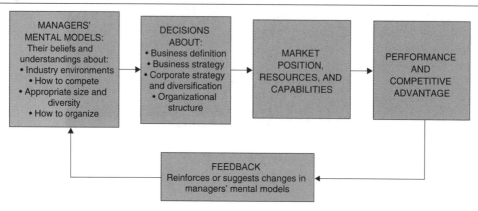

- Explore the complex relationship between corporate diversification and firm performance, and consider a number of factors that are likely to influence performance in diversified firms.
- Demonstrate how managers and managerial thinking influence and impact the relationship between diversification and performance.

The Focus of Corporate Strategy, Why Firms Diversify, and the Different Types of Diversification

As indicated in earlier chapters, business strategy focuses on how a firm or business should compete in a given competitive environment. On the other hand, **corporate strategy** focuses on the appropriate scale or scope of the enterprise. Corporate strategy therefore influences how large and how diversified firms will be. Thus, in many respects, this chapter on corporate strategy and diversification is related to the chapter on business definition because decisions about diversification and corporate strategy are really decisions about the definition of the firm. A firm can be a "single business firm" operating in a single industry environment and an easy to describe business definition. On the other hand, a large and widely diversified firm with many different businesses, each operating in a different industry, faces the challenges of defining each of its various businesses as well as developing an overall corporate or firm definition.

Steinway, the manufacturer of fine pianos, operates in a fairly small portion of the musical instruments industry, offering a limited line of pianos to a select group of customers who are willing to pay from $20,000 to $100,000 or more for a fine musical instrument. The firm's business definition is fairly straightforward. In contrast, the managers of General Electric, with businesses in such diverse industries as household appliances, entertainment, medical products, financial services, jet aircraft engines, and railroad locomotives must define or position each of the company's businesses in its respective industry, but they must also develop a unified definition for the General Electric enterprise as a whole.

Successful corporate strategies are not only the product of successful definition, however. Although we will see that diversified firms need some sort of unifying definition, or what Porter has called a "corporate theme," successful diversification is also the result of organizational capabilities or competencies that allow managers to exploit or realize the potential economies and other synergies that large size and diversity can offer.[2] We will see that diversification also often requires complex organizational structures, and, above all, diversification requires the development of unique management knowledge and skills. Thus, this chapter logically follows earlier chapters on managers, competitive advantage, definition, and business strategy because it brings together concepts and issues from all these previous chapters. Chapter 11 elaborates on the structural requirements of businesses and firms, and will give specific attention to the kinds of organizational structures required by large diversified firms.

The aim of corporate strategy and diversification is to achieve synergies across the businesses in a firm's portfolio of business units. **Synergy** is the incremental gains in value that should be derived from a particular corporate or diversification strategy. In other words, the businesses in a diversified firm's portfolio of business units should collectively perform at a higher level than the businesses would perform as standalone businesses. Later in this chapter, we will be focusing specifically on ways firms seek to achieve synergies through their corporate and diversification strategies, but first, we focus on why firms diversify and the different types of corporate and diversification strategies.

Why Do Firms Diversify?

Why do firms diversify rather than stay focused on a single business? Though not an exhaustive list, the following five objectives appear to motivate most decisions to diversify:[3]

To Grow

Growth seems to be an implicit objective in nearly all business organizations, and many managers pursue diversification strategies in order to maintain growth in sales and profitability beyond what their firm's core business can provide. Stock markets appear to reward growth companies, which may further encourage managers to pursue growth through diversification. Other research studies have documented a strong correlation between firm size and executive compensation, suggesting that managers who pursue aggressive growth strategies are engaging in self-serving behavior.[4] Still other researchers have suggested that managerial hubris—the pride or status that comes from managing a large business enterprise—may also explain decisions to diversify. Whatever motivates the desire to grow, it motivates much diversification activity.

To More Fully Utilize Existing Resources and Capabilities

Managers may also pursue diversification strategies because they believe their firms possess underutilized resources or capabilities that can be further exploited by expanding and by diversifying into other markets or industries. Obvious examples of underutilized resources include factories or distribution channels operating below capacity, but underutilized capabilities might also include skills at sales and marketing as well as general management skill and knowledge. As an example, over the last several years, the J. M. Smucker Company has acquired a wide variety of branded food products, including Jif peanut butter, Crisco oils, and Folgers coffee. Smucker clearly understands the marketing of branded food products and has expertise in grocery retailing and distribution—resources and capabilities that can be easily extended to these other food product lines.

To Make Use of Surplus Cash Flows

Firms will often generate surplus cash flows or cash flows that exceed their own investment needs. Evidence suggests that managers are reluctant to simply give these surplus cash flows to shareholders in the form of higher dividends. Yet large cash balances can also attract corporate raiders or unsolicited takeover offers because raiders or other firms can use these cash balances to pay for the acquisition. As a result, managers often pursue diversification strategies as a way to make use of cash balances and avoid a hostile takeover.

To Reduce Competition and Increase Market Power

While clearly involving legal, antitrust, and public policy issues, many merger and acquisition strategies are pursued to reduce competition and increase market power. Chapter 4 noted that the Federal Trade Commission has blocked many high-profile merger and acquisition proposals, fearing that these business combinations would result in significantly less competition in their respective markets.[5]

Highly concentrated industries can have advantages for consumers. For example, industry consolidation can produce economies and efficiencies that allow companies to pass along savings to consumers. But highly concentrated industries can also reduce competition and allow a few large firms to reap profits at the expense of consumers. And, research also suggests that large firms in highly concentrated industries tend to be less innovative than firms in more competitive industries.[6]

To "Escape" from Unattractive or Declining Industry Environments

The desire to escape from unattractive industry environments is also a powerful motivation for managers to pursue diversification strategies.[7] Managers of firms in a declining industry often face the choice of seeing their firm contract in size or even go out of business, or of pursuing diversification into a more promising industry. For such firms, diversification into markets and businesses that offer greater growth potential becomes a sort of institutional imperative.

Types of Diversification and Corporate Strategies

Although corporate strategies will be unique to some extent, we will describe four broad categories or types of corporate strategies: vertical integration, horizontal or related diversification, conglomerate or unrelated diversification, and global diversification. We will also focus on the potential advantages and possible disadvantages associated with each type.

Vertical Integration

Vertical integration refers to a strategy of acquiring control over additional links in the value chain of producing and delivering products or services. **Backward integration** refers

Exhibit 10.2 Vertical Integration and an Illustration of Forward and Backward Integration

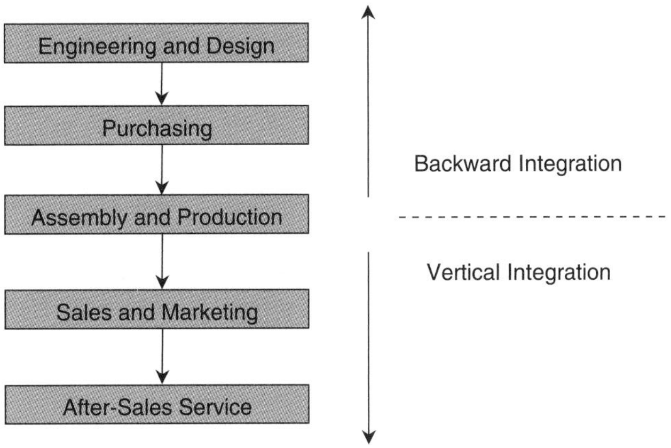

```
┌─────────────────────────────┐
│   Engineering and Design    │
└─────────────────────────────┘
              │
              ▼
┌─────────────────────────────┐
│         Purchasing          │            Backward Integration
└─────────────────────────────┘
              │
              ▼                          - - - - - - - - - - - - - - - - - - -
┌─────────────────────────────┐
│   Assembly and Production   │              Vertical Integration
└─────────────────────────────┘
              │
              ▼
┌─────────────────────────────┐
│     Sales and Marketing     │
└─────────────────────────────┘
              │
              ▼
┌─────────────────────────────┐
│     After-Sales Service     │
└─────────────────────────────┘
```

to a strategy of moving closer to the sources of raw materials by acquiring resource suppliers or by manufacturing the components needed for the production of a final product. **Forward integration** refers to a strategy of moving closer to the consumer or end user by acquiring or establishing retail outlets for the distribution, sale, or after-sale service of the company's products or services.

Firms in some industries, such as the petroleum industry, tend to be more vertically integrated than firms in other industries, but the extent of vertical integration among firms within the same industry can also vary considerably. Exhibit 10.2 illustrates the concept of vertical integration and distinguishes between forward and backward integration.

The advantages of vertical integration include greater control over the costs and supply of components (in the case of backward integration) as well as greater control over the firm's interface with its customers (in the case of forward integration). Two additional advantages of vertical integration include the ability to protect proprietary technology and to protect a company's reputation. If a firm believes it has a technology that gives it a significant advantage over its competitors, it may not wish to share that information with outside vendors that might also do business with the firm's direct competitors. Similarly, a company may wish to maintain or cultivate a reputation for outstanding quality or service. In this case, it may choose to open its own retail outlets or after-sale service centers to ensure that its customers will obtain the high level of service it wants them to receive.

For example, many fashion companies sell a large percentage of their apparel through traditional department stores, but many of the fashion companies, including Liz Claiborne and Ralph Lauren, also have their own retail outlets. These retail stores allow these companies to showcase their most innovative styles and cater to their most loyal customers in a way that department stores, which typically carry many apparel companies' products, cannot do.

Vertical integration can also have a number of disadvantages, however. First, the vertically integrated firm will almost necessarily have higher fixed overhead costs than a less integrated competitor. Only if lower direct costs (or higher sales) can compensate for these higher fixed overhead costs will the firm enjoy higher profits than its less integrated competitors.

It's possible to imagine a firm that is highly integrated and therefore incurring high fixed costs, but also failing to benefit from lower direct costs. Such a situation can really only be justified if the firm's managers are convinced that the greater integration is needed in order to insure the supply or the quality of key components or to insure adequate distribution of its products or services.

Furthermore, demand uncertainty can also create problems for the vertically integrated firm. If demand for a backward-integrated company's products exceeds the capacity of the company's component assembly operations, then the company will have to turn to outside vendors that may not be enthusiastic about dealing with a customer that only buys when demand is high and when the vendors are already operating at full capacity to meet the needs of their more reliable buyers. On the other hand, if demand is far below factory capacity, the vertically integrated firm is left with unused capacity and uncovered fixed costs.

Also, if a company operates in an industry in which technology is changing rapidly, then vertical integration can be a risky strategy for that firm. Less integrated firms can switch quickly to vendors offering the latest components or using newer, lower cost, or more sophisticated processes to produce components, leaving the more integrated firm "stuck" with older components manufactured by less efficient, more costly processes.

The advantages and disadvantages of vertical integration are usefully assessed by considering the **transaction costs** involved in contracting with outside vendors. Transactions cost analysis emphasizes that firms must consider not only the direct costs associated with either making components in house or buying them from vendors, but also the costs involved in transacting business with outside vendors.[8] Although many transactions are straightforward, firms can encounter a variety of problems in dealing with vendors, and, if disputes arise, the time and expense in resolving disagreements can become quite costly. Vertical integration avoids the transactions costs associated with dealing with suppliers or retailers.

Furthermore, although vertical integration can eliminate the costs of haggling with outside vendors or retailers, integrated firms must still deal with the **transfer pricing** dilemma—the price one division pays another division for components or services—which can create serious morale and other internal problems, potentially as serious as legal disputes with outside vendors.

Over the last few decades, many companies embraced a strategy of outsourcing and moving away from vertical integration. More recently, however, a number of firms have reversed their outsourcing strategies and become more vertically integrated. For example, Boeing, after experiencing a series of delays and glitches with the widespread outsourcing of components for its 787 aircraft, has now decided to perform more activities internally in order to insure greater control over access to, and the quality of, key components. Arcelor-Mittal, the world's largest steel manufacturer, has recently been acquiring iron ore mines in Brazil, Russia, and the United States in order to insure long-term access to a critical resource, while Nucor, the large U.S. steel manufacturer that relies on scrap metal to manufacture its steel, has acquired a large scrap dealer. Both moves are efforts to gain greater control over access to key raw materials.

Similarly, PepsiCo has proposed to acquire two of the major distributors of its products in order to gain more control over the distribution of its products, and Coca-Cola has also acquired Coca-Cola Enterprises, the largest bottler of its cola products, for the same reason.[9] And, Oracle

Exhibit 10.3 The Advantages and Disadvantages of Vertical Integration

Advantages	Disadvantages
• Greater control over costs and supply of components	• Higher overhead costs
• Avoidance of transactions costs	• Transfer pricing dilemmas
• Ability to protect proprietary technology	• Low demand can lead to underutilization of plant capacity and high demand can result in a dependence on outside suppliers
• Ability to maintain or cultivate a reputation for outstanding quality or service	• Technological change can leave vertically integrated firms stuck with older technology

acquired Sun Microsystems in order to offer products that feature more integration between hardware and software.[10]

This discussion of the advantages and disadvantages of vertical integration is summarized in Exhibit 10.3.

Horizontal or Related Diversification

Horizontal or related diversification refers to a strategy of adding related or similar product or service lines to the existing core business, either through the acquisition of competitors or through the internal development of new products or services. Horizontal or related diversification strategies can vary considerably. For example, many banks have acquired or merged with other banks over the past two decades as a wave of consolidation has swept over the banking industry. In the case of bank mergers and acquisitions, few totally new products or services are offered as a result of these combinations. Thus, it appears that the major objective of these mergers and acquisitions is to realize economies of scale by consolidating "back office" operations, such as data and check processing.

In fact, many horizontal or related acquisitions or mergers will tout some degree of expected cost savings as a motivation or a rationale for the acquisition or merger. For example, in acquiring Compaq, HP claimed that the acquisition would result in cost savings of $2.4 billion in just the first year after the acquisition with additional cost savings to result in later years. Evidence suggests that HP met many of its cost savings goals, thanks to an elaborate planning and coordination effort that went into place immediately after the Compaq acquisition was consummated.[11]

Geographical expansion can also provide a strong rationale for related diversification. For example, the drugstore giant, Walgreen, acquired Duane Reade, a drugstore chain with 257 stores in the New York metropolitan area. This acquisition of a company that was strong in a part of the U.S. in which Walgreen had few stores, allowed Walgreen to expand its geographic reach overnight. At the time of the acquisition, Walgreen CEO Greg Wasson stated, "it would have taken us many, many years, through our organic growth model, to gain that type of presence."[12]

Related diversification strategies can also allow firms to expand their product or service offerings. As mentioned above, the J. M. Smucker Company acquired the Jif brand of peanut butter and also acquired International Multifoods, the producer of Pillsbury cake mixes, Pet evaporated milk, and a number of other products, allowing it to expand its line of food products. Similarly, K2 acquired Volkl Sports, Marker Group, and Marmot Mountain Ltd. to expand its line of winter sports equipment, and it has also acquired several other sports equipment companies during the last decade, including Rawlings Sporting Goods, Worth, Inc. (a manufacturer of softball equipment), Brass Eagle and Worr Game Products (manufacturers of paintball equipment), and Football USA (an entertainment and sports marketing firm). K2 now owns more than 35 major sports brands.

According to a K2's chief executive, Richard Heckman, the company's acquisition spree is part of the company's overall growth strategy: "You don't drive growth from [cutting] cost, you do it from revenue synergies."[13] K2 aims to enhance growth by pushing a broader array of products through its existing retail distribution channels.

One key benefit of related or horizontal diversification is the opportunity to exploit economies of scale, especially in the case of mergers between firms producing the same product or service or firms that seek to get more utilization out of their existing marketing and distribution channels. This is relatively easy to do when a company acquires an almost identical business and completely absorbs the operations of that business, as in the case of one bank acquiring another bank. As we will discuss later in this chapter, companies making this type of acquisition must still work hard to *integrate* the acquired business smoothly and successfully.

Furthermore, as suggested in Chapter 4, merging firms may already be operating at minimum efficient scale, in which case a merger with a company that participates in a related industry could cause the combined firm to operate at a level of output that places it on the upward-sloping portion of the long-run average total cost curve. Certainly economies of scale can be enjoyed in many industries by increasing output, but, as we saw in Chapter 4, the minimum efficient scale in many industries occurs at fairly low levels of output. Once firms expand output beyond the minimum efficient scale, bigness for the sake of bigness is likely to yield few additional economies and is likely to create additional administrative and coordination challenges and even higher costs.

The challenges associated with achieving economies of scale can be especially vexing when firms make acquisitions of different but related businesses and then seek to maintain these businesses as separate or distinct product lines or business entities. Illustrations of this type of related diversification are firms that acquire companies or product lines that they hope will complement existing businesses or product lines, while sharing resources and capabilities to provide economies. Yet, as noted earlier, the coordination required to achieve these economies is not without cost.

Brunswick provides an example of the difficulties of managing related business lines. Over the years, Brunswick acquired a number of different companies in the bowling and boating industries that were formerly competing companies. For example, in its boating business segment, Brunswick now owns many different boating lines serving the pleasure, sport, and fishing boat markets, including Bayliner and Sea Ray. The challenge for Brunswick's top management is to coordinate the activities of these various boating lines and foster a "healthy competition" among them that benefits the company as a whole while also avoiding conflicts and disputes between the different boating lines that would be detrimental to the company. It is not an easy task to walk the fine line between managing a healthy internal competition among different product lines and an unhealthy situation in which distinct businesses cannibalize each other's sales! A senior corporate development officer at Brunswick described this challenge:

> It's actually easier to manage diversification in unrelated markets. The complexity for Brunswick comes from the management of these diversified marine businesses. The very nature of having a common industry is what creates all of our problems. Why would you buy related companies that compete with each other? In bowling and marine we have companies that compete with each other. It is this aspect of diversification that creates problems for us. Diversification is not the problem. If you had total diversification, it would be a lot easier to manage.[14]

Thus, while related diversification offers opportunities for synergies across related businesses, the coordination of these businesses in order to realize those synergies requires considerable management effort. Healthy competition and rivalries among related businesses are likely to encourage innovation and high performance. On the other hand, too much competition among these businesses is likely to stifle needed cooperation and coordination. But, too much heavy-handed coordination is likely to discourage initiative and can even de-motivate business unit managers. So, firm-level managers must find the right balance of intra-firm rivalry and healthy competition among businesses while also promoting the necessary degree of cooperation and coordination to realize synergies. A delicate management balancing act for sure!

In short, economies of scale can also be quite elusive, and significant management attention and coordination may be required in order to realize economies of scale—this management effort is not costless. Obviously, any benefits of economies of scale should exceed the management coordination costs required to realize those economies.

Unrelated Diversification

Unrelated diversification, or adding businesses or product or services lines that are unrelated to the existing core business, is, however, no panacea. Firms pursue unrelated diversification strategies for a variety of reasons. One primary reason for moving into unrelated businesses is to allow a firm to continue to grow after its core business has matured or is threatened by competitors or by declining demand. **When companies engage in extensive unrelated diversification, they are referred to as conglomerates.**

Firms will also diversify into unrelated businesses in order to reduce cyclical fluctuations in revenues and cash flows. Even small companies can benefit from this type of diversification. For example, many small sporting goods companies will sell some combination of summer and winter sports merchandise, for example, bicycles in the summer and skiing equipment in the winter. In this way, these companies are able to better balance sales revenues and cash flows throughout the year.

United Technologies illustrates the advantages a large company can enjoy from unrelated diversification. United Technologies is the parent of a diverse array of companies including Pratt & Whitney (the manufacturer of jet engines), Otis Elevator, Carrier (an air conditioning company), and helicopter manufacturer Sikorsky Aircraft. Because United Technologies's defense and aerospace businesses will fluctuate with cyclical swings in defense spending, its non-defense businesses, Otis and Carrier, offer a way to buffer these swings as they tend to have steadier sales.

The major problem or disadvantage associated with unrelated or conglomerate diversification is that there are usually few obvious product or process technologies that can be the source of synergies as there are in firms pursuing related diversification strategies. Thus, these firms must rely on financial synergies, or the efficient allocation of financial capital. Ideally, these firms take cash from businesses that generate significant positive cash flows and reallocate this cash to opportunities that have significant growth and profit potential.

Researchers in finance and strategy often question the efficiency of these financial synergies, arguing that firms are unlikely to be as efficient at reallocation as the financial markets. Still, many highly diversified firms with portfolios of many unrelated businesses rely on the efficient reallocation of capital as a source of synergies among their businesses.

Another concern about highly diversified firms is that they often acquire businesses that top managers do not understand. As a result, they may rely on strict financial controls and objectives in order to manage or gauge the success of these businesses. This can result in an emphasis on short-term performance at the expense of long-run strategic objectives.

And, when problems develop in the businesses of a firm with many unrelated businesses, top managers will probably have no detailed or technical knowledge of the businesses, their manufacturing processes, their major customers, or their investment needs, and thus, they will probably have few insights into how they should intervene to correct the problems. As a result, many conglomerate firms have explicit policies stating that low-performing businesses that cannot be quickly turned around will be divested.

Exhibit 10.4 summarizes the advantages and disadvantages of both related and unrelated diversification strategies.

Exhibit 10.4 The Advantages and Disadvantages of Related and Unrelated Diversification

Related Differentiation

Advantages	Disadvantages
• Opportunities to achieve economies of scale and scope • Opportunities to expand product or service offerings or to move into new geographical areas	• Complexity and difficulty of coordinating different but related businesses

Unrelated Differentiation

Advantages	Disadvantages
• To continue to grow after a core business has matured or started to decline • To reduce cyclical fluctuations in sales revenues and cash flows	• Managers often lack technical expertise or detailed knowledge about their firm's many businesses

Global Diversification

Although many firms, including Boeing, Caterpillar, and Kellogg, have been global companies for decades, many other firms have only "discovered" **global diversification** during the last few decades. The trend toward expansion into global markets is usually motivated by the desire to grow or by pressures from global competition. Many firms begin to venture abroad only as their rate of sales growth begins to slow in their domestic markets.

Firms can take many different routes as they seek to serve global markets. The simplest route is exporting. Other options include licensing or franchising with foreign firms. Or, companies can establish joint ventures or strategic alliances overseas. The most complex route, also involving the greatest risks, is to establish wholly owned foreign subsidiaries.

Regardless of which mode a firm uses to enter foreign markets, all global diversification efforts entail significant challenges. Probably the most difficult challenge for many managers is to appreciate the unique cultures and customs of foreign markets, and the need for products, technologies, and business practices to be modified to accommodate these markets. Sometimes, few if any changes are necessary. Starbucks began moving abroad very soon after opening its initial wave of stores in the United States. For example, when Starbucks opened its first store in Japan in 1996, more than 100 people were lined-up and waiting for the store's 6:30 a.m. opening. Today, Starbucks operates hundreds of stores in Japan (and around the world), and the sales volume at its Japanese stores is twice the level of the average Starbucks location in the U.S.[15]

Like Starbucks, IKEA, Roche-Bobois, and Mattel have found that they need to do very little tailoring of their products to match global tastes and preferences. For example, Mattel originally produced different versions of many of its toy products under the assumption that children in different countries would want different toys or at least modified versions of its toys. It has since learned, however, that some products sell well throughout the world without any modifications or tailoring. Barbie is an example—Mattel's market research found that girls everywhere like blond haired, blue eyed versions of Barbie. "Blonde Barbie sells just as well in Asia as in the U.S."[16]

Still, it would be a mistake to assume that all products or services will "travel" so well. McDonald's has carefully tailored its menu and business practices as it has entered international markets. Realizing, for example, that beef products would likely offend the Hindu population when it entered the Indian market, it carefully tailored its menu.[17] This ability to tailor product and service offerings and to adapt business practices to local tastes while also developing global advertising and marketing themes illustrates the great skill that many multinational companies have to develop in order to be successful worldwide.

Summary

This discussion about different types of diversification strategies may suggest that it is relatively easy to categorize multibusiness firms into one of the four diversification strategies just described. In fact, this is not the case at all. For example, consider again the case of United Technologies Corporation. As already noted, the company's major business subsidiaries include:

Carrier (a producer of air conditioning products), Otis (the elevator manufacturer), Pratt & Whitney (a leading manufacturer of jet engines), Sikorsky (which manufactures helicopters), Hamilton Sundstrand (an aerospace company), UTC Fire & Security (a business that produces fire detection and suppression products), and UTC Power (which manufacturers fuel cells and renewable energy products). Is this company pursuing a related or an unrelated diversification strategy?

Some of the businesses are no doubt related or have the potential for synergies. For example, there are undoubtedly some potential synergies among the company's air conditioning and fire detection and suppression businesses. They almost certainly sell their products to the same customers. Similarly, the company's Pratt & Whitney, Sikorsky, and Hamilton Sundstrand businesses share many common customers. But, one would have to wonder whether the businesses are related enough that the same sales force could sell the products of two or more businesses. Possibly not. So, perhaps the best sources of synergies across these businesses are opportunities to exploit financial synergies by reallocating financial capital to those businesses that offer the greatest growth and financial return.

The message here is that the "relatedness" of firms' diversification strategies is largely a product of top managers' own understandings and sensemaking activities—their mental models. Sara Lee, selling its famous Sara Lee food products, Ball Park, Hillshire Farm, and Jimmy Dean brands of meat products, and Kiwi shoe polishes (to name just a few of its major product lines), is widely viewed as a conglomerate firm. But, Sara Lee's top managers have a very different view, seeing all of their company's products as related along a number of dimensions:

> We like to think of ourselves as a consumer packaged-goods products company, offering products that are high repeat purchase, basic items in people's diets or wardrobes, products that are not subject to big fashion swings, product categories that are marketing sensitive that allow us to differentiate ourselves. Those commonalities you can point to in all of our businesses.[18]

Later in the chapter, we will see that how firms' managers understand the relationships among their various businesses, as well as their beliefs about how diversification should be managed, will determine to a large extent whether their firms' corporate strategies are successful.

The Aim of Corporate Strategy: Synergy

While all the corporate strategies just reviewed offer a number of potential advantages, the many disadvantages associated with each strategy can easily overwhelm the benefits of diversification. The important point is this: *The aim of diversification should be to create value or wealth in excess of what firms would enjoy without diversification.*

In discussing the performance implications of diversification, strategists and company managers frequently use the term synergy to describe the gains in value that should be derived from a particular diversification strategy. Often synergy is expressed in the mathematical "shorthand" of $2 + 2 = 5$, the point being that the whole should be greater than the sum of its parts. In the case of one firm acquiring another, for example, synergy implies that the value of the combined firm after the acquisition should be greater than the value of the two firms prior to the acquisition. Synergies can be obtained in many ways, but here we focus on three of the most often mentioned ways: 1) by exploiting economies of scale, 2) by exploiting economies of scope, and 3) through the efficient allocation of capital. Each of these three sources of synergy, and several examples of each, will be discussed here.

Economies of Scale

Of the three sources of synergy, the concept of economies of scale is probably the most straightforward. **Economies of scale** exist when unit costs decline with increases in production, as fixed costs are spread over a larger volume of output. For example, say a company can manufacture 100,000 units at $1.00 each. It will enjoy economies of scale if it can produce 150,000 units at $.90 each. A practical definition or way to think about the concept is that economies of scale occur when firms *use the same resource or resources to do more of the same* and thereby realize lower per unit costs. Building on the example just cited, a company with a factory manufacturing 100,000 units might acquire a competitor and consolidate manufacturing operations so that after the acquisition the same factory might manufacture 150,000 units at a lower per unit cost.

As noted earlier, many bank mergers appear to be motivated by a desire to achieve greater economies of scale. By centralizing "back office" activities, such as check clearing and loan processing, many banks have been able to realize significant economies of scale.

Yet, as noted in Chapter 4 as well as earlier in this chapter, economies of scale are not free and may require considerable management effort and coordination. Much of the success in achieving economies of scale rests on how effectively a firm can integrate a new business or an acquisition into its existing operations. The important point to remember about economies of scale is that diversification or any other corporate strategy pursued primarily for the sake of expansion or firm growth will not necessarily enhance shareholder value without significant management attention and effort.

Economies of Scope

The concept of economies of scope is related to yet different from economies of scale. Whereas the concept of economies of scale refers to using the same resource or resources to do more of the same thing, the concept of **economies of scope** refers to using the same resource to do different things either to take better advantage of existing resources or to achieve lower unit costs or both.

For example, one reason the decision to manufacture disposable diapers was a natural diversification move for both Procter & Gamble and Kimberly-Clark was that both companies had extensive experience in manufacturing and marketing brand-name sanitary paper products. Both companies could apply this know-how or expertise to the manufacture and marketing of a completely new brand-name paper product, disposable diapers. Similarly, PepsiCo's acquisition of Quaker Oats and its Gatorade beverage business was motivated by PepsiCo's expertise in marketing beverage products and opportunities to expand its already very effective distribution system.

Financial Synergies and the Efficient Allocation of Capital

Even though the efficient markets hypothesis proposed by finance researchers holds that stock markets take into consideration all available information in assessing the value of firms, many top executives of diversified firms believe they have the ability to find undervalued companies or other attractive investment opportunities. They then seek to acquire these undervalued companies or exploit these opportunities and, through their investments of cash obtained from other businesses in their portfolio, improve operations and add value to these companies. The following statement by a top strategic planning executive at a *Fortune* 500 firm illustrates the logic of deriving synergies through the allocation of capital:

> When [a business] is part of a larger corporation there's a larger pool of investment, and when there is recognition of a major growth opportunity in one of your companies, you can pour more money into it than a banker would or maybe the equity market would be willing to do.... When a market is growing at a double-digit rate, we're pouring a lot of money into it. I don't think [businesses] could get that kind of investment on their own.[19]

According to a top strategic planning executive at a different *Fortune* 500 firm, the main advantage of diversification is:

> the ability to shift resources from one business to another.... We ... take assets out of a business [with poor prospects] and redeploy them in other businesses that are going to turn around and do well. That's really a form of capital market. It may be saying that we are better capital allocators than Wall Street. We certainly have better information than they do.[20]

Whether firms have information better than that of Wall Street investment bankers is a controversial question, likely to generate a good deal of discussion if posed to groups of academics, top managers, and Wall Street investment bankers. It's certainly possible that corporate executives may have more direct access to information that assists them in making better investment decisions.

Portfolio management is a process that has been used by companies as a way to guide investment decision making and to achieve financial synergies across a portfolio of businesses. We describe one of these portfolio management techniques, how such techniques can be used to guide investment decision making, and also describe some of the limitations of portfolio planning models in an Appendix to this chapter.

Summary

This introduction to the ways in which companies can achieve synergies through diversification does not reflect the challenges and problems associated with actually achieving these synergies. It is one thing to believe that a particular diversification strategy might yield significant synergies or that a particular management technique might make the process of formulating corporate strategy easier. As we will see in the next section, however, it is a very difficult challenge to achieve those synergies once a business has been acquired or a new product line has been introduced.

Problems in Exploiting Potential Synergies

In this section, we explore some of the many reasons why firms fail to realize hoped-for synergies from their diversification activities.[21]

Poor Understanding of How Diversification Activities Will "Fit" or Be Coordinated with Existing Businesses

First, it appears that many diversification efforts fail to live up to their hoped for benefits because managers have given inadequate thought to how a new business will be related to their firm's existing business or businesses. Or perhaps their mental models lead them to see a business incorrectly or to overestimate the benefits of a business. As a consequence, many new businesses offer few if any potential economies or opportunities to generate synergies. For example, online auction giant, eBay, acquired Skype, the Internet phone service for $2.6 billion in 2005, believing that it would find significant synergies between its customers and Skype's online calling services, but the synergies were elusive. eBay later took an accounting charge to write-down its investment in Skype and then announced that it would spin-off Skype through an IPO.[22]

Without a complete and accurate understanding of how newly acquired or internally developed businesses are related to existing businesses, firms' managers will have few clues as to how these businesses will be able to share activities, processes, skills, and other organizational resources. And, without a plan for realizing these economies, it is unlikely that synergies will be generated or shareholder value enhanced. For example, when Hewlett-Packard first proposed its acquisition of Compaq, many industry experts doubted that Hewlett-Packard had a good understanding of how the acquisition would create value. Sun Microsystems founder, Scott McNealy, was blunt in his derision of the proposed acquisition, comparing it to the "slow-motion collision of two garbage trucks."

Porter has suggested that diversified firms need to develop "corporate themes" that explicitly suggest how businesses will be related and how synergies will be derived from firms' portfolios of businesses.[23] And, he argued that these corporate themes must do more than simply sound plausible, that they must clearly demonstrate linkages and potential synergies among businesses and suggest how those synergies will be derived. In elaborating on this concept of a corporate theme, Porter concluded:

> It is all too easy to create a shallow corporate theme. CBS wanted to be an "entertainment company," for example, and it built a group of businesses related to leisure time. It entered such industries as toys, crafts, musical instruments, sports teams, and hi-fi retailing. While this corporate theme sounded good … none of these businesses had any significant opportunity to share activities or transfer skills among themselves or with CBS's traditional

broadcasting and record businesses.... Saddled with the worst acquisition record in my study, CBS has eroded the shareholder value created through its strong performance in broadcasting and records.[24]

Apparently, other media companies learned little from the dismal experiences of CBS. Many news articles and analyses have reviewed the performance of media companies after they had made large acquisitions.[25] None of the major media giants has generated synergies that impress their shareholders, and many companies, like AOL Time-Warner, have subsequently shed many of their acquisitions. The sobering experiences of these companies suggest that it's wise to step back and reevaluate the thinking—or lack of thinking—behind many of these media mega-mergers:

> the rationale driving their megamergers—control over every aspect of their businesses—has fundamental flaws. Their operations are diffuse, stretched from R-rated movies and retail video stores to trade magazines, animated cartoons and elementary-school textbooks.[26]

Ever since the first media mega-merger, analysts and commentators have questioned whether potential synergies really exist between businesses that *provide* media content and those that *deliver* media content:

> the notion that the marriage of content and distribution is always desirable has turned out to be questionable. Mergers such as Disney/ABC and Time Warner/Turner and Viacom's purchase of Paramount Communications and Blockbuster were based on the theory that studios had to be linked with networks, TV stations, cable systems and retailers to give their product a direct pipeline to viewers and to avoid being shut out by rivals.[27]

Yet, the record of most of these media companies suggests that few synergies really exist between media content and distribution.[28] Companies producing very good media content should, in fact, want the widest possible distribution, just as companies distributing media content should want to buy the best content from any media producer.[29]

Moreover, it's important to emphasize that no corporate strategy will compensate for an unprofitable business model or a lack of competitive advantage in a core business.[30] As Gary Hamel has written:

> Perhaps the attraction [of acquisitions] lies in the fact that it is so much easier to put together a deal than it is to reinvent a company's decrepit business model.[31]

Thus, the challenge for managers is to have a conceptualization of their diversified firm that not only looks good on paper or one that sounds plausible, but a conceptualization of the firm that also makes sense from a practical, operational standpoint so that it is actually likely to produce synergies. Many diversification strategies make eminent sense on paper, but environmental changes and the difficulty of implementing these strategies ultimately doomed them to failure.

Risks Associated with the Acquisition Process

With thousands of acquisitions worth billions of dollars being made each year, mistakes are inevitable and, as we will emphasize later in the chapter, many acquisitions fare so poorly that the acquiring firm eventually divests the acquired business. Many aspects and characteristics of the acquisition process are responsible for acquisitions not living up to their expected synergies. As already noted, one of the most serious mistakes managers can make is to fail to conduct an adequate strategic analysis of the acquisition candidate, and to understand whether an acquisition candidate would really fit with a company's portfolio.

This can be due to several factors. For example, managers will often try to complete an acquisition deal quickly before other potential buyers have an opportunity to become interested in the acquisition target and begin a "bidding war" that would raise the price of the acquisition. Bidding wars can result in the price of an acquisition rising way above the true economic value of the target company.

As we will discuss in greater detail later in the chapter, most research finds few gains for acquiring firms from pursuing acquisitions, while the only real winners appear to be the shareholders of the acquired firms. These findings are, of course, only heightened when the acquiring companies pay too much for the firms they acquire. Bidding wars are an excellent example of the escalation of commitment problem described in Chapter 3. There, we discussed how managers will continue to pursue a particular course of action—in this case a bidding war—even after it becomes clear that the strategy is inappropriate or that the company will pay too much for the acquisition.

Over the years, a number of bidding wars have attracted a good deal of notoriety. Vodafone's acquisition of AirTouch also illustrates the dynamics of a bidding war:

> Rumors that Bell Atlantic was in negotiations to acquire AirTouch first surfaced on December 31, 1998. The terms of the Bell Atlantic bid were publicized four days later: it had offered $73 per share, or $45 billion, a seven percent premium above AirTouch's closing share price a week earlier of $68. Bell Atlantic's stock price immediately declined by five percent. Clearly, the market did not like the deal.
>
> Vodafone entered the fray on January 7 with a bid of around $55 billion, or $89 per share. Negotiations continued for the next several days until, on January 15, Vodafone agreed to pay $97 per share, for a total of $62 billion. That price was 33 percent more than Bell Atlantic's original offer and 43 percent more than AirTouch's share price before the first rumors of Bell Atlantic's offer had surfaced. Implicit in the deal was the fact that for its shareholders to break even, Vodafone would have to find cost savings and revenue generators worth at least $20 billion.[32]

Yet, engaging in a bidding war and paying a large premium for an acquisition does not necessarily mean that an acquisition is doomed. Companies that pay substantial premiums for acquisitions will often see very low returns, but they can sometimes pay substantial premiums and still see high returns. In the case of the Vodafone-AirTouch acquisition, even though Vodafone paid a substantial premium to acquire AirTouch:

Vodafone's stock price actually increased some 14 percent [during the bidding war].

What explains the market's negative reaction to Bell Atlantic's modest premium and its positive reaction to Vodafone's high premium? The answer is that acquiring AirTouch created more valuable synergies for Vodafone than it would have for Bell Atlantic.[33]

Thus, much more important than the absolute amount of acquisition premium paid, is whether the market perceives, and managers can deliver, synergies from an acquisition opportunity.

Furthermore, because of biases in their thinking, managers will often focus on the attractive features of an acquisition candidate, while giving less attention or weight to the candidate's negative features. This is complicated by opportunism on the part of the managers of the acquisition candidate—once they agree to the acquisition of their company, they are motivated to get the best possible price for their shareholders. As a result, they will not be forthcoming about any problems or weaknesses that would cause the acquiring company to lower its offer.

The Challenges of Integrating Acquisitions

After making an acquisition, managers must integrate the new business into their company's existing portfolio of businesses. The complexity of integrating a newly acquired business with existing operations poses a new set of challenges, especially for the managers of firms that make only occasional acquisitions and therefore lack experience at managing the integration process. Should a new business be allowed to operate on a stand-alone basis, or should the new business be absorbed or incorporated into the operations of the existing core business?

Problems of melding disparate cultures can be particularly difficult for firms making international acquisitions. The acquisition of the pharmaceutical firm Upjohn, based in Kalamazoo, Michigan, by the Swedish company Pharmacia illustrates just how severe these cultural problems can be. The combined companies clashed on everything from management styles and the appropriate length of vacations to whether cigarettes and wine would be allowed in company dining rooms.[34]

Managers of acquiring companies can, however, take some initiatives to minimize clashes between cultures. Here are some suggestions:[35]

- First, clearly divide power among top managers. Attempts to split authority among top managers by having co-CEOs or by sharing managerial responsibilities in other ways almost always fail, so acquiring companies should clearly define roles among all top executives.
- Second, managers of acquiring companies can formulate integration "teams" composed of representatives from both the acquired and the acquiring companies to relieve tension among employees; to highlight and combine the best capabilities, characteristics, and resources of both the acquiring and acquired companies; and to help in blending cultures.
- Third, managers of acquiring companies can effectively communicate with employees. Employees hold fast to their companies' cultures because they provide meaning at a time of great anxiety. Rather than contributing to employees' fears by allowing rumors to run rampant, the managers of acquiring companies should communicate clearly and

frequently with their employees. Communication methods that managers of acquiring companies have used include frequent newsletters, videoconferences, retreats, focus groups and surveys, and Internet Web sites.

- Finally, top managers can design and implement compensation plans that reward cooperation and teamwork. Compensation plans can send an important message that employees who "get on board" and emphasize teamwork and the overall organization will be rewarded.

Problems Associated with the Internal Development of New Businesses

The difficulties associated with realizing synergies are not limited to firms that choose to diversify through acquisition. Managers who start new businesses internally often encounter problems as well. Most of the problems associated with internally developed diversification activities are caused by the considerable time and investment that are required to launch new businesses. Furthermore, managers usually face a great deal of difficulty assessing the risks associated with a new investment opportunity. In addition, the available capital budgeting tools offer little assistance in helping managers weigh or assess these risks. And, the capital budgeting tools that companies do have always favor investment proposals that provide very quick returns.

It's not surprising then that, although some new product introductions are overnight successes, research suggests that, *on average*, most new product lines require ten years before generating positive cash flows and net income.[36] An investment project that doesn't return a positive cash flow during the first ten years of its life is likely to have a very low net present value no matter how large the positive cash flows are in year ten and beyond!

As a consequence, many companies are simply unwilling to fund such speculative investment proposals. Of course, low estimates of cash flow are often caused by the difficulties of accurately forecasting. Unwillingness to take risks may also explain why U.S. companies are often the first to develop the new products that are made commercial successes by other companies, especially Japanese companies. For example, the fax machine and the telephone answering machine were developed by U.S. companies, but when forecasts of demand for the products were low, their U.S. inventors allowed foreign manufacturers to introduce and enjoy success from the products that they had developed. Similarly, initial estimates of potential cell phone demand and use discouraged AT&T from aggressively pursuing product development efforts. It then had to play catch-up when consumer demand for cell phones took off.

Managing Complexity and the Costs of Coordination

Increasing the number of business units in a firm's portfolio or increasing the amount of diversity will increase organizational complexity, and the task of managing additional complexity will necessarily entail greater costs of coordination. As suggested earlier in our discussion of horizontal or related diversification, even quite similar or related units can entail significant coordination costs. Some management scholars have argued that it may well be more difficult to coordinate the businesses of a firm pursuing a related diversification strategy than it is to manage a conglomerate.[37] The rationale is that the businesses of the conglomerate are so unrelated that the firm need not make an effort to coordinate their activities, bur simply allow the businesses to operate quite autonomously. Still, as we pointed out earlier in the chapter, the businesses of a firm pursuing an unrelated diversification strategy may be so diverse that corporate level managers have little or no knowledge of the businesses, which must surely increase management complexity at the highest levels of these firms.

Brunswick again serves as a good illustration of the challenges and complexity associated with managing related businesses. Not only must Brunswick manage a set of businesses that compete with each other for customers, with the company finding ways to encourage a "healthy competition" among its brands while also getting the companies to cooperate in ways that benefit the company, but the company must also deal with the inherent cyclicality that characterizes the boat business. Brunswick's sales will fluctuate wildly with swings in the economy, sometimes selling more than twice as many times during periods of economic boom as it does during deep recessions. Thus, the company faces enormous challenges in not only managing related businesses but also the economic cycles that so greatly affect its businesses.[38]

Diversification and Firm Performance

Given the potential for corporate strategy to generate synergies as well as the very real problems of actually achieving those synergies, what is the relationship between diversification and firm performance? In other words, can corporate strategy and diversification be sources of sustained competitive advantage? Unfortunately, answers to these questions are not at all obvious or straightforward. Generally, academics, consultants, and the financial community have taken a dim view of diversification. In their well-known book, *In Search of Excellence*, Peters and Waterman exhorted managers to "stick to the knitting" and avoid extensive diversification beyond their firms' core businesses.[39] And, though this book has now been in print for 25 years, their advice to "stick to the knitting" is still often quoted and cited as a reason why firms should not diversify.

Many research studies support Peters and Waterman, suggesting that diversification beyond a core business leads to lower performance. For example, in a classic *Harvard Business Review* article, Michael Porter studied the diversification activities of 33 large companies between 1950 and 1986 and found that, on average, each of these 33 firms made 80 diversification moves, of which 70 percent were acquisitions of other businesses, 20 percent were by start-up, while ten percent were joint ventures with other firms. Porter concluded that the results of this diversification activity were largely disastrous: More than 60 percent of all the acquired businesses were subsequently divested. Of those acquisitions that involved moving into unrelated markets, more than 74 percent of the acquired businesses were divested![40]

A number of other studies have sought to sort out the influence of various factors on business unit performance. In other words, these studies have sought to determine how much various factors (including industry attractiveness, business strategy, and corporate strategy) contribute to the performance of business units. Exhibit 10.5 summarizes the findings of one of these studies, and, as the exhibit suggests, industry attractiveness (i.e., average industry performance) and business strategy together explain more than 99 percent of the variation in business unit performance. Corporate parentage, on the other hand, explains less than one percent of the

Exhibit 10.5 The Influence of Industry Attractiveness, Business Strategy, and Corporate Strategy on Business Unit Performance

	Percent of variation in performance due to:
Industry Membership	16.1%
Corporate Strategy	0.8%
Business Strategy	83.0%
Total	99.9%

Source: Rumelt, R. P. 1991. How much does industry matter? *Strategic Management Journal*, 12: 167–185.

variation in business unit performance. In short, corporate strategy has no apparent effect on business unit performance!

Additional studies have reinforced the conclusion that corporate strategy rarely makes a significant contribution to shareholder value. One study reported that firms that had "de-diversified" saw improvements in stock market performance while those that had diversified actually saw their stock market value decline.[41] A *Wall Street Journal* article reported the findings of another research study that found greater levels of diversification were associated with lower levels of productivity.[42] Thus, many research studies make a strong case against corporate diversification, and, during the past decade, many business leaders and investors have concluded that Peters and Waterman were right—firms should "stick to their knitting." Many widely diversified firms have de-diversified in order to focus on a narrower range of industries or markets.

The situation is not so simple, however, and the view that diversification is necessarily associated with lower performance overlooks much evidence of successful diversification. In fact, researchers have failed to find a consistent empirical relationship between diversification and performance, in spite of extensive research over more than 30 years. While many studies have concluded that firms pursuing single business or related diversification strategies enjoy higher performance than firms pursuing unrelated strategies, other research studies have reached the opposite conclusion.[43] Furthermore, one scholar has noted that "high-performing diversified firms exist in sufficient numbers … to throw doubt on the proposition that diversification is not a workable strategy."[44]

Other researchers have concluded that the relationship between diversification and firm performance is curvilinear (as illustrated in Exhibit 10.6)—that up to some point, diversification actually increases firm performance, but that beyond some optimal level of diversification, additional diversification is associated with declining firm performance.[45]

Part of the confusion about the relationship between diversification and performance may result from differences in the questions researchers study or the methods they employ. For example, one study cited earlier examined the relationship between *changes* in diversification and *changes* in stock market performance. It did not examine the relationship between *overall* levels of diversification and firm performance. During the period studied, the stock market may well have rewarded companies that increased their focus—indeed, those firms that de-diversified during this time may have made very poor diversification decisions in the past—

Exhibit 10.6 Is the Relationship between Diversification and Firm Performance Curvilinear?

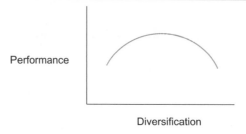

but this does not warrant the conclusion that the market necessarily penalizes all diversified companies. Similarly, the study that examined the contributions of industry attractiveness, business strategy, and corporate strategy to overall business unit performance levels did not distinguish between what we might call "successful" and "unsuccessful" diversifiers.

Another study that did distinguish between successful and unsuccessful diversified firms may offer some helpful insights on the relationship between diversification strategy and firm performance.[46] That study classified over 180 *Fortune* 500 firms into groups based on their diversification and performance characteristics. The resulting diversification-performance groups, which are illustrated in Exhibit 10.7, offered a number of surprising findings:

First, the categorization of firms into the four diversification-performance groups is remarkably balanced. In other words, high-performing firms are just as likely to be more diversified as they are to be less diversified, and low-performing firms are just as likely to be less diversified as they are to be more diversified.

Furthermore, the study found no significant performance differences between the high-performing more- and less-diversified groups of firms. In short, *higher levels of diversification are not incompatible with high performance, and higher levels of diversification do not necessarily imply that firms will suffer lower performance levels*. Such a finding is also consistent with other research that found no evidence of a "diversification discount," or that diversified firms necessarily enjoy lower performance.[47]

This same study also sought to identify how high- and low-performing diversified firms might differ along a number of strategic dimensions (including the attractiveness of the industries in which they operate, their growth rates, and their levels of capital expenditures, R&D, and leverage). Surprisingly, these analyses also revealed few significant differences.

So what do the findings of many, many research studies suggest about the relationship between diversification and firm performance? Here are some observations that seem warranted:

Exhibit 10.7 Distribution of a Sample of *Fortune* 500 Firms among Diversification-Performance Groups

	Low-Performing Firms	High-Performing Firms
Less Diversified	47	46
More Diversified	46	47

- First, though diversification has been disappointing for many firms and downright disastrous for a few, diversified firms can also be very successful and enjoy high performance.
- Second, studies have found no obvious differences between high- and low-performing diversified firms along several important strategic dimensions. In other words, high- and low-performing diversified firms do not differ from each other along many obvious dimensions or characteristics.

Thus, as suggested in Chapter 2, successful strategies result from more intangible factors or characteristics. In the next section, we argue that the specific intangible factors that are associated with effective corporate strategies are managers' beliefs about how their diversified firms' businesses are related and their understandings about how diversification should be managed.

Corporate Strategy and the Three Key Themes Emphasized in This Book

The Crucial Role of Managers

This last point—that successful diversification strategies result from the ability of managers to develop skill and competence at managing diversification—fits well with the themes we have emphasized throughout this book. We have consistently argued that competitive advantage is unlikely to emerge from factors that are obvious or resources that can be easily acquired.

Managerial beliefs, knowledge, skills, and understandings as well as supporting management processes, routines, and standard operating procedures, all of which have been developed over time, can be valuable resources that are difficult for rival firms to imitate. And, we believe that such socially complex resources are likely to be the deciding factor in predicting the success of firms' corporate strategies. Most practicing managers and most researchers in the strategic management field would agree that managers occupy a central role in the strategy formulation and implementation processes. One noted researcher has, in fact, argued that management skill is "the critical resource" of successful diversified firms.[48]

In terms of our model of strategic management, managers must develop two very important types of mental models in order to achieve successful diversification. As illustrated in Exhibit 10.8, managers must have well-developed understandings of their firms' diversity and the relatedness that defines their companies and suggests how their businesses are related to each other. Managers must also have well-developed beliefs about how diversification should be managed in order to achieve synergies. In the next two sections, we focus on these two different sets of beliefs and understandings.

Managers' Understandings of Their Firms' Diversity and Relatedness

Managers' understandings of how their firms' businesses are related are important for at least two reasons. First, understandings of diversity and relatedness will influence how managers describe their organizations to important stakeholders.[49] Such understandings of diversity and relatedness can provide diversified firms with what Michael Porter has called "corporate themes" that help "unite the efforts of business units and reinforce the ways they interrelate."[50]

Exhibit 10.8 How Managers' Beliefs and Understandings Influence the Relationship between Diversification and Performance

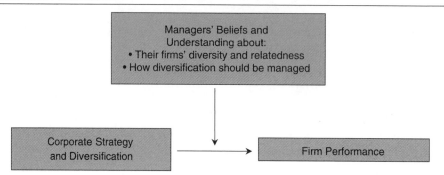

The ability to articulate a coherent identity may be especially important in the case of widely diversified firms that have business units operating in many different product markets that have no obvious linkages with one another. The task of articulating a coherent identity or understanding of how business units are related becomes not only more important but also more difficult as diversity increases because individual business units may have their own strong identities tied to strong brand names or cultures.[51]

Second, managers' understandings of diversity and relatedness will also describe or suggest how their firms' businesses are related to each other. Traditionally, we have assumed that the businesses in a diversified firm's portfolio were related if they shared product-market characteristics, such as a common production technology or similar customers or distribution channels.

Research has now demonstrated that the managers of diversified firms develop unique understandings of how their firms' businesses are related to each other that may include but also go well beyond similarities in product-market characteristics.[52]

For example, studies have shown that while some managers consider their firms' businesses to be related because their products share common physical characteristics, common manufacturing processes, or common customers, other managers tend to see their firms' businesses as related because they share a wide variety of common marketing and product differentiation characteristics. As noted earlier in the chapter, Sara Lee's businesses sell a diverse array of products, but nearly all those products share common marketing characteristics, including brand names, strong market share positions, and a reliance on advertising. Research has also shown that other managers see their firms' businesses as related because they share common financial characteristics so that even if their firms' businesses participate in many different product markets, all the businesses are expected to meet common financial objectives.

These idiosyncratic understandings of relatedness and diversity are potentially very important to the development of a competitive advantage in the management of diversification. The managers of nearly all diversified firms are likely to have understandings of such traditional concepts as economies of scale and scope, and they are probably seeking to exploit these concepts. It is the more unique understandings of relatedness and diversity that top management teams have developed over time that are much more likely to contribute to competitive advantage.[53]

Managers' Beliefs about How Diversification and Corporate Strategy Should Be Managed

A second set of understandings includes managers' beliefs about how diversification and corporate strategy should be managed. Because the management of diversification is a complex activity, managers must develop a set of beliefs about how they should manage their diversified firms. In other words, top managers of diversified firms must learn about the management of diversification "as a distinct process and skill."[54] Managers' understandings of how corporate strategy should be managed and their ability to leverage their firms' competencies will not only influence day-to-day decision making and the longer-run direction of firms' diversification strategies, but these understandings will also have the potential to be an important source of competitive advantage.

The distinct process and skill of managing diversification may include (but is not limited to) understandings and knowledge about:

- how to coordinate the activities of businesses in order to achieve synergies,
- how to allocate resources to the various businesses in a diversified firm,
- whether various functional activities, such as engineering, finance and accounting, marketing and sales, production, and research and development, should be centralized at the corporate headquarters or be decentralized and operated by business unit managers, and
- how to compensate and reward business unit managers so that their goals and objectives are best aligned with the overall goals and objectives of the organization.

The classic example of such a "formula" or "recipe" for managing corporate strategy and diversification is the case of General Electric. General Electric is a highly diversified conglomerate with businesses in such wide-ranging industries as aircraft engines, home appliances, power generation equipment, medical diagnostic imaging equipment, railroad locomotives, network broadcasting, and finance and banking. General Electric is well known for its "every business must be first or second in its respective market" dictum. GE's businesses operate quite autonomously, with division and business managers held strictly accountable for the results of their units by GE general management.

Managers of many other large diversified companies have adopted many aspects of GE's "formula," but managers of other firms have also developed unique "formulas" for managing the diversity of their own firms' portfolios of businesses.

Change and the Importance of Thinking Dynamically about the Strategic Management of Corporate Strategy and Diversification

Over the past several years, we have seen many widely diversified firms shed business units in order to "focus" on a core business or a set of core businesses. In this section, we examine this restructuring activity and assess the future of diversification while also offering some observations about possible future trends in corporate strategy.

Based on anecdotal evidence and stories from the business press, it is easy to conclude that diversification is on the wane and that the large, widely diversified firm is becoming obsolete.

Nothing could be further from the truth. Evidence supplied by Cynthia Montgomery of the Harvard Business School shows that the level of diversification among the 500 largest public companies in the United States actually increased in recent years.[55]

Furthermore, there are many good reasons to believe that diversification will continue to be an important feature of the economic landscape. Extensions of existing product lines, exploitation of economies of scale and scope, and expansion into new geographical areas remain compelling reasons for firms to move into new markets or to pursue new business opportunities. Firms will also continue to diversify into new businesses to reduce their reliance on declining business lines or industries. Given the dynamic nature of the economy, we can expect that firms will seize opportunities resulting from demographic shifts, the development of new products and services, and the emergence of new technologies, to diversify into new arenas.

Much of the de-diversification and restructuring activity that has occurred over the last two decades can be explained by the failure of these firms to develop effective understandings of how their businesses were related or fit together and how to manage those interrelationships effectively. Sears' grand strategy for developing a consumer retailing powerhouse based on its merchandising, insurance, real estate, and financial services businesses failed because the company was never able to realize the anticipated synergies. Furthermore, Sears' diversification activities had a devastating impact on the company's merchandising operations as managers "took their eye off the ball," and lost sight of the need for Sears' stores to maintain a strong and effective business definition in the ever-changing retail marketplace.[56]

In addition, as noted in Chapter 9, many companies are restructuring their operations to emphasize those value-chain activities that contribute to their competitive advantage while outsourcing other, less critical activities. We can expect to see more of this activity in the future. It is also likely that we will see fewer vertically integrated firms as many firms that are currently vertically integrated rethink this strategy. Just as the managers of Nike radically rethought their firm's value chain, many vertically integrated firms are likely to focus more attention on those links in their value chains that are or can be sources of competitive advantage while contracting with other companies for those products or services provided by less important links in their value chains.

Given that so many corporate restructurings have occurred over the past few years, it is worth asking, "What has been the impact of all this restructuring activity on bottom line performance?" Some evidence certainly suggests that restructurings have improved the performance of diversified firms. The chapter referred earlier to a research study that found the stock market rewarded firms that increased their focus on a core business or set of core businesses.[57] Other evidence also indicates that the performance levels of many businesses improve after they are divested by corporate parents, suggesting that they may have been suffering some sort of "negative synergy" when a part of a larger diversified organization. On the other hand, we have already pointed out that these studies examined the relationship between *changes* in diversity and *changes* in stock price; they say nothing about the relationship between *absolute* levels of diversification and firm performance.

It's logical to conclude that the firms most likely to de-diversify may be those that are having the most trouble managing diversification. Therefore, it is not surprising that the stock market rewards those firms when they shed the units they are having difficulty managing! Furthermore, much evidence suggests that "corporate breakups are no panacea."[58] Although the stock market often has a favorable initial reaction to announcements of spinoffs or restructuring plans, these restructuring efforts rarely correct companies' more fundamental problems.[59]

The Importance of Organizational Learning and Experience

As organizations diversify beyond a core business, they inevitably learn through trial and error.[60] Learning occurs as managers' understandings of cause and effect are shaped and influenced by their evaluations of the success of past strategic decisions.[61] Unlike management beliefs borrowed or copied from competing firms or acquired by hiring executives from other firms, the beliefs acquired through trial-and-error learning may contain unique insights that can become embedded in an organization's routine operating procedures. These insights may also be embedded in interconnected organizational processes that are difficult for other firms to imitate.[62]

Consider, for example, the daunting complexity associated with an acquisition, just one of many important corporate strategy activities pursued by diversified firms. One researcher has concluded that:

> more than 2,000 major steps and more than 10,000 non-routine decisions are required to completely integrate an acquisition of any size into a large corporation. In addition, the sequence of many of these steps is critical... which adds greatly to the complexity of the problem.[63]

Given the complexity of acquisitions, managers who have had little experience in making acquisitions will almost certainly make mistakes, often serious mistakes, and it is no surprise that some companies have simply refused to engage in significant acquisition transactions.[64] By engaging in a number of acquisitions over time, however, managers can develop an expertise about how the acquisition process should be managed. Thus, the "experience hypothesis" suggests that *those firms with management teams that have more experience at managing diversification will enjoy higher performance than those firms with management teams that are less experienced at managing diversification.*

Much evidence supports such an experience hypothesis. A *Business Week* article reported the results of a study that examined the performance of 248 acquiring firms.[65] The study found that only 54 percent of the less-experienced acquirers (i.e., those firms that had made five or fewer acquisitions) had returns above their industries' average returns, while 72 percent of the "active acquirers" (i.e., those firms that had made six or more acquisitions) enjoyed above-average returns. A *Wall Street Journal* article on the banking industry made the same observation. In many cases, active acquirers have outperformed other regional bank holding companies and have established "an excellent record of adding value through acquisition."[66] Several academic research studies also provide support for our experience hypothesis, demonstrating that active acquirers outperform firms that acquire less often.[67]

The success Hewlett-Packard has enjoyed thus far in integrating its acquisition of Compaq Computer is attributed, in part, to a team of Hewlett-Packard top managers who studied some of the best and worst previous mergers of technology companies to identify key success factors as well as pitfalls to be avoided.[68] Thus, it appears that Hewlett-Packard has done a number of things "right" as it has proceeded to implement that acquisition of Compaq. These include:[69]

- Extensive study of other large tech mergers and acquisitions to determine what must be done to insure successful integration of the two companies and what can derail efforts to bring the two companies together.
- Detailed plans for consolidating product lines and eliminating duplicate products and services.
- Extensive plans for staffing and for achieving required head-count reductions.

In addition, the company made announcements of staffing and product line changes quickly in order to minimize stress on employees and to maintain morale. Throughout the integration process, the company has emphasized open and clear communication, and has sought to bring together the best aspects of both companies' cultures.

Cisco also demonstrates the advantages an active acquirer can develop in successfully integrating acquired companies. Since 1993, Cisco has acquired scores of companies, and almost all of these companies have been successfully integrated into Cisco. Over the years, Cisco has developed an elaborate process for integrated acquired units. Managers of acquired units are usually retained, the acquired units typically remain autonomous divisions of Cisco, employees of acquired units are quickly brought into the fold by obtaining Cisco telephone numbers, email addresses, and stock options. Elaborate efforts to communicate with the employees of newly acquired units are aimed at minimizing uncertainty and calming any anxiety.[70]

These examples lend support to the observations of a McKinsey consultant, who has argued that "the people who are good at diversifying do it all the time. They have mechanisms in place, they've been through the process a number of times. They know what kinds of businesses they can and can't manage."[71]

The importance of learning and experience with managing diversification is also borne-out by the experiences of companies that have diversified globally. Kellogg provides an excellent example of the relationship between learning and performance. At Kellogg, company executives believe that two types of learning are critical. First, when Kellogg enters a new country, the company must learn how to sell cereal to the people in that particular country. In addition, however, the people in that country must learn—largely from Kellogg's teaching—to like cereal. For example, when Kellogg entered the Japanese market (where the traditional breakfast consists of warm fish and rice), it found that consumers viewed cereal as junk food—that because of their shape, cornflakes reminded consumers of potato chips. As a result, Kellogg learned that it needed to market the nutritional value of its cereal products to Japanese consumers. Kellogg very much believes that cereal consumption in a particular market is a function of how long the company has been in the country, and, therefore, how much the company has learned about selling cereal in that market.

Conclusion

Corporate strategy is concerned with the appropriate scale and scope of business firms. While this chapter has sought to introduce a number of important corporate strategy topics, to review the relevant literature and research findings, and to suggest appropriate conclusions, we have necessarily been selective in our coverage of this material. Whole books have been devoted to the subject of diversification, there are journals totally focused on mergers and acquisitions, and a large percentage of all articles in the business press focus on corporate strategy topics. As a result, this single chapter on corporate strategy is necessarily incomplete. With this caveat, however, let us now offer a few summary observations to bring this chapter to a close:

- First, size alone does not guarantee firms an advantage. Firms can achieve economies of scale through size, but, as we saw in Chapter 4, minimum efficient scale in many industries occurs at fairly low volume levels, so competitor firms can achieve economies of scale as well. The chapter has also emphasized that the coordination required to exploit economies of scale and scope is not costless. We will further emphasize in Chapter 10 that size creates additional challenges and difficulties, including problems of communication and coordination.
- At the same time, the challenges of managing diversification should not suggest that diversification is somehow a wrong or failed strategy. The evidence we have offered in this chapter indicates that high-performing firms are just as likely to be more diversified as they are to be less diversified, and low-performing firms are just as likely to be less diversified as they are to be more diversified. Furthermore, statistical tests comparing and contrasting the mean levels of performance across the high-performing more- and less-diversified groups and across the low-performing more- and less-diversified groups are not significantly different. In short, *higher levels of diversification are not incompatible with high performance, and higher levels of diversification do not necessarily imply that firms will suffer lower performance levels.*

We have argued that the critical factor in determining success is the level of management expertise in formulating and implementing corporate strategy. Few tasks are as difficult as managing a diversified firm, and even the most talented management teams are likely to encounter constraints on the amount of diversity they can manage. The evidence presented in this chapter suggests that the management teams of large, diversified firms possess a variety of well-developed mental models that provide them with powerful understandings of how to manage their firms. Experienced managers possess 1) well developed understandings that allow them to articulate clearly the purpose or definition of their firm to both external constituencies and their own employees, and 2) a highly developed set of cause-effect understandings of those factors that contribute to high performance.

These cause-effect understandings play a key role in the selection of strategies and the development of management processes to succeed with those strategies. Many diversification studies have failed to find a strong relationship between diversification and performance because they have lacked measures to assess the quality of managerial understandings.

These conclusions suggest that managers and the skills they bring to their firms are key or fundamental organizational resources that will determine whether those firms enjoy sustained competitive advantage. The quality of the mental models that managers develop is especially vital in determining the success of their firms' diversification strategies.

Key Points

- Corporate strategy is concerned with determining the appropriate scale (size) and scope (extent of diversification) of business firms. Firms can be small or large and they can focus on a single line of business or they can participate in many diverse industries.
- Firms diversify for a variety of reasons, including the desire to grow, to more fully utilize existing resources and capabilities, to escape from undesirable or unattractive industry environments, and to make use of surplus cash flows.
- Vertical integration, horizontal or related diversification, conglomerate or unrelated diversification, and global diversification are four major types of diversification. Each has a number of advantages and disadvantages associated with it and each entails a number of unique management challenges.
- The aim of all corporate strategies should be to achieve synergies. The divisions, segments, and businesses of a firm should create more value together than they would on their own as independent businesses.
- Three ways for firms to achieve synergies are to:
  - Exploit economies of scale,
  - Exploit economies of scope, or
  - Effectively and efficiently allocate financial capital.
- Several factors complicate firms' efforts to achieve synergies, including:
  - A poor understanding of how diversification activities will "fit" or be coordinated with existing businesses.
  - Dangers or risks associated with the acquisition of businesses.
  - Problems associated with the internal development of new businesses.
- As a result, the relationship between diversification and performance is complex. The conventional wisdom suggests that higher levels of diversification lead to lower levels of performance; however, this conventional wisdom has received very little empirical support. Moreover, many successful, highly diversified firms exist.
- Managers' beliefs and understandings play a key role in influencing the relationship between diversification and firm performance. Two specific beliefs or understandings that are key to the successful management of diversification are:
  - Managers' understandings of how their firms' businesses are related.
  - Managers' beliefs about how diversification and corporate strategy should be managed.
- Learning from experience is key to developing skills at managing diversification, and the chapter specifically hypothesizes that *those firms with management teams that have more experience at managing diversification will enjoy higher performance than those firms with management teams that are less experienced at managing diversification.*

Key Questions for Managers

- Have you and other managers at your firm clearly identified and articulated a view about where you are planning to take the firm and the role that diversification and corporate strategy should play in that view of your firm's future?
- What type of diversification strategy is your firm pursuing, and is your firm capitalizing on the advantages of that strategy while minimizing the disadvantages of that strategy?
- Do you and other managers at your firm have an effective understanding of your firm's diversity that describes how your firm's businesses are related and how they are expected to yield synergies? Do you and other managers have an effective understanding about how diversification and corporate strategy should be managed at your firm?

Suggestions for Further Reading

Additionally, links to further resources online—such as cases, articles, and videos—can be found on the book's website, www.routledge.com/textbooks/Duhaime.

Biggadike, E. R. 1979. The risky business of diversification. *Harvard Business Review*, 57(3): 103–111.

Carey, D. C., & Ogden, D., with Roland, J. A. 2004. *The Human Side of M&A: How CEOs Leverage the Most Important Asset in Deal Making*. New York: Oxford University Press.

Child, J., Faulkner, D., & Pitkethly, R. 2001. *The Management of International Acquisitions*. New York: Oxford University Press.

Ghemawat, P. 2007. *Redefining Global Strategy: Crossing Borders in a World Where Differences Still Matter*. Boston: Harvard Business School Publishing.

Goold, M., & Campbell, A. 1990. *Strategies and Styles: The Role of the Centre in Managing Diversified Corporations*. New York: Blackwell Publishers.

Hitt, M. A., Harrison, J. S., & Ireland, R. D. 2001. *Mergers and Acquisitions: A Guide to Creating Value for Stakeholders*. New York: Oxford University Press.

Montgomery, C. A. 1994. Corporate diversification. *Journal of Economic Perspectives*, 8: 163–178.

Porter, M. E. 1987. From competitive advantage to corporate strategy. *Harvard Business Review*, 65(3): 43–59.

Prahalad, C. K., & Bettis, R. A. 1986. The dominant logic: A new linkage between diversity and performance. *Strategic Management Journal*, 7: 485–502.

Ramanujam, V., & Varadarajan, P. 1989. Research on corporate diversification: A synthesis. *Strategic Management Journal*, 10: 523–551.

Reuer, J. J. (Ed.). 2004. *Strategic Alliances: Theory and Evidence*. New York: Oxford University Press.

Ricks, D. A. 1999. *Blunders in International Business* (3rd ed.). Malden, MA: Blackwell Business.

Rumelt, R. P. 1974. *Strategy, Structure and Economic Performance*. Cambridge, MA: Harvard University Press.

Sirower, M. 1997. *The Synergy Trap*. New York: Free Press.

Thackray, J. 1991. Diversification: What it takes to make it work. *Across the Board*, November: 17–23.

Appendix: The Use of Portfolio Management in Diversified Firms to Achieve Financial Synergies

Following the wave of diversification activity that occurred during the 1960s and early 1970s, portfolio management techniques emerged as a very popular tool for managers to develop corporate strategies. Nearly all portfolio management techniques are based on three sets of concepts. First is the concept of product or industry life cycle, introduced in Chapter 8. Life cycle models suggest that all products or services have a natural pattern of emergence, rapid growth, maturity, and eventual decline. Portfolio models build on the life cycle concept to argue that the portfolio of businesses owned by a diversified firm should include a variety of businesses at all stages of the product life cycle; firms with no mature businesses may lack stability and steady cash flows, while firms relying only on slow-growing mature businesses risk eventual decline.

Most portfolio models also build on the concepts of experience or learning curve effects and scale economies. The greater the cumulative output of a particular business the lower its per unit costs should be, and higher levels of output are likely to be associated with economies of scale, thus portfolio models emphasize the importance of businesses acquiring a large market share.

A business's competitive position—market share in most portfolio models—thus becomes a proxy for experience curve effects and scale economies. The greater a particular business's market share the more likely that it is rapidly moving down the experience curve and enjoying economies of scale.

The final concept on which all portfolio models rest is the efficient allocation of capital. Portfolio management techniques view firms as "internal capital markets." Central to all portfolio models is the idea that the businesses of diversified firms are not allowed to operate independently but that corporate managers will actively intervene to transfer capital from some businesses to others. In fact, portfolio models assume that the major task of corporate managers is to balance cash flows between those businesses that generate excess cash and those that require cash in order to grow and prosper.

Using Portfolio Models to Formulate Corporate Strategy

Use of a portfolio model such as the BCG Growth-Share Matrix (as illustrated in Exhibit 10.9) begins by analyzing and placing the diversified firm's businesses along these two dimensions. In BCG's Growth-Share Matrix, market attractiveness is assessed by the industry growth rate, while competitive position is assessed by examining each business's relative market share. As the diversified firm's businesses are analyzed along these two dimensions, they are then placed on the matrix, with each circle representing one business. The circles are scaled according to the size of the business, so that smaller and larger circles represent smaller and larger businesses.

The four quadrants in the Growth-Share Matrix illustrated in Exhibit 10.9 are labeled based on their cash flow characteristics. Businesses in the "Cash Cows" quadrant are, because of their high relative market shares but relatively low rates of growth, most likely to be successful, mature businesses. These businesses are assumed to be generating large amounts of surplus cash. This cash can be transferred to "Question Marks," emerging businesses that have the potential to become "Stars" but need additional capital to fund expansion and marketing activities. "Dogs" are businesses that, because of their low relative market shares and low growth, are deemed to contribute little value to the corporate portfolio; most portfolio models suggest that these businesses should be divested.

The ideal portfolio will vary considerably depending on the unique characteristics and circumstances of different diversified firms, but one central objective of portfolio management

Exhibit 10.9 The BCG Growth-Share Matrix

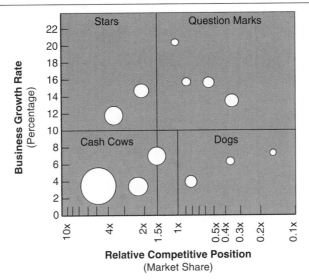

is balance across the quadrants. No managers would want their firms to have only "Dogs." Similarly, a company with a vast majority of its businesses in the "Cash Cows" quadrant might be generating a great deal of cash flow, but it may have few opportunities for future growth. Thus, portfolio management techniques, such as the BCG Growth-Share Matrix, can be very helpful tools for generating thought and discussion among managers about the various businesses of their diversified firms.

More elaborate portfolio models may offer additional insights, but they can also be much more complex and time consuming to use. Furthermore, all portfolio models must be used with caution because a number of factors (discussed below) limit their effectiveness as analytical frameworks.

Nevertheless, like all of the other frameworks and models introduced in this book, portfolio models can be very useful in stimulating thought and discussion among managers, and they may be particularly effective at getting managers to vocalize their beliefs and understandings—their mental models—about their firms' diversification strategies.

Limitations of Portfolio Management Techniques

Though widely taught and used, portfolio management models have a number of limitations, and fewer managers of large diversified companies appear to be relying much on portfolio management models to guide the formulation of their corporate strategies. One concern or limitation is whether portfolio models, such as the BCG Growth-Share Matrix, are really very useful for most companies.

Because competitive position in the BCG Matrix is determined by relative market share, by definition, only one business in an industry will be on the left side of the matrix's *relative* market share dimension. Many companies enjoy great success without their businesses having large market shares (in other words, their businesses are either "Dogs" or "Question Marks"). In addition, the emphasis that portfolio models place on cash flow management ignores the challenge of building linkages across businesses in order to achieve economies of scale and scope.

Furthermore, many of the basic assumptions underlying portfolio models do not hold upon closer examination. For example, research has shown that "Dogs" can be a "manager's best friend." In other words, these low-growth, low-share businesses do not necessarily have the unattractive profitability and cash flow characteristics that most portfolio models assume.[72]

Perhaps the main factor limiting the use of portfolio management techniques is the pressure firms receive from investors when they reallocate cash internally. Pressure from corporate raiders and institutional investors during the past decade has made it unlikely that firms can transfer large amounts of cash from profitable business units to "Question Mark" businesses with high risks. Instead, institutional investors will pressure firms to divest these "Question Mark" businesses in order to "increase shareholder value."

Chapter 11

Organizational Structure and the Implementation of Strategy

Throughout this book we have emphasized the importance of managerial thinking in the effective strategic management of firms, and noted the critical role managerial thinking plays in decisions about the formulation of organizational strategies and the implementation of those strategies. Earlier chapters addressing business definition, business strategy, and corporate strategy (the "what" of strategic management) noted that firms differ greatly in their ability to implement strategies effectively, and that managerial thinking about appropriate organizational structure for strategy implementation is an important potential source of competitive advantage.

The overall aims of any organizational structure are to implement the strategic initiatives that managers have formulated and to make organizations responsive to their managers, their shareholders or owners, and developments in their larger competitive environments. By developing especially effective structures, managers can give their organizations a significant competitive advantage.

Chapter Objectives

The specific objectives of this chapter are to:

- Define structure and describe its role in the implementation of strategy.
- Identify and describe the different components of organizational structure.
- Identify some of the problems associated with organizing and describe how the various components of organizational structure can be used to overcome these organizational problems that are common to nearly all firms and businesses.
- Discuss some of the emerging issues that are likely to have an impact on organizing and organizational structures in the future.

The Characteristics of Business Organizations

In all organizations, managers have to think about the implementation of strategy, how to accomplish the plans and achieve the goals. In the smallest entrepreneurial businesses, we may see the entrepreneurs literally "doing it all"—working tirelessly to do every task themselves in the launch of their businesses or aided only by some immediate family—the classic "started in a garage" story of a business startup. But entrepreneurs who succeed in the startup stage soon pass the point where "doing it all" themselves is possible. They must rapidly expand the number of employees they have, and sometimes locations and other factors as well, and must delegate many tasks in order to meet demand for their product or service.

Organizing for effective implementation of organizational strategy, therefore, is critical for *all* firms beyond the entrepreneurial startup stage. It is obvious that the very large size and high level of complexity of firms like General Electric and Procter & Gamble, and the challenges of managing and coordinating such large organizations, force managers to focus on developing sophisticated structures. But it is important to recognize that the topics of this chapter apply to all firms beyond the entrepreneurial startup stage—the small and medium-size firms that make up the vast majority of business organizations worldwide as well as large firms like General Electric and Procter & Gamble. Indeed, failures of small and medium-size firms too often can be traced not to weaknesses in their strategies but rather to weaknesses in the implementation of their strategies.

How managers uniquely organize their firms can have enormous consequences for organizational effectiveness and performance, and organizational structure may be one of the most powerful—if not the most powerful—tools for achieving competitive advantage. Carol Bartz, CEO of Yahoo, summed up the importance of structure for innovation, "Organizations can get in the way of innovation, because people are all bound up," and don't know if they have the freedom to make decisions.[1] Similarly, here's how two respected organizational theorists assess the importance of organizational structure:

> most of the old, reliable sources of competitive advantage are drying up. No longer can companies located in a handful of money centers rely on exclusive access to capital, no longer can the Xeroxes and Polaroids of the world rely on the exclusive, proprietary technology that once assured them of a virtual monopoly. Markets that were once the exclusive domain of local producers are now fair game for competitors headquartered halfway around the globe. And highly skilled employees, their loyalty shaken by years of corporate cutbacks and downsizing, feel free to offer their services to the highest bidder…
>
> In this volatile environment where instability is the norm, we're convinced that the last remaining source of truly sustainable competitive advantage lies in what we've come to describe as "organizational capabilities"—*the unique ways in which each organization structures its work and motivates its people to achieve clearly articulated strategic objectives.*[2]

The growing size and complexity of firms and businesses thus requires the development of organizational processes and structures in order to implement their strategies. Today, all businesses will have the following characteristics:[3]

Division of Labor

Employees in most companies generally do not perform a wide range of duties; instead, work is organized so that employees specialize in a particular task or set of related tasks. Organizations recruit or train specialists to perform these tasks, and such a division of labor allows these specialists to become increasingly adept at performing their job duties. For example, it would be very uncommon for a company to hire an individual to make some sales calls in the morning, do some manufacturing work in the early afternoon, and then perform some bookkeeping activities before leaving work at the end of the day. Instead, organizations hire marketing, manufacturing, and accounting specialists who then work within their respective areas of functional expertise.

Hierarchy

Hierarchy is another characteristic of nearly all business organizations. Hierarchy is the "organization chart," or the arrangement of managers and employees into superior-subordinate relationships. The concept of *hierarchical levels* refers to the levels of managerial decision-making activity. A "tall" structure would have many (perhaps as many as eight) hierarchical levels from the CEO down to the lowest level of subordinates, while a "flat" structure would have fewer hierarchical levels (perhaps only two or three in companies that are just beyond the startup stage). Closely related to the concept of hierarchical levels is the concept of *span of control*. Span of control refers to the number of subordinates reporting to a manager. The greater a manager's span of control, the more subordinates that manager would have reporting to him or her.

Decisions are Based on Rules, Policies, and Standard Operating Procedures That Seek to Promote Efficiency

In most organizations, employees are not free to do whatever they want in any way they wish. Instead, their actions are guided by uniform rules, policies, and standard operating procedures that aim to promote standardization and efficiency. In most organizations, such policies and standard operating procedures are a very important component of structure, and, as we shall discuss later, such rules and standard operating procedures can have significant positive benefits and, at times, some negative consequences for organizational performance.

The Tendency to Become Inflexible and Resist Change

Finally, as noted at the end of Chapter 5, one key characteristic of most organizations is their stability. Often, organizations rigidly adhere to their rules, policies, and standard operating procedures even when circumstances might suggest that exceptions or changes in policies might be warranted. Once set in motion, organizations can become quite resistant to change, preferring to "do things the way they've always been done." As a result, most organizations tend to resist leadership that initiates change. Mintzberg emphasizes this tendency, noting that all organizations are characterized by "bureaucratic momentum" and a desire for stability that can be quite pathological because businesses and firms must operate in dynamic environments.[4]

The remainder of this chapter is organized as follows: First, we define structure and take a closer look at the various components of organizational structure. We then consider some of the central issues and problems that are common to nearly all organizations and discuss how structures can be altered or modified to alleviate some of these problems. Finally, we describe several emerging issues that are likely to have an impact on how organizations structure their operations in the future.

A Definition of Organizational Structure

Although hierarchy is the most obvious or visible component of structure, organizational structure includes much more than hierarchy or organization charts.

As already noted above, another important component of organizational structure is the written and unwritten rules, standard operating procedures, and systems that constitute organizations' marketing, production, personnel, and compensation policies as well as their accounting, financial control, and information systems. In addition, the lifeblood of any organization is the information and knowledge that resides in and is passed among organizational members and their departments. We have also come to realize that an organization's culture or its "informal structure" can be just as important as if not more important than its formal hierarchical structure, policies and systems, and flows of information. Thus, we will define structure broadly to include any mechanisms that facilitate the formulation and implementation of strategy and the overall coordination of the business enterprise. These mechanisms include:

- Hierarchical reporting relationships.
- Policies, standard operating procedures, and control systems.
- Information systems and flows of information moving through organizations.
- Culture.

The challenge confronting general managers is to combine these components into appropriate organizational structures that: 1) effectively implement chosen strategies, and 2) make their firms responsive to the leadership of owners and managers as well as to changes in the larger competitive environments in which firms operate. And as we will emphasize, this means much more than a re-organization or restructuring of lines and boxes on a chart. It needs to address critical issues such as the impact on information flow and business processes, effects on customers, and interrelationships among employees, to name a few.[5] In other words, these mechanisms need to *fit* together. When a change is made in one area, such as reporting relationships on the organization chart, managers need to consider the implications in the other areas. Policies may need to change, information systems may need to be adjusted, or even new norms created. As suggested by our model of strategic management, illustrated in Exhibit 11.1, these decisions about organizational structure will be influenced by managers' beliefs about how to organize and implement strategy. Finally, as suggested in Chapter 3, managers' beliefs and understandings are likely to be developed by their own trial-and-error learning, imitation of other firms' effective structures, and their own creativity and ingenuity.

The Components of Organizational Structure

Hierarchy

Hierarchy is both the most visible and the most widely studied aspect of structure. This section focuses on three types of hierarchical structures—functional, multidivisional, and matrix—and examines the strengths and limitations of each type of structure. Later in the chapter, we examine some new types of hierarchical structures.

Exhibit 11.1 Managers' Beliefs, the Strategic Decisions Studied in This Book, and Their Influence on Performance and Competitive Advantage

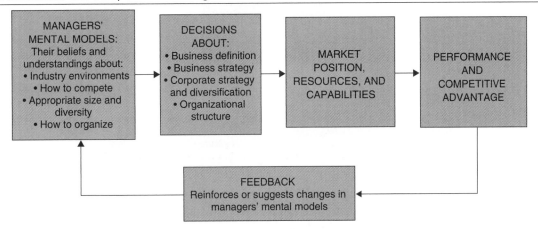

Functional Structures

Functional structures organize activities around functional activities or departments, such as manufacturing, marketing, research and development, and sales, as illustrated in Exhibit 11.2. The principal advantage of the functional structure is that its division of the organization into departments allows employees to specialize and become increasingly skilled at what they do. Because of its emphasis on specialization and efficiency, the functional structure has been described as the natural way for most firms, even fairly large firms, to organize their operations.[6] According to Naomi Stanford, a recognized expert in the field of organization design, the functional structure is well suited for firms operating with the following conditions:

- There are stable and undifferentiated markets.
- There is a successful, control-focused culture.
- There is a single product or service line.
- There is scale or expertise within each function.
- There are long product development lifecycles.
- The organization works to common standards.[7]

Yet many problems are associated with functional structures. First, communication and motivational difficulties can be particularly vexing in functional organizations. The various departments of a firm organized along functional lines must communicate with each other, but because of the structure's design, most information must flow up through functional "chimneys" before it can flow across to another functional department. Though it might seem reasonable that an employee in the manufacturing or production department who has a marketing question could simply telephone or e-mail a colleague in the marketing department, this is rarely done in practice, except in small, new organizations. Rather than simply telephoning a colleague in the marketing department, the manufacturing employee with a question would instead write a memorandum to his or her manager who might then relay the request to the vice president

Exhibit 11.2 An Illustration of Functional Structure

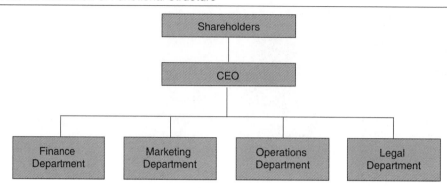

of manufacturing who would then forward the request to the vice president of marketing who would forward the memo to a marketing manager who would then deliver the memo to the employee he or she deems most qualified to answer the query.

Why this cumbersome process? Primarily because it keeps employees' supervisors informed and allows them to provide their input to policy questions.

Furthermore, the process leaves a "paper trail," allowing employees to show that they have kept supervisors informed. At the same time, however, the process increases the amount of time required to transmit data, slows decision making, and increases the likelihood that both the request for data as well as the reply will be distorted or altered as they move through the organization's hierarchy, all of which can undermine strategy implementation.

Also, in most functional organizations, some departments or divisions are designated *profit centers*—seen as responsible for generating the company's revenues, while other departments or divisions are designated *cost centers*—seen perhaps as important, but not responsible for generating revenues. Without responsibility for generating revenue, employees in cost centers can develop morale and motivation problems.

Finally, functional structures tend to overload top managers.[8] Because most information goes up before it goes across departments in functional organizations, much management time is spent just relaying information. Furthermore, top managers must referee disputes that inevitably arise between functional departments.

If these motivational and informational limitations become so severe that they prevent managers from noticing or responding to changes in their competitive environments, or if these problems limit the ability of their firms to effectively implement strategies, then changes in the hierarchy may be needed.

Most managers have found that as organizations grow and become increasingly diversified, they must make major changes to their firms' hierarchies. One response to these challenges was the development and adoption of multidivisional structures.

Multidivisional (Product, Process, Geographical, and Customer) Structures

As just suggested, the growth and increasing diversity of some early corporate giants during the first decades of the twentieth century resulted in a variety of organizational problems, including inefficiencies in information flows and top management overload. Through a process of trial-and-error learning, managers of several large firms began to develop **multidivisional structures**.[9]

Multidivisional structures are based on the reality that many firms consist of several distinct operating segments or businesses or geographical regions. Instead of operating and trying to coordinate the activities of these different businesses as if they were a single firm, the multidivisional structure explicitly divides these businesses into autonomous units or "divisions." As illustrated in Exhibit 11.3, these divisions can be made along business or product lines as illustrated in part A of the exhibit, or along geographical lines as illustrated in part B.

A few firms adopted multidivisional structures early in the twentieth century, but the adoption of the multidivisional structure by major firms quickly accelerated in the post-World War II years.[10] In fact, the adoption of the multidivisional structure—and administrative or

Exhibit 11.3 Illustrations of Multidivisional Structure

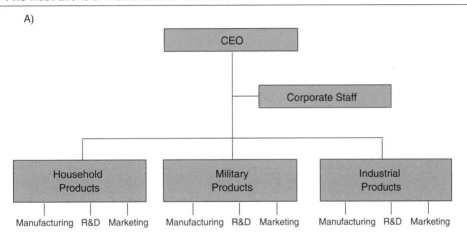

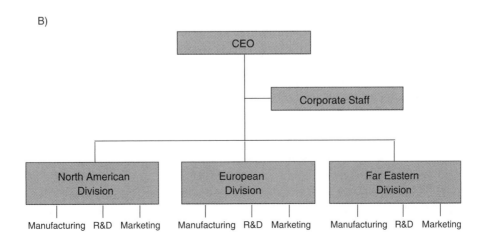

management innovation—by nearly all *Fortune* 500 firms in the years after World War II is an excellent example of how imitation by managers leads to the diffusion of innovations throughout the economy.

The divisionalization of business activities that characterizes the multidivisional structure has a number of advantages for large, diversified firms. First, the multidivisional structure decentralizes decision making, freeing firms' top managers from day-to-day decision making so they can focus on more strategic issues. In the multidivisional organization, most tactical and strategic decisions affecting each division are made by the managers in those divisions. Thus, corporate-level managers can focus on more strategic issues, including the allocation of capital to the various divisions, the overall direction of the firm, and decisions to buy or sell businesses.

Johnson & Johnson is a company that excels with its multidivisional structure and realizes this advantage. With 250 operating companies in 57 different countries, decentralization is necessary for J&J, but the advantages of the company's extreme decentralization are apparent.[11] By standardizing certain processes in staff and support areas but not in operations, the company allows leaders to focus on running their businesses and provides each business with considerable independence and motivation.

Furthermore, the multidivisional structure improves accountability. A key component of any multidivisional structure is the "corporate staff" (illustrated in Exhibit 11.3), which serves both advisory and assessment functions. The corporate staff holds division managers accountable for decisions made in their units by measuring and monitoring the performance of each division. Thus, the corporate staff "keeps score," summarizing for corporate managers how each of their firms' various businesses or geographic regions are performing.

In addition, the multidivisional structure can improve the allocation of resources by requiring all divisions to submit investment proposals to the corporate staff, which then applies common criteria (i.e., return on capital or hurdle rate requirements) to evaluate and fund these investment proposals. In many respects, this internal competition for capital is the most distinctive feature of the multidivisional enterprise. Cash flows in the multidivisional firm are always sent to the corporate treasury and

> are not automatically returned to their sources but instead are exposed to an internal competition. Investment proposals from the several divisions are solicited and evaluated by the general management. [T]his assignment of cash flows to high yield uses is the most fundamental attribute of the [multidivisional] enterprise.[12]

In other words, one business or geographic region may generate considerable cash flow, but if it has fewer profitable opportunities for reinvesting those cash flows, the cash can be reallocated to other divisions in the organization that have more profitable investment opportunities. In sum, multidivisional structures are effective when:

- There are different measurements for success across the firm's businesses.
- Divisions have different competitive environments.
- There is little synergy across product or service lines.
- There are different production processes and distribution channels.
- There are different cultures and workforce types.[13]

In spite of their many advantages over functional structures when firms become very large and diversified, multidivisional structures also suffer from a number of limitations and disadvantages. First, each division in a multidivisional firm will have its own array of functional marketing, production, and service departments as illustrated in Exhibit 11.3. Instead of centralizing all manufacturing or marketing activities in a single manufacturing or marketing department, the multidivisional firm will typically have as many manufacturing and marketing departments as it has divisions. As a result, many functional activities will necessarily be duplicated once or many times in the multidivisional firm. This duplication is costly and can prevent firms organized along multidivisional lines from realizing many potential economies of scale and scope that were envisioned when the organization's strategy was formulated.

A second problem with multidivisional firms is that top managers can become very far removed from divisional activities. In fact, it is not uncommon for top managers of multidivisional firms to have little if any expertise about the activities or operations of the various divisions of their firms. Though a key advantage of the multidivisional structure is that it provides top managers with time to focus on "the big picture" and more strategic issues, top managers may, as a consequence, lack the day-to-day experience or familiarity with operating divisions that can be crucial when reviewing investment proposals or when dealing with strategic issues or a crisis within a particular business.

The transfer pricing dilemma is another problem common to any multidivisional firm in which one division sells components, products, or services to another division in the same firm. In spite of a long history of working with transfer pricing problems, few companies have been able to develop solutions that leave both selling and buying divisions totally pleased. The key problem is determining the appropriate prices that supplying divisions should receive for the transferred goods and services. At the risk of oversimplifying the problem, it is easy to see that if prices are set equal to market prices (or higher), supplying divisions are likely to be pleased but buying divisions may feel that they should receive some sort of price break or that they are not enjoying the same sort of flexibility that they would have if they were dealing with external suppliers. On the other hand, if prices are set lower than market prices, buying divisions may be pleased but supplying divisions are likely to feel cheated. In either case, morale problems in one of the divisions may ensue, potentially undermining strategy implementation.

Multidivisional structures can result in a short-term focus and an undesirable level of competition for resources among divisions. Because investment dollars tend to be allocated to those divisions showing the most promise and because firms tend to promote those managers who show the best results, division managers may feel tremendous pressure to report strong performance in the short run. By emphasizing short-run performance goals, however, division managers may pursue activities that will actually harm their business units over the longer run. For example, expenditures for marketing and R&D efforts may be needed to maximize long-term market share and profitability, yet these expenditures will reduce a division's quarterly net income. A division executive hoping to "look good" or aiming to improve the division's results might decide to forgo these expenditures, thereby improving the next quarter's results at the expense of longer-term performance. Thus, it is important for companies to develop compensation plans that reward division managers based on their performance on multiple criteria, including short- and long-term performance of their divisions as well as their contribution to overall corporate goals and objectives.

Cross-Functional or Matrix Structures

Cross-functional or matrix structures represent a hybrid hierarchy in which a functional structure is overlaid or placed on top of a multidivisional (or geographical or product) structure. Exhibit 11.4 illustrates the types of matrix, or cross-functional team, structures that nearly all of the major automobile companies have adopted over the last two decades. The cross-functional structure illustrated in Exhibit 11.4 shows that the major automobile companies are organized along both product lines (e.g., small-car platform team, large-car platform team, truck platform team) as well as functional lines (e.g., engineering, production, marketing, and finance). Employees retain functional specialties, such as engineering, marketing, or production, but the company has placed employees in "cross-functional" product teams. As a result, engineers, marketing, and production people all work together on a "platform team" such as the small car team or the truck team. Other types of cross-functional structures are obviously possible; a firm pursuing a global strategy, for example, might be organized along both product and geographical lines.

Cross-functional structures are especially useful in a situation like that of the automobile companies when traditional functional or multidivisional structures would not be likely to distribute information adequately throughout the organization. In the past, the "chimney" problem (described earlier in the section on functional structure) has been particularly acute at U.S. automobile companies.

Engineers often designed cars that were difficult to build and/or that consumers didn't want. Ensuing discussions to correct problems and communicate across engineering, production, and marketing departments would take months or even years. Already the advantage of cross-functional product teams is seen in much shorter product development lead times and significantly lower product development costs at the major automobile companies.[14]

Exhibit 11.4 The Matrix or Cross-Functional Structure Adopted by Nearly All Major Automobile Companies

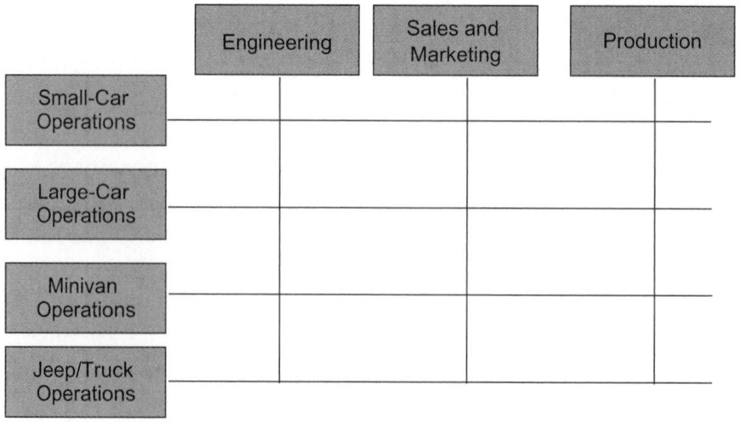

Some pharmaceutical companies are now making use of "drug discovery teams" to speed the development of new products. Like other types of cross-functional teams, these drug discovery teams consist of researchers who have different types of expertise but are focusing on a common problem. Working closely together, these discovery teams develop a common body of knowledge or team mental model that facilitates research.[15]

To summarize, a matrix or cross-functional structure is most appropriate when:

- The cost of labor is a primary driver.
- Projects require specialized skills and knowledge and these vary greatly.
- Major work is project based.[16]

Although the major advantage of the cross-functional structure is its ability to improve information flows, the matrix structure also has a number of drawbacks. One problem is often referred to as the "two-boss problem."

Employees working in a firm organized as a matrix will find that they often report to two bosses. In the automobile company example described earlier, an engineer working on the small car platform team is responsible to the head of the engineering department as well as to the head of the small car platform team.

Thus, if goals are not congruent throughout the firm or if the organization lacks an effective mechanism for settling conflicts and disagreements, the cross-functional structure can become unworkable. In fact, cross-functional structures have often produced either power struggles or outright anarchy as product managers struggle with functional managers.

Another problem that is sometimes encountered in cross-functional organizations has been referred to as "groupitis," or the tendency for cross-functional team members to believe that every decision needs to be made as a group.[17] Although group decision making offers many benefits, it can also slow progress if the group becomes bogged down in deciding too many details.

Another limitation of the cross-functional form that the major automobile companies and some high-technology companies have encountered is that specialists who are working on a product team often become so involved in working on the product that they lose touch with their specialty area. For example, some automobile companies have found a trade-off between the benefits of better information flow from having their engineers involved in product teams and the cost of having those engineers unaware of new developments in engineering technologies. Some companies have dealt with this challenge by having employees rotate into and out of product teams on fairly strict schedules.

We've already described how different hierarchies are more and less effective at moving information. For example, we noted that the automobile industry has embraced cross-functional structures and teams to better share information and overcome the limitations of moving information through or between functional silos or chimneys. Whenever the context demands the dissemination and application of information, we can expect more and more companies in different industries to adopt cross-functional structures as a way to improve decision making. Later in this chapter, we examine the *virtual* or *modular* structures and other new structural forms that many companies are adopting in order to more effectively manage information flows.

Many global companies have adopted cross-functional structures as a way to manage their international business activities and to improve coordination and information flows. Global companies have unique and significant organizational challenges. The structures that the managers of global companies adopt must assist them in their efforts to exploit opportunities to achieve economies of scale by centralizing their marketing and production activities whenever possible. At the same time, the structures of international companies must also accommodate differences in national cultures and variations in business practices. And, as in any organization, the structures of international companies must serve to coordinate business activities and to move information quickly and accurately across borders and around the world.

Policies, Standard Operating Procedures, and Control Systems

Though organizational charts or hierarchies of supervisor-subordinate relationships are the most visible aspect of structures, much of the actual work of organizations and the implementation of strategies are accomplished through their policies, standard operating procedures, and control systems. Most organizational behavior is highly routinized; rather than "reinventing the wheel" every time a unit of work must be performed, organizations standardize most activities and functions in order to increase efficiency and reduce variability.

Thus, most large and even medium-size organizations have thick policy manuals describing routines and standard operating procedures for accomplishing an array of tasks, including everything from market research, engineering, and personnel recruitment to manufacturing, marketing, sales, and after-sales service activities. Furthermore, even strategic tasks, such as performance monitoring and the review of investment proposals, are routinized. As a result, accounting data from one period are comparable with data from other periods, and investment proposals are not considered uniquely but in light of uniform financial criteria.

The importance of this component of organizational structure should not be underestimated; indeed, it is probably fair to state that organizations' policies, standard operating procedures, and control systems play a critical role in influencing their successes in implementing their strategies as well as their failures. On the positive side, high performance is almost always associated with an effective set of policies, procedures, or systems. A low-cost, high-quality manufacturing operation is based on a set of policies and procedures that reflect a great deal of learning and prior experience. And, as suggested in the preceding chapter, firms make a series of successful acquisitions not because of luck or the intuition of their top managers, but because they have developed a set of procedures that helped them identify attractive acquisition candidates, execute the purchases, and successfully integrate the new units. Managers of many organizations believe that their firms' financial control systems are important sources of competitive advantage.

At the same time, organizations' procedures and systems can harm organizational effectiveness and even be pathological. Highly routinized policies and procedures can limit organizational flexibility and adaptability, and can make organizations very unresponsive to changes in their competitive environments. Recall from Chapter 6 that we suggested that managers' understandings of their firms' definitions tend to become tightly coupled with their firms' strategies, policies, and procedures. Because of this tight coupling and because firms' policies and procedures tend to be so highly routinized, managers can come to use their organizations' policies, procedures, and systems over and over again in an automatic, almost unthinking way. Although this automatic or reflexive use of policies, procedures, and systems minimizes ambiguity and promotes rapid decision making, it can become a serious liability if environmental conditions or competitive circumstances change.

Organizational policies and procedures can also unwittingly reward the wrong types of behaviors and, therefore, produce undesirable results. One example of how a company's systems can have an adverse effect on strategy and performance is provided by the Harvard Business School case study of the Dexter Corporation.[18] In this case, one of Dexter's businesses manufactures a key component for firms in the rapidly growing semiconductor industry. One Dexter executive summarizes the company's problem this way:

> We were doing very well but we were underinvesting in what turned out to be a very high-growth industry. We weren't putting in the marketing dollars and we weren't putting in the R&D dollars. We were growing … at close to 20 percent, however, the semiconductor market was growing at 30 percent. So we were losing market share and didn't know it.[19]

And what role did Dexter's structure play in fostering this problem? First, until the time of the case, Dexter lacked some sort of monitoring system for gauging company performance against the competitive environment. The case also suggests a second factor, however. The casewriter again quotes the same Dexter executive:

> I would say going back one, two, or three years ago, that due to the constraints of the profit-sharing and the incentive program for the divisions, we probably underinvested in our two growth businesses.[20]

In other words, one of the company's control systems—its compensation system—which rewarded division executives on the basis of their division's bottom line return on investment—discouraged division executives from spending what was needed for marketing and R&D efforts in order to maximize the company's long-run performance outcomes.

Wal-Mart's attempts to enter the German market in the 1990s also show the negative effects of automatically or reflexively using certain organizational procedures and systems. Instead of being innovative and researching the local culture of the market it wanted to enter, Wal-Mart resorted to its general strategies that brought it success in the United States. The result of Wal-Mart's apparent ignorance of the local culture resulted in nothing short of a fiasco.

Information Systems and Information Flows

Although a traditional aim of structure has been the organization of work—especially physical work or tasks—to implement or achieve strategic objectives, it now appears that the implementation of strategy is becoming increasingly dependent on the acquisition, storage, distribution, and application of information. Many companies have found that information and systems for managing the flow of information can be important sources of competitive advantage. The text has already noted how Wal-Mart has successfully exploited information and information technology to provide it with the most sophisticated logistics and inventory management systems of any retailing firm. Nearly all large retailing firms have come to realize that their ability to manage information about their costs, inventories, and customer preferences and shopping patterns can have a profound impact on their success in implementing their strategies.

One important factor behind the revolution in manufacturing is the incorporation of information technology to handle the flow of materials and labor through the manufacturing process. Computerized information systems allow companies to process vast amounts of marketing, production, and human resources data. Highly sophisticated information systems, such as MRP (materials requirement planning) and SAP, not only schedule production processes but they also automatically order raw materials, control inventories, and maintain general ledgers and other accounting records.

It is not enough to simply collect and manipulate information. The proliferation of computers and other information technology has vastly increased the ability of companies to collect, store, and distribute information. How that information is used and whether it is used in a way that offers companies a competitive advantage has quickly become the central question for the managers of firms in many industries.

Online businesses have the ability to collect vast amounts of information about their customers—when they enter the website, how often they enter, whether they come back, which pages they view, how long they spend on each page, whether they buy, how much they buy, what combinations of products they buy—but they frequently lack the ability to process this information. And, even if they could, they would still have to assess whether they are analyzing the right kinds of data and whether the insights they glean from their data processing efforts are worth the cost.

Even more challenging for online business firms "is to analyze and understand the behavior of the consumer and do it in real time, while the consumer is in the middle of the transaction."[21] While this is, indeed, a lofty goal, it's easy to see how an Amazon.com or other online business firm might be able to offer its customers a truly extraordinary level of personalized service if it can develop the information processing capabilities to offer its customers recommendations and shopping advice in a real-time fashion.

Organizational Culture

If we think of organizations' hierarchical reporting relationships and their policies, procedures, systems, and information flows as more formal aspects of structure, then their cultures are a more informal, but no less important, aspect of structure. Anyone who has been involved for any length of time in businesses, schools, clubs, or religious institutions knows that nearly all organizations have cultures—widely shared norms and values—that have a powerful influence on their activities and operations. And, culture can have significant positive and negative impacts on performance. In fact, an organization's culture can be both an important source of sustained competitive advantage as well as a serious drag on its effectiveness.[22] As Edgar Schein, one of the preeminent writers on culture has said: "Culture matters. It matters because decisions made without awareness of the operative cultural forces may have unanticipated and undesirable consequences."[23]

In many cases, an organization's culture reflects the myths and realities surrounding a founder or a key leader of the company. For example, the distinctiveness of the culture at Herman Miller can be traced to its founder D. J. DePree, and his son Max, who succeeded him as chief executive officer.[24] Both valued the importance of employee involvement and ownership in the business. The company's "Scanlon plan," in which employees are also owners of the business and enjoy profit sharing, not only follows from the company's culture, but also strongly complements it. Southwest Airlines also has a celebrated culture that reflects the influence of its legendary former chief executive, Herb Kelleher. Key features of Southwest's culture include an emphasis on decentralization of decision making, employee autonomy, and the importance of having fun at work.

An organization's culture can also be derived from or associated with its definition or identity so that those characteristics that make the organization distinctive in the eyes of customers or other external constituencies are also internalized as norms or values by the organization's employees. Again, under Kelleher's influence, Southwest almost certainly developed a distinctive culture early on, but as Southwest has grown and prospered in an industry that is characterized by stiff competition and very inconsistent profitability, Southwest's employees have almost certainly internalized their company's success and view themselves as "winners" who work for a "winning" organization. In this way, even strong cultures can be further reinforced and strengthened.

These examples also suggest how culture gets transmitted to employees. Quite often, new employees are socialized into an organization's culture as veteran employees pass along stories and myths. Stories about a dynamic leader, an employee's extraordinary efforts, a remarkable turnaround that saved the company from bankruptcy, or any other epic, offer new employees a powerful model for their behavior.

The development and communication of effective cultures can be an important source of competitive advantage because they can provide employees with a sense of meaning and purposefulness. In his remarkable book, *Leadership Is an Art*, former Herman Miller CEO, Max DePree, writes,

> Every family, every college, every corporation, every institution needs tribal storytellers. The penalty for failing to listen is to lose one's history, one's historical context, one's binding values....
>
> As a culture or a corporation grows older and more complex, the communications naturally and inevitably become more sophisticated and crucial. An increasingly large part that communication plays in expanding cultures is to pass along values to new members and reaffirm those values to old hands.[25]

Effective cultures also motivate the types of behaviors that are important to organizational success in strategy implementation. For example, if culture helps to foster certain norms and behaviors that are desired by the organization or consistent with its goals and objectives, then culture can take the place of much supervisory activity.[26] In other words, organizations can establish formal supervisory and other structural controls to ensure employee compliance, and/ or they can develop informal structural mechanisms, such as a strong culture, that can socialize employees into the organization's norms, goals, and objectives and encourage appropriate employee behaviors—a less expensive and usually far more effective alternative.

On the other hand, culture can also slow or retard organizational adaptation to change. If employees become so entrenched in their organization's way of doing things that they cannot objectively evaluate new developments in their firm's environment, then culture can have devastating consequences.[27] Donald Katz, in his analysis of the decline Sears, Roebuck experienced in retailing, found that the company's strong culture had prevented its managers from understanding the changes that were occurring in retailing:

> None of the consultants [hired by Sears] had ever encountered such awesome cultural and political impediments to altering an economic organization. They all sensed the richness and religiosity of the contrived family of Sears, and though they believed it continued to be the best of America in so many ways, they believed also that the Sears system was inimical to the survival of a great enterprise.[28]

Culture can also lead to fundamental problems in a company. Take for example a *Wall Street Journal* article, "Secretive Culture Led Toyota Astray," which highlights the impact Toyota's culture had on the company's early attempts to suppress the acceleration problems with many of its vehicles.[29] Or the critique of GM's corporate culture by a one-time GM executive, "GM's culture shows little tolerance for dissent, little appetite for making hard decisions and an insularity that has made it seem sometimes "tone-deaf" to broader societal concerns like the environment."[30] Similarly, many critics familiar with Enron believe that an arrogant culture was a major reason for the downfall of the company.

Thus, culture can be a double-edged sword, providing meaning, helping to socialize new employees, and motivating desired behaviors for implementing current organizational strategies, but culture can also be dangerous if it prevents managers and employees from being open to new ideas and new developments in their firms' competitive environments.

Issues and Problems in Organizing

When an individual sits down to play a video game, his or her commands are executed immediately and precisely. General managers, in spite of impressive job titles, high-paying salaries, and willing subordinates, face a much different situation, however. In spite of their power and prestige, even the chief executive officers of the world's largest corporations find that the most carefully designed strategies often fail to get implemented because of a variety of organizational issues and problems. Here we will review some of these issues and describe how managers can use the various components of organizational structure to resolve these problems.

Centralization Versus Decentralization

Whether their firms are small or large, one important issue that all managers confront is the appropriate degree of centralization and decentralization. The more managers centralize decision making, the more control they can exercise over their firms. Centralized decision making can facilitate rapid implementation of strategies in some situations. It can also improve coordination, and a high degree of centralization may be required in vertically integrated organizations when different business units depend on each other for raw materials, components, and services. Effective management of related diversification strategies may also require a good deal of centralization in order to ensure that the related business units act on and realize the envisioned economies of scale and scope.

At the same time, decentralization can have a number of advantages. Decentralization gives lower-level employees and managers more opportunities to participate in organizational decision making. Decentralized decision making can enhance the esteem and morale of those employees and managers by making them feel as though they play important roles in their firms. Johnson & Johnson has already been mentioned as a company that excels with its decentralized structure, and its leadership development is well-respected by many people. Another decentralized company that has been a good breeding ground for leaders is the multinational conglomerate General Electric. Because lower-level employees are allowed to make important decisions, employees feel more responsible for their work.

Another example that highlights the advantages of decentralization is the contract that franchise owners of Great Harvest Bread Company Owners sign with the parent company owners. The first page of the contract emphasizes the company's desire for franchise owners to operate in a very decentralized way—"ANYTHING not expressly prohibited by the language of this Agreement IS ALLOWED"—and thereby encourages individual autonomy, initiative, creativity, and learning. Moreover, Great Harvest Bread Company provides individual franchise owners with many ways to share what they are learning at their franchise with other franchise owners. In such a way, the entire organization can get smarter and smarter.

Furthermore, because lower-level managers and employees in most organizations are more likely to be aware of unique or special circumstances surrounding various issues, decentralization of decision making is likely to lead to better decisions. And, because lower-level employees and managers are probably the first to become aware of changes or the potential for changes in the competitive environment, decentralized decision making can improve organizational flexibility and responsiveness to environmental change.

Centralization and decentralization thus have both advantages and disadvantages, and firms' unique missions and needs will determine the appropriate degree of centralization or decentralization. The various hierarchical structures that have been described here vary significantly in terms of their centralization and decentralization with functional structures being the most centralized and the cross-functional teams found in most matrix structures quite decentralized from top management. The degree of centralization can vary considerably inside any type of structure, however. For example, even in relatively decentralized multidivisional structures in which division managers are given a good deal of responsibility and control over their units' activities, accounting, finance, and treasury operations and decision making are almost always centralized in the corporation's headquarters.

Nor will managers agree on the appropriate degree of centralization or decentralization. Under its founder, Bernie Marcus, Home Depot was managed in a highly decentralized way in which each store manager was free to run his or her store in an almost completely autonomous fashion. When Bob Nardelli arrived from General Electric to take the reins as CEO, he insisted that many activities that were decentralized become much more centralized. In addition, he also required that the performance of individual stores be highly monitored by control systems in the corporate headquarters. The change in structure had a major impact on the company's formerly free-wheeling culture, and was not immediately embraced by most Home Depot employees.[31] When employee morale and firm performance declined, Nardelli was removed as CEO, and many activities were again decentralized.

Communication and Language Problems

It is interesting to consider that an organization with eight hierarchical levels and a span of control of eight individuals per manager—not unreasonable assumptions—would have the theoretical capacity to employ over two million individuals! Yet, even the world's largest corporations rarely have more than a few hundred thousand employees. And, though it is certainly conceivable that organizations could have very tall hierarchies with a dozen or more levels of superior-subordinate reporting relationships, it is rare for even the largest business organizations to have more than eight hierarchical levels. What explains the difference between "theoretical capacity" and the actual size of today's largest corporations, and why do organizations rarely have more than eight hierarchical levels?

Although several factors limit the size of organizations, the most important limiting factor is communication. All modern organizations suffer language and other communication problems; research suggests that these problems intensify as organizational size and diversity increase. An excellent illustration of these organizational communication problems is provided by the children's game of telephone, in which one child in one corner of a room relays a message to the next child who relays the message to the next child and so on until a much-distorted message reaches the last child in the far corner of the room. In the children's game of telephone, the distortion of the original message will vary directly with the number of participants in the game. The same distortion occurs in organizations as information flows across hierarchical levels or from one department to another.

Researchers have long been aware of such communication problems. One organizational scholar writing in the late 1960s noted that

> a [manager] faces a world of vast scope, and therefore he must rely primarily on a formal information system to filter out "noise" and less important data and to provide an abstraction of the real world that preserves essential information about significant events.[32]

But he also acknowledged that data flowing through the organization could become so distorted that the resulting information "cannot convey what is going on in the world." As a result, managers work "in an analogue, abstract world."[33] Other researchers have made the same observation, noting that "almost all organizational structures tend to produce false images in the decision maker, and the larger…the organization, the better the chance that its top decision-makers will be operating in purely imaginary worlds."[34]

Nor has information technology enabled firms to overcome these limitations. According to Martin S. Davis, former chairman and chief executive officer of Paramount,

> complexity has narrowed the capacity of managers. There are limits to the information they can absorb and the operating details they can monitor. Managers can be spread so thin that they overlook areas of true opportunity. The information age has not necessarily been accompanied by an ability to interpret and use the greater fund of information advantageously.[35]

In most organizations, however, the problem is even more complicated than is suggested by these concerns about information distortion and data overload because business firms are political organizations. Self-interested managers will often find it expedient to alter or otherwise intentionally distort a particular communication. Researchers have observed that information, and especially bad news, moves very slowly through organizations.[36] Managers who have unfavorable information to pass along have strong incentives either to alter or to slow down this information before passing it along. The result is a loss of management control, and strategy implementation inevitably suffers.

It is probably impossible to totally alleviate organizational communication problems. Certainly no hierarchical structure is free of communication problems. In fact, the various hierarchical structures that have been described in this chapter were all developed, at least in part, to alleviate communication problems and improve organizational responsiveness. The multidivisional structure aimed to reduce the problem of top management overload that often develops in functionally organized firms, yet it has failed to completely eliminate communication problems. As a consequence, many firms have adopted cross-functional structures to improve communication, coordination, and information flows. Future evolutions in organizational structure will almost certainly continue to address the communication problems that are inherent in all organizations. For example, some organizations have been able to develop highly effective intranets that link employees via email and the Internet to speed communication and facilitate the exchange of information. Yet even these sophisticated intranets must cope with the staggering growth of email, texting, and other forms of electronic communication, and the possibility that critical messages can be overlooked or not seen promptly.

Conflict

Because organizational life is political, conflict is an inevitable part of all organizations. Some conflict is almost unavoidable, as many business situations invite disagreements and animosities among individuals and departments. Some of these situations have already been noted. For example, the transfer pricing problem, found in any company in which one division produces a component or raw material or provides a service for another department, invites conflict. Functional rivalries are also often a source of conflict. Manufacturing managers often claim that engineers design products that are difficult to build or assemble, while engineers often feel as though manufacturing managers lack appreciation for the "elegance" of their product designs.

Sales and marketing personnel will often conclude that accounting or finance departments prevent them from selling products or services by insisting that prices be kept high, while accounting and finance personnel often claim that sales and marketing departments are trying to "give away" their companies' products or services. Because of the way our thinking tends to become socialized or influenced by our surroundings, it is only natural that managers will come to hold the values associated with their respective departments.

An emphasis on "superordinate goals" (i.e., goals that are more important to all organizational members than their individual or group goals) can do much to reduce conflict among employees, departments, and business units. Superordinate goals can have powerful motivational impacts on employees.[37] Compensation systems can also be designed to motivate employees and managers to work to achieve overall organizational objectives rather than their own parochial interests. For example, bonus plans that reward managers based on the performance of their own division or unit *and* overall company performance are much more likely to get managers focused on overall company goals than compensation plans that reward managers solely on the basis of their own unit's performance.

At the same time, it's important to emphasize that conflict is not entirely negative. If conflict brings out different opinions and leads to a greater exploration of strategic options, it can be very beneficial for managerial thinking and for organizations. In fact, organizations without any conflict or disagreements are likely to be particularly vulnerable to groupthink. They are also more likely to be vulnerable to the forces of environmental change because they are unlikely to generate a variety of ideas for how their firms should anticipate or respond to the competitive dynamics in their industries.

A related problem is referred to as the "agency problem"—the tendency for the interests of principals (owners) and their agents (managers) to diverge.[38] The same agency problems exist within organizations between top managers and their subordinates, and no organizational structure, however carefully designed, can completely alleviate these agency and motivation problems.

In fact, problems of agency afflict all organizations at multiple levels: At the senior management level, for example, the objective of maximizing shareholder wealth will often take a back seat to other objectives that may be more aligned with the interests of managers and employees. At lower levels, many employees are extremely conscientious and often willing to do the work of several of their more average performing colleagues, but other employees are shirkers who will gladly let their more ambitious colleagues take up the slack. Furthermore, employees will naturally work harder on those initiatives to which they are more committed and on those that they see as serving their own best interests.

Summary

As already noted, these issues and problems are an inevitable part of organizational life. We've already suggested some ways in which the various components of structure can be used to deal with these issues and problems. Multidivisional structures are necessarily more decentralized than functional structures, and we've already noted that one of the key advantages of the multidivisional structure is its ability to improve decision making in large and diversified companies. Cross-functional structures can further decentralize decision making to product teams and can also provide excellent forums for conflicting points of view to be heard and addressed in an effective manner. Similarly, effective organizational cultures can be highly motivational and can often minimize the need for more elaborate hierarchical structures.

Top managers' mental models—their beliefs and understandings about how to organize and implement strategy—determine how they combine the various structural components of hierarchy, standard operating procedures and policies, information systems, and culture into effective organizational structures. Unfortunately, many managers fail to give adequate attention to the structural issues and questions surrounding strategy implementation, preferring instead to focus their attention and energy on the formulation of strategy. Another common mistake is to fix one aspect of organization (e.g., the information system), and fail to consider the implications on policies or norms or reporting relationships. As a consequence, many very good strategies never live up to their potential but become "unrealized strategies" because of ineffective implementation.

Emerging Issues and New Types of Organizational Structure

This final section considers how the changing nature of work, demands for information, and emerging human resource management issues are encouraging the development of new organizational structures.

The Changing Nature of Work

The rapid rate of technological change, especially the rapid pace of developments in information technology, is having a profound impact on the nature of work in most industries. Products and services are becoming increasingly knowledge intensive. This shift toward more knowledge-intensive products and services has placed important new demands on workers. As a study prepared by the Hudson Institute suggests, these transformations in the economy will require a more educated and knowledgeable workforce.[39] Workers with four-year college or university degrees now earn, on average, more than 40 percent more than employees holding only a high school diploma, a premium that has grown considerably over the last 20 years and is likely to continue growing as our economy continues to transform the nature of work.[40]

Even more profound than these changing educational requirements, however, are the changes that are occurring in the nature of work itself. As noted earlier in the chapter, the traditional aim of structure has been to organize work—physical work—in order to implement strategies effectively. Employees were organized into functional departments so they could specialize and become increasingly proficient at their tasks. And, while Frederick Taylor aimed to remove "all possible brain work"[41] from employee's jobs, few jobs today depend solely on the physical labor or physical skills of workers. Now, workers are important for the knowledge and expertise they possess, and few tasks allow employees the luxury of working in isolation, unaware of what other employees in other parts of the organization know and are doing. Here's how one business manager described the ways this transformation in the nature of work is changing how his company views its workers:

> [W]e began to realize that when we looked at the social and technical changes that needed to take place in the work force and the workplace … that the real technology was in people's heads.
>
> The real cutting edge competitive piece to this was not the hardware that sat in front of them [the employees] or necessarily the social systems that were around them. It was the knowledge in workers' heads. That is the competitive edge.[42]

Organizational structure thus takes on added importance because of this changing nature of work. Even in manufacturing and other types of labor-intensive firms, employees are becoming less and less important for their physical labor. As in the service sector, nearly all manufacturing employees are now "knowledge workers," important not for their physical labor but for their expertise and know-how.

Further complicating the management of knowledge workers is that the knowledge employees carry around in their heads is relatively worthless unless they freely communicate and share it with others who need this information. Thus, structures that formerly sought to organize physical labor efficiently through specialization and into separate departments are almost certainly inappropriate and ineffective in encouraging employees to share their knowledge and communicate it with other employees. Companies have found information technologies such as email, the Internet, and intranets extremely helpful in disseminating the knowledge of individual employees.

At the same time, company cultures must often be altered to provide employees with incentives to share rather than hoard the knowledge and information that they possess.[43] For example, factory workers who hold a great deal of knowledge about their manufacturing processes are often reluctant to share that knowledge if their companies have a long tradition of labor-management conflict or animosity. Other workers can fear losing their jobs if they share specialized knowledge that they possess.[44]

Thomas Friedman has described how the changing nature of work and the importance of knowledge workers are requiring companies to rethink structural arrangements. In the following passage, he describes how the advertising firm, WPP, has rethought traditional modes of organization and structure:

> WPP adapted to get the most out of itself. It changed its office architecture and practices, just like those companies that adjusted their steam-run factories to the electric motor. But WPP not only got rid of its walls, it got rid of all its floors. It looked at all its employees from all its companies as a vast pool of individual specialists who could be assembled horizontally into collaborative teams, depending on the unique demands of any given project.[45]

These shifts imply that we will see major changes in human resource management and new types of organizational structures in the years ahead.

Human Resource Management Issues

As a consequence of the changing nature of work, companies need to focus more effort and energy on how jobs are designed, how work is organized, and how knowledge will be accumulated, stored, and shared with other employees as well as with customers and suppliers. In other words, companies will need to place a new emphasis on human resource management issues and policies—considerations that have frequently been downplayed.

The management of knowledge workers requires a radical rethinking of traditional organizational structures. At present, we know very little about the management of knowledge workers in any industry. The traditional, functional division of labor approach may enhance efficiency, but an unintended consequence of this approach is the "dumbing down" of work so that it becomes a repetitive, thoughtless, and mind-numbing exercise. One industry observer has argued that the problem with many traditional assembly line jobs is not the time lost as workers pass parts from one workstation to the next or the high incidence of costly repetitive stress injuries; instead, the problem is that employees "doing the same task repeatedly twenty-five hundred times a day cannot think, record data, study, teach, learn, maintain, improve, and otherwise perform as a world-class work force."[46]

A better approach is to organize work in such a way that employees become managers of their own processes, that they take responsibility for developing their knowledge and skills, and that they have opportunities for sharing their knowledge and skills with other employees, customers, and suppliers.[47] And, it is important that companies retain knowledge workers because they "become about three times more productive after ten years with the same employer than when they started work," and their "knowledge is key to keeping customers—whose longevity is the source of repeat sales and referrals."[48]

Finally, most companies are now realizing the value of adopting *high-performance work practices* that include all of the following components:

- Selective hiring.
- Extensive training.
- Decentralized decision-making.
- Extensive sharing of information.
- Use of incentive compensation.[49]

Though researchers have long known the value of adopting such work practices, their widespread adoption has only begun to take on urgency with the changing nature of work and the growing importance of managing knowledge workers. Nearly all of the components of high impact work practices have a significant and strategic role for human resource managers and staff.

Outsourcing and New Types of Hierarchical Structures

We are also seeing the emergence of new types of organizational structures that meet the information needs of the new work. Certainly we can expect that the trend toward the use of more cross-functional teams and matrix structures will continue. As discussed in Chapter 9, the managers of many firms have evaluated their value chains and concluded that many activities that their firms have traditionally performed have not contributed to competitive advantage, and they have now begun to contract with suppliers for these activities. It is conceivable, in fact, that many organizations could be radically restructured so that nearly all the activities they now perform could be supplied by outside vendors.

The resulting *virtual* or *networked* organizations focus on the one or few activities that are critical to their success while outsourcing nearly all other functional activities. Companies like Nike and Liz Claiborne operate in this way. Nike designs and markets footwear, but outsources all its production needs, leaving the company free to focus on those activities—marketing and product design—that provide it with its competitive advantage. Similarly, Liz Claiborne designs clothing lines, but, like Nike, Liz Claiborne contracts with other companies to produce its apparel products. Retail department and specialty stores sell the merchandise of both companies.

While Nike and Liz Claiborne are perhaps extreme examples, we see many organizations contracting out for services that have traditionally been handled in-house by functional departments. A large percentage of companies now outsource their payroll function, and some companies have even outsourced all of their data-processing operations. Advancements in information technology will only continue to push organizations toward greater outsourcing.

Organizational boundaries will become more fluid as firms rethink which activities and functions must be performed "inside the organization" and which activities can be outsourced to other firms.

Many observers have criticized organizations that have outsourced manufacturing and other activities, arguing that these firms are "hollowing" themselves and that they risk losing control of critical functions. Others have argued just the opposite, however. Dartmouth professor James Brian Quinn is one of the leading advocates of restructuring efforts that allow firms to focus attention on critical activities while outsourcing many less critical activities. In his defense of outsourcing, Quinn argues that:

- Intellectual and service activities now occupy the critical spots in most companies' value chains—regardless of whether the company is in the service or manufacturing sector—and if companies are not "best in world" at these critical intellectual and service activities, then they are sacrificing competitive advantage by performing those activities internally or with their existing levels of expertise.
- Each company should focus its strategic investments and management attention on those capabilities and processes—usually intellectual or service activities—where it can achieve and maintain "best in world" status.
- The specialized capabilities and efficiency of outside service suppliers have so changed industry boundaries and supplier capabilities that they have substantially diminished the desirability of much vertical integration, and, strategically approached, outsourcing does not "hollow out" a corporation, but it can decrease internal bureaucracies, flatten organizations, and give companies a heightened strategic focus, vastly improving their competitive responsiveness.[50]

In other words, companies must focus on those value-chain activities that are critical to their success, while the efficiency and quality of outside vendors allows companies to outsource their less central activities.

While much outsourcing has involved moving manufacturing jobs to low-income countries where it can be done much more inexpensively, more recent concerns over outsourcing have focused on the outsourcing of highly skilled and technical work. Many companies are now employing software developers in India and elsewhere. General Electric has opened a research and development center in India. At the same time, rapidly developing countries like India are now buying more products and services from the United States, which should help fuel U.S. domestic job growth, so economists are still struggling to reach an understanding of the full implications of this most recent wave of outsourcing for countries around the world. Clearly, different industries will be impacted differently by the opportunities and challenges posed by outsourcing.

Peter Drucker has concluded that the virtual corporation may well become the dominant form of organizational structure in the years ahead.[51] Drucker argues that it is not just because virtual organizations contract out less critical activities, allowing them to focus their attention and resources on those activities that are sources of competitive advantage. Drucker's more important observation is that contracting out these more peripheral activities may be a way to actually gain an additional advantage over competitors who keep these activities inside the organizational hierarchy. Drucker reasons that when employees are involved in an activity that is not central to the success of an organization (such as sorting the mail, janitorial work, manufacturing of components), they have only limited promotion opportunities and will therefore suffer from low morale and low job performance. By contracting out these peripheral activities, however, employees working for those contract organizations will have greater opportunities for advancement and will therefore have higher morale and be more effective in performing the duties and responsibilities of their jobs.

Another creative way of organizing to accommodate the changing nature of work is through an *ambidextrous organizational structure*. This structure addresses the need for both radical and incremental innovation. In this structure the new, exploratory, or innovative parts of the company are separated from traditional parts of the organization allowing for different processes, structures, and cultures. These new parts of the company aren't left totally by themselves; however, they are integrated into the traditional management structure so they can share important resources from the traditional units—for example talent, funds, and customers as illustrated in Exhibit 11.5. They are, however, enough outside the traditional structure that they aren't contaminated and their cultures are not overwhelmed by the forces of "business as usual."[52]

Conclusions: Organizational Structure and the Book's Three Key Themes

The Importance of Managers and Managerial Thinking

The optimal organizational structure for any firm involves balancing many different components of structure and dealing with a number of complex topics and issues, such as conflict, employee motivation, the appropriate degree of centralization and decentralization, and communication and language problems. In making important decisions about organizational structure, managers must weigh many considerations, but well-designed structures are essential if strategies are to be effectively implemented and if organizations are to be responsive to changes in the competitive

Exhibit 11.5 The Ambidextrous Organization Structure

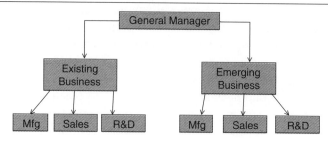

environment. Managers' beliefs about how to organize are therefore a major influence on organizational effectiveness and performance.

At the same time, this chapter has underscored that structure in organizations is a much broader concept than the organizational chart or the formal hierarchy of an organization. While organizational theorists have long understood the importance of conceptualizing structure broadly, practicing managers all too frequently underestimate the power of the less visible aspects of organizational structure—communication and information flows, organizational routines, standard operating procedures, control systems, and above all, culture. Peter Senge captures the importance of these less visible aspects of organizational structure when he writes that "structure in human systems includes the 'operating policies' of the decision makers in the system," and that "redesigning … decision making redesigns the system structure." Structure, then, is "inextricably tied to how [managers] think."[53] Thus, managerial thinking not only plays an important role in designing organizational structures, but it is itself both a product of and a key component of organizational structure. This is a profound idea because it suggests how tightly coupled managers and managerial thinking are to the formulation and implementation of strategies in business organizations.

Change and the Need to Think Dynamically about Strategic Management

As the intellectual or knowledge component of work continues to increase, managers will place ever greater pressure on their firms' structures to acquire and disseminate information and knowledge and to facilitate individual and organizational learning.[54] In addition, firms will continue to rethink their value chains as discussed in Chapter 9. This will almost surely lead to more and more companies focusing on key value-adding activities that can be sources of competitive advantage, while contracting with other firms to perform less critical functions. Finally, because yesterday's source of competitive advantage—whether it be an effective business definition, a low-cost manufacturing capability, or a strong organizational culture—can quickly become tomorrow's competitive *disadvantage*, managers and their firms must become even more responsive to changes in their competitive environments.

The Importance of Organizational Learning

Organizing and organizations will continue because they provide the necessary context and continuity that knowledge workers require in order to function effectively. In short, organizational structures convert the creativity and expertise of knowledge workers into desired firm outcomes.[55] Yet, we know very little about how firms foster individual and organizational learning or what can be done to improve their ability to exploit this learning. One of the major automobile assembly companies recently undertook a study of its product development efforts and found that it had learned very little from its past mistakes and successes; every new vehicle development effort was essentially starting at zero, and the same mistakes were being committed over and over again with each new vehicle. On the other hand, a small coffee shop in Colorado Springs asks all employees, before punching out, to write comments in a running log about what went right or wrong during their shift; likewise, before they can begin working, arriving employees must read all comments that have been added since their last shift. These two examples are anecdotal, but the extremes they illustrate suggest the pressing need for thinking and research on organizational learning.

Key Points

- Organizational structure includes *the mechanisms that facilitate the formulation and implementation of strategy and the overall coordination of the business enterprise.*
- The objectives of structure are to implement strategies and to make organizations responsive to their owners (shareholders), managers, and the competitive environment.
- Structure includes hierarchical reporting relationships, formal organizational control systems, flows of information, and organizational culture.
- Three traditional types of hierarchical structure are the functional, multidivisional, and matrix forms, each having some advantages as well as disadvantages and limitations for the effective implementation of organizational strategy.
- Though less visible than hierarchical structures, organizational control systems, flows of information, and organizational culture are other important components of organizational structure.
- Any structure will face a number of issues and problems, including communication and motivational problems, control loss, and the danger that owners' interests will be subordinated to managers' interests. Effective organizational structures can mitigate, but not completely eliminate, these problems.
- The competitive environment and the changing nature of work will lead companies to adopt new human resource management practices and to develop new structures, including virtual forms of organization.

Key Questions for Managers

- How effective is your organization's structure at allowing managers to implement strategies?
- How well does your organization respond to environmental changes? What aspects of your company's structure enhance the organization's responsiveness? What aspects of the structure inhibit responsiveness?

- How important is your organization's informal structure, i.e., its rules, processes, standard operating procedures, culture? In what ways are these informal elements effective? In what ways are they dysfunctional?
- What are some of the trade-offs your organization has made in the ways it deals with the central issues in organizing described toward the end of this chapter—centralization versus decentralization, conflict, and agency problems?
- How is the changing nature of work affecting your company? In what ways has your organization responded to the growing importance of knowledge work? What innovative structural components has your company embraced to enhance its effectiveness?

Suggestions for Further Reading

Additionally, links to further resources online—such as cases, articles, and videos—can be found on the book's website, www.routledge.com/textbooks/Duhaime.

Alvesson, M. 2004. *Knowledge Work and Knowledge-Intensive Firms.* New York: Oxford University Press.

Barney, J. B. 1986. Organizational culture: Can it be a source of sustained competitive advantage? *Academy of Management Review,* 11: 656–665.

Chandler, A. D., Jr., 1962. *Strategy and Structure: Chapters in the History of the Industrial Enterprise.* Cambridge, MA: MIT Press.

Chatzkel, J. L. 2003. *Technology and Innovation Knowledge Capital.* New York: Oxford University Press.

Child, J. 2004. *Organization: Problems and Practice for Our Times.* Malden, MA: Blackwell.

Choo, C. W., & Bontis, N. 2002. *The Strategic Management of Intellectual Capital and Organizational Knowledge.* New York: Oxford University Press.

Cortada, J. W. 2004. *The Digital Hand: How Computers Changed the Work of American Manufacturing, Transportation, and Retail Industries.* New York: Oxford University Press.

Joyce, W., Nohria, N., & Roberson, B. 2003. *What Really Works. The 4 + 2 Formula for Sustained Business Success.* New York: HarperBusiness.

Martin, R. 2009. *The Design of Business: Why Design Thinking Is the Next Competitive Advantage.* Boston: Harvard Business Press.

Nadler, D. A., & Tushman, M. L. 1997. *Competing by Design: The Power of Organizational Architecture.* New York: Oxford University Press.

Nonaka, I., & Nishiguchi, T. (Eds.) 2001. *Knowledge Emergence: Social, Technical, and Evolutionary Dimensions of Knowledge Creation.* New York: Oxford University Press.

Quinn, J. B. 1992. *Intelligent Enterprise: A Knowledge and Service Based Paradigm for Industry.* New York: Free Press.

Rapp, W. V. 2002. *Information Technology Strategies.* New York: Oxford University Press.

Williamson, O. E. 1975. *Markets and Hierarchies: Analysis and Antitrust Implications.* New York: Free Press.

Chapter 12

The Management
of Strategic Change

The importance of anticipating and responding effectively to ever-changing business environments has been consistently emphasized throughout this book. To conclude, Chapter 12 again takes up this theme and examines in some detail the factors that limit the ability of managers to anticipate and respond to changes in their firms' environments. The chapter also suggests some ways in which managers and organizations might be more responsive to, and even proactive in dealing with, environmental changes. All of these suggestions are related in some way to managerial thinking and organizational learning—the other two key themes emphasized throughout this book.

Chapter Objectives

The specific objectives of this chapter are to:

- Review and further explore the factors that inhibit managerial responsiveness to changes in industry environments.
- Describe different types of organizational learning and their relationship to strategy formulation and implementation.
- Identify factors that influence the rate and extent of organizational learning.
- Offer some recommendations for managers and their organizations that aim to make firms more adaptive, responsive, and innovative.

Introduction: "Strategic Change Management"

A key premise of this text is that nearly all business environments are in a state of on-going change or disequilibrium. For example, the main point of Chapter 5 was that the various dimensions of industries are continually shifting as customer demographics, needs, and wants change, as new technologies emerge, and as new products and services are introduced into the marketplace. Firms must either 1) stay aligned with changes in their competitive environments by responding quickly to these changes, or 2) proactively anticipate changes in customer demographics, future technologies, and potential new products and services and thereby play key roles in recreating their industries.

Exhibit 12.1 The Role Managers Play in Maintaining an Alignment between Firms and Their Industry Environments

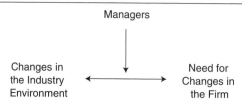

Throughout this book, we have emphasized that managers hold responsibility for anticipating or responding quickly to changes in their firms' competitive environments. Firms must stay aligned with changes in their industry environments, but it is the responsibility of firm managers to insure that this alignment is maintained. One way to depict this managerial responsibility is shown in Exhibit 12.1. The exhibit attempts to capture the important role managers play in maintaining an alignment between their firms and their industry environments.

The interactions between firms and their environments that are portrayed in Exhibit 12.1 do not occur frictionlessly, however. As illustrated in Exhibit 12.1, managers play a key role in this relationship between industry and organizational change. Because managers' mental models influence strategic decision making, managerial thinking must anticipate or respond quickly to environmental change if their firms are to stay aligned with their industries. Yet, the text has highlighted the difficulty managers have in anticipating and recognizing changes in their business environments. Chapters 1, 3, and 5 emphasized that managers' mental models do not always keep pace with changes in their firms' environment. As a consequence, managers of business firms are often unable to see industry changes or to appreciate fully the consequences these industry changes might have for their firms.

The price for failing to keep pace with industry changes can be very high. Often, firms that find themselves misaligned must restructure, and frequently a restructuring will entail laying-off employees—thousands of employees for very large companies. Along the way, these firms incur significant financial losses and will usually see their stock price fall, often leading to the loss of millions or even billions of dollars in shareholder value. In addition to direct impacts on employees and shareholders, the write-offs and reductions in investment and R&D that accompany corporate restructuring efforts have far-reaching negative consequences for the larger economy.

The danger of falling out of step with industry changes will almost certainly continue in the future as international competition intensifies, as existing and new technologies continue to be exploited, and as shifts in consumer demographics lead to new customer needs and wants. Organizational change will, therefore, be essential to firm survival. In fact, so important is the management of change to organizational success, that the field of strategic management might more appropriately be called "strategic change management."

This chapter is divided into two main sections. The first section reviews and explores further the factors that delay managerial responsiveness to environmental change. The second section offers recommendations for how managers can overcome this inertia and become more responsive to or proactive in dealing with environmental change.

Managerial Thinking and Environmental Change

Many factors slow or limit the responsiveness of managers to environmental change. The academic research literature has shown that managers can fail to anticipate or adequately respond to change for a number of reasons. First, managers can simply fail to *notice* change in their business environments. As a result, they are "blindsided" by changes that were totally unanticipated. Second, research has also shown that managers can be aware of changes in their industries, but they may fail to *interpret* these changes correctly. If they underestimate the importance of these environmental changes, they may wait too long to respond, or they may not respond at all. Finally, research evidence has also shown that managers may correctly see or notice changes, that they may even correctly interpret the likely impact of these industry changes, but that they might still fail to adopt an appropriate course of *action*. In the next few sections, we examine in more detail each of these limitations or weaknesses associated with managerial thinking. This section begins by examining some of the cognitive factors that limit the ability of managers to notice, interpret, and act on environmental stimuli.

The Problem of Noticing Change

Two researchers, Sara Kiesler and Lee Sproull, have written about the problems of responding to environmental change and have suggested that:

> [a] crucial component of managerial behavior in rapidly changing environments is problem sensing, the cognitive process of noticing and constructing meaning about environmental change so that organizations can take action.[1]

Note the implications of this statement: Noticing is crucial because if environmental changes are not noticed, action will not be taken. In many ways, the problem of noticing is similar to the "boiled frog experiment."[2] As the experiment is explained, a frog is first placed in a pot of boiling water. As soon as the frog lands in the water, it jumps out. The frog is then placed in a pot of lukewarm water and the heat is turned on. The frog fails to notice the gradually warming temperature, however, and ends up being boiled.

Considerable anecdotal and empirical evidence suggests that managers are like the frog—they swim along comfortably in their firms' current environments and fail to notice how their industries are gradually changing. How is it possible that experienced and competent managers can simply fail to notice important changes in their organizations' environments? Recall from Chapter 3 that one of the key roles played by managers' mental models is to focus their attention on those aspects of the environment that are deemed important. Indeed, without this focusing characteristic of mental models, we would be overwhelmed by the incredible array of environmental stimuli that are constantly bombarding us. In fact, without this focusing function of our mental models, few if any of us would be able to live effectively in this complex world. The downside—or what could be considered a "necessary evil"—of this focusing function is that we miss much of the activity in our environments.

As a result, managers are almost certainly scanning their environments, but their mental models are likely to be focusing attention on those aspects of their firms' business environments that are deemed most salient or most important by their *current* mental models. If managers are more committed to their firms' ongoing strategies than they are to noticing unrelated data and other environmental stimuli, they will "actively ignore" data that are inconsistent with those strategies.[3] Thus, changes may be occurring in their industries, but managers may simply fail to detect these changes because their attention is focused on their firms' strategies and other related aspects or features of their firms' business environments.

The problem of noticing industry changes is also compounded because these changes are unlikely to stand out or be overtly obvious to managers. "Most strategic decisions do not present themselves to the decision maker in convenient ways; problems and opportunities in particular must be identified in streams of ambiguous, largely verbal data."[4] Other researchers have concluded that many potentially important changes go unnoticed by managers for long periods simply because they have failed to track them.[5]

Thus, much research suggests that changes must be dramatic or have major consequences for firms before their managers will take notice of them. Noticing changes depends on those changes being seen as "breakpoints" or sharp changes from the *status quo*.[6] Stated another way, the changes that tend to be noticed are those changes that are significant, sudden, or perhaps even catastrophic. Unfortunately, when managers and their firms are eventually blindsided by significant, sudden, or catastrophic changes in their industries, it is often too late for them to respond effectively. As a result, many of these blindsided firms go into decline and some never fully recover.

Interpretation of Data and Environmental Stimuli

Even when managers notice changes in their industries, they may still fail to interpret correctly or appreciate fully the potential consequences of these changes for their firms. A number of studies suggest that "seeing is not always believing." For example, a study that examined companies in the declining railroad industry during the 1950s and 1960s found that railroad managers noticed or were aware of the significant competitive threat posed by trucks and an improved national highway system by the early 1950s, yet those same managers continued to believe that government regulation, the railroad labor unions, and even the weather were more serious problems than competition from trucks.[7]

A Harvard Business School case study that examined the Japanese entry and takeover of the U.S. motorcycle industry also illustrates how difficult it is for managers to correctly interpret the data that they do notice. The Japanese manufacturers entered at the low-end of the market, offering motorcycles with engines as small as 50 ccs. These small, easy to handle bikes, combined with creative marketing and distribution strategies, brought motorcycle riding to hundreds of thousands of new riders. After learning to ride on a small Honda or other Japanese model, many riders naturally wanted to trade-up to larger bikes. As a result, sales of Harley, BSA, Triumph, and Norton motorcycles rose dramatically, even doubling between 1960 and 1966. But even as sales of Harley and British motorcycles grew rapidly in the 1960s, their share of the motorcycle market was plummeting.

In what has to be a classic example of misinterpretation of market trends, Eric Turner, chairman of BSA Ltd. was quoted in *Advertising Age* as saying, "The success of Honda, Suzuki, and Yamaha in the States has been jolly good for us." Perhaps even more surprising was the reaction of William Davidson, the president of Harley-Davidson, who, in a *Forbes* article, stated:

> Basically we do not believe in the lightweight market... The lightweight market is only supplemental. Back around World War I, a number of companies came out with lightweight bikes. We came out with one ourselves. We came out with another one in 1947 and it just didn't go anywhere. We have seen what happens to these small sizes.[8]

William Davidson may not have "believed" in "the lightweight market," but his company's Japanese rivals, with virtually no share of the U.S. motorcycle market in 1960 had, by 1970, achieved a commanding 85 percent of total U.S. motorcycle sales!

Another illustration of the difficulty managers have in correctly interpreting data comes from a study that compared the financial performance of matched pairs of sample firms from a variety of industries.[9] In each pair, one firm went bankrupt while the other firm survived. As illustrated in Exhibit 12.2, one of the most interesting findings of this study is that significant performance differences between the bankrupt and survivor firms appeared as early as *ten years before the failing firms declared bankruptcy!*

The managers of the low-performing firms would have had to notice that their firms were underperforming industry competitors, so why, given such a long lead time, were the managers of the low-performing firms unable to formulate and implement strategies that would have changed the course of their histories and avoided eventual bankruptcy? And, in the case of the railroads, why, given managers' awareness of the threats posed by trucks, did they continue to focus their attention on other factors, such as government regulation and the weather?

One possible explanation for this problem of interpretation is that managers' mental models will allow them to rationalize away unfavorable stimuli. Chapter 3 emphasized the tendency for managers to give more weight to data that confirm their beliefs while discounting data that would require them to alter their mental models. The managers of declining firms might therefore be

Exhibit 12.2 Survivors Versus Bankrupts: Return on Assets in the Years Prior to Bankruptcy

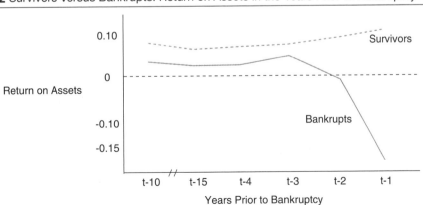

Source: Hambrick, D. C., & D'Aveni, R. A. 1988. Large corporate failures as downward spirals. *Administrative Science Quarterly*, 33: 1–23.

able to overlook poor performance on one dimension (say, return on assets) if they can focus instead on some more positive dimension of performance (such as an increase in sales).

As in the motorcycle industry in the 1960s, decline in the railroad industry was *relative* rather than *absolute*, so railroad managers could ignore market share losses and take consolation in the fact that they were continuing to handle increasing volumes of freight in spite of increasing competition from trucks. Something similar was probably happening at General Motors as the company's share of the U.S. automobile market declined from over 50 percent in 1980 to only about one-third of the market a decade later. During most of the 1980s, General Motors enjoyed very high profits, so as long as the company was profitable, its managers may have chosen to focus on that performance metric, while choosing to ignore the more negative slide in its market share.

Limits on Organizational Action

Finally, even when managers are aware of and fully appreciate the seriousness of the changes that are occurring in their competitive environments, they may still fail to formulate appropriate responses or strategies to meet these threats. Once again, a company that offers a good example of this problem of taking effective action in response to environmental change is Kodak. The available evidence suggests that Kodak's leadership has been fully aware of the potential consequences of this profound technological change. Kodak's own scientists and researchers developed digital photography technologies. In the mid-1990s, Kodak's board of directors almost certainly recruited a chief executive, George Fisher, from Motorola, because the directors knew and understood that the company needed a leader who understood and could focus the company on digital technologies. Fisher's successors have also made it clear that Kodak's future must be in exploiting digital technologies.

Yet, Kodak has yet to score any significant wins in its efforts to transform itself. Many early initiatives, such as its Photo CD and Advantix digital camera, were major product flops. Over the last decade, its digital business lines have lost hundreds of millions of dollars. And, even as the company has more forcefully put itself on the course to a digital future, it has yet to become recognized as a major player in the market for digital photography products.

The managers of the American and European automobile companies probably deserve a similar criticism for their lack of action. Since coming to a full appreciation of the threat posed by Japanese automobile manufacturers as recently as the 1980s, all of the major manufacturers have adopted new strategies to improve their manufacturing processes and the quality of their product offerings. But most of the strategies they have adopted are attempts to imitate the practices of their Japanese competitors, and few if any of their strategies are really new or novel.[10] As a result, though the U.S. and European companies have achieved remarkable improvements in manufacturing efficiency and product quality, they have also failed to leapfrog ahead of Toyota, Nissan, and Honda, and they are unlikely to do so at any time in the near future and certainly not until they have devised truly original strategies.[11]

Institutionalized industry practices are another factor that can limit the ability of managers to implement changes. In Chapter 5, we emphasized that competition among firms in the same industry results in a good deal of imitation and industry-wide institutionalization of common business practices.[12] Firms in the same industry also develop a common language and similar understandings about how to compete. Managers of these firms develop a "common body of knowledge" that is reinforced by reading the same publications, participating in professional networks and trade associations, and moving between firms within the same industry.[13]

Chapter 5 noted that these industry influences play an important, positive role in facilitating the emergence of industry standards that, in turn, encourage customer acceptance of products and services. On the other hand, Chapter 5 also described how these industry norms can blind managers to new opportunities and technologies, alternative bases of competition, and potential competitors. Thus, these institutional contexts in which firms compete will reinforce existing patterns of competition, and firms seeking to adopt new strategies will have to contest industry norms and influences. Firms that deviate from these industry standards—by introducing totally new products and services or by incorporating totally new technologies—face considerable upside, but also significant downside, risks. As a result, many firms choose the safer route of incremental changes in product or service offerings.

Furthermore, selecting a totally new course is rarely an obvious or a straightforward process for most established firms. Accounts of organizations struggling to formulate totally new strategies suggest that the process is a painful and highly uncertain one, characterized by periods in which organizations are "groping" or "in flux," without a clear definition or focus.[14] Again, many firms choose to remain content pursuing strategies that are consistent with industry norms rather than face the ambiguity and uncertainty associated with formulating and implementing totally new strategies.

The result is that incumbent firms in established industries are often quite vulnerable to the "attack" of new entrants that fill unmet customer needs or wants, offer new products or services, or exploit emerging technologies. Apple's development of the personal computer, the Japanese invasion of the U.S. automobile industry, the eclipse of the railroads by trucks, and Google's emergence in the market for search tools are just a few of examples that illustrate how vulnerable incumbent firms can be to new entrants that are motivated by ideas that lie outside industry norms and traditional patterns of competition.

Two Different Types of Organizational Learning and Change

Lower-Level Learning

In addition to the kinds of cognitive and organizational limitations just described, problems associated with organizational learning also limit organizational adaptation and change. This book has emphasized the importance of managerial and organizational learning, but has deferred until now an in-depth discussion of learning theories. Here, we examine one of the most important aspects of organizational learning, the distinction between lower-level learning and higher-level learning. **Lower-level learning** is characterized by improvements in or refinements of existing beliefs, understandings, and organizational processes. In contrast, **higher-level learning** involves developing totally new beliefs, understandings, and organizational processes.

One leading organizational scholar has distinguished between these two types of learning by describing lower-level learning as the "exploitation of the known" and higher-level learning as "exploration of the new."[15] Both types of learning are absolutely critical to organizational

Exhibit 12.3 An Illustration of Experience Effects

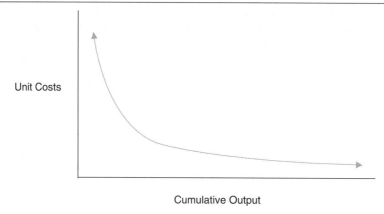

Cumulative Output

effectiveness. One of the best ways to depict the importance of lower-level learning is to refer to experience or learning curve effects that were introduced in Chapter 4. As illustrated in Exhibit 12.3, lower-level learning leads to refinements of existing organizational knowledge and processes that allow firms to reduce unit costs as cumulative output increases. Lower-level learning through experience effects offers companies important dividends. In fact, lower-level learning to refine and improve existing organizational processes is absolutely essential if firms are to develop and maintain competitive advantage.

Higher-Level Learning

Higher-level learning, or the "exploration of the new," is also critical. All organizations need to learn how to do totally new things. Without higher-level learning and the "exploration of the new," firms are vulnerable to being blindsided by new rivals, newly developed technologies, and the introduction of new products and services. When organizations emphasize lower-level learning at the expense of higher-level learning—their firms get better and better at what they already know how to do, but fail to develop new capabilities—they risk developing **competency traps** in which they become increasingly adept at routines and processes that are no longer appropriate because of changes in their environments. Thus, both types of organizational learning are absolutely essential to maintaining organizational effectiveness over the long run. Firms must get better and better at what they already do while also exploring new opportunities.

The railroads offer an excellent illustration of lower-level learning and the possibility of falling into competency traps. During the 1950s, railroad managers realized that by increasing capital intensity (i.e., by replacing steam locomotives with more powerful diesel locomotives and by acquiring larger freight cars) they could reduce the number of employees needed to move the same quantity of freight. Their investments in capital equipment had the intended effect.

Dieselization and larger freight cars allowed railroad companies to operate longer trains carrying far more freight than in the past. Because fewer trains were needed, the railroads were able to reduce the number of train crew employees. In fact, railroad employment fell from

1.2 million employees in 1950 to 780,000 employees in 1960! The railroads enjoyed great success at reducing employment levels, but fewer trains meant slower freight service at exactly the same time that trucks were beginning to offer faster and more reliable service. The railroads got more efficient at doing what they had always done, but their managers missed the most important development in transportation in the twentieth century.

Organizational Learning and Different Types of Organizational Change

Just as we have described two different levels or types of organizational learning, so too can we distinguish between two different types of organizational change. **First-order—or evolutionary—change** can be thought of as refinements to existing products or services or technologies. Product line extensions, software upgrades, and new models are all examples of first-order changes. **Second-order—or revolutionary—change** involves introducing totally new product lines or totally new services, reaching totally new groups of customers, or adopting new technologies. First- and second-order changes have also been called competence-enhancing and competence-destroying changes, respectively, because first-order change involves enhancing or extending existing knowledge and capabilities while second-order change usually means that existing knowledge and capabilities are made irrelevant by the creation of new knowledge and capabilities. Thus, the desired rate of change and the appropriate amount of first- and second-order change are key questions for general managers to address.

Just as all organizations need to engage in both lower- and higher-level learning, organizations must also engage in both first- and second-order change. Yet, acknowledging the importance of both types of organizational change is much easier than actually implementing change. More recent improvements Kodak made to its film technologies (i.e., a first-order change) did nothing to stop the rush of the marketplace to digital technologies (i.e., a second-order change).

Why Do Firms Prefer Lower-Level Learning and First-Order Change?

Unfortunately, most firms tend to allocate more resources to lower-level learning and first-order change (the "exploitation of the known"), while failing to engage in enough higher-level learning and second-order change (the "exploration of the new"). Such an allocation of resources is clearly detrimental to long-run effectiveness, but it is not surprising that managers make this trade-off. In fact, managers have good reasons to emphasize lower-level learning over higher-level learning. Lower-level learning and first-order change are likely to have fairly immediate, predictable, and positive impacts on firm performance, while higher-level learning is much more speculative and much less likely to have an immediate or a positive impact on bottom-line financial performance. In fact, it can often take a decade or more for innovations in higher-level learning to generate a satisfactory financial return.

Furthermore, lower-level learning allows managers and their firms to continue doing more or less what they have been doing, while higher-level learning may suggest pursuing totally new and different markets and strategies. In fact, as the Kodak example suggests, the exploration of the new—in Kodak's case, the company's attempts to incorporate digital technologies to develop new photography products—typically requires considerable investment and often results in many years of financial losses before firms see any significant benefits.

The capital budgeting procedures most companies use—the financial processes through which companies allocate resources for making major purchases—also tend to favor low-level learning. Capital requests that are associated with low-level learning, say the purchase of a new machine to enhance an existing manufacturing process, will almost always have benefits that are easier to quantify than the benefits associated with an investment in higher-level learning. Again, take Kodak as an example: The costs and benefits of the company's investments in improving film manufacturing capabilities were probably very easy for Kodak's managers to estimate, and if those analyses showed that the net present value of the additional revenues or lower costs outweighed the present value of the investment, then the project was approved.

On the other hand, investments in digital technologies were undoubtedly much more difficult for Kodak's managers to approve. Demand for a previously unknown end product is very difficult to estimate. Kodak's managers also have significantly less experience in evaluating investments in digital technologies, making not only the benefits and potential revenues, but also the costs associated with digital investments highly uncertain. As a result, it should not be surprising that over the last three or four decades, Kodak's managers have systematically under-funded investments in what has proven to be the future of photography.

Factors Associated with Higher-Level Learning and Second-Order Change

In spite of its costs and speculative nature, higher-level learning is essential to the survival of firms. What seems to be lacking is a clear understanding of the factors that contribute to or foster higher-level learning. Research evidence suggests that at least two factors influence the extent of higher-level learning:

Problemistic Search

First, higher-level learning is most likely to result from "problemistic search;" in other words, when routine policies or procedures fail to deal effectively with organizational problems or crises, managers initiate search activity that leads to higher-level learning in order to solve these organizational problems.[16]

Managers' aspirations—or their desired levels of performance—will be an important influence on the decision to engage in problemistic search, and so aspiration levels are also an important influence on the rate of organizational learning. When organizational performance fails to match high aspiration levels, managers will be more likely to engage in problemistic search activity. On the other hand, if aspiration levels are low, even low performance may not initiate problemistic search.[17] Thus, an important prerequisite of higher-level learning is for managers to have high aspiration levels and to notice problems and shortcomings in performance early on. Furthermore, managers must interpret these problems and performance shortcomings correctly so that, rather than rationalizing them away, they initiate problemistic search, which leads to higher-level learning.

Absorptive Capacity

Another factor that is important to the success of higher-level learning efforts is **absorptive capacity**,[18] which has been defined as the ability of firms to "recognize the value of new information, assimilate it, and apply it to commercial ends."[19] Firms with higher levels of absorptive capacity are better able to scan their external environments, recognize the importance of significant developments, such as an emerging technology, and then assimilate that knowledge into the organization.

What determines a firm's absorptive capacity? It appears as though a firm's absorptive capacity is a function of its existing knowledge base. In other words, like the old saying "it takes money to make money," the ability of an organization to recognize new developments and assimilate new knowledge is a function of its current stock of knowledge. Thus, investments in R&D, but even more importantly the development of an effective research and development infrastructure, are important to augmenting a firm's absorptive capacity.

Here again, we see the importance of time, which was also emphasized in Chapter 2 when examining the factors that are associated with the development of competitive advantage. The organization that spends considerable time studying a particular technology is much more likely to understand and to assess the value of new developments in that technology than a firm that has only recently become interested in that technology.

Absorptive capacity also underscores the importance of socially complex resources—also discussed in Chapter 2. Here's how one management researcher described the important role of socially complex resources in the development of absorptive capacity:

> The firm invests in R&D related infrastructure to facility the collection and storage of data. Employees create relationships with others both within and outside the organization and share information, both adding data and building relationships among data. Examples include purchasing computer hardware and database software, creating and supporting cross functional teams, building a culture where employees are encouraged to interact wit peers through publication and joint research, or by developing joint ventures and technology sharing alliances. All of these increase the amount of data available for learning and improve the likelihood that relationships among these data can be understood.[20]

The Value of Diversity in Managerial Thinking

Another important organizational factor that encourages managerial responsiveness to environmental change and organizational learning is diversity in managerial thinking. If all or most of a company's managers think alike, then they may not be able to "think outside the box," or generate new ideas. The most insightful ideas will often emerge from employees who think differently. Thus, it is key to have diversity in the thinking of company managers.

Yet, all too many large organizations are caught in an "Attraction-Selection-Attrition" cycle (illustrated in Exhibit 12.4) that tends to promote homogeneity in managerial thinking.[21] According to this model, only certain people are attracted to particular firms. Of those attracted, companies will select, primarily on the basis of "fit," an even more limited group of individuals to join. Over time, those employees who find that they do not "fit" well with these companies will be more likely to leave (attrition). The A-S-A cycle therefore predicts that the thinking of employees within their respective companies will become more and more homogeneous over time. As a result, those managers who are promoted from within to top management positions are likely to think very much alike.

Exhibit 12.4 The Attraction-Selection-Attrition Cycle

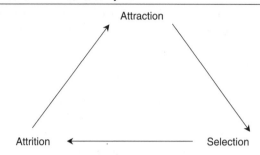

Source: Schneider, B. 1987. The people make the place. *Personal Psychology*, 40: 437–453.

Although this "thinking alike" can facilitate cohesion and rapid decision making, it can also have very serious negative consequences for firms operating in fast-changing environments. A management team composed of like-thinking individuals is much more likely to notice important environmental changes too late or to misinterpret the nature of those changes. Organizations can overcome the dangers of like-minded thinking in at least two ways.

One would be to give greater attention to "contrarian voices." Within nearly all organizations are managers and employees whose ideas are at odds with the prevailing wisdom. Often shunted aside, these individuals and their ideas tend to be ignored. Furthermore, they are the managers the A-S-A model would predict are most likely to "attrit," or leave their organizations. As the English statesman, Walter Bagehot, has written:

> One of the greatest pains to human nature is the pain of a new idea. It … makes you think that after all, your favorite notions may be wrong, your firmest beliefs ill-founded… Naturally, therefore, common men hate a new idea, and are disposed more or less to ill-treat the original man who brings it.[22]

Management researcher, Danny Miller, makes a similar observation about the culture at General Motors:

> At the once thriving General Motors, for example, many excellent suggestions regarding small cars, pollution controls and quality improvements were rejected out of hand because they challenged cherished beliefs. They were also sponsored by relatively disenfranchised groups such as engineers, dealers and suppliers rather than by the revered financial specialists. The perspective of the dominant coalition had legitimacy—all others were suppressed.[23]

Yet, it is precisely these contrarian members who are most likely to see aspects of changing industry environments that are ignored by top managers, and they are also most likely to be able to suggest new ideas and strategies for coping with these industry changes.

A second way organizations can overcome the dangers of like-minded thinking would be to encourage greater turnover among top management ranks. Most research on turnover has focused on the negative organizational consequences (such as the loss of skilled employees and added recruiting and training costs) of turnover among lower-level employees. Far fewer studies have focused on either the positive or functional aspects of turnover among top managers.

Research evidence also suggests, however, that a lack of turnover among top managers can have a negative impact on organizations. Studies have shown that executives become more and more committed to the *status quo* as they remain in the same position, continue in employment with the same company, or stay in the same industry.[24] As a result, companies with long-tenured executives run the risk of getting locked into the *status quo* and pursuing strategies that are inappropriate given changes in their industry environments.

Danny Miller, whose research has focused on the effectiveness of top managers, found that firms were much more likely to be appropriately aligned with their industry environments when their CEOs had served for less than ten years. Firms with CEOs who had served for more than ten years tended to exhibit greater misalignment with their industry environments, and this misalignment was associated with lower levels of firm performance. Based on his findings, Miller concluded that long-serving chief executives become "stale in the saddle."[25]

Research studying the impact of employee turnover and workforce heterogeneity on organizational learning has concluded that both contribute to greater knowledge generation.[26] Another study found, for example, that the absence of turnover and workforce heterogeneity can lead to situations in which all of an organization's members become well-versed in its routines and procedures. As illustrated in Exhibit 12.5, at some point, an information equilibrium is reached, and, without new personnel, ideas for changing or improving organizational routines and procedures are not forthcoming and very little new knowledge accumulates. In other words, the exhibit illustrates that without the new thinking introduced by newcomers to an organization, the rate of new knowledge acquisition will begin to deteriorate. Failure to introduce new

Exhibit 12.5 Knowledge Acquisition With and Without Turnover

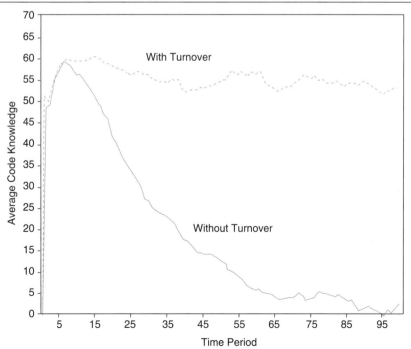

thinking into a closed system leads to stagnation, and an organization's capacity for change can fall below the rate of change in its environment.[27]

The value of introducing new individuals into an organization comes not from their superior knowledge; in fact, this same study confirmed that organizational veterans will almost always have more knowledge about their firms. Instead, the value of new individuals is the new knowledge they contribute. Newcomers may be less knowledgeable than veterans, but what they know is less redundant, can be insightful, and, as also illustrated in Exhibit 12.5, offers more opportunities for improving existing routines or suggesting new procedures.[28]

The decline of the railroad industry was probably due in large part to a lack of heterogeneity and turnover among top railroad managers. From 1885 through 1913, nearly 20 percent of all senior managers in railroad companies had come from other industries. By 1940, however, only about five percent of all senior managers had come to railroad companies from other industries.[29] One railroad industry observer has suggested that because of the tendency to promote from within,

> [o]utside inputs were often ignored or suppressed. Rather than being change seekers, the railroads attempted to accommodate the changing environment by retarding the change or accommodating the new situation with minimum change to the way business was conducted.[30]

The tendency to promote from within had also:

> contributed to an attitude of suspicion of any value or idea that is generated outside the system, and, as in many closed social systems, the belief that insiders are more worthy and trustworthy than outsiders and behavior that rejects anything "not invented here."[31]

Implications and Recommendations

The previous section implies that, without intervention, managers will be less responsive than they should be to changes in their firms' industry environments. We have also suggested that progress comes from the ability to challenge the *status quo* rather than continually accepting it. This section offers a warning and three recommendations aimed at improving the responsiveness of managers and their firms. Our warning emphasizes the dangers of complacency that comes from enjoying success, while our first two recommendations assume that managers need to think like outsiders, and we offer some specific proposals for how this "outsider" thinking can be encouraged. Our final recommendation focuses on the importance of higher-level learning, and we offer some ideas for how this higher-level learning can be institutionalized in business organizations.

Firms Can Be Poisoned by Their Own Success

The bottom-line message from research on these issues is counterintuitive: *Too much success breeds complacency and a failure to engage in higher-level learning.* One organizational researcher has summarized his findings by noting that "organizations are often poisoned by their own success" because they are "unable to unlearn obsolete knowledge in spite of strong disconfirmations." He offered the very paradoxical conclusion that *"shortages are useful to prevent organizations from dying from wealth."*[32]

Advantage can produce adversity in the long run by making firms complacent today while ignoring environmental and other factors that are sowing the seeds for the firm's failure down the road. And, it's plausible that adversity can produce advantage in the long run by forcing managers to engage in problemistic search and to formulate and implement strategies that position them well for long-run success.

Advantage Comes from Thinking (and Acting) Like an Outsider

As already suggested in Chapter 5, one clear implication of the various factors just reviewed is that advantage comes not only from thinking like an outsider, but also from taking risks that would be considered unconventional given industry norms and standards. The factors reviewed in the previous section also suggest that one important way in which firms can think and act like outsiders is for top managers to give greater credibility to contrarian voices or renegades within their own organizations.

Rather than see these contrarian individuals or renegades become alienated and eventually leave as the A-S-A cycle suggests they will, organizations would benefit by giving greater attention and credence to their maverick views. As suggested earlier, these contrarian individuals are much more likely to see and anticipate industry changes, and they are much more likely to understand how their firms could proactively respond to these changes. Gary Hamel has described the process of strategic change as "a fight with orthodoxy" and suggested that it is fueled by new voices, new conversations or connections among new voices, new perspectives, and experimentation. He concludes that *"heretics—and not prophets—create company futures!"*[33]

This recommendation has important implications for companies' human resource management practices. If most organizations select new employees on the basis of "fit," then these hiring practices are responsible for much of the "thinking alike" that can be so detrimental and stultifying for business organizations. The challenge for the future will be for firms to develop new recruitment and selection practices that ensure greater diversity in thinking among employees. It will not be enough, however, to simply alter recruitment and selection patterns in an effort to increase cognitive diversity. Employees who hold maverick views must be supported within the organization or they will leave.

Samsung offers an example of how companies can alter their hiring practices to encourage greater diversity of thinking. Instead of recruiting at a limited set of universities as is common among Korean companies, Samsung recruits widely to be certain it has the broadest possible pool of highly qualified candidates. Then, once hired, employees find an environment that encourages discussion of a wide array of ideas and a focus on developing those ideas deemed most innovative.[34]

Research by Robert Burgelman of Stanford University suggests that middle- and senior-level managers play important roles in accommodating and supporting new points of view.[35] According to Burgelman, middle-level managers play an important role as "champions" of new ideas, while senior-level managers must alter the "strategic context" of their firms in order to accommodate these new ideas. The ideas of new employees are unlikely to have any beneficial impact without managers who are willing to "champion" these ideas or an organizational "context" that welcomes them.[36]

Demographic Diversity Versus "Genetic Diversity"

Over the last few decades, an emphasis on diversity has pushed business organizations to increase both their hiring and promoting of minorities and women into top management positions. Although many firms are to be applauded for their efforts to improve diversity within their ranks, it should be remembered that the *economic* value of demographic diversity is the possibility that it will also lead to greater cognitive diversity—or what Hamel and Prahalad have called "genetic diversity"—by introducing more divergent and contrarian points of view into organizations. Hamel and Prahalad argue that:

> It is important to distinguish between genetic diversity and cultural diversity. Many laggards are international companies. Many possess enormous cultural diversity in their ranks. Many celebrate diversity as a source of strength and innovation. Yet much of the potential for creativity offered by cultural diversity is often surrendered to an allegiance to very undiverse views about the industry and how to compete in it.
>
> Enlarging managerial frames [i.e., managers' mental models] depends, more than anything else, on curiosity and humility. It is these traits that make a senior manager willing to tolerate first-level employees who think the boss is a Neanderthal, and to exercise the patience required to span the hierarchical divides that form a barrier to "upward learning."[37]

Thus, employees who bring new and diverse points of view to an organization serve to expand or enlarge companies' "gene pools," and Hamel and Prahalad argue that more than a few companies are in need of "gene replacement therapy." Managers who fail to promote demographic diversity in their firms may be missing a major opportunity to realize economic benefits by recruiting employees with new viewpoints and understandings. Equally at fault are the managers who promote demographic diversity but then fail to tap divergent points of view within their ranks.

Embracing Exploration: The Value of Higher-Level Organizational Learning and Second-Order Change

The factors noted earlier in the chapter also suggest that organizational learning is essential if organizations are going to formulate and implement strategic change successfully. The ability to balance the allocation of resources between "the exploitation of the known" *and* "the exploration of the new" is essential if firms are to develop their capabilities and competencies while also avoiding the possibility of being blindsided by changes in their industries. As business environments change, managers and firms must not only develop and deploy new knowledge, but they must also "selectively forget" knowledge that has become dated or obsolete.[38]

The points that have been made earlier in this chapter suggest that it's unlikely that managers and their firms will simply embrace or welcome change. Thus, managers must seek to institutionalize change. One way in which some firms have been successful at institutionalizing change is through product development. Traditional product planning efforts typically begin to design new products only *after* demand for old products begins to fall. At this point, the firm will have already missed important opportunities for influencing customer buying habits, and may even lose considerable ground to new products developed by more proactive rivals.

To overcome these limitations, many companies are adopting product planning strategies that attempt to *institutionalize innovation* in their product development efforts. 3M and Rubbermaid require a certain percentage of each year's sales to come from products that did not exist previously. Sony has gone a step further. When it introduces a new product, Sony also specifies the date when the next generation of that product will be introduced. One research study has suggested that an ongoing series of first-order changes creates an experimental atmosphere within organizations that facilitates timely second-order changes.[39] According to this study, ongoing change prevents managers from concluding that they've ever "learned enough" or that they can become complacent. Furthermore, experimentation and first-order change can lead to the discovery of important new areas of opportunity that result in major second-order changes.

Conclusion

In his book, *Competitive Advantage through People*, Stanford professor Jeffrey Pfeffer asks readers to go back to 1972 and predict which companies would generate the highest returns for their stockholders over the next 20 years. He goes on to note that the conventional, structuralist wisdom would suggest selecting firms in industries

> with barriers to entry, low supplier and buyer bargaining power, few ready substitutes, and a limited threat of new entrants to compete away economic returns. Within such industries, other conventional analyses would urge you to select firms with the largest market share, which can realize the cost benefits of economies of scale. In short, you would probably look to industries in which patent protection of important product or service technology could be achieved and select the dominant firms in those industries.[40]

But, Pfeffer goes on to note that you would have much better luck selecting the highest performing firms if you had taken "this conventional wisdom and turned it on its head." The highest performing firms during this 20-year time frame (ranked by stock market performance) were Southwest Airlines with a stock appreciation of 21,775 percent, Wal-Mart with an increase in stock value of 19,807 percent, and Tyson Foods, a poultry processor, whose stock increased by 18,118 percent. Pfeffer notes that

> during this period, these industries … were characterized by massive competition and horrendous losses, widespread bankruptcy, virtually no barriers to entry [after airline deregulation in 1978], little unique or proprietary technology, and many substitute products or services. And, in 1972, none of these firms was … the market share leader, enjoying economies of scale from moving down the learning curve.[41]

In Chapter 1 of this text, we argued that the field of strategic management has long been dominated by a structuralist point of view—that firm performance is largely a function of external forces, primarily industry structure, and that high performance and competitive advantage result from an ability to strategically manage these structural forces.

Pfeffer's observations should help to emphasize a point we made in Chapters 1 and 4 about the structuralist perspective: Although industry structure is almost certainly an influence on firm performance, it is not the only influence, and within both high- and low-performing industries, we find both high- and low-performing firms. Although industry structure is part of the firm performance story, it is only one part of the story.

Recapitulation: The Key Roles of Managers, the Value of Organizational Learning, and the Importance of Organizational Change

The perspective that has guided the writing of this book suggests that general managers, and *not* industry forces, are a much more important influence on organizational success. Managerial thinking, and especially the ability to think creatively and differently, influences the choice of strategies that allow high-performing firms either to occupy unique positions in their competitive arenas or to possess unique competencies that cannot be easily duplicated by their rivals. We have also emphasized that the success of Southwest Airlines comes not from competing in an attractive industry—recall that firms in the airline industry have lost more money than their total accumulated profits since the 1920s![42] Instead, Southwest's high performance results from managerial thinking that viewed the airline industry in nontraditional ways, placed the company in a unique position in the airline industry, and led the company to develop unique and difficult-to-imitate capabilities and competencies that give it the lowest cost structure of any of the major airlines.

The study of business administration has tended to focus on evaluating, financing, and accounting for investments in physical assets. One of the key lessons to be drawn from this is that *investments in physical assets are less important than the managerial thinking that guides these investment decisions.* In other words, managers' understandings of their firms' competitive environments and their beliefs about how their firms should compete are far more critical to their firms' success than is any set of physical assets. And, the relative importance of managerial thinking, organizational learning, and other intangible organizational assets will almost certainly continue to increase in the years ahead.

Throughout this chapter, we have argued that managers must pursue two types of learning and initiate two types of organizational change. They must pursue what they already know—in other words, they must seek to apply and refine existing knowledge in order to develop the capabilities and competencies that will provide their firms with a competitive advantage. At the same time, they must focus on "exploring the new" in order to proactively redefine their businesses and develop the capabilities and competencies that will be needed to enjoy a competitive advantage in the future. Unfortunately, a good deal of the evidence offered in this book suggests that managers show a preference for the known over the more speculative unknown.

Great Dramas in Business

Throughout this text, we have offered many examples of contemporary business issues and described the strategic dilemmas currently faced by many companies: The attempts of the U.S. automobile companies to regain momentum in the worldwide automobile industry, the ascendancy of digital companies like Facebook and Google, Apple's spectacular reinvention of itself as a consumer electronics company, the ongoing development of new medical technologies for fighting disease, Kodak's efforts to remake itself in a digital future—these are great dramas in the business world that are currently being acted out on a global stage. We can learn much from these companies by seeking to understand the complex relationships among the thinking of their top managers, the dynamic nature of their industry environments, their struggles to redefine themselves in a new competitive landscape, and their strategies to maintain or regain competitive advantage.

Key Points

- A lack of responsiveness to and the inability to anticipate environmental change is a major organizational problem, probably far greater than most other business problems.
- A lack of responsiveness can be due to problems of noticing, problems in correctly interpreting environmental stimuli, and problems of taking action.
- Managers and firms have a preference for, and place an emphasis on, lower-level learning over higher-level learning, which can lead to complacency and the inability to change and adapt.
- Many companies have internal processes that encourage homogeneity in managerial thinking, and this lack of diversity in thinking can make firms less responsive.
- Industry norms and standards, while important to the adoption and growth of sales of products and services, can limit openness to new ideas and suppress innovation.
- By thinking (and acting) like industry outsiders, by emphasizing higher-level organizational learning, and by institutionalizing change, managers can become more responsive to environmental change.
- Finally, the chapter closed by describing again the important roles played by general managers and by reiterating the fundamental importance of managerial decision making. Many current examples of firms working to remake themselves offer real-time "dramas" that can teach us much about the management of strategic change.

Key Questions for Managers

- Can you identify some situations—either in your professional life or your personal life—when your cognitive biases or limitations have prevented you from being as responsive to changes as you probably should have been?
- Can you identify some situations in which you or other managers in your firm have had difficulty either noticing significant changes in your company's environment, or correctly interpreting and responding to those changes?

- Distinguish between low-level and high-level learning and describe the importance of each. Why is high-level learning so important to the management of strategic change? What can you and other managers in your organization do to encourage more high-level learning?
- Does your company have a problem with homogeneity in managerial thinking, and, if so, can you recount some situations in which this "thinking alike" contributed to a lack of responsiveness to environmental change?
- What can your organization do to encourage more diversity in managerial thinking?
- What can you do to improve your ability and your company's ability to anticipate and respond effectively to strategic change?

Suggestions for Further Reading

Additionally, links to further resources online—such as cases, articles, and videos—can be found on the book's website, www.routledge.com/textbooks/Duhaime.

Argyris, C. 1999. *On Organizational Learning* (2nd ed.). Malden, MA: Blackwell Business.

Barr, P. S., Stimpert, J. L., and Huff, A. S. 1992. Cognitive change, strategic action, and organizational renewal. *Strategic Management Journal*, 13(special edition): 15–36.

Dierkes, M., Antal, A. B., Child, J., & Nonaka, I. (Eds.) 2001. *Handbook of Organizational Learning and Knowledge.* New York: Oxford University Press.

Easterby-Smith, M., & Lyles, M. A. (Eds.) 2003. *The Blackwell Handbook of Organizational Learning and Knowledge Management.* Malden, MA: Blackwell.

Hambrick, D. C., and D'Aveni, R. A. 1988. Large corporate failures as downward spirals. *Administrative Science Quarterly*, 33: 1–23.

Hamel, G., & Prahalad, C. K. 1994. *Competing for the Future.* Boston: Harvard Business School Press.

Hedberg, B. 1981. How organizations learn and unlearn. In P. C. Nystrom and W. H. Starbuck (Eds.), *Handbook of Organizational Design*, 1: 3–27. New York: Oxford University Press.

Kiesler, S., and Sproull, L. 1982. Managerial response to changing environments: Perspectives on problem sensing from social cognition. *Administrative Science Quarterly*, 27: 548–570.

March, J. G. 1991. Exploration and exploitation in organizational learning. *Organization Science*, 2: 71–87.

Mathews, R., & Wacker, W. 2002. *The Deviant's Advantage: How Fringe Ideas Create Mass Markets.* New York: Crown Business.

Schneider, B. 1987. The people make the place. *Personnel Psychology*, 40: 437–453.

Shani, A. B., & Docherty, P. 2000. *Learning by Design: Building Sustainable Organizations.* Malden, MA: Blackwell.

NOTES

Preface

1. Rumelt, R. P. 1974. *Strategy, Structure and Economic Performance*. Boston: Harvard Business School Press.
2. Bettis, R., & Prahalad, C. K. 1995. The dominant logic: Retrospective and extension. *Strategic Management Journal*, 16: 6.
3. Porter, M. E. 1980. *Competitive Strategy*. New York: Free Press.
4. Thompson, J. D. 1967. *Organizations in Action*. New York: McGraw-Hill: 101.
5. Senge, P. M. 1990. *The Fifth Discipline: The Art and Practice of the Learning Organization*. New York: Doubleday/Currency.

Chapter 1

1. Naughton, K. 2010. With Lincoln, Ford isn't in the lap of luxury. *Business Week*, May 6: 23–24; Dolan, M. 2010. Putting the luxe back in Lincoln. *The Wall Street Journal*, June 28: B1, B2.
2. Mintzberg, H. 1978. Patterns in strategy formation. *Management Science*, 24: 943.
3. Tam, P. 2004. Is Apple losing its sheen? *The Wall Street Journal*, June 28: B1, B6.
4. Thain, J. 2004. Sarbanes-Oxley: Is the price too high? *The Wall Street Journal*, May 27: A20.
5. Collins, J. C., & Porras, J. I. 1994. *Built to Last: Successful Habits of Visionary Companies*. New York: HarperBusiness; Peters, T. J., & Waterman, Jr., R. H. 1982. *In Search of Excellence: Lessons from America's Best-Run Companies*. New York: Harper & Row. See also, Resnick B. G., & Smunt, T. L., 2008. From good to great to … *Academy of Management Perspectives*, 22(4): 6–12; Niendorf, B., & Beck, K. 2008. *Good to Great*, or just good? *Academy of Management Perspectives*, 22(4): 13–20
6. Thurow, L. C. 1999. Building wealth. *The Atlantic Monthly*, June: 57–69.
7. Senge, P. M. 1990. *The Fifth Discipline: The Art and Practice of the Learning Organization*. New York: Doubleday/Currency.
8. Mintzberg, H. 1978. Patterns in strategy formation. *Management Science*, 24: 934–948.
9. Mintzberg, H. 1978. Patterns in strategy formation. *Management Science*, 24: 935.
10. Eigerman, M. R. 1988. Letter to the editor, *The Wall Street Journal,* February 26: page number?
11. Quoted in Henkoff, R. 1990. How to plan for 1995. *Fortune*, December 31: 70–77.
12. Mintzberg, H. 1978. Patterns in strategy formation. *Management Science*, 24: 934–948.
13. Henkoff, R. 1990. How to plan for 1995. *Fortune*, December 31: 70–77.
14. Pascale, R. T. 1984. Perspectives on strategy: The real story behind Honda's success. *California Management Review*, 26(3): 47–72.

15. Pascale, R. T. 1984. Perspectives on strategy: The real story behind Honda's success. *California Management Review*, 26(3): 54.

16. Pascale, R. T. 1984. Perspectives on strategy: The real story behind Honda's success. *California Management Review*, 26(3): 57, emphasis in original.

17. Holmes, E. 2009. Skimpy profits pressure Abercrombie. *The Wall Street Journal*, August 14: B1, B2. Martin, T. W., 2009. Safeway shifts tactics in grocery price war. *The Wall Street Journal*, October 16: B1, B5.

18. Boyle, M. 2009. Abercrombie bargains for a rebound. *Business Week*, November 30: 62; Talley, K. 2009. Abercrombie plans to cut more prices. *The Wall Street Journal*, August 15–16: B5.

19. Burrows, P. 2009. Cisco's extreme ambitions. *Business Week*, November 30: 26–27.

20. Bourgeois, III, L. J., & Eisenhardt, K. M. 1988. Strategic decision processes in high-velocity environments: Four cases in the microcomputer industry. *Management Science*, 34: 816–835; D'Aveni, R. 1994. *Hypercompetition*. New York: Free Press.

21. Siklos, R. 2009. Bob Iger rocks Disney. *Business Week*, January 19: 80–86.

22. Mintzberg, H. 1978. Patterns in strategy formation. *Management Science*, 24: 934–948.

23. Huselid, M. A. 1995. The impact of human resource management practices on turnover, productivity, and corporate financial performance. *Academy of Management Journal*, 38: 635–672.

Chapter 2

1. Mintzberg, H. 1978. Patterns in strategy formation. *Management Science*, 24: 935–948.

2. Prahalad, C. K., & Hamel, G. 1990. The core competence of the corporation. *Harvard Business Review*, 68(3): 79–91.

3. Cool, K., & Schendel, D. 1988. Performance differences among strategic group members. *Strategic Management Journal*, 9: 207–223.

4. Lawless, M. W., Bergh, D. D., & Wilsted, W. D. 1989. Performance variations among strategic group members: An examination of individual firm capability. *Journal of Management*, 15: 649–661.

5. Barney, J. B. 1991. Firm resources and sustained competitive advantage. *Journal of Management*, 17: 99–120; Wernerfelt, B. 1984. A resource-based view of the firm. *Strategic Management Journal*, 5: 171–180.

6. Penrose, E. T. 1959. *The Theory of the Growth of the Firm*. New York: Wiley.

7. Barney, J. B. 1991. Firm resources and sustained competitive advantage. *Journal of Management*, 17: 99–120.

8. Wernerfelt, B. 1984. A resource-based view of the firm. *Strategic Management Journal*, 5: 171–180.

9. Barney, J. B. 1986. Strategic factor markets: Expectations, luck, and business strategy. *Management Science*, 42: 1231–1241.

10. Ishikura, Y., & Porter, M. 1983. *Canon, Inc.: Worldwide Copier Strategy*. Boston: Harvard Business School.

11. McHugh, J. 1998. Don't mess with me. *Forbes*, March 23: 42.

12. Dierickx, I., & Cool, K. 1989. Asset stock accumulation and sustainability of competitive advantage. *Management Science*, 35: 1504–1511.
13. See McCartney, S. 1996. Turbulence ahead: Competitors quake as Southwest Air is set to invade northeast. *The Wall Street Journal*, October 23: A1, A6.
14. Quintanilla, C. 1994. New airline fad: Faster airport turnarounds. *The Wall Street Journal*, August 4: B1, B7.
15. Dierickx, I., & Cool, K. 1989. Asset stock accumulation and sustainability of competitive advantage. *Management Science*, 35: 1504–1511.
16. Lippman, S. A., & Rumelt, R. P. 1982. Uncertain imitability: An analysis of interfirm differences in efficiency under competition. *Bell Journal of Economics*, 13: 418–438.
17. Data for this example are drawn from Rivkin, J. W., & Porter, M. E. 1998. *Matching Dell*. Boston: HBS Case Services; Rivkin, J. W. 1999. *Matching Dell: Teaching Note*. Boston: HBS Case Services.
18. Corcoran, E. 1992. Redesigning research. *Scientific American*, June: 103.
19. Prahalad, C. K., & Hamel, G. 1990. The core competence of the corporation. *Harvard Business Review*, 68(3): 79–91.
20. Prahalad, C. K., & Hamel, G. 1990. The core competence of the corporation. *Harvard Business Review*, 68(3): 82.
21. LeVine, S. 2010. IBM piles up patents, but quantity isn't king. *Business Week*, January 25: 53.
22. Prahalad, C. K., & Hamel, G. 1990. The core competence of the corporation. *Harvard Business Review*, 68(3): 83.
23. Barney, J. B. 1992. Integrating organizational behavior and strategy formulation research: A resource-based analysis. *Advances in Strategic Management*, 8: 44; Boyd, B. K., Bergh, D. D., & Ketchen, Jr., D. J. 2010. Reconsidering the reputation-performance relationship: A resource-based view. *Journal of Management*, 36: 588–609.
24. Wasserman, M. E. 2000. *Examining the Relationship between Research and Development Resource Flows and Knowledge-Based Capabilities: Integrating Resource-Based and Organizational Learning Theory*. Unpublished dissertation, Michigan State University; Dierickx, I., & Cook, K. 1989. Asset stock accumulation and sustainability of competitive advantage. *Management Science*, 35: 1504–1511; Hall, R. 1993. A framework linking intangible resources and capabilities to sustainable competitive advantage. *Strategic Management Journal*, 14: 607–618.
25. Aaker, D. A. 1989. Managing assets and skills: The key to a sustainable competitive advantage. *California Management Review,* 31(2): 91–106; Hall, R. 1992. The strategic analysis of intangible resources. *Strategic Management Journal,* 13: 135–144.
26. Jack Welch. (n.d.). BrainyQuote.com. Retrieved April 2, 2010, from BrainyQuote.com website: http://www.brainyquote.com/quotes/quotes/j/jackwelch173305.html
27. Schlender, B. 2002. A gorilla named Sony. *Fortune*, April 1: 116.
28. Edwards, C., Hall, K., & Grover, R. 2008. Sony chases Apple's magic. *Business Week*, November 10: 48–51.
29. Edwards, C. 2009. Dell's do-over. *Business Week*, October 26: 37–40; Fortt, J. 2008. Michael Dell "friends" his customers. *Business Week*, September 15: 35–38.

30. Levitt, B., & March, J. G. 1988. Organizational learning. *Annual Review of Sociology*, 14: 319–340.

31. Kaplan, R. S., & Norton, D. P. 1996. *The Balanced scorecard: Translating Strategy into Action*. Boston: Harvard Business School Press.

Chapter 3

1. McCaskey, M. B. 1982. *The executive challenge: Managing change and ambiguity*. Marshfield, MA: Pittman Publishing: 17.

2. See, for example, Carley, W. M. 1997. Charging ahead: To keep GE's profits rising, Welch pushes quality-control plan. *The Wall Street Journal*, January 13: A1, A6.

3. See, for example, Moran, P. 2005. Structural vs. relational embeddedness: Social capital and managerial performance. *Strategic Management Journal*, 26: 1,129–1,151.

4. Southwest Airlines. 2009. *Annual report*: 4.

5. Quoted in Hoffer Gittell, J. 2003. *The Southwest Airlines Way*. New York: McGraw-Hill: 170.

6. Fisher, D. 2002. Is there such a thing as nonstop growth? *Forbes*, July 8: 82–84.

7. Quoted in Mercer, D. 1987. *IBM: How the World's Most Successful Company is Managed*. London: Kogan: 48.

8. Donaldson, G., & Lorsch, J. W. 1983. *Decision Making at the Top*. New York: Basic Books: 10.

9. Wal-Mart Stores. 2009. *Annual Report*: 15, 16, 21.

10. Quoted in Rosenthal, J. 1994. Frame of mind. *The New York Times Magazine*, August 21: 16, 18.

11. Huff, A. S. 1982. Industry influences on strategy reformulation. *Strategic Management Journal*, 3: 119–131.

12. Quoted in Stimpert, J. L., Duhaime, I. M., & Chesley, J. A. 2009. Learning to manage a large diversified firm. *Journal of Leadership and Organizational Studies*, 11: 421.

13. Letter to the editor from Frank Gaines. 2004. *Fast Company*, July: 23.

14. Amabile, T. M. 1989. *Growing Up Creative*. Buffalo: C. E. F. Press.

15. Amabile, T. M. 1983. *The Social Psychology of Creativity*. New York: Springer-Verlag; Amabile, T. M. 1989. *Growing Up Creative*. Buffalo: C. E. F. Press; Perkins, D. N. 1981. *The Mind's Best Work*. Cambridge, MA: Harvard University Press; May, R. 1975. *The Courage to Create*. New York: Norton.

16. May, R. 1975. *The Courage to Create*. New York: Norton: 71.

17. Morris, B., & Levinstein, J. 2008. What makes Apple golden? *Fortune*, March 3: 68–74.

18. Smith, E. 2005. John Mackey. *Texas Monthly*, March: 124.

19. Johnson, G. 1996. What happens when the brain can't remember? *The New York Times*, July 7(Section E): 10.

20. O'Brien, J., & Shambora, J. 2009. Amazon's next revolution. *Fortune*, May 8: 67–76.

21. Crockett, R., Kharif, O., & Ante, S. 2009. AT&T and Verizon bet on netbooks. *Business Week*, June 1: 30–31.

22. Davis, M. S. 1985. Two plus two doesn't equal five. *Fortune*, December 9: 177, 179.

23. Hamermesh, R. G. 1977. Responding to divisional profit crises. *Harvard Business Review* 55(2): 124–130; Milliken, F. J., Morrison, E. W., & Hewlin, P. F. 2003. An exploratory study of employee silence: Issues that employees don't communicate upward and why. *Journal of Management Studies*, 40: 1,453–1,477.

24. Grove, A. 1996. *Only the Paranoid Survive*. New York: Currency: 118–120.

25. Taylor, A. 2008. Can Chrysler survive? *Fortune*, August 18: 110–117.

26. Tedlow, R. 1020. Toyota was in denial. How about you? *Business Week*, April 19: 76.

27. Quoted in Foster, R. 2001. The Welch legacy: Creative destruction." *The Wall Street Journal*, September 10: A18.

28. McCaskey, M. B. 1982. *The Executive Challenge: Managing Change and Ambiguity*. Marshfield, MA: Pittman Publishing: 25.

29. Fiske, S. T., & Taylor, S. E. 1984. *Social Cognition*. Reading, MA: Addison-Wesley.

30. Barr, P. S., Stimpert, J. L., & Huff, A. S. 1992. Cognitive change, strategic action, and organizational renewal. *Strategic Management Journal*, 13(special issue): 15–36.

31. Quoted in Lashinsky, A. 2005. Look who's online now. *Fortune*, October 31: 56–65.

32. Senge, P. M. 1990. *The Fifth Discipline: The Art and Practice of the Learning Organization*. New York: Doubleday/Currency: 176.

33. Barr, P. S., Stimpert, J. L., & Huff, A. S. 1992. Cognitive change, strategic action, and organizational renewal. *Strategic Management Journal*, 13(special issue): 15–36.

34. Janis, I. L. 1971. Groupthink. *Psychology Today*, November: 43–46.

35. Staw, B. 1981. The escalation of commitment to a course of action. *Academy of Management Review*, 6: 577–588.

36. Munk, N. 2004. *Fools Rush in: Steve Case, Jerry Levin, and the Unmaking of AOL Time Warner*. New York: HarperBusiness.

37. Kiesler, S., & Sproull, L. 1982. Managerial responses to changing environments: Perspectives on social sensing from social cognition. *Administrative Science Quarterly*, 27: 557.

38. McCaskey, M. B. 1982. *The Executive Challenge: Managing Change and Ambiguity*. Marshfield, MA: Pittman Publishing: 18.

39. Gladwell, M. 2008. *Outliers*. New York: Little, Brown, and Company.

40. Hamel, G., & Prahalad, C. K. 1994. *Competing for the Future*. Boston: Harvard Business School Press.

41. Barr, P. S., Stimpert, J. L., & Huff, A. S. 1992. Cognitive change, strategic action, and organizational renewal. *Strategic Management Journal*, 13(special issue): 15–36.

42. March, J. G. 1991. Exploration and exploitation in organizational learning. *Organization Science*, 2: 71–87.

43. Drucker, P. F. 1967. *The Effective Executive*. New York: Harper & Row: 148.

44. See for example, Fortt, J. 2008. John Hurd, superstar. *Fortune*, June 9: 35–40; Lashinsky, A., & Burke, D. 2009. John Hurd's moment, *Fortune*, March 16: 90–100.

45. Der Hovanesian, M. 2009. Jamie Dimon: Lucky or good? *Business Week*, October 19: 67–68.

Chapter 4

1. This question has generated considerable empirical research among academics. Some key studies include Schmalensee, R. 1985. Do markets differ much? *American Economic Review*, 75: 341–351; Rumelt, R. P. 1991. How much does industry matter? *Strategic Management Journal*, 12: 167–185; McGahan, A. M., & Porter, M. E. 1997. How much does industry matter, really? *Strategic Management Journal* 18(special issue): 15–30.

2. Schmalensee, R. 1985. Do markets differ much? *American Economic Review*, 75: 341–351.

3. Rumelt, R. P. 1991. How much does industry matter? *Strategic Management Journal*, 12: 167–185.

4. Rumelt, R. P. 1991. How much does industry matter? *Strategic Management Journal*, 12: 167–185.

5. Porter, M. E. 1978. How competitive forces shape strategy. *Harvard Business Review*, 56(2): 137–145.

6. Porter, M. E. 1980. *Competitive Strategy*. New York: Free Press.

7. Adams, W., & Brock, J. 1990. *The Structure of American Industry (9th ed.)*. Englewood Cliffs, NJ: Prentice-Hall.

8. Bollenbacher, G. M. 1992. America's banking dinosaurs. *The Wall Street Journal*, March 18: A14.

9. AMR Corporation. 2008. *Annual Report*.

10. United Airlines. 2008. *Annual Report*.

11. Ramstad, E. 2009. Samsung's size brings big challenges. *The Wall Street Journal*, November 12: B8.

12. Garvin, D. A. 1992. *Operations Strategy*. Englewood Cliffs, NJ: Prentice-Hall.

13. Card watch: Breaching the bank card fortress. 2001. *Credit Card Management*, November: 6.

14. Pacelle, M., & Sapsford, J. 2003. The great debit-card shuffle. *The Wall Street Journal*, November 25: C1, C13.

15. See for example, Nomani, A. Q. 1996. Eastern airports still out of reach to start-ups. *The Wall Street Journal*, April 25: B1; Rose, R. L., & Dahl, J. 1989. Aborted takeoffs: Skies are deregulated, but just try starting a sizable new airline. *The Wall Street Journal*, July 18: A1, A9.

16. McCartney, S., Brady, D., Carey, S., & Nomani, A. Q. 1996. Hot seats: U.S. airlines' prospects are grim on expanding access to Asian skies. *The Wall Street Journal*, September 25: A1, A13.

17. Schlender, B. 2001. Intel unleashes its inner Attila. *Fortune*, October 15: 169–184.

18. Marr, M. 2004. Movie-theater chains are wary amid recovery. *The Wall Street Journal*, May 17: C3.

19. Lawton, C., & Tkacik, M. 2002. Foot Locker changes mix of sneakers. *The Wall Street Journal*, July 22: B3; Tkacik, M. 2003. Rubber match: In a clash of sneaker titans, Nike gets leg up on Foot Locker, *The Wall Street Journal*, May 13: A1, A10; Kang, S. 2004. Foot Locker profit jumps 25%, boosted by influx of Nike shoes. *The Wall Street Journal*, March 3: B3.

20. Shirouzu, N. 2003. Ford and GM put the squeeze on parts suppliers for price cuts. *The Wall Street Journal*, November 18: A3.
21. Edwards, C. 2009. Why tech bows to Best Buy. *Business Week*, December 21: 50–56.
22. Bianco, A. *et al.* 2003. Is Wal-Mart too powerful? *Business Week*, October 6: 100; Fishman, C. 2003. The Wal-Mart you don't know. *Fast Company*, December: 68.
23. Warner, M. 2006. Wal-Mart extending dominance of the grocery business. *The New York Times*, March 3.
24. Wilke, J. R. 1997. FTC says Staples' bid for Office Depot sought to remove most aggressive rival. *The Wall Street Journal*, May 20: A4; Harty, R. P. 1997. Antitrust: Federal judge enjoins the proposed merger of Staples and Office Depot. *International Commercial Litigation*, September: 43.
25. Smith, E. and McCracken, J. 2009. Justice agency resists music merger. *The Wall Street Journal*, October 16: B1, B2.
26. Malone, M., & Hayes, T. 2011. Bye-bye, PCs and laptops. *The Wall Street Journal*, January 7: A13.
27. Putka, G. 1991. Colleges cancel aid meetings under scrutiny. *The Wall Street Journal*, March 12: B1.
28. Bank, D. 1997. Why software and antitrust law make an uneasy mix. *The Wall Street Journal*, October 22: B1.
29. Gripsrud, G., & Gronhaug, K. 1985. Structure and strategy in grocery retailing: A sociometric approach. *The Journal of Industrial Economics*, 33: 339–347.
30. Hamel, G., & Prahalad, C. K. 1989. Strategic intent. *Harvard Business Review,* 67(3): 64.
31. Kim, W. C., & Mauborgne, R. 2005. *Blue Ocean Strategy.* Boston: Harvard Business School Press.

Chapter 5

1. Cooper, A. C., & Schendel, D. 1976. Strategic responses to technological threats. *Business Horizons*, 19(1): 61–69.
2. Hamel, G., & Prahalad, C. K. 1994. *Competing for the Future*, Boston: Harvard Business School Press: 16.
3. Abell, D. F. 1980. *Defining the Business: Starting Point of Strategic Planning*. Englewood Cliffs, NJ: Prentice-Hall.
4. Mintzberg, H. 1978. Patterns in strategy formation. *Management Science*, 24: 943.
5. The lure of the coffee bar, the smell of the grounds. 1995. *The New York Times*, August 13(Section F): 10; Helliker, K., & Leung, S. 2002. Despite the jitters, most coffeehouses survive Starbucks. *The Wall Street Journal*, September 24: A1, A11.
6. Cole, A. 2009. Makers of military drones take off. *The Wall Street Journal.* August 24: B1, B2.
7. Reilly, P. M. 1997. Booksellers prepare to do battle in cyberspace. *The Wall Street Journal*, January 28: B1, B8.
8. Morris, B., & Levinstein, J. 2008. What makes Apple golden. *Fortune.* March 17: 68–74.

9. Stern, G. 1993. The Rio Grande is mainstream for today's US. palates. *The Wall Street Journal*, January 19: B1, B10.
10. Mintzberg, H. 1978. Patterns in strategy formation. *Management Science*, 24: 948.
11. Mintzberg, H., Raìsinghanì, D., & Théorêt, A. 1976. The structure of "unstructured" decision processes. *Administrative Science Quarterly*, 21: 253.
12. Kiesler, S., & Sproull, L. 1982. Managerial response to changing environments: Perspectives on problem sensing from social cognition. *Administrative Science Quarterly*, 27: 548–570.
13. Kiesler, S., & Sproull, L. 1982. Managerial response to changing environments: Perspectives on problem sensing from social cognition. *Administrative Science Quarterly*, 27: 557.
14. Marshall McLuhan, quoted in Barber, R. J. 1970. *The American Corporation: Its Power, Its Money, Its Politics*. New York: E. P. Dalton: 3 (emphasis added).
15. Orwall, B., Peers, M., & Smith, E. 2003. Music industry presses "play" on plan to save its business. *The Wall Street Journal*, September 9: A1, A14.
16. Hall, R. I. 1984. The natural logic of management policy making: Its implications for the survival of an organization. *Management Science*, 30: 905–927.
17. Foust, D. 2004. Things go better with … juice. *Business Week*, May 17: 81–82.
18. Holstein, W. J. 2002. Canon takes aim at Xerox. *Fortune*, October 14: 215–225.
19. Schmalensee, R. 1978. Entry deterrence in the ready-to-eat breakfast cereal industry. *Bell Journal of Economics*, 9: 318 (emphasis added).
20. Staw, B. M., Sandelands, L. E., & Dutton, J. E. 1981. Threat-rigidity effects in organizational behavior: A multilevel analysis. *Administrative Science Quarterly*, 26: 501–524.
21. Urban, G. L., Carter, T., Gaskin, S., & Mucha, Z. 1986. Market share rewards to pioneering brands: An empirical analysis and strategic implications. *Management Science*, 32: 645–659.
22. Huff, A. S. 1982. Industry influences on strategy reformulation. *Strategic Management Journal* 3: 119–131; Powell, W. W., & DiMaggio, P. J. (Eds.). 1991. *The New Institutionalism in Organizational Analysis*. Chicago: University of Chicago Press.
23. Hambrick, D. C. 1982. Environmental scanning and organizational strategy. *Strategic Management Journal*, 3: 159–174.
24. Adams, R. 2008. Gannett profit tumbles 53%. *The Wall Street Journal*, October 20: B4.
25. Drucker, P. F. 1985. *Innovation and Entrepreneurship*. New York: Harper & Row: 230.
26. Cooper, A. C., & Schendel, D. 1976. Strategic responses to technological threats. *Business Horizons*, 19(1): 61–69.
27. Cooper, A. C., & Schendel, D. 1976. Strategic responses to technological threats. *Business Horizons*, 19(1): 61–69.
28. Shapiro, E. C. 1991. *How Corporate Truths Become Competitive Traps*. New York: Wiley: 52–53.
29. Johnson, K. 2003. Small supermarket chain on the rise. *Sacramento Business Journal*, October 17.
30. Porter, M. E. 1980. *Competitive Strategy*. New York: The Free Press.
31. Cooper, A. C., & Schendel, D. 1976. Strategic responses to technological threats. *Business Horizons*, 19(1): 61–69.

32. Mintzberg, H. 1978. Patterns in strategy formation. *Management Science*, 24: 941.

33. Hamel, G. 1998. Will merger with DEC be Compaq's last hurrah? *The Wall Street Journal*, March 2: A18.

34. Mitchell, R. 1989. Masters of innovation: How 3M keeps its new products coming. *Business Week*, April 10: 58–63.

35. Rubbermaid, Inc. 1989. *Annual Report*.

36. Bank, D. 1997. Why Microsoft wants to hook into cable TV. *The Wall Street Journal*, October 16: B1, B19; Shapiro, E. 1997. TCI may get investment by Microsoft. *The Wall Street Journal*, October 15: A3, A4.

Chapter 6

1. Albert, S., & Whetten, D. 1985. Organizational identity. In Cummings, L. L., & Staw, B. M. (Eds.), *Research in Organizational Behavior*, 7: 263–295. Greenwich, CT: JAI Press.

2. Abell, D. F. 1980. *Defining the Business: Starting Point of Strategic Planning*. Englewood Cliffs, NJ: Prentice-Hall.

3. Exhibit 6.2 illustrates an industry that expands over time, suggesting that new customers are being served, new products or services are being introduced, and new technologies are being incorporated. It's important to emphasize that not all industries expand over time as illustrated in the exhibit. The newspaper market, for example, has contracted considerably since the end of World War II. At that time, many households subscribed to two major daily newspapers and, to meet this demand, many cities had at least two daily newspapers. For example, in Washington, DC, the *Washington Post* was the "morning" newspaper while the *Evening Star* was published in the afternoon to summarize the day's news. The advent of television has had a major impact on newspaper readership, and today, less than half of all American households subscribe to a daily newspaper. Thus, the newspaper market has contracted considerably over the past several decades.

4. Porter, M. E. 1987. From competitive advantage to corporate strategy. *Harvard Business Review*, 65(3): 43–59.

5. Selznick, A. 1957. *Leadership in Administration: A Sociological Interpretation*. New York: Harper & Row; Collins, J. C., & Porras, J. I. 1994. *Built to Last: Successful Habits of Visionary Companies*. New York: HarperBusiness; Larwood, L., Falbe, C. M., Kriger, M. P., & Miesing, P. 1995. Structure and meaning of organizational vision. *Academy of Management Journal*, 38: 740–769; Albert, S., & Whetten, D. 1985. Organizational identity. In Cummings, L. L., & Staw, B. M. (Eds.), *Research in Organizational Behavior*, 7: 263–295. Greenwich, CT: JAI Press.

6. Harley-Davidson: Ride your heritage. 2004. *Fast Company*, August: 44.

7. Charan, R. 1982. How to strengthen your strategy review process. *Journal of Business Strategy*, 2(3): 53.

8. Hamel, G., & Prahalad, C. K. 1994. *Competing for the Future*. Boston: Harvard Business School: 146.

9. Collins, J. C., & Porras, J. I. 1994. *Built to Last: Successful Habits of Visionary Companies*. New York: HarperBusiness: 227.

10. Sloan, Jr., A. P. 1963. *My Years with General Motors*. New York: Doubleday/Currency: 58.
11. Sloan, Jr., A. P. 1963. *My Years with General Motors*. New York: Doubleday/Currency: 68.
12. Sloan, Jr., A. P. 1963. *My Years with General Motors*. New York: Doubleday/Currency: 441.
13. Abrahams, J. 2007. *101 Mission Statements from Top Companies: Plus Guidelines for Writing Your Own Mission Statement*. Berkeley: Ten Speed Press.
14. Abell, D. F. 1980. *Defining the Business: Starting Point of Strategic Planning*. Englewood Cliffs, NJ: Prentice-Hall.
15. May, R. 1975. *The Courage to Create*. New York: Norton: 21–22.
16. May, R. 1975. *The Courage to Create*. New York: Norton: 88.
17. Amabile, T. M. 1983. *The Social Psychology of Creativity*. New York: Springer-Verlag.
18. May, R. 1975. *The Courage to Create*. New York: Norton: 88.
19. Hamel, G., & Prahalad, C. K. 1994. *Competing for the Future*. Boston: Harvard Business School Press: 145.
20. Quoted in Morris, B, & Levinstein, J. 2008. What makes Apple golden? *Business Week*, March 17: 68–74.
21. We are grateful to Anne Huff for sharing this insight.
22. Sloan, Jr., A. P. 1963. *My Years with General Motors*. New York: Doubleday/Currency: 60, emphasis added.
23. Drucker, P. F. 1964. *Managing for Results: Economic Tasks and Risk-Taking Decisions*. New York: Harper & Row: 7–8.
24. Cooper, A. C., & Schendel, D. 1976. Strategic responses to technological threats. *Business Horizons*, 19(1): 61–69.
25. Adams, R. 2010. Magazine-sales decline slows at newsstands. *The Wall Street Journal*, February 9: B6.
26. Wyman, B. 2010. What newspapers can learn from Craigslist. *The Wall Street Journal*, February 13–14: A13.
27. Miller, K. 1990. Repair industry struggles to survive cars' high quality. *The Wall Street Journal*, January 5: B2.
28. Sull, D. N. 2003. *Revival of the Fittest: Why Good Companies Go Bad and How Great Managers Remake Them*. Boston: Harvard Business School Press: 110.
29. Holusha, J. 1992. American snapshot, the next generation. *The New York Times*, June 7: F1, F6.
30. Vilaga, J. 2004. HP's digital desires. *Fast Company*, August: 32.
31. Deutsch, C. H. 1996. Picture it: More paths to profits. *The New York Times*, December 2: C1, C10.
32. Deutsch, C. H. 1996. Picture it: More paths to profits. *The New York Times*, December 2: C10.
33. Deutsch, C. H. 1996. Picture it: More paths to profits. *The New York Times*, December 2: C10.
34. Fisher, L. M. 1992. The Gallos go for the gold, and away from the jugs. *The New York Times*, November 22: F5.

35. King, Jr., R. T. 1996. Grapes of wrath: Kendall-Jackson sues Gallo Winery in a battle over a bottle. *The Wall Street Journal*, April 5: B1, B2.
36. Rigdon, J. I. 1997. Wine-bottle design suit could have a spillover effect on other products. *The Wall Street Journal*, March 31: B9D.
37. Hamel, G., & Prahalad, C. K. 1994. *Competing for the Future*. Boston: Harvard Business School Press: 312.
38. Arner, F., & Tiplady, R. 2004. No excuse not to succeed. *Business Week*, May 10: 96–98.
39. Lloyd, M. E. 2010. Kodak hits Apple, RIM over patents. *The Wall Street Journal*, January 15: B6.
40. Burrows, P. 2009. Cisco's extreme ambitions. *Business Week*, November 30: 26–27.
41. Hamel, G., & Prahalad, C. K. 1989. Strategic intent. *Harvard Business Review*, 67(3): 63–76.
42. See, for example, Starbuck, W. H. 1992. Strategizing in the real world. *International Journal of Technology Management*, 8: 77–85.

Chapter 7

1. Miles, R. E., & Snow, C. C. 1978. *Organizational Strategy, Structure, and Process*. New York: McGraw-Hill.
2. Porter, M. E. 1980. *Competitive Strategy*. New York: Free Press.
3. Reed, D. 2004. Low-fare carriers' service bests big rivals. *USA Today*, April 6: 2B; Estabrook, B. 2004. In the air, on the cheap. *The New York Times*, April 4: TR 9.
4. Brady, D., & Brasileiro, A. 2010. Getting over the jet blues. *Business Week*, February 15: 52–54.
5. Porter, M. E. 1980. *Competitive Strategy*. New York: Free Press.
6. Brush, M. 1997. At Morton, much more than a dash of cash. *The New York Times*, June 1: Section III, 5.
7. Mitchell, R. 1991. Intel isn't taking this lying down. *Business Week*, September 30, 32–33.
8. Overholt, A. 2004. Smart strategies: Putting ideas to work. *Fast Company*, April: 63.
9. Roberto Goizueta in his own words. 1997. *The Wall Street Journal*, October 20: B1.
10. Welch, D. 2010. Oh, what a (hideous) feeling. *Business Week*, February 15: 21–22.
11. Danziger, P. N. 2002. *Why People Buy Things They Don't Need*. Ithaca, NY: Paramount Market Publishing.
12. Porter, M. E. 1980. *Competitive Strategy*. New York: Free Press.
13. Brown, T. 2009. Change by design. *Business Week*, October 5: 54–56; Price, D. 2009. The shape of things to come. *The Wall Street Journal*, October 9: W8.
14. Neil, D. 2010. Rolls-Royce builds a real car. *The Wall Street Journal*, April 10–11: W6.
15. Larsen, P. F. 2003. Better is … better. *The Wall Street Journal*, September 22: R6, R11.
16. Berner, R., & Grow, B. 2004. Out-discounting the discounter. *Business Week*, May 10: 78–79.
17. Gray, S. 2004. How Applebee's is making it big in small towns. *The Wall Street Journal*, August 2: B1, B4.

18. Carey, S. 2010. Alaska Airlines reaps benefits of flying under big rivals' radar. *The Wall Street Journal*, January 29: B4.

19. Minter, R. 1998. The myth of market share. *The Wall Street Journal*, June 15: A28.

20. Porter, M. E. 1980. *Competitive Strategy*. New York: Free Press.

21. Conlin, M. 2009. Look who's stalking Wal-Mart. *Business Week*, December 7: 30–33.

22. Eisinger, J. 2004. Ahead of the tap: Seared. *The Wall Street Journal*, April 21: C1.

23. Bustillo, M., & Trachtenberg, J. A. 2009. Wal-Mart strafes Amazon in book war. *The Wall Street Journal*, October 16: A1, A15; Trachtenberg, J. A., & Bustillo, M. 2009. Amazon, Wal-Mart cut deeper in book duel. *The Wall Street Journal*, October 17–18: B1.

24. Magretta, J. 2002. Why business models matter. *Harvard Business Review*, 80(3): 91.

25. Senge, P. M. 1990. *The Fifth Discipline: The Art and Practice of the Learning Organization*. New York: Doubleday/Currency.

26. Forelle, C. 2004. Gillette to launch vibrating razor. *The Wall Street Journal*, January 16: A8; Byron, E. 2010. P&G razor launches in recession's shadow. *The Wall Street Journal*, February 12: B1, B7.

27. Meeks, F. 1994. Watch out, Motorola: Newcomer to cellular phone equipment making inroads. *Forbes*, September 12, 192–198.

28. Jannarone, J. 2010. Wal-Mart spices up private label. *The Wall Street Journal*, February 6–7: B16.

29. Burns, G. 1995. A Froot Loop by any other name…: Ralcorp's private-label cereals are gobbling market share. *Business Week*, June 26: 72, 76.

30. Lundegaard, K., & Freeman, S. 2004. Detroit's challenge: Weaning buyers from years of deals. *The Wall Street Journal*, January 6: A1, A2.

31. Linebaugh, K., & Bennett, J. 2010. Marchionne upends Chrysler's ways. *The Wall Street Journal*, January 12: B1, B2.

32. See for example, Byron, E. 2009. Tide turns "basic" for P&G in slump. *The Wall Street Journal*, August 6: A1, A10; Byron, E. 2009. P&G plots course to turn lackluster Tide. *The Wall Street Journal*, September 11: B3; Byron, E. 2009. P&G meets frugal shoppers halfway. *The Wall Street Journal*, September 11: B1, B2; Byron, E. 2010. P&G puts up its dukes over pricing. *The Wall Street Journal*, April 30: B8; Byron, E. 2010. P&G wages offensive against rivals, risks profits. *The Wall Street Journal*, August 19: A1, A14.

33. Balu, R. 1998. "Orphan" brands grow with new parent. *The Wall Street Journal*, April 2, B1, B14; Elliott, S. 1993. The famous brands on death row. *The New York Times*, November 7: F1, F6.

34. Elliott, S. 1993. The famous brands on death row. *The New York Times*, November 7: F1, F6.

35. Linebaugh, K., & Bennett, J. 2010. Marchionne upends Chrysler's ways. *The Wall Street Journal*, January 12: B2.

36. Narisetti, R. 1997. Too many choices: P&G, seeing shoppers were being confused, overhauls marketing. *The Wall Street Journal*, January 15: A1.

37. Narisetti, R. 1997. Too many choices: P&G, seeing shoppers were being confused, overhauls marketing. *The Wall Street Journal*, January 15: A1.

38. Narisetti, R. 1997. Too many choices: P&G, seeing shoppers were being confused, overhauls marketing. *The Wall Street Journal*, January 15: A1.

39. Brat, H., Byron, El, & Zimmerman, A. 2009. Retailers cut back on variety, once the spice of marketing. *The Wall Street Journal*, June 26: A1, A12.

40. Zimmerman, A., & Beatty, S. 2004. Wal-Mart's fashion fade. *The Wall Street Journal*, July 2: B1, B2; Zimmerman, A. 2010. A fashion identity crisis at Wal-Mart. *The Wall Street Journal*, July 29: B1.

41. Brush, M. 1997. At Morton, much more than a dash of cash. *The New York Times*, June 1(Section 3): 5.

42. Homes, E. 2010. Forever 21 pursues big-store branding. *The Wall Street Journal*, June 24: B16.

43. Ishikura, Y. 1983. *Canon, Inc.: Worldwide Copier Strategy*. Boston: HBS Case Services, Harvard Business School.

44. Ball, J. 1999. Productivity improves among U.S. auto makers. *The Wall Street Journal*, June 18: A2.

45. Welch, D., & Rowley, I. 2009. Toyota gets stuck in a pair of ruts. *Business Week*, November 30: 60; Ingrassia, P. 2010. Toyota: Too big, too fast. *The Wall Street Journal*, January 29: A15; Welch, D. 2010. Oh, what a (hideous) feeling. *Business Week*, February 15: 21–22.

46. Kim, W.C. & Mauborgne, R. 2005. *Blue Ocean Strategy*. Boston: Harvard Business School Press.

47. Marin, R. 2009. *The Design of Business. Why Design Thinking is the Next Competitive Advantage*. Boston: Harvard Business Press: 62.

48. Michaels, D. 2009. O'Leary pilots Ryanair into lead with "mad" ideas for cost cuts. *The Wall Street Journal*, December 9: B1, B2.

Chapter 8

1. Porter, M. E. 1980. *Competitive Strategy*. New York: Free Press.

2. Urban, G. L., Carter, T., Gaskin, S., & Mucha, Z. 1986. Market share rewards to pioneering brands: An empirical analysis and strategic implications. *Management Science*, 32: 645–659.

3. Schnaars, S. P. 1986. When entering growth markets, are pioneers better than poachers? *Business Horizons* 29(2): 27–36.

4. Technology titans battle over format of DVD successor. 2004. *The Wall Street Journal*, March 15: A1, A8.

5. Bartlett, C. A. 1983. *EMI and the CT Scanner*. Boston: HBS Case Services, Harvard Business School.

6. Teece, D. J. 1987. Profiting from technological innovation: Implications for integration, collaboration, licensing, and public policy. In Teece, D. J. (Ed.), *The Competitive Challenge: Strategies for Industrial Innovation and Renewal*. Cambridge, MA: Ballinger.

7. Taylor, III, A. 1994. Iacocca's minivan: How Chrysler succeeded in creating one of the most profitable products of the decade. *Fortune*, May 30: 56–66.

8. Ishikura, Y. 1983. *Canon, Inc.: Worldwide Copier Strategy*. Boston: HBS Case Services, Harvard Business School.

9. Bartlett, C. A. 1983. *EMI and the CT Scanner*. Boston: HBS Case Services, Harvard Business School.

10. Shapiro, E. 1989. NutraSweet's bitter fight: A bid to defend its sole product as patents fall. *The New York Times*, November 19: Section 3, 4.

11. Horvath, S. M. 2004. NutraSweet gets FDA approval for strong sweetener Neotame. *The Wall Street Journal*, July 8: A21.

12. Fowler, G. A., & Bustillo, M. 2009. Wal-Mart, Amazon gear up for holiday battle. *The Wall Street Journal*, October 19: B3; The e-biz surprise. 2003. *Business Week*, May 12: 44.

13. The e-biz surprise. 2003. *Business Week*, May 12: 44–49.

14. Mullaney, T. J. 2004. E-biz strikes again! *Business Week*, May 10: 80–90.

15. Yelkur, R., & DaCosta, M. M. N. 2001. Differential pricing and segmentation on the Internet: The case of hotels. *Management Decision*, 39: 252–261.

16. Wang, F., Head, M., & Archer, N. 2002. E-tailing: An analysis of Web impacts on the retail market. *Journal of Business Strategies*, 19: 73–93.

17. Robert, M. 1003. *Strategy Pure and Simple*. New York: McGraw-Hill.

18. Head, M., Archer, N. P., & Yuan, Y. 2000. World Wide Web navigation aid. *International Journal of Human-Computer Studies*, 53: 301–330.

19. Yelkur, R., & DaCosta, M. M. N. 2001. Differential pricing and segmentation on the Internet: The case of hotels. *Management Decision*, 39: 252–261.

20. Porter, M. E. 2001. Strategy and the Internet. *Harvard Business Review*, 79(2): 62–78.

21. Head, M., Archer, N. P., & Yuan, Y. 2000. World Wide Web navigation aid. *International Journal of Human-Computer Studies*, 53: 301–330.

22. Porter, M. E. 2001. Strategy and the Internet. *Harvard Business Review*, 79(2): 62–78.

23. Kim, S., & Kim, C. 2000. *Pricing Strategy in the Digital Marketing Age*. Seoul: LG Economic Research Institute; Bakos, Y. 1998. The emerging role of electronic marketplaces on the Internet. *Communications of the ACM*, 41(8): 35–42.

24. Porter, M. E. 2001. Strategy and the Internet. *Harvard Business Review*, 79(2): 62–78.

25. Merrilees, B. 2001. Do traditional strategic concepts apply in the e-marketing context? *Journal of Business Strategies*, 18: 177–190.

26. Porter, M. E. 1980. *Competitive Strategy*. New York: Free Press.

27. Merrilees, B. 2001. Do traditional strategic concepts apply in the e-marketing context? *Journal of Business Strategies*, 18: 177–190.

28. Bulik, B. S. 2000. Survival of the fattest. *Business 2.0*, July 11: 184–187.

29. Brynjolfsson, E., & Smith, M. D. 2000. Frictionless commerce? A comparison of Internet and conventional retailers. *Management Science*, 46: 563–585; Griffith, V. 1999. Branding. com: How brick-and-mortar companies can make it on the Internet. *Strategy + Business*, 15: 54–59.

30. Xiong, C. 2003. Online stores try new pitch: Fetch it yourself. *The Wall Street Journal*, November 19: D4.

31. Schlauch, A. J., & Laposa, S. 2001. E-tailing and Internet-related real estate cost savings: A comparative analysis of E-tailers and retailers. *Journal of Real Estate Research*, 21: 43–54.

32. Yang, Z., & Jun, M. 2002. Consumer perception of e-service quality: From Internet purchaser and non-purchaser perspectives. *Journal of Business Strategies*, 19: 19–41.

33. Porter, M. E. 2001. Strategy and the Internet. *Harvard Business Review*, 79(2): 62–78.

34. Forster, S. 2004. When one hand doesn't know what the other hand is doing, customers notice. And they aren't pleased. *The Wall Street Journal*, March 22: R3.

35. Head, M., Archer, N. P., & Yuan, Y. 2000. World Wide Web navigation aid. *International Journal of Human-Computer Studies*, 53: 301–330.

Chapter 9

1. Ellison, S. 2003. In lean times, big companies make a grab for market share. *The Wall Street Journal*, September 5: A1, A6.

2. Whitehouse, M. 2010. Radical shifts take hold in U.S. manufacturing. *The Wall Street Journal*, February 3: B1, B4.

3. Book excerpt: *Execution: The Discipline of Getting Things Done*, by Larry Bossidy and Ram Charan. 2002. *Fortune*, June 10: 150.

4. Walleck, A. S. 1991. A backstage view of world-class performers. *The Wall Street Journal*, August 26: A10.

5. Morrison, D. J. 1996. Retail's shrinking middle. *The Wall Street Journal*, October 21: A20.

6. Siemers, E., & Harris, E. 1999. Airlines begin to click with Internet-booking services. *The Wall Street Journal*, August 2: B4; Fonti, N. 1999. Airlines, amid rising costs, try to steer customers to new destination: The Web. *The Wall Street Journal*, April 19: B7A; Cameron, D. 2011. American Air seeks pacts with Expedia and Orbitz. *The Wall Street Journal*, January 5: B3; Esterl, M. 2011. Dogfight erupts in plane ticket sales. *The Wall Street Journal*, January 6: A1, A14.

7. Barrett, J. 2009. Whirlpool cleans up its delivery act. *The Wall Street Journal*, September 23: B1, B2; Ihlwan, M. 2010. Creative when no one's looking: LG is re-engineering its supply chain so its innovative products will cost less. *Business Week*, April 25: 37.

8. Barringer, B. R., & Bluedorn, A. C. 1999. The relationship between corporate entrepreneurship and strategic management. *Strategic Management Journal*, 16: 7–19; Chandler, G. N., Keller, C., & Lyon, D. W. 2000. Unraveling the determinants and consequences of an innovation-supportive organizational culture. *Entrepreneurship Theory and Practice*, 25(1): 59–76; Zahra, S. A., & Neubaum, D. O. 1998. Environmental adversity and the entrepreneurial activities of new ventures. *Journal of Developmental Entrepreneurship*, 3(2): 123–140.

9. Shirouzu, N. 2003. Ford's new development plan: Stop reinventing its wheels. *The Wall Street Journal*, April 16: A1, A14.

10. Kim, K., & Chhajed, D. 2000. Commonality in product design: Cost saving, valuation change and cannibalization. *European Journal of Operational Research*, 125: 602–622.

11. Ingrassia, L. 1992. The cutting edge: Using advanced technology, Gillette has managed an unusual feat. *The Wall Street Journal*, April 6: A6.

12. Maremont, M. 1998. How Gillette brought its MACH3 to market. *The Wall Street Journal*, April 15: B1, B4.

13. Forelle, C. 2003. Schick seeks edge with four-blade razor. *The Wall Street Journal*, August 12: B1, B9.
14. Byron, E. 2010. P&G razor launches in recession's shadow. *The Wall Street Journal*, February 12: B1, B7.
15. Byron, E. 2010. New Schick razor will counter Gillette. *The Wall Street Journal*, February 20–21: B5.
16. Schonberger, R. J. 1996. *World Class Manufacturing: The Next Decade*. New York: Free Press.
17. Hammer, M., & Champy, J. 1994. *Reengineering the Corporation: A Manifesto for Business Revolution*. New York: HarperBusiness.
18. Lee, L. 1995. Rent-a-techs: Hiring outside firms to run computers isn't always a bargain. *The Wall Street Journal*, May 18: A1, A9.
19. Srikanth, K., & Puranam, P. 2010. Advice for outsourcers: Think bigger. *The Wall Street Journal*, January 25: R7.
20. White, J. B. 1996. Next big thing: Reengineering gurus take steps to remodel their stalling vehicles. *The Wall Street Journal*, November 26: A1, A10.
21. Harper, L. 1992. Hazardous cuts: Travel agency learns service firms' perils in slimming down. *The Wall Street Journal*, March 20: A1, A9.
22. Fishman, C. 2004. Toll of a new machine. *Fast Company*, May: 90–95.
23. McGregor, J. 2010. USAA's battle plan. *Business Week*, March 1: 40–43.
24. Wysocki, Jr., B. 2004. To fix health care, hospitals take tips from factory floor. *The Wall Street Journal*, April 9: A1, A6.
25. Van Biema, M., & Greenwald, B. 1997. Managing our way to higher service sector productivity. *Harvard Business Review* 75(4): 95.
26. Fishman, C. 2004. Toll of a new machine. *Fast Company*, May: 95.
27. Leung, S. 2002. Local restaurants find big chains eating their lunch. *The Wall Street Journal*, July 9: A1, A8.
28. Kunstler, J. H. 1993. *The Geography of Nowhere: The Rise and Decline of America's Manmade Landscape*. New York: Simon & Schuster.
29. Beaumont, C. E. 1994. *How Superstore Sprawl Can Harm Communities and What Citizens Can Do about It*. Washington: National Trust for Historic Preservation.
30. Leung, S. 2002. Local restaurants find big chains eating their lunch. *The Wall Street Journal*, July 9: A1, A8.
31. Leung, S. 2002. Local restaurants find big chains eating their lunch. *The Wall Street Journal*, July 9: A1, A8.

Chapter 10

1. Senge, P. M. 1990. *The Fifth Discipline: The Art and Practice of the Learning Organization*. New York: Doubleday/Currency.
2. Porter, M. E. 1987. From competitive advantage to corporate strategy. *Harvard Business Review*, 65(3): 43–59.

3. Also see, for example, Bower, J. L. 2001. Not all M&As are alike—and that matters. *Harvard Business Review*, March: 93–101.

4. Lane, P. J., Cannella, A. A., & Lubatkin, M. H. 1998. Agency problems as antecedents to unrelated mergers and diversification: Amihud and Lev reconsidered. *Strategic Management Journal*, 19: 555–578.

5. Wilke, J. R., & Bank, D. 2004. U.S. sues to block Oracle's offer to buy PeopleSoft. *The Wall Street Journal*, February 27: A1, A2.

6. Why the sudden rise in the urge to merge and form oligopolies? 2002. *The Wall Street Journal*, February 25: A1, A10.

7. Rumelt, R. P. 1974. *Strategy, Structure and Economic Performance*. Cambridge, MA: Harvard University Press.

8. Williamson, O. E. 1975. *Markets and Hierarchies: Analysis and Antitrust Implications*. New York: Free Press.

9. Cimilluca, D., McKay, B., & McCracken, J. 2010. Coke near deal for bottler. *The Wall Street Journal*, February 25: A1, A6.

10. Worthen, B., Tuna, C., & Scheck, J. 2009. Companies more prone to go "vertical." *The Wall Street Journal*, November 30: A1, A16.

11. Tam, P.-W. 2003. An elaborate plan force H-P union to stay on target. *The Wall Street Journal*, April 28: A1, A10.

12. Lattman, P., & Martin, T. W. 2010. Walgreen agrees to buy New York's Duane Reade. *The Wall Street Journal*, February 18: B3.

13. K2 to buy three ski-gear makers as it continues acquisition spree. 2004. *The Wall Street Journal*, June 16: B4.

14. Stimpert, J. L. 1992. *Managerial Thinking and Large Diversified Firms*. Unpublished doctoral dissertation, University of Illinois at Urbana-Champaign: 141.

15. Belson, K. 2001. As Starbucks grows, Japan, too, is awash. *The New York Times*, October 21(Business): 6.

16. One-toy-fits-all: How industry learned to love the global kid. 2003. *The Wall Street Journal*, April 29: A1, A12.

17. Biers, D., & Jordan, M. 1996. McDonald's in India decides the Big Mac is not a sacred cow. *The Wall Street Journal*, October 14: A13.

18. Stimpert, J. L. 1992. *Managerial Thinking and Large Diversified Firms*. Unpublished doctoral dissertation, University of Illinois at Urbana-Champaign: 157.

19. Stimpert, J. L. 1992. *Managerial Thinking and Large Diversified Firms*. Unpublished doctoral dissertation, University of Illinois at Urbana-Champaign: 164.

20. Stimpert, J. L. 1992. *Managerial Thinking and Large Diversified Firms*. Unpublished doctoral dissertation, University of Illinois at Urbana-Champaign: 154.

21. See also Zweig, P. L. 1995. The case against mergers. *Business Week*, October 30: 122–130.

22. Fowler, G. 2009. eBay to unload Skype in IPO, citing poor fit. *The Wall Street Journal*, April 15: B1, B5.

23. Porter, M. E. 1987. From competitive advantage to corporate strategy. *Harvard Business Review*, 65(3): 43–59.

24. Porter, M. E. 1987. From competitive advantage to corporate strategy. *Harvard Business Review*, 65(3): 59.

25. Landro, L. 1997. Back to reality: Entertainment giants face pressure to cut costs, get into focus. *The Wall Street Journal*, February 11: A1, A10.

26. Landro, L. 1997. Back to reality: Entertainment giants face pressure to cut costs, get into focus. *The Wall Street Journal*, February 11: A 1.

27. Landro, L. 1997. Back to reality: Entertainment giants face pressure to cut costs, get into focus. *The Wall Street Journal*, February 11: A 10.

28. Peers, M. 2009. Word to Comcast: Just don't touch that dial. *The Wall Street Journal*, October 2: C10.

29. Orwall, B., & Pope, K. 1997. Relativity: Disney, ABC promised "synergy" in merger; so, what happened? *The Wall Street Journal*, May 16: A1, A9.

30. Philips, J. 2009. What matters in the media. *The Wall Street Journal*, October 7: A19.

31. Hamel, G. 2004. When dinosaurs mate. *The Wall Street Journal*, January 22: A12.

32. Eccles, R. G., Lanes, K. L., & Wilson, T. C. 1999. Are you paying too much for that acquisition? *Harvard Business Review*, 77(4): 136–147.

33. Eccles, R. G., Lanes, K. L., & Wilson, T. C. 1999. Are you paying too much for that acquisition? *Harvard Business Review*, 77(4): 136–147.

34. Frank, R., & Burton, T. M. 1997. Side effects: Cross-border merger results in headaches for a drug company. *The Wall Street Journal*, February 4: A1, A12.

35. Lublin, J. S., & O'Brian, B. 1997. Merged firms often face culture clash. *The Wall Street Journal*, February 14: B7.

36. Biggadike, E. R. 1979. The risky business of diversification. *Harvard Business Review*, 57(3): 103–111.

37. Jones, G. R., & Hill, C. W. L. 1988. Transaction cost analysis of strategy-structure choice. *Strategic Management Journal*, 9: 159–172.

38. Carey, S. 2010. Boat makers steer through choppiness. *The Wall Street Journal*, February 22: B1, B2.

39. Peters, T. J., & Waterman, R. H. 1982. *In Search of Excellence: Lessons from America's Best Run Companies*. New York: Harper & Row.

40. Porter, M. E. 1987. From competitive advantage to corporate strategy. *Harvard Business Review*, 65(3): 45.

41. Jarrell, G. A. 1991. For a higher share price, focus your business. *The Wall Street Journal*, May 13: A14.

42. Lichtenberg, F. R. 1990. Want more productivity? Kill that conglomerate. *The Wall Street Journal*, January 16: A22.

43. Ramanujam, V., & Varadarajan, P. 1989. Research on corporate diversification: A synthesis. *Strategic Management Journal*, 10: 523–551.

44. Leontiades, M., quoted in Thackray, J. 1991. Diversification: What it takes to make it work. *Across the Board*, November: 17–23.

45. Palich, L. E., Cardinal, L. B., & Miller, C. 2000. Curvilinearity in the diversification-performance linkage: An examination of over three decades. *Strategic Management Journal*, 21: 155–175.

46. Stimpert, J. L., & Duhaime, I. M. 1996. *Theoretical Perspectives on Diversification: An Empirical Examination*. Paper presented at the Academy of Management, Cincinnati, August.

47. Villalonga, B. 2004. Does diversification cause the "diversification discount?" *Financial Management*, 33(2): 5–27.

48. Rumelt, R. P. 1974. *Strategy, Structure and Economic Performance*. Cambridge, MA: Harvard University Press: 156.

49. Halloran, K. D. 1985. The impact of M&A programs on company identity. *Mergers and Acquisitions*, 20(1): 60–66.

50. Porter, M. E. 1987. From competitive advantage to corporate strategy. *Harvard Business Review*, 65(3): 59.

51. Hall, G. E. 1987. Reflections on running a diversified company. *Harvard Business Review*, 65(1): 84–92.

52. Stimpert, J. L., & Duhaime, I. M. 1997. In the eyes of the beholder: Conceptualizations of relatedness held by the managers of large diversified firms. *Strategic Management Journal*, 18: 111–125.

53. Barney, J. B. 1992. Integrating organizational behavior and strategy formulation research: A resource-based analysis. *Advances in Strategic Management*, 8: 39–61.

54. Prahalad, C. K., & Bettis, R. A. 1986. The dominant logic: A new linkage between diversity and performance. *Strategic Management Journal*, 7: 488.

55. Montgomery, C. A. 1994. Corporate diversification. *Journal of Economic Perspectives*, 8: 163–178.

56. Patterson, G. A., & Schwadel, F. 1992. Back in time: Sears suddenly undoes years of diversifying beyond retailing field. *The Wall Street Journal*, September 30: A1, A16.

57. Comment, R., & Jarrell, G. A. 1995. Corporate focus and stock returns. *Journal of Financial Economics*, 37: 67–87; Jarrell, G. A. 1991. For a higher share price, focus your business. *The Wall Street Journal*, May 13: A14.

58. Guyon, J. 1996. Hanson spinoff plans haven't raised shareholder value. *The Wall Street Journal*, September 26: B4; Lowenstein, R. 1997. Corporate breakups are no panacea. *The Wall Street Journal*, June 5: C1.

59. Lowenstein, R. 1997. Corporate breakups are no panacea. *The Wall Street Journal*, June 5: C1.

60. Kazanjian, R. K., & Drazin, R. 1987. Implementing internal diversification: Contingency factors for organization design choices. *Academy of Management Review*, 12: 342–354.

61. Porac, J. F., Thomas, H., & Baden-Fuller, C. 1989. Competitive groups as cognitive communities: The case of Scottish knitwear manufacturers. *Journal of Management Studies*, 26: 397–416; Salancik, G. R., & Porac, J. F. 1986. Distilled ideologies. In Sims, H., & Gioia, D. (Eds.), *The Thinking Organization*. San Francisco: Jossey-Bass.

62. Barney, J. B. 1992. Integrating organizational behavior and strategy formulation research: A resource-based analysis. *Advances in Strategic Management*, 8: 39–61; Dierickx, I., & Cool, K. 1989. Asset stock accumulation and sustainability of competitive advantage: Reply. *Management Science*, 35: 1504–1511.

63. Wallace, F. D. 1969. Some principles of acquisition. In Alberts, W. W., & Segal, J. E. (Eds.), *The Corporate Merger*. Chicago: The University of Chicago Press: 173.

64. Boudette, N. E. 2003. Peugeot's formula for success: Steering clear of megamergers. *The Wall Street Journal*, August 4: A1, A6.

65. Zweig, P. L. 1995. The case against mergers. *Business Week*, October 30: 122–130.

66. Frank, S. E. 1996. In bank deals, consider this: Buy the buyer. *The Wall Street Journal*, September 11: C1.

67. Halbeblian, J., & Finkelstein, S. 1999. The influence of organizational acquisition history on acquisition performance: A behavioral learning perspective. *Administrative Science Quarterly*, 44: 29–56; Hayward, M. L. A. 2002. When do firms learn from their acquisition experience? Evidence from 1990–1995. *Strategic Management Journal*, 23: 21–39.

68. Tam, P.-W. 2003. An elaborate plan force H-P union to stay on target. *The Wall Street Journal*, April 28: A1, A10.

69. Tam, P.-W. 2003. An elaborate plan forces H-P union to stay on target. *The Wall Street Journal*, April 28: A1, A10.

70. Thurm, S. 2000. Under Cisco's System, mergers usually work; that defies the odds. *The Wall Street Journal*, March 1: A1, A12; Wysocki, Jr., B. 1997. Why an acquisition? Often, it's the people. *The Wall Street Journal*, October 6: A1.

71. Thackray, J. 1991. Diversification: What it takes to make it work. *Across the Board*, November: 18.

72. Hambrick, D. C., & MacMillan, I. C. 1982. The product portfolio and man's best friend. *California Management Review*, 25(1): 84–95.

Chapter 11

1. A question of management: Carol Bartz on how Yahoo's organization structure got in the way of innovation. 2009. *The Wall Street Journal*, June 2: R4.

2. Nadler, D. A., & Tushman, M. L. 1997. *Competing by Design: The Power of Organizational Architecture*. New York: Oxford University Press: 5.

3. Weber, M. 1947. *The Theory of Social and Economic Organization*. New York: Free Press.

4. Mintzberg, H. 1978. Patterns in strategy formation. *Management Science*, 24: 934–948.

5. Stanford, N. 2007. *Guide to Organization Design*. London: Profile Books Ltd.

6. Williamson, O. E. 1975. *Markets and Hierarchies: Analysis and Antitrust Implications*. New York: Free Press.

7. Stanford, N. 2007. *Guide to Organization Design*. London: Profile Books Ltd. 49.

8. Williamson, O. E. 1975. *Markets and Hierarchies: Analysis and Antitrust Implications*. New York: Free Press.

9. Chandler, Jr., A. D. 1962. *Strategy and Structure: Chapters in the History of the Industrial Enterprise*. Cambridge, MA: MIT Press.

10. Chandler, Jr., A. D. 1962. *Strategy and Structure: Chapters in the History of the Industrial Enterprise*. Cambridge, MA: MIT Press; Rumelt, R. P. 1974. *Strategy, Structure and Economic Performance*. Cambridge, MA: Harvard University Press.

11. Colvin, G., & Shambora, J. 2008. "J&J: Secrets of success." *Fortune*, April 22: 116–221.

12. Williamson, O. E. 1975. *Markets and Hierarchies: Analysis and Antitrust Implications.* New York: Free Press: 147, 148, emphasis in original.

13. Stanford, N. 2007. *Guide to Organization Design.* London: Profile Books Ltd.: 51–53.

14. Blumenstein, R. 1997. Tough driving: Struggle to remake the Malibu says a lot about remaking GM. *The Wall Street Journal*, March 27: A1, A8.

15. Wasserman, M. E. 1998. *Examining the Relationship between Research and Development Resource Flows and Knowledge-Based Capabilities: Integrating Resource-Based and Organizational Learning Theory.* Unpublished doctoral dissertation, Michigan State University.

16. Stanford, Naomi. 2007. *Guide to Organization Design.* London: Profile Books Ltd.: 57.

17. Davis, S. M., & Lawrence, P. R. 1978. Problems of matrix organizations. *Harvard Business Review* 56(3): 131–142.

18. White, R. 1979. *The Dexter Corporation.* Boston: HBS Case Services, Harvard Business School.

19. White, R. 1979. *The Dexter Corporation.* Boston: HBS Case Services, Harvard Business School: 11.

20. White, R. 1979. *The Dexter Corporation.* Boston: HBS Case Services, Harvard Business School: 12.

21. Bank, D. 1999. Know your customer: Companies have more data on their customers than ever. The trick is how to use it. *The Wall Street Journal*, June 21: R18. See also Clark, D. 1999. Managing the mountain. *The Wall Street Journal*, June 21: R4; Totty, M. 2002. So much information… *The Wall Street Journal*, December 9: R4.

22. Barney, J. B. 1986. Organizational culture: Can it be a source of sustained competitive advantage? *Academy of Management Review* 11: 656–665.

23. Schein, E. H. 1999. *The Corporate Culture Survival Guide,* San Francisco: Jossey-Bass.

24. DePree, M. 1989. *Leadership is an Art.* New York: Dell Publishing.

25. DePree, M. 1989. *Leadership is an Art.* New York: Dell Publishing: 82, 108.

26. Etzioni, A. 1965. Organizational control structure. In March, J. G. (Ed.), *Handbook of Organizations*. Chicago: Rand McNally.

27. See, for example, Terlep, S. 2010. GM's plodding culture vexes its impatient CEO. *The Wall Street Journal*, April 7: B1, B7.

28. Katz, D. R. 1987. *The Big Store: Inside the Crisis and Revolution at Sears.* New York: Viking: 41.

29. Linebaugh, K., Searcey, D., & Shirouzu, N. 2010. Secretive culture led Toyota astray. *The Wall Street Journal*, February 10: A1, A6.

30. GM culture: A problem that cash can't fix. 2009. *The Korea Herald*, March 3: 9.

31. Morse, D. 2003. A hardware chain struggles to adjust to a new blueprint. *The Wall Street Journal*, January 17: A1, A6.

32. Emery, J. C. 1969. *Organizational Planning and Control Systems: Theory and Technology.* New York: Macmillan.

33. Emery, J. C. 1969. *Organizational Planning and Control Systems: Theory and Technology.* New York: Macmillan: 114.

34. Boulding, K. R. 1966. The economics of knowledge and the knowledge of economics. *American Economic Review* 56(2): 8.

35. Davis, M. S. 1985. Two plus two doesn't equal five. *Fortune*, December 9: 177, 179, emphasis added.

36. Hamermesh, R. G. 1977. Responding to divisional profit crises. *Harvard Business Review* 55(2): 124–130; Milliken, F. J., Morrison, E. W., & Hewlin, P. F. 2003. An exploratory study of employee silence: Issues that employees don't communicate upward and why. *Journal of Management Studies*, 40: 1453–1477.

37. Kramer, R. M. 1991. Intergroup relations and organizational dilemmas: The role of categorization processes. In Staw, B., & Cummings, L. (Eds.), *Research in Organizational Behavior*, 13: 191–228. Greenwich, CT: JAI Press.

38. Berle, A. A., & Means, G. C. 1932. *The Modern Corporation and Private Property*. New York: Macmillan.

39. *Workforce 2000: Work and Workers for the Twenty-First Century*. 1987. Indianapolis: Hudson Institute: xxvii.

40. Wessel, D. 2004. The future of jobs: New ones arise, wage gap widens. *The Wall Street Journal*, April 2: A1, A5.

41. Quoted in Worthy, J. 1959. *Big Business and Free Men*. New York: Harper & Row: 67.

42. Kevin P. Boyle, quoted in U.S. Department of Commerce and U.S. Department of Labor. 1993. *The Work Place of the Future*. Washington, DC: U.S. Government Printing Office: 222.

43. Thurm, S. 1999. What do you know? *The Wall Street Journal*, June 21: R10, R19.

44. Aeppel, T. 2002. On factory floors, top workers hide secrets to success. *The Wall Street Journal*, July 1: A1, A10.

45. Friedman, T. L. 2005. *The World Is Flat: A Brief History of the Twenty-First Century*. New York: Farrar, Straus and Giroux: 209.

46. Schonberger, R. J. 1996. *World Class Manufacturing: The next decade*. New York: Free Press.

47. Senge, P. M. 1990. *The Fifth Discipline: The Art and Practice of the Learning Organization*. New York: Doubleday/Currency.

48. Senge, P. M. 1990. *The Fifth Discipline: The Art and Practice of the Learning Organization*. New York: Doubleday/Currency: 213.

49. See, for example, Becker, B., & Gerhart, B. 1996. The impact of human resource management on organizational performance: Progress and prospects. *Academy of Management Journal*, 39: 779–801; Pfeffer, J., & Velga. J. F. 1999. Putting people first for organizational success. *Academy of Management Executive*, 13(2): 37–48.

50. Quinn, J. B. 1992. *Intelligent Enterprise: A Knowledge and Service-Based Paradigm for Industry*. New York: Free Press: 32–33.

51. Drucker, P. F. 1989. Sell the mailroom. *The Wall Street Journal*, July 25: A16.

52. O'Reilly, III, C. A., & Tushman, M. L. 2004. The ambidextrous Organization. *Harvard Business Review*, 82(2): 76.

53. Senge, P. M. 1990. *The Fifth Discipline: The Art and Practice of the Learning Organization*. New York: Doubleday/Currency: 53.

54. Senge, P. M. 1990. *The Fifth Discipline: The Art and Practice of the Learning Organization.* New York: Doubleday/Currency.

55. Drucker, P. F. 1994. The age of social transformation. *Atlantic Monthly*, November: 53–80.

Chapter 12

1. Kiesler, S., & Sproull, L. 1982. Managerial response to changing environments: Perspectives on problem sensing from social cognition. *Administrative Science Quarterly*, 27: 548.

2. Senge, P. M. 1990. *The Fifth Discipline: The Art and Practice of the Learning Organization.* New York: Doubleday/Currency.

3. Kiesler, S., & Sproull, L. 1982. Managerial response to changing environments: Perspectives on problem sensing from social cognition. *Administrative Science Quarterly*, 27: 548–570.

4. Mintzberg, H., Raìsinghanì, D., & Théorêt, A. 1976. The structure of "unstructured" decision processes. *Administrative Science Quarterly*, 21: 253.

5. Starbuck, W. A., & Milliken, F. J. 1988. Executives' perceptual filters: What they notice and how they make sense. In Hambrick, D. C. (Ed.), *The Executive Effect: Concepts and Methods for Studying Top Managers*. Greenwich, CT: JAI Press.

6. Kiesler, S., & Sproull, L. 1982. Managerial response to changing environments: Perspectives on problem sensing from social cognition. *Administrative Science Quarterly*, 27: 548–570.

7. Barr, P. S., Stimpert, J. L., & Huff, A. S. 1992. Cognitive change, strategic action, and organizational renewal. *Strategic Management Journal*, 13(special issue): 15–36.

8. These quotes are found in Purkayastha, D., & Buzzell, R. D. 1978. *Note on the Motorcycle Industry—1975*. Boston: HBS Case Services, Harvard Business School: 5–6.

9. Hambrick, D. C., & D'Aveni, R. A. 1988. Large corporate failures as downward spirals. *Administrative Science Quarterly*, 33: 1–23.

10. Stertz, B. A. 1992. Importing solutions: Detroit's new strategy to beat back Japanese is to copy their ideas. *The Wall Street Journal*, October 1: A1, A12; White, J. B. 1992. For Saturn, copying Japan yields hot sales but no profits. *The Wall Street Journal*, October 1: A10.

11. Womack, J. P., Jones, D. T., & Roos, D. 1990. *The Machine that Changed the World.* New York: Rawson Associates.

12. DiMaggio, P. J., & Powell, W. W. 1983. The iron cage revisited: Institutional isomorphism and collective rationality in organizational fields. *American Sociological Review*, 38: 147–160; Huff, A. S. 1982. Industry influences on strategy reformulation. *Strategic Management Journal*, 3: 119–131.

13. Hambrick, D. C. 1982. Environmental scanning and organizational strategy. *Strategic Management Journal*, 3: 159–174.

14. Mintzberg, H. 1978. Patterns in strategy formation. *Management Science*, 24: 934–948.

15. March, J. G. 1991. Exploration and exploitation in organizational learning. *Organization Science*, 2: 71–87.

16. Cyert, R. M., & March, J. G. 1963. *A Behavioral Theory of the Firm*. Englewood Cliffs, NJ: Prentice Hall.

17. Cohen, W. M., & Levinthal, D. A. 1989. Innovation and learning: The two faces of R&D. *Economic Journal*, 99: 569–596; Cohen, W. M., & Levinthal, D. A. 1990. Absorptive capacity: A new perspective on learning and innovation. *Administrative Science Quarterly*, 35: 128–152; Lant, T. K., & Montgomery, D. B. 1987. Learning from strategic success and failure. *Journal of Business Research*, 15: 503–517.

18. Cohen, W. M., & Levinthal, D. A. 1989. Innovation and learning: The two faces of R&D. *Economic Journal*, 99: 569–596; Cohen, W. M., & Levinthal, D. A. 1990. Absorptive capacity: A new perspective on learning and innovation. *Administrative Science Quarterly*, 35: 128–152.

19. Cohen, W. M., & Levinthal, D. A. 1990. Absorptive capacity: A new perspective on learning and innovation. *Administrative Science Quarterly*, 35: 128.

20. Wasserman, M. E. 2000. *Examining the Relationship between Research and Development Resource Flows and Knowledge-Based Capabilities: Integrating Resource-Based and Organizational Learning Theory*. Unpublished doctoral dissertation, Michigan State University: 42–43.

21. Schneider, B. 1987. The people make the place. *Personnel Psychology*, 40: 437–453.

22. Walter Bagehot quoted in Rogers, E. M. 1983. *Diffusion of Innovations* (3rd ed.). New York: Free Press: 312.

23. Miller, D. 1994. What happens after success? The perils of excellence. *Journal of Management Studies*, 31: 325–358.

24. Finkelstein, S., & Hambrick, D. C. 1996. *Strategic Leadership: Top Executives and Their Effects on Organizations*. St. Paul: West Publishing.

25. Miller, D. 1991. Stale in the saddle: CEO tenure and the match between organization and environment. *Management Science*, 37: 34–52.

26. March, J. G. 1991. Exploration and exploitation in organizational learning. *Organization Science*, 2: 71–87.

27. March, J. G. 1991. Exploration and exploitation in organizational learning. *Organization Science*, 2: 80.

28. March, J. G. 1991. Exploration and exploitation in organizational learning. *Organization Science*, 2: 79.

29. Wyckoff, D. D. 1976. *Railroad Management*. Lexington, MA: Lexington Books.

30. Wyckoff, D. D. 1976. *Railroad Management*. Lexington, MA: Lexington Books: 87.

31. Wyckoff, D. D. 1976. *Railroad Management*. Lexington, MA: Lexington Books: 99, emphasis added.

32. Hedberg, B. 1981. How organizations learn and unlearn. In Nystrom, P. C., & Starbuck, W. H. (Eds.), *Handbook of Organizational Design*. New York: Oxford University Press: 19, emphasis added.

33. Hamel, G. 1996. *Strategy in the New Economy: Issues and Opportunities*. Talk presented at the annual meeting of the Strategic Management Society. Phoenix.

34. Siegel, J. I., & Chang, J. J. 2009. *Samsung Electronics*. Boston: Harvard Business School Publishing.

35. Burgelman, R. A. 1983. A process model of internal corporate venturing in the diversified major firm. *Administrative Science Quarterly*, 28: 223–244.

36. See also, Martin, R. L., & Riel, J. 2010. Innovation's accidental enemies. *Business Week*, January 25: 72.

37. Hamel, G., & Prahalad, C. K. 1994. *Competing for the Future*. Boston: Harvard Business School Press: 63.

38. Hamel, G. 1996. *Strategy in the New Economy: Issues and Opportunities*. Talk presented at the annual meeting of the Strategic Management Society. Phoenix.

39. Barr, P. S., Stimpert, J. L., & Huff, A. S. 1992. Cognitive change, strategic action, and organizational renewal. *Strategic Management Journal*, 13(special issue): 15–36.

40. Pfeffer, J. 1994. *Competitive Advantage through People*. Boston: Harvard Business School Press: 4.

41. Pfeffer, J. 1994. *Competitive Advantage through People*. Boston: Harvard Business School Press.

42. Dempsey, P. S. 1993. The bitter fruits of airline deregulation. *The Wall Street Journal*, April 8: A15.

Index